PROPORTIONALITY IN EU DIGITAL LAW

This book addresses the interplay between the proportionality principle and EU digital law.

Does EU digital law provide a fair balance of rights and interests? How does proportionality limit legislation in the digital economy? How can it be used to balance competing rights and interests? Diving into the dialectics of law and technology, the book analyses the relevance of the proportionality principle in regulating the digital world and as a vital tool for balancing competing rights and interests.

The chapters analyse how conflicting rights and interests are resolved in EU digital law through the proportionality principle and critically reflect on its application. They scrutinise recent EU regulatory initiatives such as the GDPR, AI Act, Copyright Directive, DSA, and more. They reflect on the unique context of AI systems regulation, digital marketing, and data protection, illuminating the application and impact of proportionality in these arenas.

Providing an in-depth examination of legal actors and real-life conflicts resolved by applying EU digital law, the book explains the pivotal role of the principle of proportionality in achieving an optimal balance of rights in our digital era.

Proportionality in EU Digital Law

Balancing Conflicting Rights and Interests

Edited by
Jan Czarnocki
and
Przemysław Pałka

·HART·
OXFORD · LONDON · NEW YORK · NEW DELHI · SYDNEY

HART PUBLISHING

Bloomsbury Publishing Plc

Kemp House, Chawley Park, Cumnor Hill, Oxford, OX2 9PH, UK

1385 Broadway, New York, NY 10018, USA

29 Earlsfort Terrace, Dublin 2, Ireland

HART PUBLISHING, the Hart/Stag logo, BLOOMSBURY and the Diana logo are trademarks of Bloomsbury Publishing Plc

First published in Great Britain 2024

A catalogue record for this book is available from the British Library.

A catalogue record for this book is available from the Library of Congress.

Library of Congress Control Number: 2024940690

ISBN: HB: 978-1-50997-451-1
ePDF: 978-1-50997-453-5
ePub: 978-1-50997-452-8

Typeset by Compuscript Ltd, Shannon

FOREWORD

In the context of its 2020 European Strategy for data, the European Union has embarked on an ambitious project of 'putting people first in developing technology, and defending and promoting European values and rights in the digital world'. As a result, the EU will soon have a comprehensive and diverse 'digital rulebook' that, apart from the GDPR, comprises the Digital Markets Act, Digital Services Act and the Data Governance Act, with the Data Act and the AI Act in the legislative pipeline.

As we know, the European values underpinning all these initiatives reflect the fundamental rights enshrined in the Charter of the Fundamental Rights of the European Union ('the Charter') including the fundamental rights to privacy and to the protection of personal data (Articles 7 and 8 of the Charter). Both rights are not absolute and may be limited, provided that the limitations comply with the requirements laid down in Article 52(1) of the Charter. The lawfulness, necessity and proportionality of a legislative measure entailing a limitation on the fundamental rights to privacy and the protection of personal data are essential requirements with which any proposed measure that involves processing of personal data must comply. These conditions are among the most important features of the Charter because they determine the extent to which fundamental rights can effectively be enjoyed. At the core of the notion of proportionality lies the concept of a balancing exercise. On one hand, the weighing up of the importance of the objective to be achieved and the effectiveness of the proposed measure to achieve it; on the other hand, the scope and intensity of the interference on the fundamental rights to privacy and to the protection of personal data.

Therefore, it is clear in my view that – to use Czarnocki's words – 'Proportionality Matters'. Indeed, the requirement of proportionality is one of the most striking and engaging developments in European data protection law, in particular over the last decade.

Given the central role that the concept of proportionality plays in EU law, the analysis of its place in digital regulation in this volume is a very timely contribution and makes it a compelling read. It is particularly worth mentioning the interesting and innovative approach followed by this book, consisting in applying *in concreto* the balancing test to situations as diverse as the use of artificial intelligence systems, the possible liability regimes under the proposed Artificial Intelligence Liability Directive the Revised Product Liability Directive, online advertising, biomedical research, data processing by manufacturers and users of connected devices under the proposed Data Act, and measures taken for the prevention of the diffusion of COVID (the EU Digital COVID Certificate).

As legislative advisor, I would like to point out in particular the role that 'profiling' plays in the way the EDPS assesses how serious an interference is with the right to protection of personal data. When the personal data collected can potentially draw a detailed picture of how a person 'is', notably having regard to her or his health conditions[1] or of her or his whereabouts,[2] the interference is particularly serious and a higher level of scrutiny is warranted, including possibly measures avoiding the most intrusive forms of data collection. In 2019, the EDPS issued Guidelines on assessing the proportionality of measures that limit the fundamental rights to privacy and to the protection of personal data.[3] This complemented the publication of the EDPS Necessity toolkit in 2017.[4] We have traditionally addressed the *vertical* dimension of proportionality, namely interferences with this right by public authorities for reasons of public interests.

In the future, we may increasingly need to address the *horizontal* dimension of proportionality too. This entails increasingly analysing interferences with fundamental rights to privacy and data protection, not only by public authorities, but also by private parties (for instance, the AdTech industry, the subject of one of the contributions in the book).

The challenge ahead consists of preserving the core values of the Union as laid out in the Treaties, starting with freedom, democracy, rule of law, fundamental rights, and balancing privacy and data protection against possibly countervailing rights and interests of controllers, as well as access to information and services provided by the economic actors of the digital economy.

This book is a valuable contribution to the increasingly urgent literature on checks and balances to public and private powers in the new digital economy. I recommend it highly. It will surely help – as regulators, lawyers, IT experts and, more broadly, everyone in the 'data protection epistemic community' – to face the challenge ahead, given the profound changes that our increasingly digital society may face in the near future!

Wojciech Wiewiórowski
The European Data Protection Supervisor

[1] See the EDPB-EDPS Joint Opinion 2/2022 on the Proposal of the European Parliament and of the Council on harmonised rules on fair access to and use of data (Data Act), adopted on 4 May 2022, para 55, referring to 'the particularly sensitive nature of certain categories of data' and para 56, available at www.edpb.europa.eu/system/files/2022-05/edpb-edps_joint_opinion_22022_on_data_act_proposal_en.pdf.

[2] See EDPB Guidelines 04/2020 on the use of location data and contact tracing tools in the context of the COVID-19 outbreak, in particular paras 4–5, available at www.edpb.europa.eu/our-work-tools/our-documents/guidelines/guidelines-042020-use-location-data-and-contact-tracing_en.

[3] See the EDPS Guidelines on assessing the proportionality of measures that limit the fundamental rights to privacy and to the protection of personal data (25 February 2019), available at www.edps.europa.eu/data-protection/our-work/publications/guidelines/edps-guidelines-assessing-proportionality-measures_en.

[4] See the EDPS Necessity toolkit on assessing the necessity of measures that limit the fundamental right to the protection of personal data (11 April 2017), available at www.edps.europa.eu/data-protection/our-work/publications/papers/necessity-toolkit_en.

CONTENTS

LIST OF CONTRIBUTORS

Jan Czarnocki is a doctoral researcher and Maria Skłodowska-Curie Fellow at the KU Leuven Centre for IT & IP Law in Belgium. His work intersects the domains of law, philosophy, technology and policy. Jan is also recognised as a Non-Resident Fellow at the Stanford Law School Transatlantic Technology Law Forum and an Affiliated Fellow at the Jagiellonian University Private Law of Data Project.

Fatma Sümeyra Doğan is an early-stage researcher and Marie-Sklodowska Curie Action's Fellow at Jagiellonian University under the Legality Attentive Data Scientists (LeADS) project. In her PhD, she focuses on the protection of health data.

Marcu Florea is a PhD researcher at the Security, Technology and e-Privacy (STeP Research Group) at the Faculty of Law of the University of Groningen. His work is part of KnowGraphs, a project funded under the EU Research Framework Program Horizon 2020/Marie Skłodowska-Curie Actions, Grant Agreement No 86080.

Konrad Gliściński has a law PhD and is a researcher at the Department of Intellectual Property Law at the Jagiellonian University. Intellectual property expert at Centrum Cyfrowe Legal advisor to the Board of the Jagiellonian Center of Innovation. Lecturer at the H Grotius Center for Intellectual Property Rights. He collaborates with the Kalecki Foundation. He completed doctoral studies at the Faculty of Law and Administration of the Jagiellonian University in Kracow and postgraduate studies in company law at the Warsaw School of Economics. He holds an LLM from the University of Turin in the field of intellectual property law. A graduate of the Top 500 Innovators programme at Stanford University on management and commercialisation of scientific research. Laureate of the 2010 Minister of Science and Higher Education award for best master's thesis organised by the Patent Office of the Republic of Poland, and the 2021 Minister of Development and Technology award for best doctoral dissertation (third prize) organised by the Patent Office of the Republic of Poland. Author of *All rights reserved. The history of disputes over copyright. 1469–1928*. Co-author of the commentary to the Industrial Property Law Act (2016) and the Copyright and Related Law Act (2019).

Aleksandra Gliszczyńska-Grabias is assistant professor at the Institute of Law Studies, Polish Academy of Sciences and member of the Board of Governors of the International Association of Jewish Lawyers and Jurists. Expert in constitutional law, freedom of speech, vulnerable groups rights and legal governance over memory. Co-editor and co-author of *Constitutionalism under Stress* (OUP, 2020) and *Law and Memory: Towards Legal Governance of History* (CUP, 2017). She has held numerous fellowships, including at the University of Cambridge, Yale University and the European University Institute. Principal Investigator in international research consortiums 'Memory Laws in European and Comparative Perspectives' (2016–2019) and 'The Challenge of Populist Memory Politics for Europe: Towards Effective Responses to Militant Legislation on the Past' (2021–2024).

Paul De Hert is full professor at the Faculty of Law & Criminology at Vrije Universiteit Brussel (VUB) and an associate professor at the Law School/Tilburg Institute for Law and Technology (TILT), University of Tilburg. He is Director of the VUB's Research Group on Human Rights, Vice-Dean of the Faculty of Law & Criminology, and a former director of the Research Group on Law, Science, Technology and Society Studies (LSTS) and of the Department of Interdisciplinary Studies of Law, and Senior Researcher for the iBOF project, 'Future-proofing human rights, Developing thicker forms of accountability'.

Michał Jabłoński is an experienced academic lecturer, affiliated with the Faculty of Law and Administration of the University of Warsaw. Advocate with more than 10 years of experience in handling court and administrative disputes (having previously practiced in one of the largest law firms in the world), representing clients before courts and tribunals at all instances, including the Supreme Administrative Court, the Supreme Court, the Constitutional Tribunal and the Court of Justice of European Union. The author of several dozen scholarly publications.

Vasileios Michail Karkatzounis is an attorney at law with significant experience in projects related to IT law and legal technology. He holds a degree in law from the Faculty of Law, University of Athens, and an LLM from the Queen Mary University of London. He is currently a PhD candidate at the University of the Aegean, Department of Information and Communication Systems Engineering. His research interests focus on online advertising, electronic communications, artificial intelligence, data protection and privacy. He is currently working with the Hellenic Ministry Digital Governance on projects in the fields of IoT, blockchain, cybersecurity and AI. He is a certified privacy professional (CIPP/E) and a regular member of the Scientific Committee of the Ministry of Justice for the impact of AI on the judicial system.

Krzysztof Koźmiński is head of the Department of Economic Analysis of Law, head of the Centre for Regulatory Impact Assessment and head of Postgraduate Studies in Legislative Issues at the Faculty of Law and Administration, University of Warsaw. Author of dozens of scholarly publications, including books on liability for damages for unlawful exercise of public authority, banking institutions offering loans indexed and denominated to foreign exchange rates, and the theory and practice of legislation. Speaker at numerous foreign international scientific conferences (including in China, India, South Africa, England, Portugal, Croatia and Ukraine).

Mateusz Kupiec is a research assistant in the Department of Administrative Law at the Institute of Law Studies, Polish Academy of Sciences. He specialises in data protection and privacy laws, with a particular focus on the legal position of children in the algorithmic society. He also works as a lawyer at Traple Konarski Podrecki & Partners. (ORCID: orcid.org/0000-0001-7280-8955).

Shu Li is assistant professor in Law and Artificial Intelligence at Erasmus University Rotterdam. His research focuses on liability and regulation of new technologies, data protection and digital harms. Dr Shu Li is also adjunct professor in Law and Technology at School of Law, City University of Hong Kong and visiting fellow at University of Helsinki.

Jeanne Mifsud Bonnici is a full professor at the Faculty of Law of the University of Groningen where she holds the Chair in European Technology Law and Human Rights. Professor Bonnici co-leads the Security, Technology and e-Privacy (STeP Research Group), which she also co-founded.

Lilian Mitrou is a professor at the University of the Aegean, Greece (Department of Information and Communication Systems Engineering) and visiting professor at the Athens University of Economics and Business and the University of Piraeus (Postgraduate Studies Programs). She is president of the Institute for Privacy Law, Data Protection and Technology (IPL), established by the European Public Law Organization, and Editor in Chief of *Technology and Communication Law Journal*. Lilian studied law in Athens and holds a PhD in Data Protection (Supervisor Spiros Simitis, University of Frankfurt, Germany). She was Member of the Hellenic Data Protection Authority (1999–2003) as well as of many committees working on law proposals in the fields of privacy and data protection, communications law, e-government, etc. She served (2016–2023) as member of the Greek National Council for Radio and Television (NCRTV). Her professional experience includes senior consulting and researcher positions in a number of private and public institutions, and national and international research projects. She has published books, chapters in books and many journal and conference papers (in English, German and Greek).

Przemysław Pałka specialises in the intersections of law, technology and social justice. His research interests include private law, consumer law, data law, the automation of law, and legal aspects of artificial intelligence, virtual objects and interoperability. Pałka has served as the Principal Investigator for the Private Law of Data: Concepts, Principles, Practices, and Politics project. He was previously a Fellow in Private Law at Yale (2018–2020) and a Researcher at the European University Institute in Florence (2016–2018). He holds a PhD (2017) and an LLM (2014) from the European University Institute, and an MA (2013) from the University of Warsaw, Poland. His contributions and roles in various projects and seminars also emphasise his focus on consumer law and technology's impact on inequality and social justice.

Bart van der Sloot specialises in questions of law and technology, privacy and Big Data. He is an associate professor at the Tilburg Institute for Law, Technology, and Society, Tilburg University, and is the General Editor of the *European Data Protection Law Review*. Bart has a dual background in philosophy and law. He has won three prestigious prizes and grants: the NWO Top Talent Grant; the NWO Veni Grant; and the KNAW Early Career Award.

Apostolos Vorras is a partner and Head of Data Protection & Digital Technologies for Deloitte Legal Greece. He is a certified privacy professional (CIPP/E), founder of the Greek Chapter of the International Association of Privacy Professionals, founder of Athens Legal Hackers, member of the Hellenic Association of Data Protection and Privacy, and expert in the pool of experts' list of EDPB. Apostolos holds a law degree from the National and Kapodistrian University of Athens, an LLM in European Law from the Johann Wolfgang Goethe Universitaet Frankfurt am Main and an LLM in Competition Law from the Vrije Universiteit Brussel. He is a PhD candidate at the University of the Aegean, Greece (Department of Information and Communication Systems Engineering), whereas his research interests focus on artificial intelligence, data protection and new technologies.

Bohdan Widła is an assistant professor at the Jagiellonian University in Kraków, where he obtained his PhD *cum laude* after defending a thesis on the protection of scientific and critical editions of public domain works (2019, published by Wolters Kluwer Polska in 2020). His research interests are focused on two areas: the future of copyright protection of computer software; and IP (over)protection of cultural heritage. Before joining academia, he was a practising lawyer (attorney-at-law) for nearly a decade. During that time, he was an associate and senior associate in leading Polish law firms specialising in IT and copyright law.

Wojciech Wiewiórowski has been the European Data Protection Supervisor (EDPS) since December 2019. Adjunct professor in the Faculty of Law and Administration of the University of Gdańsk. The Inspector General for the Protection of Personal Data (Polish Data Protection Commissioner) 2010–2014 and the Vice Chair of the Article 29 Working Party in 2014. In December 2014, he was appointed Assistant European Data Protection Supervisor. His research areas include IT law, processing and security of information, legal information retrieval systems, informatisation of public administration, and application of new IT tools in legal information processing.

TABLE OF CASES

TABLE OF LEGISLATION

Guidelines and recommendations

1

Introduction

JAN CZARNOCKI AND PRZEMYSŁAW PAŁKA

The beginning of the 2020s was a tumultuous time. The COVID-19 pandemic, amidst significant human suffering, accelerated and deepened the digitalisation of socioeconomic life. As people were switching to remote work, school or healthcare, the importance of online services grew, together with ubiquitous data collection. The deplatforming of then-American-president Donald Trump, following the storm of the US Capitol, yet again underscored the power social media give to, and hold over, individuals and communities. The war in Ukraine, where the underdog is managing to resist the Russian invasion, is being fought by soldiers in the tranches but also using drones, X (Twitter) accounts and cyber measures. Finally, the emergence of generative AI systems, most significantly Open AI's Chat GPT and DALL·E, began transformations whose endpoint is difficult to imagine. The first four years of the 2020s sped up decades-old processes and began new ones; they changed the sociotechnical world but also made it the same-just-more. When analysed through the lens of legal sensitivities, digitalisation can be considered one of the most pertinent contemporary challenges to the broadly understood constitutional order and the values the law holds dear.

In the same timeframe, the European Union adopted a number of regulations aimed at taming the excesses of digitalisation while facilitating the desired developments. With the Digital Services Act (DSA),[1] the Digital Markets Act (DMA),[2] the Data Governance Act (DGA)[3] and the Data Act (DA)[4] adopted, and with

[1] Regulation (EU) 2022/2065 of the European Parliament and of the Council of 19 October 2022 on a Single Market For Digital Services and amending Directive 2000/31/EC (Digital Services Act) [2022] OJ L 277/1.

[2] Regulation (EU) 2022/1925 of the European Parliament and of the Council of 14 September 2022 on contestable and fair markets in the digital sector and amending Directives (EU) 2019/1937 and (EU) 2020/1828 (Digital Markets Act) [2022] OJ L 265/1.

[3] Regulation (EU) 2022/868 of the European Parliament and of the Council of 30 May 2022 on European data governance and amending Regulation (EU) 2018/1724 (Data Governance Act) [2022] OJ L 152/1.

[4] Regulation (EU) 2023/2854 of the European Parliament and of the Council of 13 December 2023 on harmonised rules on fair access to and use of data and amending Regulation (EU) 2017/2394 and Directive (EU) 2020/1828 (Data Act) [2023] OJ L 2854.

political agreement reached over the contents of the Artificial Intelligence Act (AI Act), the EU has put in place a body of digital-tech-specific legislation. This occurred as a part of the broader trend of the development in the fields belonging to digital law such as, eg, privacy law, data protection law, cybersecurity and crime online, e-health, media and telecommunications, online competition protection, intellectual property protection online or open data. These regulations emerge at the crossroads of constitutional, private, criminal and administrative law.

From the viewpoint of legal academia, this is a significant shift. Regardless of whether these regulations change a lot or little, or whether we judge them a success or a missed opportunity, one fundamental aspect is different: there now exists a robust *system* of the EU's digital law.[5] Law and technology scholars, for a while now, have been discussing how various sociotechnological phenomena *should* be regulated.[6] Now, however, many of these phenomena *have been* regulated and, given how long the EU's legislative process lasts, these regulations will accompany us for the foreseeable future. Consequently, the tasks of academic lawyers interested in technology are also shifting: in addition to the critique of the status quo and proposing new measures, legal scholars will now have to engage in doctrinal work, making sense of the EU's digital law and helping others navigate it. Digital law could be understood as a branch of inquiry studying changes that information technology brought to law, its theory and practice. One should remember, however, that these socioeconomic and legal changes have not occurred in a normative vacuum. On the contrary, the laws predating them co-shaped them,[7] and the new regulations will be embedded in a much broader system of the EU's primary and secondary law, with the existing principles, concepts and traditions. Among these, a prominent place is held by the principle of proportionality.

The proportionality principle holds a central place in the contemporary legal and constitutional thought,[8] including in the EU law.[9] At the constitutional level,

[5] Of course, it would be false to claim that digital technologies were not regulated in the EU pre-2020s. Examples include the e-Commerce Directive 2000/31 governing the platforms' liability, e-Privacy Directive 2002/58 governing the use of cookies, the Data Protection Directive 95/46 (later replaced by the GDPR) establishing the EU's robust system of personal data protection law, the Database Directive 96/9 and the InfoSoc Directive 2001/29 in the field of intellectual property, as well as several privotal decisions by the ECJ. However, the breadth and depth of the EU's digital law has expended significantly with the recent series of regulations, accompanied by the drive towards unification of laws and not just their harmonisation.

[6] What Roger Brownsword calls 'law 2.0' and BJ Ard and Rebecca Crootof refer to as 'normative uncertainties'. See R Brownsword, 'Law, Regulation, and Technology: The Bigger Picture of Good Governance' in B Brożek (ed), *Research Handbook on Law and Technology* (Edward Elgar Publishing, 2023); BJ Ard and R Crootof, 'Legal Responses to Techlaw Uncertainties' in ibid.

[7] On the law's facilitative role in sociotechnological changes, see JE Cohen, *Between Truth and Power: The Legal Constructions of Informational Capitalism* (Oxford University Press, 2019) 5–9.

[8] On the role of the proportionality principle see esp R Alexy, *Law's Ideal Dimension* (Oxford University Press, 2021); R Alexy, *A Theory of Constitutional Rights*, 1st edn (Oxford University Press, 2010); A Barak, *Proportionality: Constitutional Rights and Their Limitations* (Cambridge University Press, 2012).

[9] T-I Harbo, 'The Function of the Proportionality Principle in EU Law' (2010) 16 *European Law Journal* 158.

the proportionality principle provides a legal methodology or procedure to judge whether the legislative limitation to the right that pursues a particular policy objective is legitimate and reconcilable with a constitution.[10] It does so through the evaluation of: a) the legitimacy of the aim pursued by the measure limiting a right; b) rational connection or suitability between aim pursued and a measure; c) necessity that is existence or lack thereof of alternative, less restrictive measures able to achieve the same objective; and d) balancing, that is weighting the social benefits and detrimental effects to the right caused by a measure.[11] Scholars agree that proportionality is a general principle of the EU law, 'having some universal quest',[12] even if they are eager to point out that the courts do not always use it in a consistent manner.[13] Regardless of whether one is enthusiastic about the proportionality principle[14] or remains critical of it,[15] one cannot question the pivotal role it plays in the EU law. And it will also continue to do so in the EU's digital law.

The proportionality principle will remain central to the EU's digital law not only because of its constitutional, EU Treaty level significance[16] and role as a general principle of the EU law.[17] It will also be pivotal because it is often explicitly ingrained in the structure of the aforementioned laws.[18] Moreover, numerous rights and interests are at stake in the digital milieu, requiring balancing, reconciliation or authoritative decisions as to their respective priority. As this book shows, the EU's digital law is greatly impacted by retrospective and prospective application of the proportionality principle, by the public and private actors. Indeed, as is demonstrated throughout the book, the proportionality analysis is, and should be, undertaken not only by the constitutional and ordinary courts and relevant authorities, but also sometimes by private parties operating in the digital world.

These reasons motivated the creation of this book. On the one hand, we firmly believe that one cannot properly understand, apply or further develop the EU's digital law without a serious consideration of the proportionality principle. As the EU's new legislation has been adopted, to fully comprehend its significance, law

[10] Or other quasi constitutional law, such as EU Treaties.

[11] The last element of the proportionality test – *stricto sensu* balancing – might be understood differently in the European and American doctrine. Whereas European judges often skip the last step, focusing on the rational connection between ends and means, American judges tend to engage in the policy dimension of the cost–benefit analysis directly. See the work of Bomhoff for a further explanation: J Bomhoff, 'Genealogies of Balancing as Discourse' (2010) 4 *Law & Ethics of Human Rights* 109; J Bomhoff, 'Balancing, the Global and the Local Judicial Balancing as a Problematic Topic in Comparative (Constitutional) Law' (2008) 31 *Hastings International and Comparative Law Review* 555.

[12] Harbo (n 9) 159.

[13] See Paul De Hert's and Bart van der Sloots's contributions in this volume, see also: ibid 160–78.

[14] Theoretical and doctrinal work on the constitutional role of proportionality by Barak cannot be interpreted as not enthusiastic. See in general A Barak, *Proportionality: Constitutional Rights and Their Limitations* (Cambridge University Press, 2012).

[15] For a comprehensive account of the exisiting criques, see FJ Urbina, *A Critique of Proportionality and Balancing* (Cambridge University Press, 2017).

[16] Art 52 Charter on the Fundamental Rights of the European Union.

[17] See P Craig and G de Búrca, *EU LAW: Text, Cases, and Materials* 7th edn (Oxford University Press, 2020) ch 5.

[18] See Jan Czarnocki's contribution in this volume.

and technology scholars can no longer constrain their analysis to the field of tech law and will have to take into account the much broader context of the EU's legal system.[19] As a matter of theory, to fully grasp the contents and the logic of the EU's digital law, one must wrestle with the questions posed by the principle of proportionality. On the normative level, we hypothesise, the proportionality principle can help answer many difficult questions that will inevitably arise while applying the EU's digital law, or when critiquing it and proposing new developments. Hence, as a matter of practice, the proportionality principle can be a useful tool or a method for answering, in a lawyerly manner, normative questions regarding the (proper) balancing of various rights and interests at stake.

On the other hand, the developments in the EU's digital law will also affect the proportionality principle. As the proportionality test will inevitably be deployed both when applying the digital laws by the private parties, and when resolving disputes by courts, these new decisions will become part of the larger *acquis* needed to fully grasp the position of the principle of proportionality in the broader context of the EU law. Hence, our hope is that this book will prove useful to scholars of legal theory or constitutional law who, until now, did not treat the digital policy questions as central to their scholarship. By rendering proportionality so pivotal to the body of digital law, the EU lawmakers have begun a process of transformation of the principle itself.

Put simply: the EU's digital law and the principle of proportionality have been, and will remain, in a dialectical relationship: influencing one another and growing in importance towards one another. Regardless of whether readers come to this tome from a tech law background, or a theoretical or doctrinal background, the times when one can ignore the other side of this dialectical relationship are over. Thus, the goal of this book is to closely scrutinise these new legal developments.

This book is based on the conviction that the proportionality principle needs special scholarly attention when applied in the EU digital law. Three factors justify this need: a) the inherent embeddedness of proportionality in any EU law given its constitutional role; b) the challenge posed by digitisation and new types of power; and c) the direct application of the principle in the secondary digital laws. In consequence, in this book, we ponder whether there is something distinct to proportionality application in EU digital law and what lessons can be learned from the principle's application therein. In this spirit, the book provides a critical overview of the dialectical relationship between the proportionality principle application and regulations of information technology in the EU's digital laws. The question of whether there is something distinct to proportionality application in digital law is crucial both from a theoretical and practical perspective. Surprisingly,

[19] Of course, many tremendous scholars have been doing so already; see eg G De Gregorio, *Digital Constitutionalism in Europe* (Cambridge University Press, 2022) and the work and community gathered by the Digital Constitutionalist association: digi-con.org. However, for academics who have been more interested in the political economy of technology, this will constitute a shift that we hope this volume will assist with.

this question has not yet been comprehensively addressed. The book aims to fill this gap by critically scrutinising the EU's approach to regulating the digital world, from the standpoint of proportionality. The book also reexamines the principle itself in the context of the EU digital law.

In theory, proportionality is a balancing tool for the rights and interests of different stakeholders. It is can also serve as an empowerment tool for the weaker party, ie, the party whose rights and interests might be at stake (though often it will be the rights of the structurally stronger party that might be affected). Caution is needed to balance competing fundamental rights and economic interests to allow for high legal protection standards for citizens and dynamic IT and digital economy growth. The proportionality principle is often seen as a suitable tool for this purpose, as it limits the scope of allowed regulation to only what is strictly required. It also necessitates the application of legal norms with due regard to competing rights and interests. Still, given the dynamic development of IT and the digital economy, it is an open question of what is strictly necessary regulation (and how to assess it) in each instance or necessity of a given measure when limiting a particular right. It is also uncertain whether lawmakers gave due regard to structural changes brought by IT and, in consequence, to proportionality application in these various contexts. Explicitly, this is a question of whether the extent to which lawmakers succeeded in providing for a structural balance between stakeholders in the regulation is sufficient, given the changes IT brings to applying the law.

From this perspective, proportionality can be seen as: a) a matrix of conflicting rights and interests; b) a regulatory virtue as to whether to regulate or not; c) a principle defining the limits of the law, and where politics and decision-making take the law's place; d) a law's interpretative virtue, balancing conflicting rights and interests; and e) an empowerment tool, through assumptions protecting rights on behalf of a weaker party in a liberal democracy.

We think that there is a need to pause and reflect on these issues since, as much as IT brought differences in how the law is applied, it must have also brought differences in how proportionality, as one of the central legal virtues, is applied. Consequently, the first supplementary question posed in the book is what limits proportionality introduces for the legislators and how to regulate IT and the digital economy proportionally. The second question is how to balance rights and interests proportionally in the digital economy. The third is, in consequence, what separates the application of the proportionality principle in the EU digital law from the traditional application of the proportionality principle?

To answer these questions, the book brings together experts on the proportionality principle and researchers dealing with regulatory issues related to information technologies and the digital economy. The book aims to answer these questions by focusing on legal actors and conflicts that aim to be legally remedied between them by the proportionality principle. Therefore, the book is not focused merely on technology, but also on legal actors. Consequently, the book concentrates on how real-life conflicts and power struggles are resolved through digital law and whether proportionality therein applied fulfils the role of a balance-bringer.

Although the law is a mechanism of social coordination, it is imperfect in foreseeing and solving *ex ante* all conflict. Therefore, there is a need for an analysis of who is positioned structurally in digital law in any given case (and how), and whether proportionality can provide or amend a structural balance in a particular situation, providing for the highest possible level of fundamental rights protection, safeguarding digital economy development at the same time.

Hence, the book also focuses on various social roles in which a natural and legal person appears in digital law. These roles range from, eg, a data subject and data controller in data protection, consumer and trader in consumer protection, or user and provider in AI systems regulation. All these legal roles correspond to different rights and obligations vis a vis multiple stakeholders engaged in the given context. When rights and interests conflict, proportionality is almost always used to bring balance in each case when there is uncertainty regarding the law's application.

However, it is uncertain whether there is an authoritative and clear-cut answer to the question of distinctiveness of proportionality in the digital law context. The proportionality principle is all-encompassing in recently proliferated EU digital law. It appears in various contexts, with multiple stakeholders acting in different legal roles. However, what scholarship can provide from a pragmatic perspective is an analysis of crucial parts of digital law and answers to particular legal conflicts, which proportionality aims to reconcile. In this way, the practical effects of proportionality application in crucial subfields of digital law which impact people the most can be understood. In this way, common necessary elements will appear that distinguish proportionality in digital law.

To achieve this goal, the book first describes and analyses the theory and history of the proportionality principle. Second, it critically reflects on recent regulatory initiatives in the EU's digital law, from the proportionality perspective, and inquires into the theory of structural differences setting proportionality apart as applied in the IT context. The choice of subjects is determined by the need to provide a detailed analysis of the proportionality principle in digital law with, at the same time, broad cross-examination of as many as possible instances of proportionality in digital law. However, the vastness of digital law and many new legislative initiatives preclude thorough analysis of every instance of the proportionality principle in digital law in one book. Therefore, the book chooses the most important theoretical and practical instances in which, according to the authors' view, the proportionality principle reveals itself most fully: where proportionality shows its most salient features it provides insight into the book's leading questions.

The book's foreword is by Professor Wojciech Wiewiórowski, European Data Protection Supervisor, who reflects on the constitutional and social dimensions of the challenges that digitalisation brings. He states that proportionality should be at the forefront of not only scholarly reflection but policy debate. Professor Wiewiórowski also underscores the special place data protection law has in EU digital law, and explains why.

The first part of the book is dedicated to the historical, theoretical or meta-level at which the proportionality principle functions in EU digital law. Therefore, the chapter two, by Bart van der Sloot, empirically traces the origins of proportionality and balancing in the jurisprudence of the European Court of Human Rights and shows how the principle was used increasingly frequently as the number of the cases related to the right to privacy in the ECHR rose. The chapter provides an empirical and historical analysis that positions the proportionality principle in the context of how European human rights law has developed, and how judges started to use the principle more frequently to solve the conflicts between human rights and public interest.

In chapter three, Paul De Hert discusses at length the history of the proportionality principle and its role in Western constitutional thought. He critically examines the principle from the constitutional and theoretical perspective as a cornerstone in European legal theory. His bold analysis deconstructs the principle, criticises it and then lavishly reconstructs it again, arguing that how legal scholars and judges have very different approaches to how they perceive and apply the principle. However, the principle is necessary given axiological ambiguities and the need to decide in the Western constitutions. In this spirit De Hert's contribution demystifies the actual and perceived benefits and functionalities of the proportionality principle, distinguishing between the realities of its application in courts and the normative frameworks proposed in academic literature. Therefore, De Hert offers us a must-read framework for an in-depth understanding of the proportionality principle.

In chapter four, Przemysław Pałka warns against the phenomenon of 'proportionality washing' used by the EU policymakers to justify limited legislative interventions. He also shows how the 'proportionality mindset', in his view, constrains the lawmakers' imagination, ambition and ability to address the digital challenges in an appropriate way. The chapter explains how the EU policymakers, by realising the EU Digital Agenda and Strategy, 'do too much, by doing too little' and what role the proportionality principle-based thinking plays in the pursuit of suboptimal means to the problems posed by digitalisation. He calls for a more imaginative and ambitious rule-making, going beyond self-imposed proportionality thinking constraints.

Disagreeing with Pałka, in chapter five, Jan Czarnocki argues that although imperfect, the proportionality principle is inevitable in EU digital law. Given the principle's omnipresence in the law and inherent conflict between rights and interests, but also the dependence of numerous EU digital laws on the risk-based approach, the proportionality principle is a necessary solution. To make his point, Czarnocki relies on Alexy's theory of proportionality and legal argumentation to support it. He argues that we should focus on transparency and quality of arguments supporting given proportionality decisions, rather than the principle's methodology ideal application. The proportionality should be accepted even if imperfectly applied by courts. The argument claims that the principle's numerous imperfections are its feature, rather than a bug, which, although irremediable, are not in themselves disqualifying.

The second part of the book inquires into how proportionality has been implemented in particular digital laws. It starts with chapter six by Li Shu, who discusses the proportionality principle as applied to the Proposed Artificial Intelligence Liability Directive and the Revised Product Liability Directive. He discusses the main roles and responsibilities of the parties given the proportionality principle's role, including the problem of the burden of proof in the context of the AI systems' related harm.

Looking at the principle of proportionality from the subsidiarity perspective, and as a proper legislative approach, in chapter seven Aleksandra Gliszczyńska-Grabias Krzysztof Koźmiński and Michał Jabłoński reflect on whether there is a balance between the users and providers of the digital services. They reflect on the proportionality principle based on how consumer protection law constructs the relationship between users and service providers, as exemplified by digital payments and social media platforms' service provision. Against the tide, the article criticises privileging the position of a consumer based on fundamental rights over and without due regard for the interests of service providers. Such an imbalance is, in the view of the authors, against the fundamental principles of contract law.

Vasileios Michail Karkatzounis, Lilian Mitrou and Apostolos Vorras dedicate chapter eight to the interplay between regulation and the advertising technology ecosystem. They address the way the proportionality principle influences the related rights and interests of individuals and online marketing actors. They argue that the proportionality principle is crucial to understanding the reasoning behind legislative initiatives to mitigate individualistic and societal risks related to targeted advertising, such as the newly adopted DSA.

In chapter nine, Bohdan Widła explores how the DA manages the relationship between device purchasers and manufacturers. From the proportionality principle perspective, he argues that property rights are losing a tug-of-war against copyright and trade secrets in the Internet of Things industry and that the position of the manufacturer is stronger, against the interests of the purchasers. The proportionality principle aids understanding of why this is the case.

In chapter ten, Marcu Florea and Jeanne Mifsud Bonnici reflect on the limitations and proportionality of consent when applied to personal data processing in biomedical research. Their analysis reflects on the limits of the right to data protection, as balanced against the public interest in biomedical research. They provide in-depth analysis and methodology for evaluating what happens if a data subject withdraws his consent for his personal data processing for such a sensitive purpose. They suggest that, in order to comply with the law, the design of withdrawal mechanisms should incorporate the result of a balancing exercise based on the principle of proportionality.

In chapter eleven, Konrad Gliściński criticises interpretations of the notion of necessity in the proportionality principle in favour of copyright holders in the context of online content-sharing service providers. He asserts that the way the CJEU interprets the notion of necessity limits the rights to freedom of expression and information and is thus unnecessarily disproportionate. He uses the notion of Civil Law Policy, taken from Leon Petrażycki, to look for a better way to interpret the concept of necessity in copyright law, which in turn points to the insufficient rational grounding of the CJEU jurisprudence.

Coming back to data protection and reflecting on the proportionality of the EU Digital COVID Regulation, in chapter twelve, Fatma Dogan and Paul De Hert criticise the proportionality of the implemented measures. They provide a legal analysis of why the measures implemented were overtly restrictive and therefore do not meet the proportionality test demands. Their research not only enables a critical reflection about the ways in which the EU reacted to the COVID-19 emergency, but also supports lawmakers in their responses to similar crises in the future.

Finally, in chapter thirteen, Mateusz Kupiec reflects on the proportionality of prohibiting the targeted advertisement for minors in the DSA. He argues that such a solution might be patronising and give rise to numerous unintended consequences, negatively impacting other rights and interests of minors. In his view, the prohibition may be disproportionate, so he calls for a more nuanced approach.

***

Working on this book has been a joy and a challenge, not only because the subject matter is so complex, but also because the legal and socioeconomic landscape has been shifting so quickly. When we began, most of the EU's legislative action in the area of digital law was still in the proposal stage; at the time of completing the manuscript, everything other than the AI Act has been adopted. In a way, digital law will always be characterised by this dynamism. However, it is also always developing in a dialectical relationship to existing legal systems, tradition and concepts. Our hope is that the contents of the book will be illuminating both for the authors trying to understand the EU's digital law better, those willing to critique it, and those proposing how to change it.

At the same time, understanding the intricacies of the EU's digital law will take an increasingly central role in theorising the role the proportionality principle plays in the legal system as a whole. To put it simply, and somewhat provocatively: in a decade from now, the specific challenges will have shifted, and the laws might have been amended, though the deep structure of the problem – the need to balance competing interests and rights through law – will remain largely similar. With this book we hope to advance the thought of both the readers in the foreseeable future, and those coming back to the early 2020s from afar, willing to understand the collective mindset of the time. As always in academic pursuits, the work is far from over.

2

The Origins of Proportionality and Balancing in the Jurisprudence of the European Court of Human Rights

BART VAN DER SLOOT

I. Introduction

There is quite some controversy over the notion of balancing.[1]

On the one hand, the term is increasingly deployed in legal, political and administrative discourse. It is one of the most frequently used notions by legislators, policymakers and courts. When approaching matters through a balancing lens, the interests of two private parties can be weighed against each other, or the private interest can be weighed against the public interest. Such an approach is intuitive and builds on a layperson's understanding of fairness and approach to moral and legal complexities. It is also grounded in one of the archetypal symbols of law: blindfolded lady justice with a sword in one hand and a weighing scale in the other, suggesting that the ultimate role of law is to ensure that the weightiest of interests prevails.

On the other hand, there are quite a number of problems with deploying the notion of balancing in the legal sphere. Balancing is a metaphor, drawn from the physical realm, where two or more objects can be weighed and balanced against each other. But different from physical objects, interests or rights have no weight; weight can only be (metaphorically) attributed. There is no standard or objective measure for how to assign weight to interests or rights, meaning that it is

[1] P Van Dijk, 'Some Reflections on Balancing Conflicting Human Rights' in Y Haeck et al (eds), *The Realisation of Human Rights: When Theory Meets Practice* (Intersentia, 2013) 53–72; B Cali, 'Balancing Human Rights? Methodological Problems with Weights, Scales and Proportions' (2007) 29 *Human Rights Quarterly* 251; TA Aleinikoff, 'Constitutional Law in the Age of Balancing', (1987) 96 *The Yale Law Journal*. J Habermas, *Between Facts and Norms* (Polity, 1996); S Tsakyrakis, 'Proportionality: An Assault on Human Rights?', Jean Monnet Working Paper 09/08 (2008); B Van der Sloot, The Practical and Theoretical Problems with 'Balancing' Delfi, Coty and the Redundancy of the Human Rights Framework (2016) 23 *Maastricht Journal of European and Comparative Law* 439.

ultimately a subjective, moral or political decision by judges, legislators or administrators. There is no standardised measure or unit for weight in the legal realm, like a kilogram, and, different from the physical realm, there is no objective device for weighing the different interests or rights at stake, such as a weighing scale. Thus, while concepts like balancing and weighing have an aura of objectivity, when deployed in the legal realm, the effect is the exact opposite; without any standard, unit or scale, it is ultimately a subjective interpretation that prevails.

Because what weight is assigned to a right or interest and how the various rights and interests are balanced against each other is devoid of objective standards, each judge will have to find their own path, leading to legal uncertainty and legal inequality. The lack of objective criteria means that each matter is judged on its own merits, on a case-by-case basis, leading to a highly incident-driven body of jurisprudence. This leads to an increase in the number of cases and decisions that focus on the circumstances of a particular case: it is the rights and interests relevant to that specific case that should be weighed. This generally means that when rights or interests are balanced in light of the specific circumstances of a particular case, no legal precedents are developed and the larger, societal questions at stake are left untouched.

Balancing also runs counter to the very idea of law, in particular human rights law. Most modern human rights instruments were adopted in the wake of the Second World War, in which the most basic of human rights were trampled. Law and in particular human rights instruments are introduced to counterbalance acts that normally prevail in moral and political discourse. It sets out minimum standards that such decisions must always accord to; these minimum standards cannot be balanced themselves, but must be respected at all times. Balancing is intrinsic to one of the major ethical theories: utilitarianism.[2] In its most basic form, utilitarianism looks at every particular action and asks: does this action inflict more pain than it brings pleasure? If so, the action is morally wrong and should not be pursued. If the action provides more pleasure than pain, the action should be pursued. It was precisely this philosophy against which post-WWII human rights frameworks, such as the European Convention on Human Rights (ECHR), guarded. A utilitarian approach can easily lead to minorities being suppressed. If an act is to the detriment of a small minority, but to the joy of the majority, it is easy to see how the pleasure of the masses will quickly outweigh the pain of the few. The human rights framework explicitly aims at protecting the rights of minorities; the rule of law sets limits to democratic (majority) decision-making. Hence, the human rights framework distances itself from a utilitarian philosophy and is based on the opposed deontological ethics, which emphasises the respect for absolute

[2] A Sen and B Williams (eds), *Utilitarianism and beyond* (Cambridge University Press, 2016); B Williams, JJC Smart and B Williams, *A critique of utilitarianism* (Cambridge University Press, 1983); JJC Smart and B Williams, *Utilitarianism: For and against* (Cambridge University Press, 1973); G Scarre, *Utilitarianism*. (Routledge, 2020). T Mulgan, *Understanding utilitarianism* (Routledge, 2014); D Lyons, *Forms and limits of utilitarianism* (Clarendon Press, 1965).

prohibitions and minimum requirements.[3] Reintroducing the notion of balancing in the human rights framework might hence defeat its very purpose.

There are consequently serious arguments against using notions of balancing and weighing in legal discourse. Today, their use is so omnipresent that most lawyers and legal scholars can simply not see how one could come to a legal decision without them. When pointing to the fact that human rights instruments are not based on the fluid and relative notions of weighing and balancing, but on the binary tests of necessity and legality (an interference either has a legal basis or it has not; an interference either serves a public interest or it does not; an interference either is necessary in a democratic society or it is not), the counter-argument is that necessity by definition entails a test of proportionality and that a proportionality test requires weighing the different rights and interests at stake. Thus, balancing is engrained in the human rights frameworks and intrinsic to decisions by human rights courts.

This chapter will verify to what extent this suggestion is true and does so by studying the jurisprudence of the European Court of Human Rights (ECtHR). Section II will discuss some of the most important aspects of the Convention and the way in which it was designed. Section III will discuss the methodology used for this study. Sections IV and V will discuss the role of the notion of proportionality and balancing in the case law of the Court respectively. The period covered by this research is 1950–2000, which allows for a detailed assessment of whether the two legal metaphors were always part of the Court's legal reasoning and, if not, how these notions entered its jurisprudence and developed over time. Finally, section VI provides an analysis.

II. The Convention

When the European Convention on Human Rights[4] was drafted, the first proposal was to have one article include a list of human rights protections, a second providing ancillary rights and a third laying down a general limitation clause reading:

> The rights specified in Articles 1 and 2 shall be subject only to such limitations as are in conformity with the general principles of law recognized by civilized nations and as are prescribed by law for: (a) Protecting the legal rights of others; (b) Meeting the just requirements of morality, public order (including the safety of the community), and general welfare.[5]

[3] B Hooker (ed), *Developing deontology: New essays in ethical theory* (John Wiley & Sons, 2012); N Naaman-Zauderer, *Descartes' Deontological Turn: Reason, Will, and Virtue in the Later Writings* (Cambridge University Press, 2010); N Rosenstand, *The moral of the story: An introduction to ethics* (Mayfield Publishing, 1997); EV García, *Ethics, Law and Professional Deontology* (ESIC Editorial, 2021); G Wu and Y Li, *Between Deontology and Justice: Chinese and Western Perspectives* (Routledge, 2019).

[4] Convention for the Protection of Human Rights and Fundamental Freedoms Rome, 4.XI.1950.

[5] *Collected edition of the 'Travaux préparatoires' of the European Convention on Human Rights / Council of Europe = Recueil des travaux préparatoires de la Convention européenne des droits de l'homme / Conseil de l'Europe* (Martinus Nijhoff, 1975–85) 8 vols.

This formula incorporated the prescribed by the law criterion and a reference to public interests and the rights of others; though it did not speak of 'necessity', it did allow only such limitations as were in conformity with the general principles of law recognised by civilised (read democratic) nations. Later, a new proposal was put on the table which, instead of enumerating the rights in one article and working with a general limitation clause provided in another, was based on what was called 'precise definition'; each provision contained one specific right and indicated per right whether, and if so, under which conditions that right could be curtailed. This is the version that ultimately prevailed. Although the notions of proportionality and balancing did not figure in any of the discussions of the authors of the Convention found in the *travaux préparatoires*, the ECHR does make use of the term 'necessity', most prominently in the so-called qualified rights, Articles 8 (right to privacy), Article 9 (freedom of religion), Article 10 (freedom of speech) and Article 11 (freedom of association):

> **Article 8**
>
> …
>
> 2. There shall be no interference by a public authority with the exercise of this right except such as is in accordance with the law and is necessary in a democratic society in the interests of national security, public safety or the economic well-being of the country, for the prevention of disorder or crime, for the protection of health or morals, or for the protection of the rights and freedoms of others.
>
> **Article 9**
>
> …
>
> 2. Freedom to manifest one's religion or beliefs shall be subject only to such limitations as are prescribed by law and are necessary in a democratic society in the interests of public safety, for the protection of public order, health or morals, or for the protection of the rights and freedoms of others.
>
> **Article 10**
>
> …
>
> 2. The exercise of these freedoms, since it carries with it duties and responsibilities, may be subject to such formalities, conditions, restrictions or penalties as are prescribed by law and are necessary in a democratic society, in the interests of national security, territorial integrity or public safety, for the prevention of disorder or crime, for the protection of health or morals, for the protection of the reputation or rights of others …
>
> **Article 11**
>
> …
>
> 2. No restrictions shall be placed on the exercise of these rights other than such as are prescribed by law and are necessary in a democratic society in the interests of national security or public safety, for the prevention of disorder or crime, for the protection of health or morals or for the protection of the rights and freedoms of others. …

Besides the qualified rights, there three other articles that have similar formulations. Article 2 (right to life), uses the term 'absolutely necessary', Article 6 (right to a fair trial) speaks of 'strictly necessary' and Article 15 (state of necessity) refers to 'strictly required':

Article 2

…

2. Deprivation of life shall not be regarded as inflicted in contravention of this Article when it results from the use of force which is no more than absolutely necessary:

(a) in defence of any person from unlawful violence;
(b) in order to effect a lawful arrest or to prevent the escape of a person lawfully detained;
(c) in action lawfully taken for the purpose of quelling a riot or insurrection.

Article 6

1. … Judgment shall be pronounced publicly but the press and public may be excluded from all or part of the trial in the interests of morals, public order or national security in a democratic society, where the interests of juveniles or the protection of the private life of the parties so require, or to the extent strictly necessary in the opinion of the court in special circumstances where publicity would prejudice the interests of justice.

Article 15

1. In time of war or other public emergency threatening the life of the nation any High Contracting Party may take measures derogating from its obligations under this Convention to the extent strictly required by the exigencies of the situation, provided that such measures are not inconsistent with its other obligations under international law.

No explanation is provided in the *travaux préparatoires* on the difference between 'strictly necessary', 'strictly required' and 'absolutely necessary',; rather they all seem to emphasise the same, elevated threshold. Both Article 15 and Article 2 seem to foreshadow a proportionality test when they emphasise 'to the extent strictly required' and 'no more than absolutely necessary', as this refers to the relation between means and ends. Most provisions in the Convention, however, do not use the notion of necessity. For example:

Article 3

No one shall be subjected to torture or to inhuman or degrading treatment or punishment.

Article 5

1. Everyone has the right to liberty and security of person. No one shall be deprived of his liberty save in the following cases and in accordance with a procedure prescribed by law:

(a) the lawful detention of a person after conviction by a competent court;
(b) the lawful arrest or detention of a person for non-compliance with the lawful order of a court or in order to secure the fulfilment of any obligation prescribed by law;
(c) the lawful arrest or detention of a person effected for the purpose of bringing him before the competent legal authority on reasonable suspicion of having committed an offence or when it is reasonably considered necessary to prevent his committing an offence or fleeing after having done so;

(d) the detention of a minor by lawful order for the purpose of educational supervision or his lawful detention for the purpose of bringing him before the competent legal authority;

(e) the lawful detention of persons for the prevention of the spreading of infectious diseases, of persons of unsound mind, alcoholics or drug addicts or vagrants;

(f) the lawful arrest or detention of a person to prevent his effecting an unauthorised entry into the country or of a person against whom action is being taken with a view to deportation or extradition.

Article 14

The enjoyment of the rights and freedoms set forth in this Convention shall be secured without discrimination on any ground such as sex, race, colour, language, religion, political or other opinion, national or social origin, association with a national minority, property, birth or other status.

Article P1-1

Every natural or legal person is entitled to the peaceful enjoyment of his possessions. No one shall be deprived of his possessions except in the public interest and subject to the conditions provided for by law and by the general principles of international law.

The preceding provisions shall not, however, in any way impair the right of a State to enforce such laws as it deems necessary to control the use of property in accordance with the general interest or to secure the payment of taxes or other contributions or penalties.

Article P1-2

No person shall be denied the right to education. In the exercise of any functions which it assumes in relation to education and to teaching, the State shall respect the right of parents to ensure such education and teaching in conformity with their own religious and philosophical convictions.

There are two important points to make to assist general understanding of the Convention.

First, Articles P1-1 and P1-2, quoted above, are Articles 1 and 2 of the First Protocol to the Convention.[6] The First Protocol was adopted at the same time as the Convention, yet the right to property and the right to education were left outside of the Convention mechanism itself. Being adopted against the backdrop of the Second World War, the ECHR was predominantly concerned with providing negative rights to citizens and imposing negative obligations on states. The Convention sets limits to the powers of the state: it can never use its powers to torture citizens; it can only deploy emergency measures to the extent strictly required; and it can only enter the home of a citizen in accordance with the law and when necessary in a democratic society.

The rights contained in the Convention are so-called civil and political rights, or first-generation human rights, while the rights to property and education are so

[6] Protocol to the Convention for the Protection of Human Rights and Fundamental Freedoms Paris, 20.III.1952.

called socio-economic rights, or second-generation human rights. The essential difference is that these are positive rights of citizens, namely to enjoy property and education, and that it requires positive action by the state, namely to lay down a regime for property ownership and to facilitate or organise an educational system.[7] What was required from the state in light of these positive obligations was deemed vague by the authors of the Convention and ultimately a political, rather than a legal, question. Thus, these rights were moved to an optional protocol.

Second, the authority of the Court was under discussion when setting up the Convention mechanism.[8] Many countries felt that having a Commission (the European Commission of Human Rights, which did the majority of the work until the end of the twentieth century, when its tasks were transferred to a separate branch of the ECtHR)[9] was sufficient. The Commission had the authority to assess cases and decide on their admissibility; the Court could give an ultimate substantive decision on the matter. Many states felt that if the Commission declared a case admissible, that would signal to the state against which the case was brought that it should reconsider its stance and enter into negotiations with the claimant. Many authors of the Convention believed that the embarrassment of the Commission declaring a case admissible would be enough to put the state to action. This was so, because the number of cases was expected to be low (each case that was declared admissible would thus get due media coverage and political attention) and this in turn was so because the ECHR was set up not to provide protection to incidental problems for individual claimants, but to structural and systemic problems, such as those that had emerged during the Second World War.

Ultimately, the Court was set up as a matter of compromise. But to emphasise that the Convention mechanism should not be used by natural persons to pursue their particular interests, individual applicants were denied the right to petition to the ECtHR. Thus, though they could bring a case to the Commission, even if the Commission declared their case admissible, they could not put their case before Court. Only the Commission itself or a Member State could do so. And they would only do so, it was believed, when the case had a significance that went beyond its particularities, if the case exemplified a wider, societal problem, or revealed a structural injustice in the legal system of the state.

[7] K Vasak, 'A 30 Year Struggle: The Sustained Efforts to Give Force of Law to the Universal Declaration of Human Rights' (2021) *Law Journal of Social & Labor Relations* 20.

[8] B Van der Sloot, *Privacy as Virtue: Moving beyond the Individual in the Age of Big Data* (Intersentia Ltd, 2017).

[9] See for several important changes to the Convention mechanism: 'Protocol No. 9 to the Convention for the Protection of Human Rights and Fundamental Freedoms' (1990), available at www.echr.coe.int/documents/d/echr/Library_Collection_P9_ETS140E_ENG; 'Protocol No. 11 to the Convention for the Protection of Human Rights and Fundamental Freedoms, Restructuring the Control Machinery Established Thereby' (1994), available at rm.coe.int/168007cda9; 'Protocol No. 14 to the Convention for the Protection of Human Rights and Fundamental Freedoms, Amending the Control System of the Convention' (2004), available at www.echr.coe.int/documents/d/echr/library_collection_p14_ets194e_eng.

III. Methodology

This chapter is based on empirical research. The Hudoc database was consulted to find the relevant documents.[10] All judgments, decisions, advisory opinions, reports and resolutions until the year 2000 are included; legal summaries and communicated cases are not, because they have no legal effect. For finding the relevant documents on proportionality, the following search was used: 'proportionate OR proportionality OR proportion OR disproportionat'. For finding the relevant cases on balancing, the following search query was used: 'balance OR balancing OR balanced OR weighing'. For proportionality, this resulted in 2,035 hits, for balancing, 1,551. These documents were subsequently assessed on their relevance. The following caveats apply to the selection:

1. Not all cases and reports have been published on Hudoc. Some are not published or are published in the Yearbook and have not been digitised. These have consequently not been included.
2. The search terms used are in English, although there are two official languages in the Council of Europe: English and French. Though most cases and reports are published in both languages, some appear only in French. These are consequently not included in this research.
3. It may well be that the Court balances interests or rights or uses a proportionality test, without making that explicit or without using the terms used for the query as indicated above. These cases and reports are consequently not included.
4. Not all results for the words 'proportionality' or 'balancing', or variations thereof, were used, for the following reasons:
    a. Sometimes, the terms are not used in the judgment of the Court, but in a dissenting or concurring opinion. These were outside the scope of this research because they have no legal effect.
    b. Sometimes, the terms are used when discussing the facts of the case or the relevant laws at domestic level. Thus, it may appear that an Austrian court has balanced several rights and interest at domestic level; if the Commission or Court has not adopted this language itself, such cases have been left outside the scope of this research.
    c. Sometimes, the terms are not used by the Commission or Court itself, but by either one of the parties, or both. These have been mostly left outside the scope of this research, unless it is clear that the Court agrees with the reasoning of one of the parties when using the terms. An assessment of this point is not a matter of exact science; other researchers may come to different conclusions when making their own evaluation.
    d. Sometimes, the terms are used, but in a non-legal way. For example, 'balance sheet' is a term commonly used in cases on Article 1 Protocol 1;

[10] ECHR, 'HUDOC–European Court of Human Rights', available at hudoc.echr.coe.int/eng.

or the Court could say that, on the balance, it is convinced that the house that was entered by the police was owned by the claimant. These have not been included in this research. Again, a decision on this point is not a matter of exact science – there are many grey areas – and again, other researchers may come to different conclusions when making their own evaluation.

5. A judgment can contain several parts on different aspects of the case. When the Court has used the terms with respect to a decision on two different rights, eg, Article 3 and Article 8 ECHR, these have been counted twice, as one of the goals of this study was to see under which doctrines the terms were introduced and subsequently used most. When there were two different claims under the same right, for example one regarding the secrecy of correspondence and the other on the inviolability of the home, both provided protection under Article 8 ECHR, and the Court used the terminology with respect to both parts, this has only been counted once.
6. When a decision, judgment or report uses both 'proportionality' and 'balancing', it has been included both under the calculations with respect to the first and with respect to the second term. This means that there is overlap between the numbers.

Given these and other limitations, the numbers presented in this study should be taken to be indicative rather than exact.

IV. Proportionality

Proportionality as a legal concept was not deployed in the first years after the Convention was adopted (1950), although it was sometimes referred to by applicants. It was only in the famous *Belgian Linguistic* case (1968) that the Court used that notion itself.[11] Belgium has two main languages (Dutch and French) and is divided in two main regions (Flanders and Walloon). Brussels, the capital, is bilingual and was surrounded by Flemish municipalities, while the main language in the capital increasingly tilted towards French. The school system was roughly divided along these linguistic lines, with Dutch education being offered in the Flemish region, French education in the Walloon and education in both languages in the metropolitan area of Brussels. The complaints concerned the inequality in treatment between parents with a different tongue in the Flemish region, and the interference with the family life of French-speaking parents when their children were taught in a different language than they spoke at home.

The provisions that played a role were Article 2 of the First Protocol (the right to education), Article 8 ECHR (the right to privacy) and Article 14 ECHR (the

[11] ECtHR, *Case 'Relating To Certain Aspects Of The Laws On The Use Of Languages In Education In Belgium'*, application no 1474/62, 1677/62, 1691/62, 1769/63, 1994/63 and 2126/64, 23 July 1968.

prohibition on discrimination). Article 14 ECHR, it should be remembered, cannot be invoked in isolation, but only in relation to another material provision in the Convention. Thus, discriminatory policies as such cannot lead to a violation of the Convention, but only when they have an impact on one of the rights provided protection under the ECHR.

Right at the start of the judgment, at [5], the Court made a general reference in relation to the right to education in which it mentions the notion of balancing.

> The right to education guaranteed by the first sentence of Article 2 of the Protocol (P1-2) by its very nature calls for regulation by the State, regulation which may vary in time and place according to the needs and resources of the community and of individuals. It goes without saying that such regulation must never injure the substance of the right to education nor conflict with other rights enshrined in the Convention. The Court considers that the general aim set for themselves by the Contracting Parties through the medium of the European Convention on Human Rights, was to provide effective protection of fundamental human rights, and this, without doubt not only because of the historical context in which the Convention was concluded, but also of the social and technical developments in our age which offer to States considerable possibilities for regulating the exercise of these rights. The Convention therefore implies a just balance between the protection of the general interest of the Community and the respect due to fundamental human rights while attaching particular importance to the latter.

This reference to the notion of balancing should be understood as a general consideration on the approach taken by the Court rather than a concept that it deployed to determine the outcome of a legal question *in concreto*.

Subsequently, it found at [7] that although the right to education had explicitly been moved to the First Protocol by the authors of the Convention because this is a socio-economic right, it could

> not to be excluded that measures taken in the field of education may affect the right to respect for private and family life or derogate from it; this would be the case, for instance, if their aim or result were to disturb private or family life in an unjustifiable manner, inter alia by separating children from their parents in an arbitrary way.

Thus, the strict separation envisaged by the authors of the Convention between civil and political rights on the one hand and socio-economic rights on the other was nuanced by the Court, stressing that educational matters could also be relevant to the right to privacy, Article 8 ECHR.

The Court found a violation with respect to the policies by the state on the ground that they were discriminatory (Article 14 ECHR) in relation to the right to education (Article P1-2). It was when considering the criteria for assessing whether there had been a violation of Article 14 ECHR when the Court first used the notion of proportionality.

> It is important, then, to look for the criteria which enable a determination to be made as to whether or not a given difference in treatment, concerning of course the exercise of one of the rights and freedoms set forth, contravenes Article 14. On this question the Court, following the principles which may be extracted from the legal practice of a

large number of democratic States, holds that the principle of equality of treatment is violated if the distinction has no objective and reasonable justification. The existence of such a justification must be assessed in relation to the aim and effects of the measure under consideration, regard being had to the principles which normally prevail in democratic societies. A difference of treatment in the exercise of a right laid down in the Convention must not only pursue a legitimate aim: Article 14 is likewise violated when it is clearly established that there is no reasonable relationship of proportionality between the means employed and the aim sought to be realised.[12]

After the *Belgian Linguistic* case, the proportionality test was regularly used with respect to Article 14 ECHR.[13] It was only in 1976, more than 25 years after the Convention was adopted, that the notion of proportionality was first linked to the necessity test of Articles 8–11, namely in the case of *Handyside*.[14] The case regarded restrictions posed to the freedom of expression in light of the 'protection of morals'. The Court noted first that by

> reason of their direct and continuous contact with the vital forces of their countries, State authorities are in principle in a better position than the international judge to give an opinion on the exact content of these requirements as well as on the 'necessity' of a 'restriction' or 'penalty' intended to meet them. The Court notes at this juncture that, whilst the adjective 'necessary', within the meaning of Article 10 para. 2, is not synonymous with 'indispensable' (cf., in Articles 2 para. 2 and 6 para. 1, the words 'absolutely necessary' and 'strictly necessary' and, in Article 15 para. 1, the phrase 'to the extent strictly required by the exigencies of the situation'), neither has it the flexibility of such expressions as 'admissible" 'ordinary' (cf. Article 4 para. 3), 'useful' (cf. the French text of the first paragraph of Article 1 of Protocol No. 1), 'reasonable' (cf. Articles 5 para. 3 and 6 para. 1) or 'desirable'. Nevertheless, it is for the national authorities to make the initial assessment of the reality of the pressing social need implied by the notion of 'necessity' in this context.[15]

It continued to stress the importance of plurality in a democratic society and attached to this the possibility for citizens to receive and impart information and ideas that went beyond those generally deemed favourable, including those that shock, offend and disturb. It was in this light that it introduced the proportionality test. 'This means, amongst other things, that every "formality", "condition", "restriction" or "penalty" imposed in this sphere must be proportionate to the legitimate aim pursued.'[16] The same approach was later taken by the Commission with respect to the same provision, Article 10 ECHR, in the *Sunday Times* case.[17] Later, it extended this approach to other qualified rights, such as Article 8 and 11 ECHR.

[12] ibid [10].

[13] For example, in *Svenska v Sweden*, regarding a claim on the discriminatory restrictions on the right to association (Art 11 ECHR), the Court devoted a separate section to the question of proportionality under Art 14 ECmHR, *Svenska Lokmannaförbundet v Sweden*, application no 5614/72, 27 May 1974.

[14] ECtHR, *Handyside v The United Kingdom*, application no 5493/72, 7 December 1976.

[15] ibid [48].

[16] ibid [49].

[17] ECmHR, *The Sunday Times v the United Kingdom*, application no 6538/74, 18 May 1977.

Finally, both in *X v Austria* (1978)[18] and *Sporrong* (1979), the notion of proportionality was introduced with respect to Article 1 of the First Protocol. For example, in the latter case, the Commission observed that

> while the necessity for such legislation seems to be left to the discretion of the State, Article 1 appears to provide for a limited supervision of the enforcement measures as regards their lawfulness and purpose. Even where their lawfulness is beyond doubt and the purpose at the outset appears legitimate, the question may arise whether the prolonged existence of restrictions amounts to an interference which could become unjustified as going beyond or being disproportionate to their legitimate purpose.[19]

All in all, the use of the term 'proportionality' or variations thereof by the Commission and the Court in the first 30 years of the Convention was very limited. Only Article 14, under which the concept is part of the standard approach by the Court, had significance. This is evidenced in Figure 2.1 below, showing the number of cases in which the term 'proportionality' was used, diversified per provision it was deployed under.

Figure 2.1 Use of proportionality or variations thereof, 1950–1980

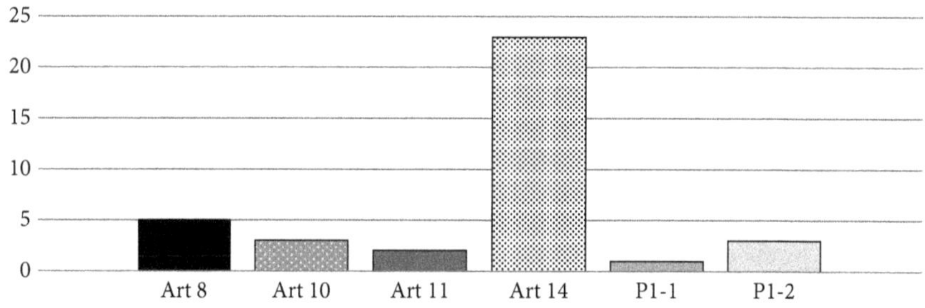

It was only in the next decade that the role of proportionality gained more prominence, though the numbers stayed low, as evidenced in Figure 2.2. Interestingly, although the notion of proportionality is still commonly deployed with respect to Article 14 ECHR, in fact, it is used more often in cases on the right to property (Article P1-1) and in particular the right to privacy (Article 8 ECHR). It is interesting to see that the use of the proportionality test as part of the necessity test in Article 8 ECHR also overshadows its application with respect to Article 10 ECHR, under which provision the notion of proportionality was first linked to the concept of necessity. In fact, Article 10 ECHR is only fourth in line when it comes to the frequency in use of the term 'proportionality'.

[18] ECmHR, *X v Austria*, application no 7287/75, 3 March 1978.
[19] ECmHR, *Sporrong and Lonnroth v Sweden*, application nos 7151/75 and 7152/75, 5 March 1979.

Figure 2.2 Use of 'proportionality' or variations thereof, 1958–1990

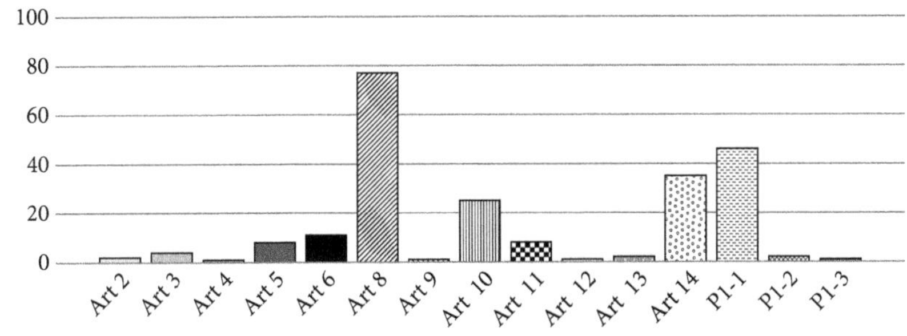

Finally, it is clear that the notion of proportionality is used more frequently over the years. It is only in the 1990s that proportionality is finally predominantly linked to the necessity tests, as the notion or proportionality is used most often in cases relating to Article 8 ECHR and subsequently to cases concerning Article 10 ECHR. Only then, it is used most in Article 1 of the First Protocol, followed by a fair number of cases with respect to Articles 6 and 14 ECHR.

Figure 2.3 Use of 'proportionality' or variations thereof, 1990–2000

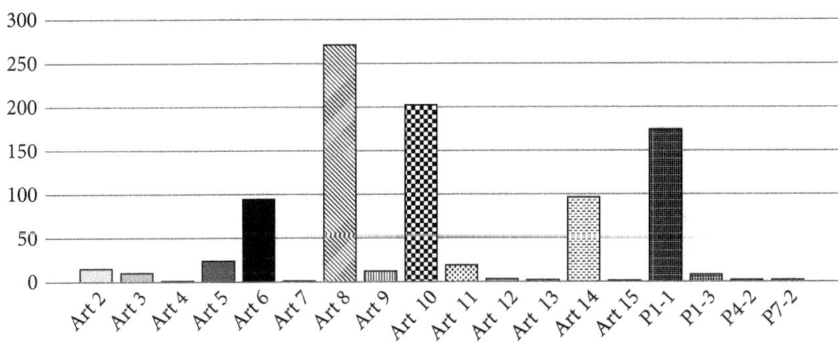

The notion of 'strict proportionality' arrived only late in the jurisprudence of the Court. As might be expected, it was first deployed with respect to a claim under Article 2 ECHR, which indeed seems to suggest a strict test of scrutiny, in the case of Stewart from 1974.[20] Again, the first, and in this case only, other provision under which this concept was also applied was Article 8 ECHR, recorded for the first time in 1991.[21]

[20] ECmHR, *Stewart v the United Kingdom*, application no 10044/82, 10 July 1984.
[21] ECmHR, *Chave nee Jullien v France*, application no 14461/88, 9 July 1991.

Figure 2.4 Use of 'strict proportionality', 1950–2000

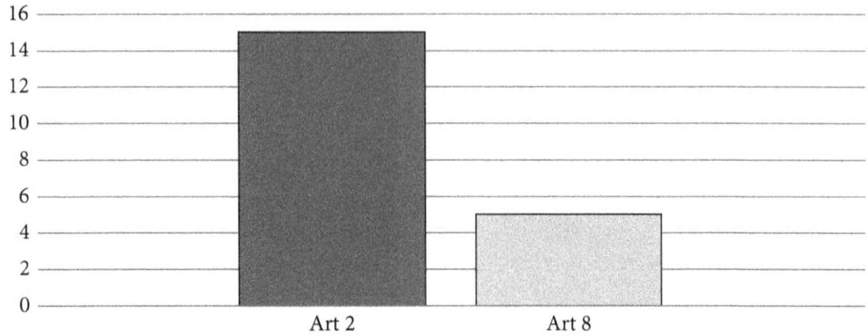

V. Balancing

The history of the notion of balancing under the ECHR is largely similar to that of proportionality. It was first used, as discussed above, in the *Belgian Linguistic* case from 1968, where it was used as a general caveat. Then, in *Kjeldsen et al* (1975), the Commission expanded on that doctrine, again in relation to Article P1-2:

> Here it becomes necessary to balance the right of the State to regulate education 'according to the needs and resources of the community and. of (the) individuals' (Belgian Linguistic Case), and its obligations to respect the right of the parents protected in the same Article. Two considerations seem to be of importance in order to achieve this balance. The first is that the State must have good reasons for the introduction of a subject in the public schools which may interfere with the religious or philosophical convictions of some parents. Secondly, and most important, the State must show respect for these convictions in the way in which the subject is taught. Respect must therefore mean tolerance towards the different religious and philosophical convictions which are involved in a particular subject.[22]

The Commission also copied that language to its discussion on Article 8 ECHR.

> The Commission considers unanimously that there has been no violation of Art. 8 in this case. As the Court has pointed out in the Belgian Linguistic Case, measures in the field of education may come into conflict with this Article 'if their aim or result were to disturb private or family life in an unjustifiable manner, inter alia; by separating children from their parents in an arbitrary way'. If sex education is handled with all due respect for the different convictions of parents, the danger of such a disturbance will be greatly diminished. If in specific cases that disturbance would still result, and it cannot be completely avoided, sex education would not be unjustifiable or arbitrary for the reasons given above. It would be the unavoidable result of the difficult balancing between the interests of the community and the individual in the sphere of education which is implied in the Convention.[23]

[22] ECmHR, *Kjeldsen, Madsen Pedersen v Denmark*, application nos 5095/71, 5920/72 and 5926/72, 211975, [159]–[160].

[23] ibid [169].

It is interesting that in this case, there was an objection to the use of the notion of balancing by one of the judges voiced in a separate opinion. Judge Opsahl warned explicitly for the consequences of minority rights when the notion of balancing would be used, stressing that for

> the task of interpreting P1-2 and applying it in this case, it is, in my opinion, unnecessary and, indeed, inadvisable or incorrect for the Commission to enter into the balancing of needs. Nor should it consider such controversial distinctions as that between 'information' and 'indoctrination' or make its findings dependent on the conclusion that the purpose of the legislation in question is not to impose a certain view of life. The emphasis should be placed elsewhere. As I understand Art. 2 and its reference to the right of parents, the purported objectives of State education are not in themselves decisive. Parents may feel that their convictions, within the meaning of Art. 2, could nevertheless be infringed. An assessment of whether or not the necessary respect had been shown must ultimately be left to the parents themselves. Neither the opinion of the State nor that of a majority of parents, nor even that of the Commission can claim precedence here. To decide otherwise would make the position of minorities much too precarious.[24]

Subsequently, the notion of balancing was used in the previously discussed *Sunday Times* and *Handyside* cases, with respect to Article 10 ECHR in both. In doing so, the Commission explicitly referred to the ethical theory of utilitarianism.

> The questions which then fall to be considered are the needs or objectives of a democratic society in relation to freedom of expression; for without a notion of such needs the limitations essential to support them cannot be evaluated. The Commission agrees with the applicant who stated that freedom of expression is based on the need of a democratic society to promote the individual self-fulfilment of its members, the attainment of truth, participation in decision-making and the striking of a balance between stability and change. The aim is to have a pluralistic, open and tolerant society. Of necessity this involves a delicate balance between the wishes of the individual and the utilitarian 'greater good of the majority'. But democratic societies approach the problem from the standpoint of the importance of the individual and the undesirability of restrictions on the individual's freedom. The Commission accepts, however, that in striking the balance, certain controls on the individual's freedom of expression may, in appropriate circumstances, be acceptable in order to respect the sensibilities of others. It notes, in this context, that 'freedom of expression is commonly subject in a democratic society' to laws importing restrictions considered 'necessary to prevent seditious, libellous, blasphemous and obscene publications' (de Becker case).[25]

In the case of *Klass and others v Germany* (1978), the notion was applied to Article 8 ECHR, where the Commission found: 'As regards the duty to inform the persons concerned, a balance must be struck between the State's interest in its security and the individual's interest in being informed.'[26] And in the case of *Sporrong*, discussed earlier, the notion of balancing was used with respect to a discussion of Article P1-1:

> In considering this question, the Commission will have to balance the applicants' individual interest in protection of their right to peaceful enjoyment of possessions

[24] ibid, Separate opinion of Mr Opsahl [2]–[3].
[25] *Handyside* (n 14) [146]–[148].
[26] ECmHR, *Klass and others v Germany*, application no 5029/71, 18 December 1974.

> and the interest of the State or, as in the present cases, the City of Stockholm, of being able effectively to realise their town plans.[27]

All in all, the notion of balancing was applied in just eight cases until 1980. It was only after 1980 that the notion of balancing became a more standard way of approaching legal questions. The notion was applied regularly to determine the outcome of cases only with respect to two provisions, Article 8 ECHR and P1-1. The notions of balancing and weighing are used less frequently than terms related to proportionality. When the term 'balancing' is used, it is mostly in relation to a proportionality test, while the proportionality test is also deployed without reference to the notion of balancing.

Figure 2.5 Use of 'balancing' or variations thereof, 1950–1990

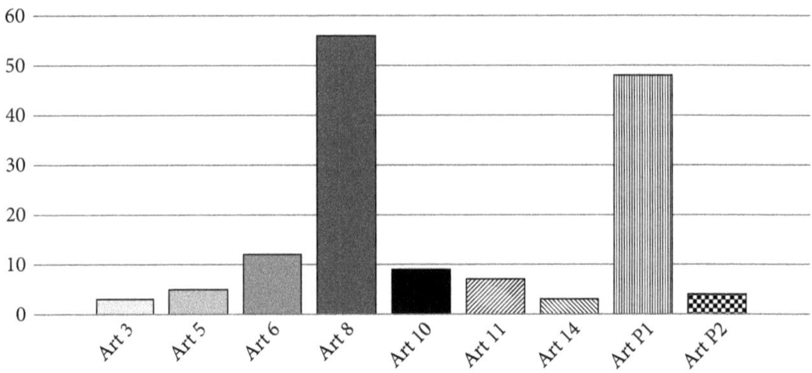

Between 1990 and 2000, the notion of balancing was used more frequently. It continues to be used primarily in relation to Articles 8 ECHR and P1-1, but it is also deployed regularly with respect to Articles 6 and 10 ECHR.

Figure 2.6 Use of 'balancing' or variations thereof, 1990–2000

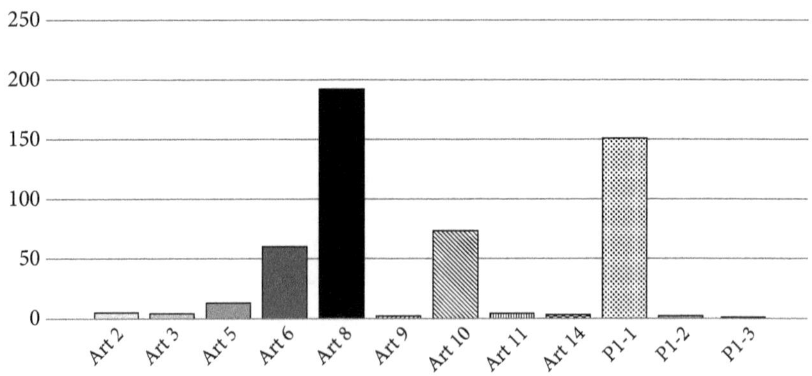

[27] *Sporrong and Lonnroth* (n 19).

VI. Conclusion

From the previous two sections, the following picture emerges.

1. The notion of proportionality is not intrinsic to the necessity test. It was introduced first under provisions in which the concept of necessity is absent.
2. Neither was the proportionality test developed under the provisions that foreshadow such an approach, namely Articles 2 and 15 ECHR.
3. The history of the notion of balancing by and large runs along the same path as the notion of proportionality. When balancing is used, most often, it is in light of the proportionality test, though the reverse does not hold true. Thus, there is a strong link, but no intrinsic connection, between the notions of balancing and proportionality.
4. Proportionality or the variations thereof where more popular than the notion of balancing or variations thereof.

Figure 2.7 Frequency of the use of 'proportionality' and 'balancing'

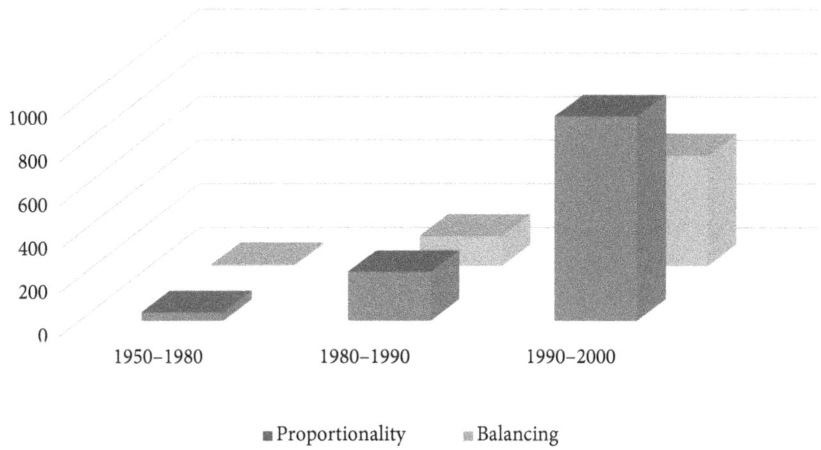

5. The frequency in which the terms are used, even in the last decade included for this study, relative to the total number of cases, is not high.[28] For the first period, proportionality is used in about five per cent of the case and balancing in about one per cent. For the period 1980–1990, the ratio is around 13 per cent and eight per cent respectively. Finally, although used more frequently, the ratio to the total number of cases declines in the period 1990–2000, namely to about 10 per cent and 5.5 per cent respectively. On the one hand, the relatively low percentage might be explained by the fact that many decisions, concerning the admissibility of the case, are taken on the basis of

[28] For the total number of cases, only the English documents have been included, to allow for a better comparison to the documents found through the use of English search queries in Hudoc (section III).

formalities (was the application submitted on time; were the domestic remedies exhausted; etc) and the question whether the claim falls to be considered under the Convention at all (*ratione personae; ratione materiae; ratione loci; ratione temporis*), which do not normally entail either a test of necessity, proportionality or balancing. On the other hand, the following points must be underlined:

a. In most cases in which either the term 'proportionality' or 'balancing', or both, were used, they did not play a role of significance. Rather, the Court would mention the concept once, as a side note or in its general approach to the case. These cases are nevertheless included in the numbers presented in Figure 2.8.
b. Also, it must be stressed that the fact that the terms 'proportionality' or 'balancing' are used with respect to one part of the claim means that the case is included in the Figure 2.8, while may not have used the term with respect to the legal assessment of claims under other provisions invoked in the same case.
c. In most cases in which 'proportionality' was used, the term 'balancing' was also used, so that these two figures cannot be added up to arrive at a total number.
d. As explained in the methodology section, when 'proportionality' or 'balancing' is used in two different parts of a judgment or report, on two different provisions, these have been counted twice.

Figure 2.8 Frequency of the use of 'proportionality' and 'balancing', and the total number of documents

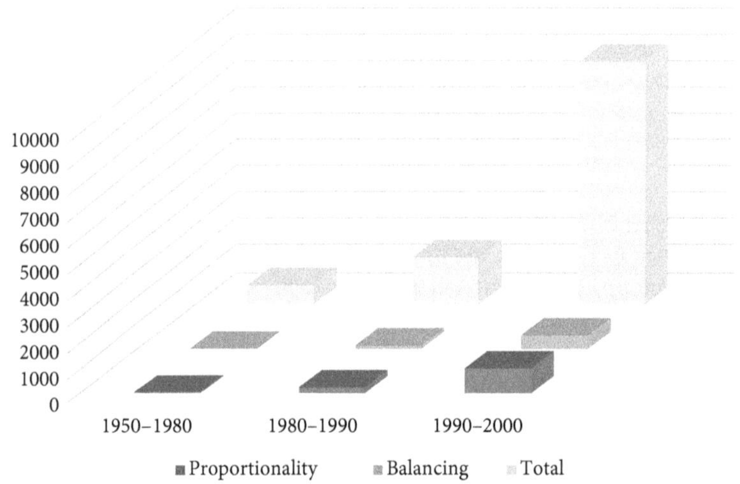

6. There are some articles under which both notions seem to have played a more prominent role, in particular Articles 8, 10 and 14 ECHR and Article P1-1. Figures 2.9–2.12 below show the extent to which the use of the notions of proportionality and balancing are significant in relation to the total number of cases on these provisions. The following should be taken into account when interpreting the figures:
   a. Cases may concern more articles, eg both a claim with respect to Article 8, with respect to Article 10 and with respect to a violation of Articles 6 and 14 ECHR. These cases have consequently be counted in each relevant category.
   b. Although applicants may invoke a provision, the Court does not always discuss the arguments concerning that right in detail, for example merely stating that the provision is not relevant to the case or that all questions have already been dealt with under another provision. This is especially so for Article 14 ECHR.
   c. For the selection of the relevant documents, the Hudoc database allows the selection of cases that were issued per provision in the Convention. However, cases are not always categorised accurately and consistently in this respect.

   Hence, it should be underlined again that the numbers below are indicative only.

Figure 2.9 Frequency of the use of 'proportionality' and 'balancing', and the total number of documents in relation to matters on Article 8 ECHR

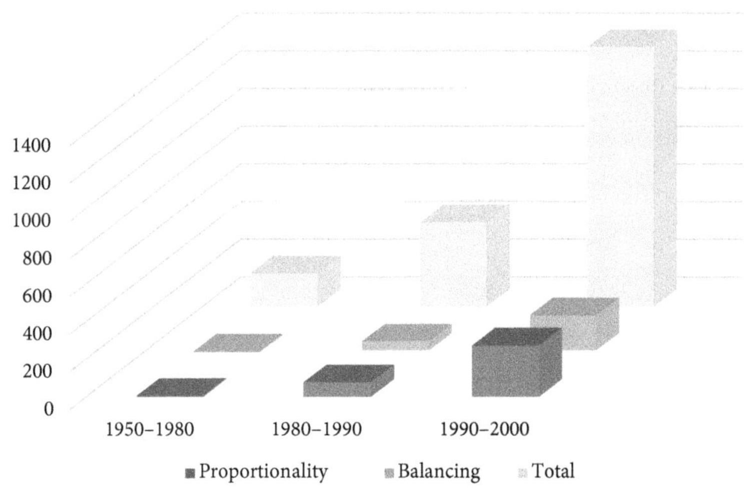

Figure 2.10 Frequency of the use of 'proportionality' and 'balancing', and the total number of documents in relation to matters on Article 10 ECHR

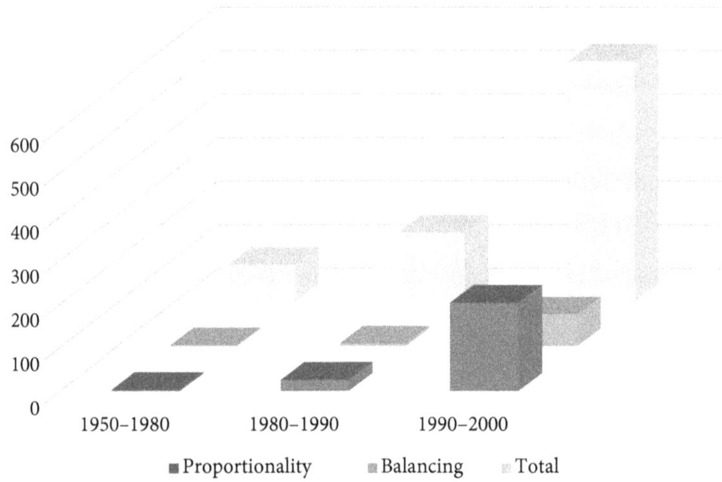

Figure 2.11 Frequency of the use of 'proportionality' and 'balancing', and the total number of documents in relation to matters on Article 14 ECHR

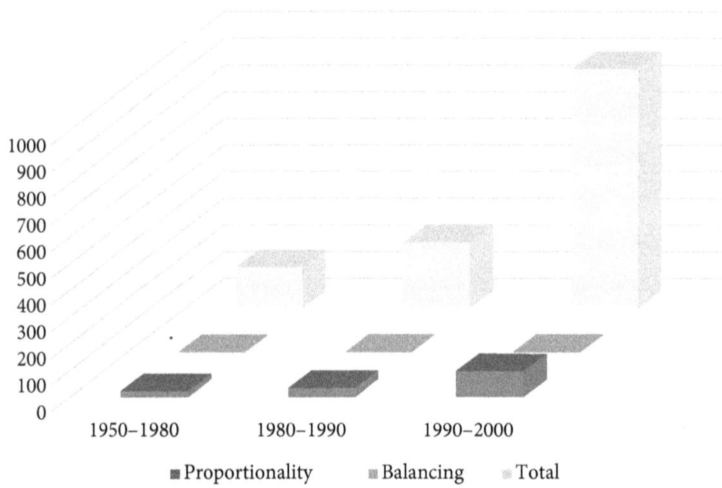

From Figures 2.9–2.12, it appears that the use of the terms proportionality and balancing is low compared to the total number of matters, even though it are these provisions under which the two terms have played the most prominent role. There is a marked difference between Articles 10 and 14 ECHR, under which the notion of balancing is seldom used, and Article 8 ECHR and Article P1-1, under which the ratio is more equal (353-248 for Article 8 ECHR; 221-199 for P1-1).

Figure 2.12 Frequency of the use of 'proportionality' and 'balancing', and the total number of documents in relation to matters on P1-1

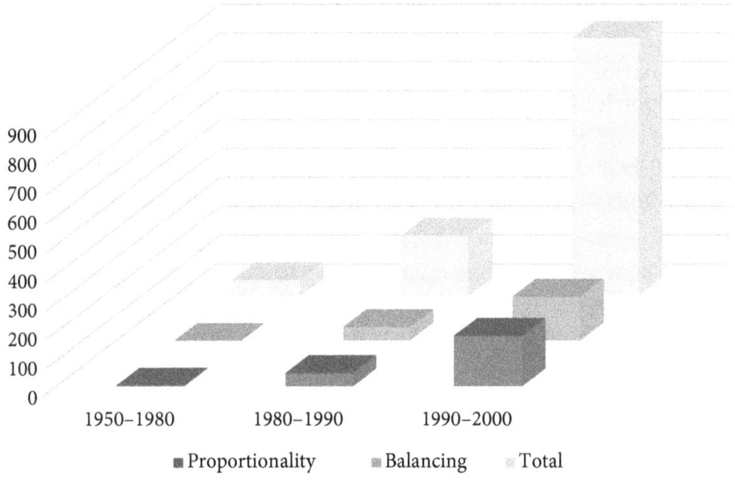

7. The terms 'proportionality' and 'balancing' were introduced via the Protocol, in particular with respect to Article 2 of the First Protocol, and have gained prominence under Article 1 of the First Protocol. As explained, this should not come as a surprise, as the precise reason for putting these provisions in a separate Protocol instead of the Convention was that they are socio-economic or second generation rights which require positive action by states. Positive obligations, different from negative obligations, entail financial costs. Generally speaking, all states would want the most perfect educational system, as they would want the best healthcare with universal coverage, the most effective police force and the cleanest living environment, and so on. But the budget is limited and so choices have to be made. Economic issues are typically discussed in terms of balance, costs and benefits, and weighing. There is a scale, there is a standardised unit (monetary value such as the euro) and there is an objective way for arriving at a calculation of the costs and benefits. It seems more intuitive to apply a utilitarian than a deontological approach to economic and financial matters.
8. From this perspective it also becomes clear why the notion of 'proportionality' may have been introduced in respect to Article 14 ECHR. The term was used first in the *Belgian Linguistic* case, in which the Court also explicitly rejected the distinction between negative and positive rights and obligations, both by blurring the lines between the rights in the Convention and those in the Protocol, and by stressing that the provisions in the Convention also entail positive rights by citizens and positive obligations by states. 'No distinctions should be made in this respect according to the nature of these

rights and freedoms and of their correlative obligations, and for instance as to whether the respect due to the right concerned implies positive action or mere abstention.'[29] Obviously, the reason why the Belgian state did not offer education in two (or three, when German is also included) languages throughout Belgium was for reasons of costs. It is also from this perspective that proportionality and balancing have their background in economic and financial considerations.

9. Article 8 ECHR seems to have functioned as the perfect vehicle for popularising both the notion of proportionality and balancing, for the following reasons:
   a. The high number of cases with respect to this provision.
   b. As seen in the *Belgian Linguistic* case, it is this provision that the Court uses to include rights and interests that were left outside the scope of the Convention by the authors, most often entailing positive obligations by states.[30]
   c. The Court also prefers to refer to Article 8 ECHR rather than other provisions in the Convention or its protocols; the right to privacy has become a super-right of sorts that encompasses almost all aspects of life.
   d. This also means that many economic interests are provided protection under the right to privacy, and that many cases under Article 8 ECHR haa an economic angle to it,[31] such as compensation for being fired at work, for destruction of property, or for reputational harm, matters concerning inheritance and the fair distribution of family property.
   e. Article 8 tends to overshadow Article 14 ECHR as, again, the Court prefers to discuss questions only under the former provision, especially when they include discriminatory aspects, such as against homosexual, transgender or queer people.
10. The Court explicitly linked the introduction of balancing to utilitarian philosophy and it ignored criticism by judges warning for the consequences for minorities.[32]

[29] *Case 'Relating To Certain Aspects Of The Laws On The Use Of Languages In Education In Belgium'* (n 11) [9].

[30] B van der Sloot, 'Privacy as personality right: why the ECtHR's focus on ulterior interests might prove indispensable in the age of Big Data' (2015) 80 *Utrecht Journal of International and European Law* 25.

[31] This trend is described up to 2010 in B van der Sloot, 'Where is the harm in a privacy violation? Calculating the damages afforded in privacy cases by the European Court of Human Rights' (2017) 4 *Journal of Intellectual Property, Information Technology and Electronic Commerce Law*.

[32] For more recent criticism, see the opinion of Pinto De Albuquerque, inter alia in ECtHR, *Muhammad and Muhammad v Romania*, application no 80982/12, 15 October 2020.

3

Proportionality in Modern Regulatory States Confused about Priorities. Judges Like, but do not Comply with Academic Doctrines

PAUL DE HERT

> In Germany, the professor is God: in England, the judge is God.[1]

> A doctrine … is a way of dealing with problems across a range of problems … The overall picture in each jurisdiction is, I believe, a messy blend of cases in which judges employ a loose form of structured proportionality analysis and an equally loose version of categorical reasoning.[2]

> The first model, described in this way, has great plausibility, and most laymen and lawyers, I think, would respond to it warmly. The metaphor of balancing the public interest against personal claims is established in our political and judicial rhetoric, and this metaphor gives the model both familiarity and appeal. Nevertheless, the first model is a false one, certainly in the case of rights generally regarded as important, and the metaphor is the heart of its error.[3]

I. Proportionality and Europe's Expert-Driven Paternalism (Introduction)[4]

Academics approach cases not bottom-up from the facts, but top-down from the law. This allows them to offer the judiciary a bigger picture of the law, to position a

[1] L Goff, *The Search for Principle* (Maccabean Lecture, 1983), reprinted in W Swadling and G Jones (eds), *The Search for Principle: Essays in Honour of Lord Goff of Chieveley* (Oxford University Press, 1999) 327.

[2] M Tushnet, 'Is There a Doctrine of Proportionality in Asia (or Anywhere)?' in P Yap (ed), *Proportionality in Asia* (Cambridge University Press, 2020) 269–83.

[3] R Dworkin, *Taking Rights Seriously* (Harvard University Press, 1977) 198.

[4] This contribution is written as part of the iBOF project 'Future-proofing human rights. Developing thicker forms of accountability'. The author thanks the editors and Bárbara da Rosa Lazarotto (LSTS,

particular case and to offer critiques of past decisions. But are they right to insist on structured testing of state limitations to human rights? A critical investigation of dominant narratives on the priority of rights in Europe and its commitment to the rule of law tradition, mixed with legal and political theory (incorporating authors like Ronald Dworkin, Kai Möller, Alasdair MacIntyre and Jens Meierhenrich), shows how an appearance of structured testing 'fits' an historical tradition of paternalism and managerialism, and related values of foreseeability. Using the expert language of (structured) proportionality offers advantages for the judiciary, but in practice the courts give themselves leeway when applying it.

The doctrine of proportionality in the wide sense is the name given to the set of tests used to establish whether a limitation of rights is justifiable. Proportionate limitations of rights are justifiable; disproportionate ones are not. Academics present a more elaborated version of the doctrine. Following their account, proportionality requires answers about rights limitations by states: that state measures pursue a legitimate objective and can be rationally related to this objective; that they are necessary in the sense that there must be no less restrictive but equally effective alternative, and that a balancing exercise demonstrates that the importance of the state interest invoked outweighs the seriousness of the restriction of the rights of the individual.

This chapter assesses the proportionality principle in European case law and legal thought. The focus is on the different interpretations of the principle in courts as opposed to those defended in literature, mainly by those who work in the slipstream of Robert Alexy. The chapter prioritises a judicial perspective over an academic one when assessing proportionality. It leans towards an inductive approach and shows that courts often lack a strict structure in their legal reasoning. Academic literature suggests a fully matured doctrine with a structured test that is applied quasi-systematically by courts with only small variations. But the formulation in literature of the components of the test is often more normative than descriptive. Judgments that do not deal with the proportionality test in a structured way are abundant but disregarded by scholars as poorly motivated.

A broad historical approach is proposed as a background for a deeper understanding of the rise and pretended use of the principle in Europe. The argument is structured as follows. It begins by discussing the European struggles with giving clear priority to rights (section II.A). Rights in Europe are prima facie trumps (section II.B), in line with a tradition of paternalism and priority of the modern state where experts with expert-language become central characters (section II.C–D). The use of proportionality hints is a way for judges to secure recognition as experts (section V.C) and to play a role of peacemaking or truce-keeping in a world without shared first moral principles (section VI.)

Vrije Universiteit Brussels), Dr Mritunjay Kumar (Centre for Comparative Public Law, Himachal Pradesh National Law University, Shimla, India) and César Augusto Fontanillo López (CITIP KU Leuven) for comments.

The traditional story about the role of World War II as a transition point towards societies based on the rule of law and the priority of rights, with judicial review of laws by courts (section III.A–B) and strong review by the two European Courts (section III.C–section IV.AB) is not downplayed. Rather, it is situated in a historical tradition of bureaucratic states that conceive individuals as independent rational beings, prescribing their moral standpoint to themselves, but also as anomic products of circumstances whose happiness must be contrived for them.[5] The analysis voices a seldom-heard message about a European tradition on the Continent (the countries of Europe except for Great Britain and Ireland) of state managerialism and paternalism. This tradition retarded the transition away from authoritarian rule and interfered with transitions to democracy and the rule of law. At the same time, it created the conditions for the emergence of the welfare state in the late nineteenth century. State dirigisme – so integral to the German idea of freedom – is anathema to the Anglo-American way of thinking about the relationship between the state and the individual. The reception of these ideas in Continental Europe was made from a paternalistic and managerial stance. It explains the absence of any European ideal of human rights as trump cards and warrants a cautious understanding of the European post-World War II move towards the priority of rights and proportionality (section VI.C).

The chapter looks at the historical roots of proportionality in court (section IV.D) and its interpretations by CJEU) (section IV.A–B). The supposed adherence of judges in general to the test is but one of the myths surrounding the test that prevent a clear vision (section IV.D). Inspired by proportionality scholars, textual analysis of the way in which rights are formulated is downplayed to address a broader range of values and interests, making no attempt to bring them into a systematic relationship. Rights lose their assumed priority status and are opened to balancing with other interests. The insistence on balancing is quasi-religious and the idea of categoric reasoning is extruded. But drift sand – antipode of legal certainty and predictability – has its limits. Hidden behind the balancing rhetoric, judges often implicitly reintroduce categorical reasoning, sometimes in ways that undermine the pretended functions of the test (section V.A–C). It is a broad test, and the components invite reasoned analysis. But its openness to a broad range of considerations allows judges to bring in openly or below the level of consciousness categorical preferences that are often state-friendly, but not faithful to the idea of balancing that is respectful of all interests at stake (sections V.B and VI).

Poorly rooted, easily captured, one is amazed to note how many 'technicalities of the test' (burden of proof, nature of the interest (any state interest?) to limit rights; relationship with levels of scrutiny) remain vague when compared with the US doctrine on testing and scrutiny (section V.B).

The priority of rights and the idea of preserving the constitution through the judiciary is only half of the truth, the other half being cautiousness and judicial

[5] A MacIntyre, *After Virtue* (University of Notre Dame Press, 2007) 228.

restraint, and deference to step on the seat of the legislator and reluctance to overrule state laws and actions based on human or constitutional rights (section V.B). The proportionality inquiry, starting from the premise that it is frequently justifiable to infringe, or to interfere, with these rights, is perfectly compatible with a culture of state managerialism and enlightened paternalism. So, what are academics supposed to do (section VI.)? Advocate more structured testing to enhance human rights accountability? American concepts such as 'constitutional generosity' and the introduction of various levels of scrutiny (strict scrutiny; intermediate scrutiny; and rational basis scrutiny) in the legal practice of courts are discussed. The author does not necessarily subscribe to the former, but the latter might clear the (political) air in which the courts operate and lessen academically fueled expectations about proportionality testing in Europe.

II. Societies without Priorities

A. European Fundamental Rights as Trump Cards? (Ronald Dworkin)

Dworkin is famously known for his metaphor of human rights as trumps. These rights are overriding demands by individuals to society and states for respect for them and their positions. Rights constrain governmental use of its power. Human rights have a high moral status and should trump simple state policies. Even if the community were better off by violating rights, it must not do so.[6] Kai Möller has recently brought together all Dworkin's writings on the topic and distinguished older and more recent writings. In the older writings (of the 1970s) rights were based on a liberal conception of equality and, once recognised, were considered fundamental and in need of strong protection. In Möller's understanding of Dworkin's *Taking Rights Seriously*-era, rights are presented by Dworkin in a more absolute way: rights categorically trump any interest advanced by the state that clashes with them to combat excessive utilitarianist thinking.[7] A subtlety is lost when the trump

[6] R Dworkin, *Taking Rights Seriously* (Harvard University Press, 1977) 199: 'if rights make sense at all then the invasion of a relatively important right must be a very serious matter. It means treating a man as less than a man, or as less worthy of concern than other men. The institution of rights rest on the conviction that this is a grave injustice, and that it is worth paying the incremental cost in social policy or efficiency that is necessary to prevent it'.

[7] Later writings (R Dworkin, *Law's Empire* (Hart Publishing, 1998); R Dworkin, *Justice for Hedgehogs* (Belknap Press, 2013)) go deeper into the structure of rights and bring us a more familiar theory of rights based on human dignity. K Möller, 'Dworkin's Theory of Rights in the Age of Proportionality' (2018) 12 *The Law and Ethics of Human Rights* 281, 287. It would bring us too far to comment on Möller's characterisation of Dworkin's work. In *Taking Rights Seriously* Dworkin identifies equal concern and respect as a source of human rights, although human dignity is also mentioned as a possible candidate (198). The emphasis of human dignity will grow in time with *Justice for Hedgehogs* celebrating dignity the essential core of living well. This shift has no impact on Dworkin's view that the requirement that

metaphor is taking as an absolute. Dworkin accepts utilitarian-based policies by the states but does not believe that elections alone will be sufficient to orient and frame these policies. Voting based on external preferences might greenlight policies that threaten minority views.[8] A society respectful of rights will therefore recognise that rights must be sufficiently strong to withhold (only these) utilitarian policies that infringe rights. Balancing between the rights of the individual and the demands of the society at large, Dworkin stresses with insistence, is not the way to uphold fundamental rights. Balancing must only be done when there is a conflict of rights between individual. In all other cases – where the individual faces the government – it should be avoided since it relies on a confusion of society's rights with the rights of members of society.[9] In reality governments do not represent the rights of the members of a society, but solely their own governmental interest. In these cases, a system of law must work not with balancing, but with proper, recognised grounds limiting a right that recognises the importance of rights and only allows limitations in cases of emergency (such as to prevent a catastrophe), clear and substantial risk, and clear and major benefit.[10]

European human rights law knows very few absolute rights (see below) and the formulation of most rights does not suggest any 'strong' adherence in the sense of Dworkin's theory. With regard to rights such as communication, privacy and freedom of expression, this is made clear in the text of the 1950 European Convention on Human Rights (ECHR), where rights are most often followed by specific or more generic formulated exception or limitation grounds.[11] Article 8 ECHR, for example, proclaims the right of every person to respect for 'his private and family life, his home and his correspondence', but provides for a system of restrictions if these are 'prescribed by law', 'necessary in a democratic society' and pursue a legitimate aim.[12]

political rights recognised in a society should be 'strong' to protect minoritarian views against utilitarian policies. Dworkin does not consider strong rights as absolutes (that would be against his general theory) but favours strict scrutiny along the lines of the doctrine of levels of scrutiny developed by the Supreme Court (see below).

[8] On utilitarianism as a theory respectful of liberal equality and the phenomenon of external preferences, Dworkin, *Taking Rights Seriously* (ibid) 235, 358.

[9] '*Balancing* is appropriate when the Government must choose between competing claims of right – between the Southerner's claim to freedom of association, for example, and the black man's claim to an equal education. Then the government can do nothing but estimate the merits of the competing claims, and act on its estimate. The first model assumes that the 'right' of the majority is a competing right that must be balanced in this way; but that, as I argued before, is a confusion that threatens to destroy the concept of individual rights' (Dworkin, *Taking Rights Seriously* (n 6) 199).

[10] Dworkin, *Taking Rights Seriously* (n 6) 191, 203–04.

[11] In older literature the term 'accommodation clause' is used (eg, TA O'Donnell, 'The Margin of Appreciation Doctrine: Standards in the Jurisprudence of the European Court of Human Rights' (1982) 4 *Human Rights Quarterly* 474, 477. I will use that term occasionally, but prefer the more straightforward term 'limitation ground'. The rights with generic limitation grounds include Arts 8 (right to privacy and family life), 9 (freedom of thought and religion), 10 (freedom of expression), and 11 (freedom of association), and Art 2 of the Fourth Protocol (liberty to travel and to choose place of residence).

[12] Similar limitation grounds are provided for in subsequent articles, including Art 10 (freedom of expression) and Art 11 (freedom of assembly). Similar limitation grounds are to be found in the 2000

The contrast with the 1787 US Constitution and its 1791 Amendments is striking; it suffices to look at freedom of expression and assembly. In the ECHR these rights, only mentioned in Articles 10 and 11, are accompanied by long second paragraphs with extensive limitations. In the US these rights are concentrated in the first (!) Amendment and given almost absolute protection.[13]

As said, most European rights are recognised with specific or generic limitation grounds. There are rights formulated, in the spirit of the First Amendment, in a succinct way with some exceptions, but no generic limitation clause (like the provision prohibiting torture, inhuman or degrading treatment or punishment).[14] However, in many cases the Strasbourg-based European Court of Human Rights (ECtHR) has read an implicit possibility for limitation into these rights.[15] This European 'de-trumping' in the relevant texts and in the work of the courts, raises question about the strong rights rhetoric omnipresent in today's European landscape. In our view the strength of European rights is seldom acknowledged in practice. In the bureaucratic welfare state, human rights can never be more than prima facie trumps.[16]

B. European Human Rights as Prima Facie Trumps (Fitting Welfare State)

English codification of human rights started with the *Magna Carta* (1215) and was further elaborated in seventeenth-century documents (*Petition of Right* (1628), *Habeas Corpus Act* (1679), *Freedom of Conscience* and *Bill of Rights under constitutional monarchy* (1689)). On the Continent, the adoption and codification were called for by 1789 *French Declaration of the Rights of Man and of the Citizen*,

European Union Charter on Fundamental rights (CFR) and in all state Constitutions. They can take the form of limitations in relation to specific rights, along the lines of the European Convention, or they can take the form of one single chapeau clause or general limitation clause, as is the case in the EU Charter of Fundamental Rights (Art 52(1)). But the limitations are there, and nowhere is this made more visible than in the ECHR, where the text of the limitations often added as a second paragraph to a right contained in a first paragraph is usually longer and more detailed than the text parts with the formulation of the rights.

[13] First Amendment: 'Congress shall make no law respecting an establishment of religion or prohibiting the free exercise thereof; or abridging the freedom of speech, or of the press; or the right of the people peaceably to assemble, and to petition the Government for a redress of grievances'.

[14] The other three are: the right not to be held in slavery or servitude; the right not to be convicted for conduct which was not an offence at the time it occurred; and the right not to have a heavier penalty imposed for an offence than the one applicable at the time the offence was committed. See S Greer, *The Margin of Appreciation: Interpretation and Discretion Under the European Convention on Human Rights* (Human rights files 17, Council of Europe Publishing, 2000) 27.

[15] J Gerards, 'How to improve the necessity test of the European Court of Human Rights' (2013) 1 *International Journal of Constitutional Law* 466.

[16] The official human rights narrative about the post-World War II turn of Europe to rights and the rule of law after the World War II experience of state violence led by majorities seizing power is discussed in section III.

and the message was picked up in some European states in subsequent years. Further European codifications would have to wait until after World War II.

At that point of time, the welfare state was already well on its way. The drafters of the 1950 ECHR took care to formulate these European rights in such a way that ambitious state interventions in all sectors of life would not be rendered impossible.[17] Hence, the long list of possible limitation grounds in 1950 ECHR-provisions like Article 10 (freedom of expression),[18] including a reminder that humans do not only have rights but also 'duties and responsibilities' and a clarification in the first paragraph that the right of free expression 'shall not prevent States from requiring the licensing of broadcasting, television or cinema enterprises'.[19]

Why this state-friendly tone of the ECHR? Some authors insist on the different constitutional histories of the Continental states and the UK (and US).[20] Bernard Edelman sees culturally conflicting world views at work with regard to the position of the individual.[21] A most benevolent understanding of the state-friendliness of the ECHR points at European aversion of (American) excessive individualism and the risk of a possible disconnect between individual and community in a rights-based culture. In Europe, human rights are clearly not 'self-evident' or God-given. They are only prima facie trumps.[22] They are the result of careful drafting by humans considering a necessary needed space between law and politics, to make politics possible, be it left or right, conservative, or progressive. Hence, in the (original) text of the ECHR, there is no right to property and no strong

[17] F Ewald, *L'Etat providence* (Grasset, 1986) 608; F Ewald, *Histoire de l'état providence* (Grasset, 1996) 317.

[18] Art 10(2) ECHR: 'The exercise of these freedoms, since it carries with it duties and responsibilities, may be subject to such formalities, conditions, restrictions or penalties as are prescribed by law and are necessary in a democratic society, in the interests of national security, territorial integrity or public safety, for the prevention of disorder or crime, for the protection of health or morals, for the protection of the reputation or rights of others, for preventing the disclosure of information received in confidence, or for maintaining the authority and impartiality of the judiciary.'

[19] Dworkin's trump theory grounded on US constitutionalism is seemingly irreconcilable with the European concern for state interest in a human rights document. Human rights in Dworkin's view need an extraordinary moral force to avoid horse trading, even in the name of the welfare state. Policies that might further the community's overall best interests should not justify acceptable limitations to human rights in Dworkin's view. See on this, Möller (n 7) 284.

[20] F Macchiarola, 'Finding the Truth in an American Criminal Trial: Some Observations' in J Nijboer and J Reijntjes (eds), *Proceedings of the First World Conference on New Trends in Criminal Investigation and Evidence* (Koninklijke Vermande, 1997) 85–93; C Blakesly, 'The Role and Impact of Constitutionalism, Constitutional Courts and Supreme Courts on the Evolution and Development of Criminal Justice Systems: The Strange Trip in the U.S.' (1998) 17 *Nouvelles Etudes Pénales* 271.

[21] B Edelman, 'What Rights for Those on Trial? Universality and Human Rights' in M Delmas-Marty (ed), *The Criminal Process and Human Rights. Towards a European Consciousness* (Martinus Nijhoff, 1995) 99–110. See also J Whitman, 'No Right Answer' in J Jackson, M Langer and P Tillers (eds), *Crime, Procedure and Evidence in a Comparative and International Context: Essays in Honour of Professor Mirjan Damaska* (Hart 2008) 371–392.

[22] J Donnelly, 'Human Rights' in JS Dryzek, B Honig and A Phillips (eds), *The Oxford Handbook of Political Theory* (Oxford University Press, 2006) 601, 617. Donnelly extends this observation to most other human rights systems, by observing that the United Nations 1966 International Covenant on Civil and Political Rights (Art 4) also permits derogations from most enumerated rights.

formulation of liberty rights, but lavish attention to limitation grounds, amplified by the famous margin of appreciation doctrine developed by the ECtHR.[23] Due to this doctrine all predictability about the prevalence of state interest is low. The margin can either be narrow or broad, but when?[24]

The ECtHR is not alone in seeking judicial discretion while judging. The other European Court, CJEU, in *Coty Germany*, avoided testing a German law on bank confidentiality on the 'essence' requirement in Article 52(1) of the 2000 European Union Charter on Fundamental rights (CFR) ('is the law affecting the essence of the right to personal data protection or not?'). The CFR's essence requirement might speak strongly to concerned citizen, but for judges it is often categorical and not flexible enough.[25] European judges clearly shy away from using 'strong' human

[23] This margin-doctrine initiated by the now abolished European Commission on Human Rights and confirmed by the ECtHR in *Handyside* (1976) grants the Contracting States a space for maneuvering that the Strasbourg judges are willing to grant national authorities, in fulfilling their obligations to respect rights under the Convention. O'Donnell (n 11) 474–96; Greer (n 14) 60. ECtHR, *Handyside v United Kingdom*, judgment of 7 December 1976, Series A no 24. The Court had to consider whether a conviction for possessing an obscene book could be justified under Art 10(2) as a limitation upon freedom of expression that was 'necessary for the protection of morals'. The applicant in *Handyside* had been convicted under the Obscene Publications Acts 1959 and 1964 for publishing *The Little Red Schoolbook*, anti-authoritarian work including sexually explicit information targeted at school children between the ages of 12 and 18.

[24] The Court constantly reformulates the doctrine to avoid unwanted consequences about the margin drawn by parties based on former judgments. To grant itself this discretion, the ECtHR 'plays' with the broadly formulated European list of legitimate purposes (including 'the protection of morals') to limit rights and textual differences between the respective limitation grounds (O'Donnell (n 11) 489). See on the 'confusing' use of the ECtHR in its three judgments on the pandemic, R McQuigg, 'The COVID-19 Pandemic and the European Court of Human Rights' (*QPOL Blog*, 11 April 2022), available at qpol.qub.ac.uk/covid-19-pandemic-the-european-court-of-human-rights. An older example is *Dudgeon* (ECtHR, *Dudgeon v United Kingdom*, judgment of 23 September 1981, Series A, no 45) where the British Government, relying on the reasoning about the margin by the Court in *Handyside*, asked the Court to recognise a broad margin for Northern Ireland to preserve criminal sanctions on homosexuality to protect the conservative moral climate of this region, just like the Court had recognised a broad margin for the UK in *Handyside*. The Court in *Dudgeon* did not like to be cornered and give up its discretion in setting the margin and complemented *sur place* its doctrine with novel elements to counter this undesired consequence made by the British Government of its previous judgments. It for instance 'clarified' (read: added to its formerly composed doctrine) that the margin left to states to impose limitations not only depends on their envisaged purpose (like defending morality) but also on the citizen activities that are inflicted by the limitation: 'not only the nature of the aim of the restriction but also the nature of the activities involved will affect the scope of the margin of appreciation. The present case concerns a most intimate aspect of private life. Accordingly, there must exist particularly serious reasons before interferences on the part of the public authorities can be legitimate for the purposes of paragraph 2 of Art 8' [52]. It also added a relevant textual observation. Privacy rights (including sexual rights) can only be limited when 'necessary in a democratic society' says the Convention, and this means, in the view of the Court, tolerance and broadmindedness: 'in Art 8 as in several other Arts of the Convention, the notion of "necessity" is linked to that of a "democratic society". According to the Court's case law, a restriction on a Convention right cannot be regarded as 'necessary in a democratic society' – two hallmarks of which are tolerance and broadmindedness – unless, amongst other things, it is proportionate to the legitimate aim pursued' [52] with reference to *Handyside* [49] and *Young, James and Webster v the United Kingdom* (judgment of 13 August 1981, A 44) [63]).

[25] See T Tridimas and G Gentile, 'The Essence of Rights: An Unreliable Boundary?' (2019) 20 *German Law Journal* 794, 808. This might explain why the CJEU avoided using or testing the essence

rights language, as they do with all 'political' concepts that figure in human rights provisions.[26]

Judges are no academics, and the latter perhaps should show 'understanding' when judges avoid the political road and prefer to concentrate on the concrete case brought before them.[27] Judges deal with cases that oblige them to work bottom-up from the facts. Academics take these facts as a given for a top-down approach and are primarily interested in the law and its application to the given facts. They approach cases not bottom-up from the facts but top-down from the law. This allows them to offer the judiciary a bigger picture of the law (including the position of a particular case in it), to offer critiques of past decisions, and to explain relevant policies.[28]

In a lecture on the increased influence of academics on judges in the English system, where academic influence was traditionally restrained ('better read, when dead'), Lord Burrows, Justice of the Supreme Court of the United Kingdom, identifies a string of relevant features that distinguish the work of a judge from this of an academic.[29] Most of these features are practical or formal in nature, but they do

requirement and opted for the self-invented language of 'serious impairment'. CJEU, Case C-580/13 *Coty Germany GmbH v Stadtsparkasse Magdeburg*, ECLI:EU:C:2015:485, judgment of 16 July 2015. The Court was called upon to reconcile, on the one hand, the right to a trademark and the owner's right to an effective remedy, which included the right to access information in the context of proceedings for the infringement of trademark rights and, on the other hand, the right to protection of personal data. The CJEU pointed out that a measure which results in serious infringement of a Charter right does not provide for a fair balance between conflicting rights and found that the unlimited and unconditional authorisation to invoke banking secrecy provided by German law was liable to impair seriously the effective exercise of the fundamental right to intellectual property. See Tridimas and Gentile (ibid) 794, 808.

[26] Academics have invited the ECtHR to better explain what is meant by the idea in the ECHR that rights limitations should be compatible with a 'democratic society', but all they get are vague references to concepts such as 'pluralism', 'tolerance' or 'broadmindedness'. These three features of democracy are mentioned in *Handyside* [49]: ECtHR, *Manoussakis and others v Greece*, judgment of 26 September 1996, App no 18748/91 [44].

[27] '[B]eyond this, little attempt has been made to define the needs of democracy. The Strasbourg institutions have instead chosen to concentrate upon the necessity of a given restriction in the context of the interference complained of. This is understandable since the Convention suggests that interferences with the right in question are permissible only if they are necessary in pursuit of one or other of the legitimate aims stated. Nevertheless, given their vital role in the development of a European human rights culture it would not be unreasonable to expect the Court and Commission gradually to construct a deeper and more comprehensive 'democratic needs' theory than they have to date' (S Greer, The exceptions to Articles 8 to 11 of the European Convention on Human Rights, Human rights files No 15 (Council of Europe Publishing, 1997) 15). See also Greer (n 14) 18: 'little attempt has been made to articulate a distinctive theory of democracy with the Strasbourg institutions instead choosing to concentrate upon the necessity of a given interference on public interest grounds in the context concerned. Ideally the Court should have a coherent and consistent conception of the general relationship between rights, democracy, and the public interest. But since the task of successfully constructing one is enormously difficult, with few insights from jurists and others to go on, it is perhaps not surprising that this is not the case.'

[28] L Burrows, 'Judges and Academics, and the Endless Road to Unattainable Perfection' (2022) 55 *Israel Law Review* 50.

[29] ibid 58–63. Time spent on a case (as opposed to an article); freedom to criticise colleagues or to respond to academic critique on decisions; the obligation to work in a collegiate way; consequences of

have an impact. That judges 'speak' the law is a misunderstood expression. They produce what is law while being constraint by their methods and sources, the legal rules and text being one of them, principles being another.[30] In the realm of human rights and constitutional rights, the political relevance of their work is probably at its peak, and it is up to these judges to manage and uphold the legitimacy of their work amid this landscape.

C. Rights under Bureaucratic Individualism (Alasdair MacIntyre)

The previous analysis of European human rights texts does not suggest 'strong' human rights protection capable of meeting the high standards of Dworkin in his analysis of American constitutionalism. However, the rhetoric on the priority of rights is as strong in Europe as in the US, maybe even stronger. Strong or firm language on fundamental rights serves several purposes.[31] On both sides of the Atlantic, the communication and claims about human rights are very similar but Europe, in particular, sees itself as the continent where the idea of human rights was to a large degree invented,[32] and pushed to the extreme of what is legally possible.[33] Even today, major historical overviews frame human rights as

non-correct results; a lesser need to articulate their own methodology; limitations to scope of enquiry; and the need for a decision to be decisive.

[30] See Dworkin, *Taking Rights Seriously* (n 6) 14–45. Dworkin argues that settled law embodies not only rules but also principles. These principles – such as 'no person may profit from wrong' – operate as reasons that can be accorded different degrees of 'weight' according to both the case at hand and interplay with other principles. On the mix of personal and legal preferences that account for the work of judges partly explaining why not all in law is politics), see J Segal, 'Judicial Behavior' in G Caldeira, D Kelemen and K Whittington (eds), *The Oxford Handbook of Law and Politics* (Oxford Academic, 2008); S Gutwirth, 'Le contexte du droit ce sont ses sources formelles et les faits et moyens qui exigent son intervention' (2013) 70 *Revue Interdisciplinaire d'Etudes Juridiques – Droit en context*, available at works.bepress.com/serge_gutwirth/96.

[31] Tridimas and Gentile (n 26) 815. Signaling and legitimising are among these possible purposes. In a party-political contemporary world, strong rights talk signals to all branches of government, but primarily to the legislature, that there are (counter-majoritarian) limits to what parties in power can do. Emphasising the historical connection between today's human rights regime with the legacy of the French Revolution and the British natural rights tradition seeks to legitimise. The signal to the *populus* is reassuring: today the whole of Europe has converted to liberal, rule of law-based democracy where governments can be trusted.

[32] See eg, S Trautweiler, 'Human Rights' (10 December 2017) 4, available at www.europewatchdog.info/en/council-of-europe/core-values/human-rights.

[33] There are the foundations laid by the Ancient Greek in developing the precursors of human rights. There is the further development of the modern concept of human rights as a philosophical idea in the 18th century during the European Age of Enlightenment. There is a first codification of human rights with the French Revolution Declaration of the Rights of Man and of the Citizen (1789) together with the US Bill of Rights (1789) – but preceded by the American Declaration of Independence (1776) and the Virginia Declaration of Rights (1776) or the US Bill of Rights (1789). There is the broad scope of European human rights, including social, economic and cultural rights (eg the right to food, housing and health; the right to work or education). Most of all there is the pioneering role of Europe in using human rights as an international organisation and as a monitoring tool, with strong supranational supervision of Member States on human rights compliance by both the Strasbourg-based EctHR and the Luxembourg-based CJEU.

quintessentially European.[34] The message is one of progress and strength: human rights in Europe, like constitutional rights in the US, are legally top-ranked and strongly enforced instruments to shield the individual against excessive or unwarranted state intervention.

Human rights narratives need to be understood in the light of their function and role in historical nation-state formation. Historians today dismiss these long-term success narratives and insist on historical realism.[35] Alasdair MacIntyre's *After Virtue*, written in 1981, combines historical and philosophical analysis. His work remains remarkable: very early in the history of critical human rights studies, MacIntyre was first in highlighting the diminishing role of virtues in Western history and the use of human rights as the new surrogate for defining the good life.[36]

The point of departure in *After Virtue* is the Weberian rationalisation thesis about the societal development from charismatic over traditional, to rational authority in modern times.[37] Due to the growing complexity in modernity a 'Rational-Legal Authority' is established.[38] Its power is no longer based on charismatic or traditional leadership, but associated with legal office, not with the office holder. The bureaucrat – a new social actor – functions on basis of an impersonal logic of objective selection, expertise, professionalism and neutrality.[39] MacIntyre pushes the Weberian analysis a step further and positions the *expert manager working for the state* as one of the key new characters of modernity. This manager is confronted on a daily basis with 'the fragmentised but autonomous individual'. Both operate and live in a society unbound by a common *telos* with only the market mechanism at work that separates people rather than unites them. These subjects of modernity are bearers of rights but in need of the state to enforce them,

[34] P Pasture, 'The Invention of European Human Rights' (2018) 103 *History* 485.

[35] S Moyn, *The Last Utopia. Human Rights in History* (Harvard University Press, 2010) 352. Only after World War II and in the 1970s when US President Carter started using human rights as a foreign policy instrument, did rights become the things that we know or think to know they are. See also S Gutwirth and P De Hert, 'Human Rights: A Secular Religion with Legal Crowbars. From Europe with Hesitations' (2021) 33 *National Law School of India Review* 420.

[36] The context of modernity is not ideal for the pursuit of a virtue-driven culture, but the concept of rights fares much better 'at least at the level of perception' (MacIntyre (n 5) 68).

[37] Weber saw rationalisation as the basis of modern western society at work in all areas of life, including economy and politics. States evolve historically towards more rationalised organisation forms of their troops and resources. Weber's analysis was published as *Economy and Society* posthumously in 1921/22. See F Sager and C Rosser, 'Weberian Bureaucracy' in *Oxford Research Encyclopedia of Politics* (Oxford, 2021) 20, available at oxfordre.com/politics/view/10.1093/acrefore/9780190228637.001.0001/acrefore-9780190228637-e-166.

[38] A division of labour, written procedures and rules and impersonal hierarchies become the norm in state (but also in corporate) administrations.

[39] *cf* 'Their appointment is based on qualification and performance. A vocational ethos characterizes bureaucrats as specialized, full-time professionals. They share an esprit de corps, and their mode of interaction with both policy principals and the public must be neutral. In view of this, their household must be strictly separated from their profession, which in turn requires that they be employed and receive a pension. Considering these principles, one notes that they refer to both formal organizational structures and bureaucratic personnel' (Sager and Rosser (n 38) 2).

although that same state is on the one hand driven by its own interests, and, on the other hand, incapable of making up for a lost societal telos or of taming market mechanisms.

For MacIntyre our era is one of a culture of bureaucratic individualism, where concepts such as rights and utility serve to find a delicate balance between the bureaucratic state organisations and the individual: the latter makes its claims in terms of rights, the former in terms of utility and effectiveness. These concepts look quasi-technical, capable of providing us with a rational criterion, but in practice, MacIntyre holds, they do not. They are matching pairs of incommensurable fictions.[40]

After Virtue's unmasking of rights and governmental expertise as contemporary political myths is important.[41] Rights today only have a relative role and must compete with other societal goods (utility, equality, redistribution of resources, security, economic competitiveness) in a complex relationship between individual and the state.[42] When individuals claim human rights protection they turn to the state, with more state intervention as a consequence. Meanwhile, intervening states never lose track of their own interest brought and supported with claims of utility and effectiveness. Proportionality, as will be discussed below, functions in this give-and-take framework of exchanging agendas. Its seemingly objective structure allows one to find provisional 'solutions' for conflicting interests.

D. The Paternalist Political Vision and the Priority of the State (Meierhenrich)

A useful complement to MacIntyre's counternarrative of European modernity is Jens Meierhenrich's recent *Rechtsstaat versus the Rule of Law*. This author invites us to understand the advent of the modern state in the light of three (not two!) alternative political visions: absolutism, liberalism *and* paternalism. The three visions

[40] '[I]t will be the case that the moral idiom employed at best provide a semblance of rationality for the modern political process, but not its reality. The mock rationality of the debate conceals the arbitrariness of the will and power at work in its resolution' (MacIntyre (n 5) 71).

[41] See equally on the importance of mental constructions, on les *homo fabulator* and the narrative communities that we live in, F Ost, 'L' État de droit, une notion paradoxale à l'épreuve de la pandémie' in S Parsa and F Tulkens (eds), *État de droit, état d'exception et libertés publiques* (Anthemis, 2022) 11, 43. *cf* the more optimistic account of rights as ideals by Jack Donnelly: 'Human rights are at once a utopian ideal and a realistic practice for implementing that ideal; a sort of self-fulfilling moral prophecy. If the underlying moral vision of human nature is within the 'natural' limits of possibility, then implementing those rights will make real that previously ideal nature'(Donnelly (n 23) 604).

[42] MacIntyre is not only critical about rights talk, but also about expert talk and claims of effectiveness of contemporary managers (whether in corporations or in office). A myth, he holds, but a successful one. When we see a manager, we project beliefs about their expertise and efficiency on them. The manager will of course do nothing to correct the image. See on Erwin Goffman's sociology of role-playing and the normative emptiness transcending Goffman's social world, MacIntyre (n 5) 115: 'The goal of the Goffmanesque role-player is effectiveness and success in Goffman's social universe is nothing but what passes for success. … Goffman's is a sociology which by intention deflates the pretentions of appearance to be anything more than appearance.'

offer fundamentally different perspectives on the relationship between state and society.[43] The story of liberalism in Meierhenrich's account is merely an English one,[44] whereas the story of the European continent and its view on law is neither liberal, nor absolutist,[45] but paternalist.

Paternalism is the forgotten political force of Europe. Enlightenment is often understood as a development from absolutism to liberalism, culminating in a final victory of liberalism characterised by a central role of the individual, human rights, equality and legalism.[46] In reality, a third vision existed among the elite on the Continent this of paternalism characterised by a condescending view of society and of its citizens: founded on the assumption that individuals are not capable of acting in their own best interests, nineteenth-century ruling elites, incorporated a blend of absolutism and liberalism in their policies, be it for opportunistic reasons (to stave off revolution) or out of genuine beliefs (to initiate reform).[47]

The European paternalist regimes were not identical. French aristocratic liberalism with its preference for constitutional monarchism,[48] sided with German enlightened authoritarianism of sovereigns like Prussia's Frederick II. They were attracted by reason as a tool of state-building and driven to perfect their societies by maximising utility, by pursuing reasons of state.

Compared to the French paternalist developments, equality and human rights played a lesser role in the early developments of the German *Rechtsstaat*,[49] but

[43] J Meierhenrich, 'Rechtsstaat versus the Rule of Law' in J Meierhenrich and M Loughlin (eds), *The Cambridge Companion to the Rule of Law* (Cambridge University Press, 2021) 39–67, 43–44.

[44] 'In England, liberalism, not paternalism, was the guiding vision of politics, and thus central to the construction of law as a social imaginary. In accordance with this construction, law was widely regarded as a check on – not channel of – sovereign power' (Meierhenrich (n 44) 46).

[45] The differences between the traditions of absolutism and liberalism are well known. Meierhenrich quotes Quentin Skinner to summarise both traditions: 'One speaks of sovereignty as a property of the people, the other sees it as the possession of the state. One gives centrality to the figure of the virtuous citizen, the other to the sovereign as representative of the state. One assigns priority to the duties of citizens, the other to their rights. It hardly needs stressing that the question of how to reconcile these divergent perspectives remains a central problem in contemporary political thought' (Meierhenrich (n 44) 42 with reference to Q Skinner, *Visions of Politics, vol. 3: Renaissance Virtues* (Cambridge University Press, 2002) xi.

[46] Rousseau, in some ways an idiosyncratic Enlightenment thinker, stressed the positive function of laws in promoting cherished values and a negative one in restraining rules in *Discourse on Political Economy*: 'It is to law alone that men owe justice and liberty. It is this salutary organ of the will of all which establishes in civil rights the natural equality between men. It is this celestial voice which dictates to each citizen the precepts of public reason and teaches him to act according to the rules of his own judgment and not to behave inconsistently with himself. It is with this voice alone that political leaders should speak when they command' (JJ Rousseau, *A Discourse on Political Economy*, available at www.files.ethz.ch/isn/125495/5020_Rousseau_A_Discourse_on_Political_Economy.pdf).

[47] Meierhenrich (n 44) 42.

[48] See also A de Dijn, 'Aristocratic Liberalism in Post-Revolutionary France' (2005) 48 *Historical Journal* 661.

[49] German enlightened authoritarianism with its belief in a 'science' of government was a strategic ruse, a cooptation of Enlightenment values in the service of unfreedom (Meierhenrich (n 44) 44–45 with reference to C Ingrao, 'The Problem of "Enlightened Absolutism" and the German States' (1986) 58 *Journal of Modern History* 161). Enlightenment's importance for human rights is often overrated. *cf* L Hunt, *Inventing Human Rights: A History* (New York, 2007). This author highlights the role of humanitarian culture (rather than Enlightenment thought) in explaining how human rights became prominent in European political discourse – how they became 'evident' as she astutely comments. See

legalism was as important in the German states as it was in France. Clear laws were desired to reduce arbitrary government and to spell out clear rules, albeit often of an authoritarian nature ('authoritarian legalism'). This legalism – the embodiment of 'paternalistic authoritarianism' or 'enlightened despotism' – was *not* primarily designed to protect the individual, but to realise the policy agenda of the state.

In the continental European landscape after the social upheavals of 1848 the climate became even more austere for rights optimism. The rights rhetoric was still there, but the heart was not involved. For Hegel, whose influence in this era was unparalleled, the primary goal of good political institutions like the constitutional monarchy is 'to reconcile the subjective freedom of individuals with the free and rational direction of public affairs'.[50]

The quote illustrates *After Virtue*'s core message about modernity's constant balancing of the role of rights with public utility.[51] For Meierhenrich the German idea of freedom is one of unfreedom or limited freedom. This less-known bedfellow of European history did however create the conditions for the emergence of the welfare state in the late nineteenth century. This welfare state *to become* was based on state dirigisme ('so integral to the German idea of freedom'). In its laws and codifications, the *Rechtsstaat* tradition headed by sovereigns in Germany and the

also Pasture (n 35) 486; D Pendas, 'Toward a new politics? On the recent historiography of human rights' (2012) 21 *Contemporary European History* 95. In what follows, I will use the term 'legalism' several times. Legalism in this context is used in its plain sense. There are authors, like Hildebrandt, who, in talking about the rule of law, distinguish between legality and legalism. In her view, grounded on Fuller's principles, the latter implies a formal legal ground for justified intervention, while the former is broader: it both justifies and limits governmental intervention. I do not distinguish, since I do not necessarily view legalism as inherently imbuing the law with an inner moral element. M. Hildebrandt, 'Radbruch's Rechtsstaat and Schmitt's Legal Order: Legalism, Legality, and the Institution of Law', available at cal.library.utoronto.ca/index.php/cal/article/view/22514/18311.

[50] GWF Hegel, *Elements of the Philosophy of Right*, HB Nisbet (trans), AW Wood (ed) (Cambridge University Press, 1991) quoted by Meierhenrich (n 44) 46.

[51] MacIntyre's diagnosis is of a general nature and applicable to all Western systems, whereas Meierhenrich underlines the 'key difference', at least in historical perspective between the *Rechtsstaat* tradition, with its deep roots in Europe, and the rule of law tradition, with its Anglo-American heritage, where the rights of the individual have a higher status, compared to the continental tradition where these rights are a byproduct or leftover of state policies (Meierhenrich (n 44) 64). A more diplomatic way of understanding differences with regard to where the rights of individuals originate is to hold that the *Rechtsstaat* tradition prioritises political liberty, whereas the Anglo-American tradition prioritises the liberty of the individual (Meierhenrich (n 44) 62, with reference to the distinction between individual liberty and political liberty, as theorised by Benjamin Constant in 'The Liberty of the Ancients Compared with that of the Moderns' [1819]). In the light of the success of utilitarianism and the move to parliamentary sovereignty in the late 17th and 18th century in Great Britain, we assume, however, that the differences on both sides of the Channel and of the Atlantic might in practice not be so 'key', as Meierhenrich suggests. See on the question whether the British lost the rule of law in the late 17th and 18th century, SC Stimson, 'Constitutionalism and the Rule of Law' in Dryzek, Honig and Phillips (n 23) 317–32. We feel more attracted to MacIntyre's more general analysis of Western systems assuming avoiding the risk of giving too much weight to the idea and the impact of the rule of law idea in Britain and the US, where the phrase 'rule of law' has proven to be one of those meaningless and 'self-congratulatory rhetorical devices that grace the public utterances of Anglo-American politicians' (Stimson (ibid) 317). Meierhenrich's account of German paternalistic authoritarianism or enlightened despotism – where rights exist only when they are recognised by the state – is however particularly relevant of this discussion of the 'German' proportionality principle.

rest of the European continent emphasised the individual's duties at the expense of his rights.[52] The agenda of (legal) institutionalisation amplified the leadership's role and the secondary role of the citizen. In the late nineteenth century, citizens were put to serve the state's requirement of ongoing modernisation.[53]

III. Post-World War II Moving to Priorities?

A. Move from Legalism to Priority of Rights (State Level): Moral Constitutional Standards

Only after World War II did the human rights picture become more familiar to contemporary eyes. The transition from authoritarian or paternalist rule to democracy was by now more or less completed. Another transition, caused by the experiences of World War II atrocities, was that of the continental *Rechtsstaat* tradition to the rule of law tradition.[54]

This second transition was realised by bringing morality into constitutional law. Formal conceptions of the *Rechtsstaat*, based on the perceived virtue of legalism, gradually gave way, in both theory and practice, to substantive understandings of what it means to govern by way of law.[55] In legal philosophy, Lon

[52] Meierhenrich (n 44) 63, borrowing from M Raeff, 'The Well-Ordered Police State and the Development of Modernity in Seventeenth- and Eighteenth-Century Europe: An Attempt at a Comparative Approach' (1975) 80 *American Historical Review* 1221, 1240.

[53] 'It was the last step in the conversion of the single individual from a creative force into an instrument of modernity for the benefit of the state' (Meierhenrich (n 44) 63, quoting Marc Raeff).

[54] By now, it was sufficiently clear that the virtues of law (promoting values and restraining rulers) could not prevent morally fallible laws by becoming instruments of tyranny, inequality or injustice. See L Green, 'Book Review: Law's Rule – The Rule of Law: Ideal or Ideology, by A. C. Hutchinson & P. Monahan (eds)' (1986) 24 *Osgoode Hall Law Journal* 1023, 1023. See on the contemporary notion of rule of law, Ost (n 42) 39–44.

[55] 'What Hayek dismissed as "mere legality", most theorists of the *Rechtsstaat* long regarded as the institution's cardinal virtue, certainly up until 1945. After the initial perversion and eventual destruction of the previous *Rechtsstaat* tradition during the Nazi dictatorship, a reinvention, in Germany at least, was attempted. It was a successful experiment in legal reimagination. In this period, the postwar-*Rechtsstaat* began to resemble the rule of law, which is why the likes of MacCormick and Allan and Krygier are in the habit of equating the *Rechtsstaat* and the rule of law, of thinking both concepts express 'the same ideal'. They do not, except in normative accounts that generalise about the idea of the *Rechtsstaat* solely on the basis of its late modern instantiation' (Meierhenrich (n 44) 53). 'The *Rechtsstaat* tradition, not unlike that of the rule of law, has been anything but static. Rather, it has been subject to reinvention from the get- go. In the nineteenth century, as we have seen, procedural conceptions of the *Rechtsstaat* held sway. In the twentieth century, especially in its latter half, these formal conceptions of the *Rechtsstaat* gradually gave way, in both theory and practice, to substantive understandings of what it means to govern by way of law. In post-war Germany, this has meant that conceptions of the *Rechtsstaat* and of the rule of law have, for all intents and purposes, converged, a trend that has continued in the 21st century. It is this recent convergence that likely convinced MacCormick to equate the idea of the *Rechtsstaat* with that of the rule of law. His monochromatic snapshot, however, was just that – a rendering in black and white that concealed the colorful histories of the *Rechtsstaat*, in Germany and elsewhere' (Meierhenrich (n 44) 66).

Fuller proposed eight, by now classic, formal standards for the rule of law in *The Morality of Law* (1964).[56] Together they defined and made possible what he called 'the inner morality of law', indispensable prerequisites for legitimate law-making. In the discussion that followed Fuller's ideas, more substantive requirements for legitimate laws were added. Dworkin rejected the idea that moral principles can be established by deliberate acts and pushed for standards of substantive rather than formal morality.[57] In *Law's Empire*, he added the requirement that laws could be rationally defended.[58]

In Germany, this process of tempering unrestrained legalism with moralism produced and inspired the 1949 the German Constitution or *Grundgesetz*, insisting on human dignity and the equal status of the person (rule of law as moral standards) *and* introducing the American idea of constitutional review of laws by judges (rule of law as constitutionalism).[59] The adoption of these two 'rule of law' ideas tempering continental legalism proved to be successful.

A first idea or device to tame legalism by bringing morality into post-World War II laws was to define constitutional standards with a substantive moral nature. A prime illustration is the introduction of human dignity in the opening article of the 1949 German Constitution. This standard is formulated as the mother of all rights (constituting the supreme value of the Constitution), as an absolute right, and as an eternal right. It became an influential hallmark for legal governance followed by many other states *and* the EU.[60]

[56] LL Fuller, *The Morality of Law* (Yale University Press, 1969). See K Rundle, 'The Morality of the Rule of Law: Lon L. Fuller' in J Meierhenrich and M Loughlin (n 44) 186–201. Laws should be (1) general; (2) publicly promulgated; (3) non-retroactive; (4) sufficiently clear; (5) non-contradictory; (6) possible to comply with; (7) relatively constant through time; and (8) that there be congruence between official action and declared rule.

[57] R Dworkin, 'Philosophy, Morality, and Law: Observations Prompted by Professor Fuller's Novel Claim' (1965) 113 *University of Pennsylvania Law Review* 668. See on the Dworkin–Fuller debate, D Dyzenhaus, 'The Rule of Law as the Rule of Liberal Principle' in A Ripstein (ed), *Ronald Dworkin* (Cambridge University Press, 2007) 56, 73–75.

[58] Dworkin, *Law's Empire* (n 7). For criticism, see Stimson (n 53) 319–20; J Shklar, 'Political theory and the rule of law' in A Hutchinson and PJ Monahan (eds), *The rule of law: Ideal or ideology* (Carswell, 1987) 1–16. Reprinted in J Shklar, *Political Thought and Political Thinkers*, S Hoffman (ed) (Chicago University Press, 1998) 21–37.

[59] On these two dimensions of the rule of law (rule of law as standards and as constitutionalism), see Stimson (n 52) 319–23.

[60] Human dignity is enshrined in the first Article of the German Constitution, which reads: 'Human dignity shall be inviolable. To respect and protect it shall be the duty of all state authority. The German people therefore acknowledge inviolable and inalienable human rights as the basis of every community, of peace and of justice in the world. The following basic rights shall bind the legislature, the executive and the judiciary as directly applicable law.' See A Barak, *Human Dignity. The Constitutional Value and the Constitutional Right* (Cambridge University Press, 2015) 215, 225–42. The book also contains a discussion of human dignity provisions in other constitutions inspired by the German example. See also the discussion of the consensus on dignity amongst left and right, east and west, south and north before and after World War II: C McCrudden, 'Human Dignity and Judicial Interpretation of Human Rights' (2008) 194 *European Journal of International Law* 655. Although values such as equality or liberty equally qualify as basic values grounding other rights, the moral impact of human dignity leaves very few people untouched. When in 2000 the EU drafted its own fundamental rights catalogue and followed the German example of prioritising human dignity as a constitutional foundation,

Equally successful, at least at the symbolic level, is Article 19(2) *Grundgesetz* stating categorically that 'in no case may the essence of a basic right be affected.'[61] Again, this is a strong moral message with a cathartic value signaling a definite break with totalitarianism and illiberalism, that found its way into a number of European and non-European constitutions, *and* in Article 52(1) CFR that lays down respect for the essence of rights as one of the requirements that limitations on rights must respect.[62]

B. Move from Legalism to Priority of Rights (State Level): Judicial Review

A second device to inject morality into the German post-World War II legal system was the idea of constitutional review – the power of courts to strike down incompatible legislation and administrative action. The new Constitution was enriched with a Constitutional Court armed with American- and Austrian-inspired (see below) judicial review powers. Again, we have a success that spread around the world.[63] The German Constitutional Court, like its American counterpart, is a *strong-form court*,[64] mandated to interpret the Constitution and bind other branches with their interpretations. It became the model for the constitutional courts adopted by other nations after World War II.[65] Later in the twentieth century some countries, also in the Western sphere, introduced weaker

criticism was barely heard, even from constitutionalists living in countries with more egalitarian or liberty-based constitutions. See P De Hert, 'John Rawls on Constitutionalism and the Charter of Fundamental Rights of the European Union' in WP Heere (ed), *From Government to Governance. The Growing Impact of Non State Actors on the International and European Legal System* (TCM Asser Press, 2004) 443–53.

[61] Tridimas and Gentile (n 26) 795. An earlier reference to the essence can be found in the Hessen Constitution of 1946.

[62] Tridimas and Gentile (n 26) 796 and 815.

[63] T Ginsburg, 'The Global Spread of Constitutional Review' in Caldeira, Kelemen and Whittington (n 31) 81–99. In 1942, there were only two countries where laws could be reviewed by judges, the U.S. and Norway, while some other countries were experimenting with weaker variants of judicial review. Today, most Western states have adopted judicial review of laws and/or have accepted judicial review of state actions (including of law-making) by international courts like the ECtHR, or the EU Court of Justice.

[64] Strong-form courts have *general* authority to determine what the Constitution means, *and* their constitutional interpretations are authoritative and binding on the other branches, at least in the short to medium run (Tushnet (n 2) 17). Strong judicial review by courts with a power to strike down incompatible legislation and administrative action is an innovation of the American constitutional order. In *Marbury v Madison* (1803) the US Supreme Court confirmed it had the power to declare unconstitutional a statute enacted by Congress. Without an explicit textual mandate, increasingly vigorous constitutional review was developed by the Court. Tushnet holds that strong-form review existed by the 1890s (19). See also Ginsburg (n 64) 81–99.

[65] See M Hailbronner, *Traditions and Transformations: The Rise of German Constitutionalism* (Oxford University Press, 2015) 201; M Jestaedt et al, *The German Federal Constitutional Court: The Court Without Limits* (Oxford University Press, 2020); M Tushnet, 'Alternative forms of judicial review' (2021) 280 *Revista De Direito Administrativo* 15, 20, available at doi.org/10.12660/rda.v280.2021.85146.

forms of review,[66] partly as a response to democratic concerns about the legislative prerogatives raised by strong-form review of laws by the judiciary.[67]

Distinctions like the one between strong and weak review teach us that constitutionalism knows no fixed formulae, but allows design choices.[68] Another design choice is whether to create or not specialised constitutional courts. Systems with constitutional courts (including the Constitutional Council in France) have higher frequencies of unconstitutional declarations of laws (in the formal sense).[69]

The post-World War II development of constitutional devices such as constitutional courts is impressive, but hard to reconcile with the previous sections about European paternalism and its priority of state interest. As a matter of fact these courts with their power of judicial review were indeed serving state interest. The choice for a federalist structure of North America explains the mandate of the Supreme Court in the US Constitution of 1789. The turn to federalism and a court safeguarding it in Germany (*above*) was preceded by similar Austrian

[66] Tushnet (n 2) 17. Courts in weak-form systems still have the power to evaluate all legislation to determine whether it is consistent with all the constitution's provisions, but ordinary legislative majorities can displace judicial interpretations of the constitution in the relatively short run (Tushnet (n 2) 22). One should not too easily assume that mainly weak rule of law democracies opt for weak-form review. Experiments in strong rule of law democracies with weak-form review catch the eye. Canada's 1981 Charter of Rights, the New Zealand Bill of Rights and the UK Human Rights Act of 1998, all are rebalancing the relationship parliament and judiciary in one way or another, and are referred to by Tushnet as examples of weak-form judicial review.

[67] The democratic argument can be phrased as follows: 'courts lack the democratic legitimacy to displace decisions taken by bodies with stronger democratic legitimacy'. See Tushnet (n 2) 22; R Bellamy, 'Rights as Democracy' (2012) 15 *Critical Review of International Social and Political Philosophy* 449. See also J Waldron, *Law and Disagreement* (Oxford University Press, 1999) 302 and J Waldron, 'The Core of the Case Against Judicial Review' (2006) *The Yale Law Journal* 1346. Critical of the democratic argument used against judicial review, R Dworkin, 'The Majoritarian Premise and Constitutionalism' in T Christiano (ed), *Philosophy and Democracy: An Anthology* (Oxford University Press, 2003) 241–57. Critical of Dworkin's critique of democracy and its self-fulfilling prophecy, R Bellamy, 'Ronald Dworkin, *Taking Rights Seriously*' in JT Levy (ed), *The Oxford Handbook of Classics in Contemporary Political Theory* (Oxford, 2015) 7.

[68] In most European countries, there is now a form of constitutional review of formal laws, while before the mid-20th century inviolability of the formal law was the rule and judicial review was non-existent or in principle excluded. There is great diversity in the design of the system (whether there is a separate constitutional court and its powers and functions, the standards of review and the alignment of review against the constitution on the one hand and review against treaties and EU law on the other). For a detailed discussion see M de Visser, *Constitutional Review in Europe: A Comparative Analysis* (Hart, 2015) 528; M Claes, AW Heringa, M van der Sluis and M Stremler, *Rechtsvergelijkend onderzoek constitutionele toetsing* (Maastricht University, 2021) 70, available at open.overheid.nl/documenten/ronl-4a5c6e1a-ae9c-4fa3-a717-6a2c0421541e/pdf.

[69] The constitutional courts set up in Germany, Belgium and France have great authority. Their mandate and jurisdiction, through legislation and their own interpretative practice, has gradually expanded. Scandinavian and British ordinary courts can review the constitutionality of laws. In comparison these courts are however more reluctant to review formal laws against the Constitution. This reluctance is explained by the constitutional culture (the deeply rooted constitutional views regarding the specific position of the judiciary in the division of branches), the (constitutional) provisions that establish judicial review (the Human Rights Act in the UK, the Constitution in Sweden, which in so many words instructs the court to take into account the fact that Parliament is the representative of the people when reviewing the Constitution) and by the very fact that no separate body has been established with the specific mandate to review the constitutionality of laws. See Claes, Heringa, Sluis and Stremler (n 69) 65.

developments. A federalist structure for the young Austrian democracy, emerging from the ashes of the Habsburg Empire, explains Kelsen's successful efforts to establish the Austrian Constitutional Court based on the Constitution of 1920s, with new and stronger review powers as compared to its predecessors (the Imperial Court (1867–1919) and the (German-) Austrian Constitutional Court (1919–1920)).[70] A constitutional court was set up in 1980 in Belgium when it evolved from a unitarian state to a federal state. The focus on state interest rather than on individual rights interest clearly rang through the name of this court: 'Arbitragehof', 'Cour d'arbitrage' or 'Schiedshof'. Not the priority of rights, but institutional and functional concerns about the concrete necessities of federalism, are the bedrock of constitutional politics in many countries, allowing ideas such as judicial review to be enshrined in constitutions.[71]

C. Move to Priority of Rights (European Level): ECtHR's Concept of Law and Foreseeability

After our discussion of the Europe's societal context – its culture of bureaucratic individualism, its welfare state, and its post-World War II commitment to the rule of law and judicial review – let us now move to the European institutional level and the European human rights law as created after World War II. Human rights can easily be endangered in a legalistic system (rule by laws), with instrumental laws realising every possible state agenda. The ECHR, in the spirit of the Anglo-Saxon rule of law tradition, rests on the assumption that human rights can only thrive in a system that goes beyond legalism (in the ordinary formal sense of based on laws) and its pitfalls.[72]

This does not mean diminishing the importance of the legality. On the contrary: faithful to Fuller's belief in the morality of the legality principle, the principle stands firm in European human rights law. Concerns for rights are and were perfectly compatible with this morality.[73]

Although the ECtHR relaxed the legality requirement in its formal sense by a broad understanding of the term 'law' (for instance, prison rules drafted by

[70] Verfassungsgerichtshof Österreich, 'The History of the Constitutional Court' available at www.vfgh.gv.at/verfassungsgerichtshof/geschichte/history_overview.en.html accessed 12 December 2023.

[71] StG Hinghofer-Szalkay, 'The Austrian Constitutional Court: Kelsen's Creation and Federalism's Contribution?' (2017) 17 *Fédéralisme*, available at popups.uliege.be/1374-3864/index.php?id=1671. See also Ginsburg (n 64) 81–99, who highlights that the success and authority of constitutional courts in federal states, like Germany and Belgium, is due to both federalism and rights rationales.

[72] The message of the 1950 ECHR is congruent with the constitutional developments at state level: although only *some* rights in Europe are absolute (not capable of being limited by law), *all other* rights limitations need, from now on, more than just a legal basis. Passing all sorts of laws to run a state is not enough. These laws and the limitations on rights herein need to be 'necessary in a democratic society'. We will see that this concept of the Convention has been repackaged in the case law of the EctHR as a proportionality requirement.

[73] From its early days – end of the 18th-century codification of rights in France and the US – the only limitations to rights allowed for were those incorporated by domestic law, preferably voted in parliaments. This guaranteed arbitrary tampering of rights by the executive and by courts. Greer (n 28) 9.

the prison management and court decisions),[74] it has added a defendable new doctrine insisting on the accessible, foreseeable nature of laws that need to contain legal safeguards against abuse of state powers.[75] This doctrine clearly limits state practices to vote far-going, undefined powers.

This enriched or 'thick' legalism has had important consequences. First, it ensured the grounding of legitimate interferences with the relevant European rights in national law *and* in European rule of law standards as defined by the ECtHR itself and European organisations such as the Council of Europe.[76] Second, it allowed the Court to behave as a de facto constitutional court addressing itself directly to legislators in Member States with recommendations to improve national laws.[77] Important judgments in this context are *Zakharov* (2015) on individual surveillance methods – where the Court for the first time abandoned its rejection of *in abstracto claims*[78] – and *Centrum för Rättvisa* (2018) and *Big Brother Watch* (2018), both on mass surveillance methods.[79] Surveillance laws, in the ECtHR's view, have to respect no less than nine 'minimum requirements of law'.[80] It is

[74] *cf Handyside* [49]: 'The domestic margin of appreciation thus goes hand in hand with a European supervision. Such supervision concerns both the aim of the measure challenged and its "necessity"; it covers not only the basic legislation but also the decision applying it, even one given by an independent court. In this respect, the Court refers to Article 50 of the Convention ("decision or … measure taken by a legal authority or any other authority") as well as to its own case-law (Engel and others judgment of 8 June 1976, Series A no 22 [100]).'

[75] P De Hert and G Malgieri, 'One European Legal Framework for Surveillance: The EctHR's Expanded Legality Testing Copied by the CJEU' in V Mitsilegas and N Vavoula (eds), *Surveillance and Privacy in the Digital Age. European, Transatlantic and Global Perspectives* (Hart, 2021) 255–95. See also the contribution of van der Sloot (below).

[76] Greer (n 28) 9–10; B van der Sloot, 'The quality of law: How the European Court of Human Rights gradually became a European Constitutional Court for privacy cases' (2020) 11 *Journal of Intellectual Property, Information Technology and E-Commerce Law* 160, available at www.jipitec.eu/issues/jipitec-11-2-2020/5098. van der Sloot shows that the doctrine of qualitatively based legalism developed from the 1980s onwards has allowed the EctHR to reduce its role as a traditional human rights court, that assesses *in concreto* whether one of more of the human rights of an applicant have been violated and if so, whether damages should be awarded. Instead, its role as a constitutional court was enhanced, assessing (where needed) laws *in abstracto*, and testing them on general principles deriving from the rule of law and the separation of powers.

[77] Three decades characterised by a logic of individual justice were followed by the current era of constitutional logic. The Court gave up its initial refusal to consider as admissible *in abstracto* claims (revolving around the legitimacy of a law or policy as such) or did not longer reject a priori claims (complaints about injury that has not yet materialised). This development was confirmed in the beginning of the century by the new powers and competences of the Court, such as the competence to adoption a pilot judgment where the facts of an application reveal the existence of a structural or systemic problem or another similar dysfunction which has given rise or may give rise to similar applications.

[78] EctHR, *Roman Zakharov v Russia*, application no 47143/06, judgment of 4 December 2015. The Court made explicit that in cases revolving around secret surveillance, where people generally do not know whether they have been the target of data-gathering activities, this principle could no longer be upheld. See van der Sloot (n 77) 184.

[79] EctHR, *Centrum för Rättvisa v Sweden*, application no 35252/08, judgment of 19 June 2018; EctHR, *Big Brother Watch and others v the United Kingdom*, application nos. 58170/13, 62322/14 and 24960/15, judgment of 13 September 2018.

[80] These requirements are: (1) accessibility of the domestic law; (2) scope of application of the secret surveillance measures; (3) the duration of secret surveillance measures; (4) the procedures

not difficult to see a parallel between the ECtHR's minimum requirements of law and Lon Fuller's minimum requirements of law.[81] Hence the 'inner morality of law' is present in post-World War II European human rights law. What about more external moral reference points?

D. Move to Priority of Rights (European Level): ECtHR's Concept of Necessity

The core message of European human rights law is not about legality, but about states no longer being able to do whatever they think fit, simply by voting laws. Human rights limitations, say the ECHR limitation clauses, must be based on laws and respect the legality requirement (above) but also be 'necessary in a democratic society'. This last formulation is extremely rich. Insisting on a democratic *telos* of laws that constrain rights limitations and on the need for limitations to respect necessity (as opposed to usefulness) are additional rule of law ingredients that complete the rule of law-enhanced legality requirement discussed above.

The expression 'necessary in a democratic society' was sacrificed as such by the drafters of the 2000 CFR. This text on fundamental rights, a corollary of the ECHR, only copies the term 'necessary' and integrates it into the proportionality test defined in Article 52 CFR ('subject to the principle of proportionality, limitations may be made only if they are necessary'). Omitting the notion of a democratic society in Article 52(1) CFR only adds to the technocratic feel that emanates from the proportionality principle central in that provision.[82] Terms like 'necessary' ('necessary for what?) and 'proportional' ('proportional for or to

for processing data; (5) authorisation procedures; (6) ex post supervision of the implementation of secret surveillance measures; (7) conditions for communicating data to and receiving data from other parties; (8) notification of interception of communications; and (9) available remedies. See van der Sloot (n 77) 184. The Court found multiple violations of these minimum requirements in *Zakharov* and *Big Brother Watch*. In *Centrum för Rättvisa*, no violation was found, but the EctHR stressed that there was room for improvement of the Swedish legal system on several points.

[81] van der Sloot's understanding of the EctHR's approach through a Fullerian lens is rich. For Fuller the minimum requirements of law are characterised by a morality of aspiration, aimed at the ideal, the maximum, something that shall never be attained. Such a conception, requirements as an ideal rather than a mandatory result, solve the puzzle, van der Sloot writes, of why the EctHR allows exceptions to its own list of minimum requirements of law: when in each case there is no arbitrary use of power or when a legal system remedies for its weaker performing on certain requirement with exceptionally strong performing on other minimum requirement of law. 'Like Fuller had proposed, the EctHR does not so much treat these principles as "minimum" requirements of "law", but as principles of aspiration. If a law fails to meet all these principles, it clearly cannot be called a law proper, but there is no law that accords in full to all these standards' (van der Sloot (n 77) 184).

[82] *cf* Greer (n 14) 18. On the anchoring of democracy in the Preamble and Art 2 of the TEU, see D Kostakopoulou, 'Liberty and democracy as fundamental constitutional principles of EU law' in K Ziegler, P Neuvonen and V Moreno–Lax (eds), *Research Handbook on General Principles in EU Law Constructing Legal Orders in Europe* (Edward Elgar, 2022) 254–66.

what?') hang in the air, without a definition of their societal context. The Greek understanding of virtues was not of a universal nature, but localised. A virtuous man is a Greek living in one of the city states and the moral nature of his behaviour is assessed in that context. Human rights provisions with reference to guiding values such as social justice, pluralism, tolerance or broadmindedness, or which refer to political concepts such as 'democratic society', localise human rights in a meaningful way.

I already discussed the relative failure or reluctance of the ECtHR in *Handyside* to theorise the notion of 'democracy' in the ECHR.[83] Instead, it concentrated on textual and conceptual analysis of the term 'necessary'. Interesting in the conceptual part of ECtHR's analysis, is the introduction of the term 'proportionality' (absent in the text of the Convention) to explain 'necessary'.[84] This approach was introduced in *Handyside* (1976) and consolidated in *Dudgeon* (1981) – both dealing with the severity of criminal sanctions on certain expressions and conduct.[85]

[83] See section II.B discussing *Handyside*. In *Handyside*, followed by judgments such as *Dudgeon* (above), the EctHR clarified some of the characteristics of a democracy that might or might not warrant certain proposed limitations. This method makes sense from a political theory perspective. If the choice for a democratic system means something, it cannot be compatible with whatever law that is voted in Parliament. These laws must be congruent with the democratic society they are meant to regulate.

[84] Judges are not easily nudged into political theorising about the nature of democracy and to draw from thereof legal conclusions. That is why they introduced in the seminal *Handyside* judgment the proportionality method or device for checking on states that use legal instruments or decisions to limit rights. It allows them to replace the question 'is this limitation necessary in a democratic society?' with the question 'is this limitation proportional?'. I will discuss other methods, amongst them a more internal way of clarifying this requirement: text exegesis ('what is meant by 'necessary' in common language and in the context of the 'Convention'). The method of using proportionality to clarify the necessity-requirement is more external. Using the idea of proportionality as a clarification brings in an external notion absent in the text of the 1950 Convention. German scholars like to think the EctHR brought in proportionality inspired by German constitutional law (below). It is however useful to remember that *Handyside* is a case against the UK and one that dealt with a matter of criminal law. This area of law has a long tradition going back to Beccaria's *Dei delitti e delle pene* (1764) of insisting on the proportionality of the sanctions. See on the connection between proportional punishment and civilisation, F Kuty, 'La proportionnalité de la peine en droit belge: une exigence de l'État de droit érigée en droit pour le justiciable' in C Guillain and F Kuty (eds), *Actualités en droit pénal et exécution des peines* (Larcier, 2020) 7–48.

[85] The essential paragraph of *Handyside* ([9]) where one finds (first) attempts to explain the concept of 'a democratic society', followed by a (equally first) clarification of 'necessary' as meaning 'proportional', is worth extra attention: 'The Court's supervisory functions oblige it to pay the utmost attention to the principles characterizing a "democratic society". Freedom of expression constitutes one of the essential foundations of such a society, one of the basic conditions for its progress and for the development of every man. Subject to paragraph 2 of Article 10, it is applicable not only to "information" or "ideas" that are favorably received or regarded as inoffensive or as a matter of indifference, but also to those that offend, shock or disturb the State or any sector of the population. Such are the demands of that pluralism, tolerance and broadmindedness without which there is no "democratic society". This means, amongst other things, that every "formality", "condition", "restriction" or "penalty" imposed in this sphere must be proportionate to the legitimate aim pursued' (*Handyside* [49]).

IV. Proportionalities in Law

A. Proportionality and the ECtHR's Understanding of 'Necessary in a Democratic Society'

Dudgeon contains a first comprehensive presentation of the ECtHR's understanding of the necessary limits of rights limitations based on laws in a democracy. In these paragraphs the ECtHR, five years after *Handyside*, structures and synthesises its principles on assessing laws constraining rights found so far in its previous decisions:

> 50. A number of principles relevant to the assessment of the 'necessity', 'in a democratic society', of a measure taken in furtherance of an aim that is legitimate under the Convention have been stated by the Court in previous judgments.
>
> 51. Firstly, 'necessary' in this context does not have the flexibility of such expressions as 'useful', 'reasonable', or 'desirable', but implies the existence of a 'pressing social need' for the interference in question (see … Handyside judgment, par. 48).
>
> 52. In the second place, it is for the national authorities to make the initial assessment of the pressing social need in each case; accordingly, a margin of appreciation is left to them (ibid). However, their decision remains subject to review by the Court (ibid., par. 49). …
>
> 53. Finally, in Article 8 as in several other Articles of the Convention, the notion of 'necessity' is linked to that of a 'democratic society'. According to the Court's case-law, a restriction on a Convention right cannot be regarded as 'necessary in a democratic society' – two hallmarks of which are tolerance and broadmindedness – unless, amongst other things, *it is proportionate to the legitimate aim pursued* (see … Handyside judgment, par. 49 …).
>
> 54. The Court's task is to determine on the basis of the aforesaid principles whether the reasons purporting to justify the 'interference' in question are relevant and sufficient under Article 8 par. 2 (see … Handyside judgment, par. 50). The Court is not concerned with making any value-judgment as to the morality of homosexual relations between adult males.[86]

[86] *Dudgeon* [50]–[54] (author's emphasis). A first principle – we rather speak of a first method or methodological step (the term 'method' is used in *Handyside* [51], but is not repeated in later judgments) – is textual analysis of the term 'necessary' (*Dudgeon* [51]). We will come back to this later, but the outcome of this query is that the existence of a pressing social need might be a pointer to the 'necessity'. The second methodological step is to determine the precise margin of appreciation in each case (*Dudgeon* [52]). A third and fourth method uses the lens of a democracy and the lens of proportionality to assess laws adopted to limit rights (*Dudgeon* [53]). *Dudgeon*'s [54] concludes this presentation of principles or methodological steps. All four previous steps allow the EctHR to ascertain whether the reasons given by the national authorities to justify their measures are both 'relevant' and 'sufficient'. So, limiting rights at the European level is about argumentation: the reasons given by states to limit rights must be convincing in one way or another. In *Dudgeon* it is about 'relevant' and 'sufficient'. Other judgments express the same idea in other terms like 'the necessity for a restriction must be convincingly established' (EctHR, *Autronic AG v Switzerland*, judgment of 22 May 1990, A 178 [61]; *Weber v Switzerland*, judgment of 2 May 1990, A 177 [47]; *Barthold v Germany*, judgment

Several remarks can be made about these principles, all of which have equal relevance.

First, the ECtHR seems to suggest in the last part of [53] that assessing the democratic nature of a measure is secondary to checking on proportionality: Democracy is about tolerance and broadmindedness, 'amongst others', but a proportional law can pass the threshold of 'necessary in a democratic society'. A restriction cannot be necessary in democracy unless it is proportionate to the legitimate aim. So, a restriction must be proportionate to be necessary, or, otherwise, unproportionate restrictions cannot be necessary. This suggest that proportionality is a broader category than necessity. This paragraph heralds the future ECtHR's approach to privilege the proportionality tool, while refraining from democratic theory deduction or semantic analysis.[87]

Secondly, the paragraphs suggest a structured test applied by the ECtHR to assess the necessity of rights limitations based on four methodical steps, but the Court does not promise to apply all methods in every case. On the contrary, what is developed in *Dudgenon* is *not* a structured test, and the ECtHR does *not* commit to adapting it.[88] It is also not a complete test and does not include other principles or methods, like the method of assessing whether a rights limitation affects the essence of a right or not.[89] It has, finally, also not proven to be a sustainable test to clarify the requirement of 'necessary in a democratic society. Later versions of it would show significant differences in composition and finality.[90]

of 25 March 1985, A 90 [58]); and 'the exceptions to Arts 8 to 11 should be narrowly construed' (EctHR, *Klass v Germany*, judgment of 6 September 1978, A 28 [42]; EctHR, *Sunday Times v United Kingdom*, judgment 26 April 1979, A 30 [65]). See Greer (n 28) 15.

[87] Constitutional language, including fundamental rights language, serves several purposes, like signaling messages to the population or branches of government (see above). However, 'democracy' proves to be a constitutional concept only triggering minimal engagement by the judges. It performs a powerful defensive role in political debates, but in courts lacks the malleability of proportionality (Tridimas and Gentile (n 26) 815–16). We will see other examples of boundary-setting but apparently unsuitable judicial tools below.

[88] See on this section VI.B below.

[89] Tridimas and Gentile (n 26) 802.The first reference to essence was made in EctHR, *Winterwerp v The Netherlands*, judgment of 24 October 1979, App no 6301/73. In this case, the EctHR found a breach of the very essence of the right to liberty as protected by Art 5(4) ECHR. An older reference this time to the protection of 'the substance' of Convention rights appears in the *Belgian Language* Case. See *Case Relating to Certain Aspects of the Laws on the Use of Languages in Education in Belgium' v Belgium*, judgment of 23 July 1968, App Nos 1474/62, 1677/62, 1691/62, 1769/63, 1994/63, 2126/64. A more recent illustration is *Young, James and Webster v United Kingdom* (1989) A 44 regarding an arrangement British Rail had with its trade unions to require union membership as a condition of employment. The plaintiffs complained about a violation of Art 11 ECHR, protecting the freedom of assembly and association and their view was shared by the EctHR that held that the introduction of any obligation to join a trade union is a form of compulsion that interferes with the very substance of the freedom guaranteed by Art 11 ECHR.

[90] When Robert Spano – then president of the ECtHR – was asked to contribute a foreword to a book on proportionality, the whole issue of assessing rights-limiting laws under the Convention is presented as 'a proportionality test' comprising four independent but closely related components; the essence-method is one such component: 'first, there must be a reasonable relationship between the means and the ends; secondly, there must also be a fair balance between the demands of the general interest and the interest of the individual concerned; thirdly, the limitation must not impair the very essence of the

Thirdly, there is the final outcome of the proposed test: paragraph [54] suggests that the principles – proportionality amongst them – allow the ECtHR to verify the 'relevance and sufficiency' of a measure that then will determine whether the requirement of 'necessary in a democratic society' is met. In later practice the proportionality test will dominate the ECtHR's approach; the question of relevance and sufficiency will become less central.[91] The proportionality test seems to seduce judges, more than any other tool or method suggested in *Dudgeon* to test the necessity of rights limitations.[92]

Fourthly, and linked to the previous remark, proportionality proves to be cuckoo's egg. Once introduced in a constitutional toolkit, is aspires to dominance and finds strong support among the judiciary.[93] Together with the equally malleable tool or concept of 'margin for states', it takes precedence over other assessment criteria developed in written or unwritten law. Recently Paul Tavernier has made an inventory of proportionality's success. It has not only colonised the analysis of Articles 8–11 ECHR with their mention of 'necessary', but equally of Article 15(1) ECHR that contains a general limitation clause devoted to rights limitations in time of emergency.[94] The ECtHR even went further and 'found' the proportionality principle also in provisions that do not have terms like 'necessary' and 'strictly required',[95] including in the group of extra sensitive ECHR-rights protected by

right; and fourthly, these components are relative to the scope of margin of appreciation afforded to the state in the field in question' (R Spano, 'Foreword' in E Billis, N Knust and JP Rui (eds), *Proportionality in Crime Control and Criminal Justice* (Hart Publishing, 2021) v, vi).

[91] In the German structuring of the test that will be discussed below, relevance and sufficiency will become a component of the proportionality test. In Judge Spano's 2002 presentation of the rights limitation test of the EctHR (above) relevance and sufficiency were simply not mentioned, neither as the outcome of the limitation test, nor as a component.

[92] A central message is developing in this chapter: lawmakers and drafters of human rights or constitutional text can draft guidelines and requirements, but judges have agency and specific working constraints that push them towards a certain autonomy, towards tools or concepts that are malleable in the sense that no fixed consequences arise from their use, and all this without making them vulnerable to political tensions with other branches. The last aspect explains the lack of engagement with political concepts such as democracy (discussed above) or essence (see below) as a brake or test on state laws contested in the name of fundamental rights.

[93] We will see below that proportionality can (and should) also attract the virtuous legislator.

[94] Art 15 ECHR creates general exception to all the specific limitation provisions previously mentioned in the Convention. These can be disregarded in times of emergency, and are replaced by one general test: measures are allowed only 'to the extent *strictly required* by the exigencies of the situation' (author's empahsis).

[95] 'Mais la jurisprudence de Strasbourg a été très audacieuse et elle a étendu ces hypothèses à d'autres dispositions de la Convention qui ne se référaient ni à la nécessité démocratique, ni à la stricte mesure' (P Tavernier, 'La Cour de Strasbourg et le Principe de Proportionnalité. La Jurisprudence Récente concernant la France' (2015) *Ordine internazionale e diritti umani* 241, 243, available at www.rivistaoidu.net/wp-content/uploads/2021/12/2_Taverneir_2.pdf). Hence Tavernier's proposal to distinguish between an ordinary proportionality or a quasi-explicit proportionality in the case of Arts 8–11 and 15 ECHR, as opposed to an implicit proportionality. Particularly troublesome is that the EctHR started reading in rights provisions that apart from explicit exceptions in the Convention have no further limitation grounds – rights such as the right to a fair trial (Art 6), to protection to arbitrary detention (Art 5) and the prohibition of discrimination (Art 14). None of these rights foresees unwritten exceptions, but in all cases the Court recognised them by applying an 'implicit'

Article 15(2) ECHR.[96] This can be characterised as an interpretative leap from quasi-explicit proportionality to implicit (or invented) proportionality.

Finally, a remark about neutrality in the light of Weber's characterisation of the impersonal logic of 'rational-legal authority' today (see above). *Dudgeon*'s paragraph [54] concludes the ECtHR's presentation of its method to test the necessity in a democracy of rights limitation. This test, says the Court, is about assessing the relevance and sufficiency of the reasons given by the state for the interference (in this case prohibiting homosexual acts). We are 'not concerned with making any value-judgment as to the morality of homosexual relations between adult males'.[97]

This last clarification gives us an understanding of the 'good' the ECtHR is expecting from the proportionality exercise: it can be applied without forcing the Court to take a moral stand. Neutrality seems guaranteed when judges look at rights limitations. Hence, all the benefits are there. A certain structure that suggests a method to test whether laws are 'good' in a democracy and thus to go beyond legalism respectful to the sour World War II lessons. A method that is presumed to work without moral stands. A method that, moreover, creates more hands-free working conditions for the European judges in need of malleable concepts. Euphoria guaranteed? I will come back to this last question, after a brief presentation of the rise of proportionality in the EU fundamental rights system.

B. Proportionality in the CJEU's Methodology to Assess Rights Limitations

In the previous paragraph I discussed proportionality as a cuckoo's egg. Once introduced, it pushed aside other 'methods' and made us collectively forget that the ECHR requires 'necessity in a democratic society' and not 'proportionality'. The leap from the former to the latter was so evident, and the leap from quasi-explicit proportionality to implicit proportionality was so attractive, that it inspired other legal systems to follow. One of the systems that followed was the

proportionality principle. In one Art 5 case the Court simply stated that 'it was entitled to do so' (EctHR, *François v France*, judgment of 21 April 2015 [52]. See Tavernier (ibid) 248). In an Art 6 case (equally on procedural rights) proportionality is simply read into the provision, since 'the procedural right in question (access to court) is not an absolute right therefore allows for implicit limitations' (EctHR, *Viard v France*, judgment of 9 January 2014 [29]). Trumps?

[96] Art 15(2) ECHR states that 'No derogation from Article 2, except in respect of deaths resulting from lawful acts of war, or from Articles 3, 4 (paragraph 1) and 7 shall be made under this provision'. These provisions about life, torture, slavery and the no punishment without law rule are the closest Europe comes to the concept of rights as trump. Still, the EctHR has applied a proportionality test to assess limitations by states of these rights. This time it is a 'reinforced proportionality' test, but it is a proportionality test, nevertheless. *cf* 'La jurisprudence de la Cour de Strasbourg a reconnu que l'exigence de proportionnalité était renforcée dans certaines hypothèses, notamment en ce qui concerne les articles de la Convention qui ne sont pas susceptibles de dérogation au titre de l'article 15' (Tavernier (n 96) 246).

[97] EctHR, *Dudgeon v United Kingdom* [54].

EU legal system of fundamental rights codified in the CFR.[98] In the text of the CFR proportionality is explicitly given a pole position, with 'necessary' in a subordinate role as its subset.[99] In CJEU practice proportionality has even reached top status. Although Article 52(1) CFR demands the verification not only proportionality, but also essence and legality as autonomous requirements,[100] the practice of the CJEU points in another direction. In that practice, the CJEU does not always refer to the CFR, treats CFR rights only as principles,[101] (although the CFR makes an explicit distinction),[102] or does not examine Article 52(1) CFR systematically, and omits checking on the essence requirement.[103]

These practices might not surprise in the broader picture of modernity sketched by MacIntyre. Essence reflects 'an unconditional moral imperative' derived from human dignity and owed to every individual,[104] and this unconditional character explains perfectly why courts, be it national or European, shy away from establishing any concrete criteria for distinguishing between the

[98] Compare MA Eissen, 'Le principe de proportionnalité dans la jurisprudence de la Cour européenne des droits de l'Homme' in LE Pettiti, E Decaux and PH Imbert (eds), *La Convention européenne des droits de l'Homme, Commentaire article par article* (Economica, 1999) 65–81; E Bjorge and J Zglinski, 'The principle of proportionality in EU law and its domestic application: ni tout à fait le même, ni tout à fait un autre' in K Ziegler, P Neuvonen and V Moreno-Lax (eds), *Research Handbook on General Principles in EU Law. Constructing Legal Orders in Europe* (Edward Elgar, 2022) 191, 193.

[99] This in striking contrast with the 1950 ECHR where 'necessary' is the only term mentioned in the Convention and where 'proportionality' is only an unwritten law tool introduced by Court to clarify 'necessary'. Hence, 'proportionality' in the Charter has moved up in rank and 'necessary' has been downplayed and deprived of its important connection to 'democratic society'. 'Necessary' thus becomes a technical tool, deprived of its political dimension.

[100] Under Art 52(1) CFR any limitation must be (a) provided for by law; (b) respect their essence; and (c) comply with the principle of proportionality. Art 52(1) CFR: 'Any limitation on the exercise of the rights and freedoms recognised by this Charter must be provided for by law and respect the essence of those rights and freedoms. Subject to the principle of proportionality, limitations may be made only if they are necessary and genuinely meet objectives of general interest recognised by the Union or the need to protect the rights and freedoms of others.'

[101] B Zalar, 'Basic values, judicial dialogues and the rule of law in the light of the Charter of Fundamental Rights of the European Union: judges playing by the rules of the game' (2013) 14 *ERA Forum* 323. For Zalar the CJEU often disregards a careful application of the Charter and even minimises or discards the Charter's structure of rights and principles. Indeed, the Court has often appeared to abuse the concept of principles to downplay rights contained in the Charter by interchangeably referring to rights as mere principles or values without coherent reasonings. Besides, the Court seems to favour interpreting EU law not based on the provisions contained in the CFR, which is primary law, but more pursuant provisions contained in secondary law.

[102] Art 52(5) CFR provides for the distinction between the rights and principles, introduced to find a compromise as to the justiciability of economic and social rights. The rights contained in the Charter may be fully judicially operational – they can be invoked and enforced before courts and be a direct legal basis for judicial decisions, while the principles should be implemented by legislative or executive acts and their judicial operationality is limited to the interpretation and legality of such acts. See more in detail, N Poltorak, 'The application of the rights and principles of the Charter of Fundamental Rights' (2021) 34 *Robert Schuman Centre for Advanced Studies Research Paper*, available at ssrn.com/abstract=3821682 or dx.doi.org/10.2139/ssrn.3821682.

[103] Reference to the essence requirement, for example, is often made in *passim* as part of outlining the conditions which limitations of rights must respect under Art 52(1), and in practice, proportionality is by far the most important of the limiting conditions provided for in Art 52(1). See Tridimas and Gentile (n 26) 806.

[104] Tridimas and Gentile (n 26) 802.

essence and the periphery of fundamental rights.[105] Essence allows no compromise or malleability, putting the judiciary in a difficult position towards the state.[106] Lacking a clear moral *telos* for our society explains why a moral imperative 'no' to affect the essence of rights is difficult to enforce.[107] Irony wants it that proportionality is called upon by judges in to assess the question whether a limitation affects an essence or not:[108] proportionality as a tool for the judiciary to do the work![109]

Note also that the 'principle' of proportionality in the CFR is hardly defined or clarified.[110] The vague set-up of the general limitation clause (that should logically require the utmost precision) has allowed the CJEU to continue doing what it has been doing from the start of its proportionality journey: making sure the proportionality principle was under its definitional control, avoiding annoying consequences of coming out the cuckoo's egg.[111]

[105] See the comparative analysis of Tridimas and Gentile (n 26) 797.

[106] Tridimas and Gentile (n 26) 815. These authors in their comparative analysis also point at the Italian Constitutional Court's attempts to 'save' the essence criterion from legal oblivion by making or defining it as a malleable standard.

[107] In a similar vein, Dworkin in *Taking Rights Seriously* (n 6) argues that a society needs a political theory to guide its rights selection and practice.

[108] Tridimas and Gentile (n 26) 808: 'The appreciation of the essence of a right, and the nature of the infringement that affects the essence (think about the length of an infringement) cannot easily occur outside the assessment of proportionality. For how long should offenders be deprived of their voting rights for the violation to be considered to interfere with essence? … The truth is that essence is defined by reference to qualities the assessment of which requires a balancing exercise and therefore, at the very least, implies a proportionality analysis.'

[109] *cf* about the essence-tool: 'None of the above functions can hide the limitations of essence as a judicial tool. It does not do away with the need for balancing nor does it guarantee a higher level of protection than would otherwise apply. The value of the concept lies much more in offering a constitutional posture and a legitimizing device than a judicial tool that provides a firm dividing line' (Tridimas and Gentile (n 26) 815). The idea behind the essence of rights requirement should precisely be one of a rule (and not a principle) that bars any balancing, or weighing, no matter how weighty or pressing the legitimate aims of any restriction are, or any other legal arguments made. See T Ojanen, 'Making the Essence of Fundamental Rights Real: The Court of Justice of the European Union Clarifies the Structure of Fundamental Rights under the Charter' (2016) 12 *European Constitutional Law Review* 318, 328.

[110] The text suggests a definition of the principle of proportionality, but a proper look reveals only a suggestion that the principle is vaguely about reasonable or necessary relationships between means and certain legitimate ends ('Subject to the principle of proportionality, limitations may be made only if they are necessary and genuinely meet objectives of general interest recognized by the Union or the need to protect the rights and freedoms of others').

[111] See Bjorge and Zglinski (n 99) 193. This journey started with *Internationale Handelsgesellschaft* (1970), judged six years before the ECtHR's *Handyside* (1976). The Advocate General invited the CJEU to affirm the principle of proportionality in a case with fundamental rights dimensions. The CJEU recognised the existence and role of the principle. Contrary to the suggestion of the AG, it did however not undertake any effort to anchor the principle in the wordings of the Treaty but decided to base the principle on unwritten law rather than on textual arguments. Amid this creative moment, the CJEU looked at German law, but insisted on a European law solution. This was found! The Court detected the presence of a general principle in European law requiring that limitations must be 'appropriate and necessary' to attain the relevant EU policy objective of the measure. The term proportionality was not used, but the cuckoo's egg was added to the basket, and it was under the full control of the European judges.

There is little difference between the approaches of the two European courts. Both are bound by legal text that contain indications about how to assess laws that limit rights, but both approaches form part of an interpretative ethic that favours teleology and conceptual autonomy over literary interpretation and textual anchors.[112]

The rest of the CJEU proportionality story should therefore by now be familiar.[113] Different formulas are used in different areas of EU law.[114] A stable definition of the principle or a stable commitment by the CJEU to apply such a definition would never follow. Neither the definition, nor components of the principle, were clarified.

C. Proportionality: Its Historical Legacy

One can safely state that proportionality is by far the most important of the limiting conditions provided for European and national human rights law practice.[115] But is it only a tool for judges? History teaches us that the concept addresses itself to all, including the virtuous citizen and legislator.

Proportionality is by no means a modern concept. It is present in the moral thought and practices of the Ancient Greeks with their moral code based on physical and mental virtues, adapted by the Romans and by Christians. Proportionality can be attached to all four cardinal virtues: fortitude (*andreía* or *fortitude*), prudence (*phronesis* or *prudentia*), temperance (*sōphrosýnē* or *temperantia*) and justice (dikaiosýnē or *iustitia*).

The affinity for acting in a proportionate manner with the virtues of temperance and prudence (also understood as wisdom (*sophia*)) is clear.[116] But justice

[112] Tridimas and Gentile (n 26) 802.

[113] Once entered in EU law, the principle became a popular adjudicative technique. The CJEU resorted to it in a wide range of fields and contributed to the export of the principle to domestic legal systems withing the EU that were unfamiliar with it (Bjorge and Zglinski (n 99) 195). The EU's take on proportionality will typically consist of an examination of the suitability and necessity of the relevant measure – the *Internationale Handelsgesellschaft* stage of the proportionality test-, as well as, where appropriate the right balance between the interest of the rights holder and the competing policy concerns-the balancing stage of the test that was added in subsequent cases.

[114] 'While sometimes requiring that a measure must be no more than "appropriate for attaining a legitimate objective and must no go beyond what is necessary to achieve it" on other occasions it has found that state action must, in addition, not constitute a "disproportionate" interference and respect the "substance" of a right' (Bjorge and Zglinski (n 99) 195). With regard to the number of limbs, components or prongs, we will discuss the German law-inspired academic version of a structured proportionality test with three limbs and three sub-limbs (see below), but the CJEU will frequently omit one or two steps during its review of proportionality, or only examine the matter where it is explicitly raised by the applicant or where it is otherwise significant to the dispute in issue (Bjorge and Zglinski (n 99) 195).

[115] Tridimas and Gentile (n 26) 806.

[116] See on the connection between *phronesis* and *sophia*, A Kinneging, *De Onzichtbare Maat* (Prometheus, 2021) 523. *Pronesis*, once mastered, gives one the ability to do the good and to bring a concrete case under the right general category. It is about considering well, judging well, and prescribing rightly, using not only rational powers, but also intuition taking into consideration context and potential consequences.

seems to guide most straightforwardly towards the basic ideas of proportionality. This cardinal virtue that regulates all our relationships with others, is usually defined as 'to each his own' or 'may all get their due'.[117]

It was Thomas Aquinas (1225–1274) in *Summa Theologica* (written around 1270) who made the explicit connection between justice and proportionality.[118] Aristotle's worldview – insisting on *telos* as an important part of the explanation of the world, and on the central role of virtues in ethics as they allowed a human to live the most human live – had a strong impact on Aquinas. The latter used the term 'proportion' to explain the role of virtues. These help to do the 'good', a term that denotes ideas such *modus, species* and *ordo*, the right measure towards the individual, the species and the world as a whole. Everything has a certain weight, and what is heaviest must 'weight the heaviest'. Aquinas uses *proportio* to express this idea of weight and the right measure that God has wanted for the world.[119]

So, proportionality has ancient roots. It is about creating proportion and harmony between things and demands of life – not only in morals, art and architecture, but also in mathematics and law.[120] Criminal law, for instance, has played an important role in the development of the principle and its introduction in law.[121] Jeremy Bentham's famous calculus applied proportionality in legislation in *all* areas of law: weighing each time the pros and cons of one or more future actions against the degree of happiness they can provide.[122] Bentham's ideas on

[117] Respectively '*Suum cuique*' and '*Unicuique suum*'.

[118] 'Now each man's own is that which is due to him according to equality of proportion. Therefore, the proper act of justice is nothing else than to render to each one his own' (*Hoc autem dicitur esse suum uniuscuiusque personae quod ei secundum proportionis aequalitatem debetur. Et ideo proprius actus iustitiae nihil est aliud quam reddere unicuique quod suum est.*) (ST, II-II.58.11C). I use the version available at www.corpusthomisticum.org/sth3057.html. On the treatment of the virtues by Aquinas, see Kinneging (n 117) 518–30; J Finnis, *Aquinas, Moral, Political and Legal Theory* (Oxford University Press, 1989).

[119] 'Praeterea, ea quae sunt ad finem, proportionantur fini' (ST, I.47.3.ad 1). 'Further, those things which are for the end are proportioned to the world.' See Kinneging (n 117) 496.

[120] Jean-Marc Sauvé, vice-président du Conseil d'État, 'Le principe de proportionnalité, protecteur des libertés', 17 March 2017, *Conseil d'État* 9, available at www.conseil-etat.fr/publications-colloques/discours-et-interventions/le-principe-de-proportionnalite-protecteur-des-libertes.

[121] See, N Courakis and V Polyzoidou, 'The Principle of Proportionality: Tracing its Historical Evolution' in E Billis, N Knust and JP Rui (eds), *Proportionality in Crime Control and Criminal Justice* (Hart Publishing, 2021) 101, 110–14 (discussing Montesquieu, Beccaria, Bentham and the different legal codifications with regard to proportional punishment). Courakis and Polyzoidou study the proportionality principle in the context of criminal law and highlight the many philosophers, starting with Socrates and Cicero who have advocated a basic understanding of it in punishment against the prevailing rule of the *lex talionis* ('an eye for an eye'). During the Enlightenment the idea of proportional punishment was on every liberal or utilitarian philosopher or politician's mind, culminating in demands for explicit rights on proportional judgment and for clear limits to disproportional punishment. These claims were recognised in the 17989 French Declaration, the 1791 US Eight Amendment, the 1794 Prussian Civil Code and several laws initiated by the likes of Thomas Jefferson in Virginia and Jean-Paul Marat in France.

[122] J Bentham, *Traités de législation civile et pénale*, vol 1 (Paris, 1820) ch V, 28ff, available at isidore.science/document/ark:/12148/bpt6k5692310z; Courakis and Polyzoidou (n 122) 111–12.

ideal legislation were actively discussed on both sides of the Channel and must without doubt have contributed to laws voted with a grain of proportionality in areas characterised by human rights or other sensitive concerns.[123]

Some contemporary authors suggest that the proportionality principle is in the first place a principle to adjudicate in conflicts, but they admit that the principle has the potential to become a principle of good governance, not only addressed to judges, but to all public authorities, including the legislator.[124] More proportionality in laws would be ideal, but the historical sketch is more subtle. Our previous discussion suggests that the tradition of injecting proportionality in laws by legislators is not new.

The history of proportionality in court as a tool for judges to deliver judgments is more complex. Our analysis of Greek virtues like justice and prudence suggests a strong connection between proportionality and judging well, a connection that might well have existed in medieval times. The connection got lost when Enlightenment (arguably following Newton's physics) *abandoned* the idea of *telos* as a necessary part of the explanation of how the world works. A reliance on proportionality by judges must have experienced a setback during this period mesmerised by scientific objectivity and rules. Law and adjudication needed to be conceived after the model of natural sciences. Enlightenment's insistence on the primacy of laws and the subordinate role for judges that would follow were relaxed towards the end of the nineteenth century.[125] Post-World War II's understanding of the need for a rule *of* law system to amend the rule *by* law practice brought the principle back into law, where it moved to the fore of the judicial activity. The gate was again open for proportionality as a corrective principle controlled by judges.[126]

Today the principle of proportionality has made a stellar rise in the moral and legal landscape.[127] Proportionality, authors hold, is *the* criterion used by most

[123] A good example is the French Act on the separation of Church and State of 9 December 1905. This law aimed to 'respect as far as possible local customs and traditions and … interfere with them only to the extent that it is strictly necessary in the interest of keeping public order'. The act is discussed by Bjorge and Zglinski (n 99) 192. I will return to it in the next section.

[124] Jean-Marc Sauvé (n 121) 4. Sauvé's example is the presence of the principle in the Act of 15 March 2004 prohibiting students in French public primary schools, secondary schools and lycée from wearing symbols and clothing manifesting a religious affiliation.

[125] See Whitman (n 22) 371–92; S Dauchy, 'Le juge, bouche de la loi. A propos de la célèbre métaphore de Montesquieu' (2014) 256 *Nagoya University Journal of Law and Politics* 325, available at hal.univ-lille.fr/hal-02959170/document. The French revolutionaries never envisaged judicial power as a balancing element vis-à-vis legislative power, nor did they intend to associate it with legislative power, or with the executive function. On the contrary, from the outset, the judiciary was conceived as subordinate to the legislature, with only a modest interpretative role. In the UK judicial proportionality was present from the 17th century. See, Bjorge and Zglinski (n 99) 191–92 with further references.

[126] Meierhenrich (n 44). This author insists on the distinction between the German or continental *Rechtsstaat* tradition and the more Dicean or Anglo-American rule of law tradition. Both traditions, however, came to be invented as responses to the rule by law tradition. The invention of these traditions took place at around the same time, but in response to very different local exigencies.

[127] K Möller, *The Global Model of Constitutional Rights* (Oxford University Press, 2015); K Möller, 'The Proportionality of Lockdowns' in P Sutoris, S Murphy, A Mendes Borges and Y Nehushtan (eds),

courts in the liberal-democratic world to determine the justifiable and legitimate nature of repressive measures taken by the state. Proportionality is then 'simply' a structure that allows judges to engage in the practical reasoning necessary to assess the justifiability of a policy.[128] It is based on the idea of creating 'proportion' in human action contained in many proverbs worldwide like 'not using a sledgehammer to crack a nut'.[129] Its use in court promises to reintroduce the virtue of justice after centuries of modernity's legalistic monopoly. The specific conditions of every case can be looked at again, the irreducible singularity of life and people is respected, and human justice (*un droit sur mesure*) can be realised.[130]

D. Proportionality in Courts: Superior Features Compared to Other Review Methods (Möller)

Proportionality review is not based on legal interpretation or a special hermeneutical method, but is about justification and instrumental and normative rationality control.[131]

Modern proportionality review is said to be a creation of German courts that spread out in the legal word.[132] In European human rights case law the review is done after the analysis of the legality criterion (is there a legal basis for a limitation of a right?) and the legitimate aim criterion (does the limitation envisaged pursue a legitimate aim?). The foundation for the EU principle of proportionality was laid in an already mentioned case regarding Germany – *Internationale Handelsgesellschaft* (1970) – where the CJEU looked at the German case law but decided to look for its own version and found it in the EU general principles of law. As developed in the EU's law and doctrine, the proportionality assessment typically entails a three- or four-step (with three to four components/questions depending on how to count) test examining suitability (whether the measure is suitable, appropriate to reach the aim pursued); necessity/alternatives (whether the measure is necessary, the least restrictive to achieve this aim); and proportionality in the strict (narrow) sense (whether the measure imposes a burden that is excessive having regard to the aim pursued).[133]

Pandemic Response and the Cost of Lockdowns: Global Debates from Humanities and Social Sciences (Routledge, 2023) 157–70, also available at eprints.lse.ac.uk/113726/1/Moller_proportionality_of_lockdowns_paper_13_2021.pdf.

[128] Möller, 'The Proportionality of Lockdowns' (ibid) 158.

[129] S Van Drooghenbroeck and X Delgrange, 'Le principe de proportionnalité: retour sur quelques espoirs déçus' (2019) 7 *Revue du droit des religions* 41.

[130] ibid 42.

[131] 'It does not demand a justification with reference to an authoritative text but rather an instrumental and normative justification of governmental measures on the basis of rational standards' (R Poscher, 'Proportionality and the Bindingness of Fundamental Rights' in E Billis, N Knust and JP Rui (eds), *Proportionality in Crime Control and Criminal Justice* (Hart Publishing, 2021) 49, 57.

[132] P Craig and Gr de Búrca, *EU Law: Text, Cases, and Materials* (Oxford University Press, 2015) 551.

[133] Craig and Búrca (ibid) 551; R Schütze, *An Introduction to European Law* (Cambridge University Press, 2015) 204–05. See further literature supporting these three steps: M Cohen-Eliya and I Porat,

Kai Möller, a leading expert on the work of Robert Alexy, presents the principle as a series of basic questions and sub-questions that respect and follow the human rights limitation logic. The question of the proportionality of a rights-limitation is addressed after answering the legality question ('is there a legal basis?'; Q Legality) and the question about the legitimate aim ('does the limitation envisaged pursue a legitimate aim?'; Q Legitimacy). The answer to the legitimacy question then forms the starting point for the proportionality inquiry with questions about appropriateness or rational connection (Q1 Proportionality–rationality), questions about possible relevant alternatives (Q2 Proportionality–necessity), and finally very specific questions about balancing (Q3 Proportionality–balancing). These very specific sub-questions about the balancing component of proportionality are said to give more depth to the balancing exercise, avoiding superficial balancing.

These four components combined – legitimacy, rationality, necessity, balancing – give the following:

- Do state measures pursue a legitimate objective and meet a 'compelling social need'? (Q Legitimacy)
- Are they rationally related to this objective/are they suitable (relevant and sufficient means to achieve it)? (Q1 Proportionality–rationality)
- Are they necessary in the sense that there must be no less restrictive but equally effective alternative? (Q2 Proportionality–necessity)
- Are they appropriate[134] or 'proportionate in the strict sense', the establishment of which requires a balancing exercise between the severity of the restriction and the importance of the public interest pursued? (Q3 Proportionality–balancing).

Q3.1. How serious is the infringement of the rights protected interest of the individual; for example, the burdens that the measures impose on the ability of individuals to live their lives freely)?

Q3.2. How important is the competing public interest (the importance of the motive called upon by the state; for example, protecting health and life)?

Q3.3. What is the relationship between the two (to determine whether the importance of the public interest in the protection of rights outweighs the severity of the restriction of freedom)?

'American balancing and German proportionality: The Historical Origins' (2010) 8 *International Journal of Constitutional Law* 263, 267; Y Arai-Takahashi, 'Proportionality – A German Approach' (1999) 19 *Amicus Curiae* 11, 12. For the CJEU's case law on these three steps, see Case C-343/09 *Afton Chemical Limited v Secretary of State for Transport* [2010] OJ C234/14 [45] (with further references).

[134] Some German scholars use the term 'appropriateness' as an alternative term for the proportionality *stricto sensu* whereas the CJEU in some cases refers to appropriateness in the sense of suitability. Here the German scholars' approach is followed.

As said, today most courts in the world apply this proportionality test or a variation of it, and in many cases, they apply the test equally to review laws. Evidently, this infringes on the institutional prerogatives of the lawmaker.[135] To create a culture of respect for rights this is said to be indispensable. Anticipating proportionality review by judges, invites lawmakers to respect a standard of care. The questions of proportionality typically require the state, when imposing measures restrictive of rights and freedoms, to pursue legitimate objectives; to prove that impugned measures are rationally related to those objectives; and to guarantee that the impugned measures are no more than necessary to achieve legitimate objectives.

The added value of proportionality as opposed to other review methods of acts and laws, is its ability to push forward the interrogation of state's motives.[136] Older judicial standards only screened for unreasonableness and abuse of power. Proportionality review is more ambitious and considers not only rationality or lack of it. It is about legitimacy, rationality, and necessity and balancing. Hence, a *first advantage* of proportionality testing is its explicit consideration of a plurality of rationally relevant considerations.[137]

A *second advantage* is that all this review work is delivered in a transparent and structured way. As said, older judicial standards only screened for unreasonableness and abuse of power. The move to standards of reasonableness in some legal systems already constituted a more restrictive approach towards state's discretion. The reasonableness test excludes disproportionate measures, but is satisfied with a proper or reasonable balance between all the competing interests at stake when state measures interfere with rights.[138] However, compared to the proportionality test with its structured questioning (see above), the reasonableness test is more

[135] 'Why have judicial proportionality controls – in all their different nuances – found their way into so many different constitutional and human rights jurisdictions? A legal realist explanation could simply point to the attractiveness of the proportionality control to the courts that claim it. It provides constitutional and other courts with a broad and flexible power of judicial review with which to overturn legislative decisions. But even if the temptations associated with judicial power are part of the explanation, it would be strange if courts could assert this power in so many jurisdictions without losing acceptance if there were no underlying reasons of political morality upon which the proportionality control could lean. Theories of democracy certainly cannot explain the widespread use of the proportionality control: as critics never tire of emphasizing, the democratic legitimacy of courts is much less than that of parliaments when it comes to balancing conflicts of interest. Thus, there must be other normative foundations of the liberal constitutional state upon which the courts can base their use of the proportionality control over the more democratically legitimated legislature.' (Poscher (n 132) 56–57).

[136] 'Unlike ordinary substantive review standards, such as *Wednesbury* unreasonableness, structured proportionality is, as the High Court of Australia observed in Palmer v Western Australia … transparent and in principle hostile to legal fictions that might justify disproportionate measures: EC Ip, 'Courts, Proportionality and COVID-19 Lockdowns' *IACL-AIDC Blog* (23 September 2021), available at blog-iacl-aidc.org/covid19-future-constitutionalism/2021/9/23/courts-proportionality-and-covid-19-lockdowns.

[137] This amount of context-sensitivity is absent in constitutional systems like the US, where courts engage in categorical reasoning focusing only on one or a handful of characteristics of the reviewed measure or circumstances in which it is invoked.

[138] NH Grohmann, 'Tracing the Development of the Proportionality Analysis in Relation to Forced Evictions under the ICESCR' (2022) 22 *Human Rights Law Review* 1, 4.

ad hoc, vague, and not guided by a framework of questions that states need to answer.[139] Proportionality is also said to be more transparent in comparison with modern constitutional review in the US based on categorical constitutional analysis ('What rule does the Constitution give for this case?') tempered in some cases by a balancing doctrine.[140] US balancing compares between the burden on the right and the importance of the governmental interest. Proportionality testing does that, too, but only as the final subtest after other tests that do not rely on balancing with its risk of subjectivity.[141]

So, proportionality is about deep interrogation of state actions (advantage 1) based on a structured transparent inquiry (advantage 2). Together they explain the heuristic benefits of the judicial turn to proportionality: it makes judicial reasoning more intelligible for other state actors and contributes to a culture of justification in a liberal constitutional state.[142] The proportionality requirement forces the majority to present this justification to an appropriate and independent constitutional institution.[143]

Proportionality, with its superior testing of state actions, not only benefits citizens, but also state actors. Subordination to its use also has strong legitimising effects on state actions in today's societies where legitimacy can no longer be based on references to external sources like religion.[144] Proportionality review in court facilitates the confrontation of the legal sphere with non-legal spheres in a controlled manner.[145] Review by judges carrying out their own assessment can

[139] ibid.

[140] Cohen-Eliya and Porat (n 134) 263–65. Balancing has never attained the status of an established doctrine in US constitutional law in the same way that proportionality has in European constitutional law and remains controversial as a doctrine in US constitutional law.

[141] ibid 268. Proportionality testing therefore allows less vagueness and judicial subjectivity in balancing, proponents of proportionality analysis hold: the balancing done in the framework of the final subtest of proportionality is only the end of the testing. It is preceded by the subtests of suitability or rationality and necessity that are not based on balancing. The test of suitability and necessity do not involve balancing and do not require comparisons between the end and the right. All that suitability and necessity require is a better fit between the means and the end, one which does less harm to the right.

[142] In political theory, a right to a justification is seen as a counterpart of the democratic process. It allows the individual to call upon the democratically elected legislature to justify the need to infringe on fundamental rights (Poscher (n 132) 56–57, with references to recognition approaches in ethics and philosophy (M Kumm, N Petersen, A Honneth, etc)). A democracy that takes justification seriously is more than a majority machine based on power struggle. It seeks additional legitimation by considering all citizens as rational subjects and to make sure its democratic decisions can be reasonably justified. The right of justification as a component of the democratic principle is through the proportionality standards equipped to be exercised in court.

[143] Poscher (n 132) 57. See also E Herlin-Karnell, 'The domination of security and the promise of justice: on justification and proportionality in Europe's 'Area of Freedom, Security and Justice' (2017) 8 *Transnational Legal Theory* 79.

[144] Remember that in bureaucratic modernity, power can no longer be based on traditional or charismatic grounds, but only on rational grounds, resting on a belief in the legality and rationality of laws to guarantee that the rationality applies to the system's bureaucratic structure as a whole. See also E Billis, N Knust and JP Rui, 'The Typology of Proportionality' in E Billis, N Knust and JP Rui (eds), *Proportionality in Crime Control and Criminal Justice* (Hart Publishing, 2021) 3, 12–13.

[145] Proportionality also facilitates the meeting of spheres within the multilevel legal order. It facilitates for instance the work of the ECtHR as a European court that must operate with respect of

irritate the other social systems (eg politics, army, police, economy), but the irritations are limited through the selective linkage of the proportionality test that is carried out only after a state decision is based on a law. While doing so, it strengthens both the checks and balances of the legal and political system and facilitates obtaining and maintaining social legitimacy for desired state policies,[146] through showing a standard of care (see above).

E. Is there a Doctrine? (Descriptive Question). Three Myths about Proportionality in Court

Many myths surround the proportionality test.[147] The first is about the neutrality of the principle.[148] Proportionality does more than simply ask a series of questions. Courts carry out a proper assessment, have a law-constitutive role, and might take law-constitutive decisions on topics with an immediate impact on the political

subsidiarity. Domestic judicial review of the proportionality of rights-infringing measures has become an obvious cornerstone of the subsidiary nature of the Convention system. Lack of judicial review of the proportionality of the COVID-19 measure entails a procedural violation of the ECHR. Its complete absence in the face of executive action that restricts Convention rights logically leads to the finding of a violation (ECtHR, *Communauté genevoise d'action syndicale (CGAS) v Suisse*, judgment of 15 March 2022, Application no 21881/20). See S Smet, 'First violations in a Covid-19 case: Communauté Genevoise d'Action Syndicale (CGAS) v Switzerland' (9 May 2022) *Strasbourg Observers* 9, available at strasbourgobservers.com/2022/05/09/first-violations-in-a-covid-19-case-communaute-genevoise-daction-syndicale-cgas-v-switzerland; JH Gerards, 'Communauté genevoise d'action syndicale (CGAS) t. Zwitserland (EHRM, 21881/20) – Demonstratieverbod in coronatijd: er zijn grenzen' 2022 *European Human Rights Cases Updates* 12. In practice this process of 'proceduralisation' of the proportionality test is a way of avoiding a proportionality test in (the European) court by relying largely on the legislative proportionality test (if any) done in the Member State that has authorised the rights infringing measure. See critically, Van Drooghenbroeck and Delgrange (n 130) 51–55. Equally, N le Bonniec, *La procéduralisation des droits substantiels par la Cour européenne des droits de l'homme. Réflexion sur le contrôle juridictionnel des droits garantis par la Convention européenne des droits de l'homme* (Larcier, 2017); E Brems and J Gerards (eds), *Procedural Review in European Fundamental Rights Cases* (Cambridge University Press, 2017); OM Arnardóttir, 'The "procedural turn" under the European Convention on Human Rights and presumptions of Convention compliance' (2017) *International Journal of Constitutional Law* 9; P Popelier and C Van De Heyning, 'Subsidiarity Post-Brighton: Procedural Rationality as Answer?' (2017) *Leiden Journal of International Law* 5; LM Huijbers, 'The European Court of Human Rights' procedural approach in the age of subsidiarity' (2017) 6 *Cambridge International Law Journal* 177; M Saul, 'The European Court of Human Rights' Margin of Appreciation and the Processes of National Parliaments' (2015) *Human Rights Law Review* 745.

[146] Billis, Knust and Rui (n 145) 14–15.

[147] One myth about proportionality as more protective of rights than US categorical balancing, will be addressed below (section V.C). About the inaccuracy of this myth in principle and in legal practice of the courts, see Cohen-Eliya and Porat (n 134) 270.

[148] In *Dudgeon* (as discussed in section IV.A) the ECtHR insisted on its method of testing rights limitations on relevance and sufficiency freed it from value-based reasoning. *cf* ECtHR, *Dudgeon v United Kingdom* [54] (author's emphasis): 'The Court's task is to determine based on the aforesaid principles whether the reasons purporting to justify the 'interference' in question are relevant and sufficient under Art 8 par. 2 .... *The Court is not concerned with making any value-judgment as to the morality of homosexual relations between adult males*'.

system, thus causing irritations within other social systems.[149] The application of the principle entails more than rationality control but demands work of interpretation (hermeneutics) that is hardly neutral.[150]

The second myth to debunk is the 'Germanness' of proportionality testing. It is true that the Supreme Administrative Court of Prussia in *Kreuzberg* (1883) applied the principle to assess police interventions – a judgment that provoked a commentator's catchphrase 'Police should not shoot sparrows with cannons'.[151] It is equally true that the German Constitutional Court authoritatively set the tone of post-World War II judicial review of laws in the *Pharmacy Decision* where it introduced and spelled out the principle into constitutional law and required the legislator to respect it.[152]

However, there are competing genealogies[153] that point at proportionality-type judicial review in public law of the UK (seventeenth century) and in the case law of the French *Conseil d'État* (early twentieth century).[154]

The full history of the proportionality principle can be better grasped when considering the presence of proportionalities (plural).[155] Today's proportionality

[149] Billis, Knust and Rui (n 145) 14. Perhaps a claim can be made that the neutrality resides in the structured form of the test, contrary to the reasonably test (above) that has no guiding framework like the questioning framework of proportionality, but this claim has to be tested to its merits (do the courts follow the framework? Is the sheer fact that there is a structure in a reasoning enough to speak about 'neutrality' of the reasoning?).

[150] Poscher (n 132) 64–66. This hermeneutical work is needed, when the judge reflects about possible alternatives that the legislator could have chosen and the question of balancing in a particular case, with the sub-question about how binding upon the legislator a specific right is. Not every right-limitation is as serious from a constitutional perspective, and, the German Constitutional Court at least, attentively looks at the relevant provisions in the German Constitution and their position in the whole of the Constitution to better understand the balancing to be done to find the answer to the question of appropriateness of the measure and the kind of safeguards that need to accompany powers to limits rights.

[151] Prussian Supreme Administrative Court *Kreuzberg*, judgment of 14 June 1882, *PrOVG* 9, 353. See Bjorge and Zglinski (n 99) 192–94; J Schwarze, *Droit administratif européen* (Bruylant, 2009) 731; Cohen-Eliya and Porat (n 134) 263–86.

[152] BVerfG 7, 377, judgment of 11 June 1958. See Poscher (n 132) 52–53. On top of a rationality or suitability test, the German Court insisted on the need for assessing the necessity of a rights-limiting measure in the light of other equally effective options. It completed the by now classical standard of proportionality with a development of the balancing test, that *Pharmacy Decision* heavily relied on a comparison of the infringement with possible alternative infringements. The proportionality test as an instrument to test limitations of fundamental rights was born.

[153] Bjorge and Zglinski (n 99) 192–94; Y Arai, 'Proportionality – a German Approach' (1999) 19 *Amicus Curiae* 11.

[154] Bjorge and Zglinski (n 99) 192–94 with further references. Their examples show how judges made sense of domestic laws, like the French Act on the separation of Church and State (above), that contained proportionality elements in their provisions.

[155] Billis, Knust and Rui (n 145) 15. A distinction can be made between proportionality as a virtue, proportionality in taste and arts and science, legislative proportionality, and proportionality in adjudication (*cf* Billis, Knust and Rui (n 145) 17). I already discussed Courakis and Polyzoidou's study of the proportionality principle in the context of criminal law (Courakis and Polyzoidou (n 122) 104–05). Within this legal field different notions of proportionality coexist: substantive criminal law (with respect to criminalisation and the limits of self-defence), procedural criminal law (regarding the applicability conditions for coercive measures such as searches, communication interceptions, arrest

testing in court is made possible and nourished by these proportionalities.[156] *Proportionality in adjudication* would not have been possible without *legislative proportionality* paving the way. The history of French proportionality testing started when French judges needed to consider a national law that included an idea of proportionality in its principles. There is a history to be written about lawmaking that is respectful of the proportionality principle. Such a study would also give a different perspective on its uptake by judges, for whom legal materials are a key point of departure.[157]

The third, and most troubling, myth regards the commitment of judges to structured proportionality testing. There is a normative stance in the discussions built upon an assumption of commitment.[158] Whether the assumption is correct is something that academic analysis will have to be attentive to.[159] Did courts commit to the principle, and if yes, did they commit to the full package as identified by scholars? Does the appearance of the structured test in one case or several cases equal an explicit commitment of the Court in question to adhere to the structured test?

Take for instance, the CJEU's *Digital Rights Ireland*. It could appear as a model judgment respectful of the German-based version of the proportionality test.[160]

warrants and pre-trial detentions) and sentencing law (concerning the assessment of the seriousness of crimes and penalties). Billis, Knust and Rui insists on this coexistence of different notions of proportionality. Proportionality in constitutional law does not mean the same thing as proportionality in administrative law or criminal law, and within each legal field more than one notion might circulate (Billis, Knust and Rui (n 145) 15). See for an overview of areas of application of the principle in EU law, Bjorge and Zglinski (n 99) 196–98).

[156] This also explains certain differences in judicial review. *cf* Poscher (n 132) 65. Poscher goes to great lengths to remind us that the proportionality principle in the *Pharmacy Decision* is hermeneutically developed from the so-called bindingness clause to Art 1(3) of the German Basic Law: 'The following basic rights shall bind the legislature, the executive and the judiciary as directly applicable law.'

[157] This devotion or *pairedness* of judges to their texts also partly explains why the review approach of the CJEU differs from this of the ECtHR: not only the primary texts (we recall that Art 52(1) CFR is formulated differently from Art 8(2) ECHR), but equally the secondary laws tested by the CJEU are different and the latter are taken from different legal areas with each their own notion of proportionality. One unique model of proportionality testing that applies always is a myth.

[158] During the pandemic, for instance, we thus could read the following: 'Unfortunately, several courts around the world have been watering down structured proportionality in the judicial review of COVID-19 emergency measures … ignoring wholesale the steps required by structured proportionality. A public health emergency per se neither suspends entrenched fundamental rights nor invalidates the continued applicability of structured proportionality and similar doctrines in the countries that recognise them. The transparent analytical steps that these doctrines obligate authorities to openly undertake should not be sidestepped by public health officials or courts, especially in times of high stress and emotionality' (Ip (n 137)).

[159] *cf* 'le Conseil constitutionnel a approfondi son contrôle, initialement limité au contrôle de l'adéquation et parfois de la nécessité, au profit du triple test de proportionnalité' (Sauvé (n 7)).

[160] CJEU, Joint cases C-293/12 and C-594/12 *Digital Rights Ireland and Seitlinger and others* [2014] [46] (with further references). In this case, the retention on the basis of the Directive 2006/24/EC was found appropriate for fighting against serious crime (*Digital Rights Ireland* [49]). Moreover, after stating that the existence of alternatives (like anonymous communication that could be deemed less harmful) did not affect appropriateness, the CJEU stressed that the retention could not be justified by the objective pursued, despite importance of this objective (*Digital Rights Ireland* [50]–[51]). Citing *IPI*, which in turn referred to *Satakunnan Markkinapörssi and Satamedia* and *Volker und Markus*

But closer analysis reveals that the 'less restrictive alternative' test is swapped with a less demanding 'limited to what is strictly necessary' test.[161] Other CJEU judgments are more superficial or less complete.[162]

Likewise, the ECtHR, without clarification, shifts between broad proportionality testing[163] and narrow proportionality testing.[164] The latter is done by omitting the 'pressing social need' question or 'relevant and sufficient reasons' element. The ECtHR not only amends the number, but also the nature of the components of the proportionality test whenever it deems it appropriate. The first proportionality question – whether the interference promote legitimate state interests – will usually be dealt with as 'promoting any legitimate state interest', but now and then is made stricter by adding a textual argument about 'necessity' or a consideration of the intimate aspect of the right that is affected.[165] In those rare cases, the ECtHR

Schecke and Eifert, the CJEU addressed proportionality in the strict sense. After highlighting the need for precise safeguards based on *Marper* (*Digital Rights Ireland* [54] and [55]), the CJEU found that the interference was not limited to what was strictly necessary, since the Directive, among (many) others, affected anyone in a generalised manner and did not provide for adequate safeguards against abuse or misuse (*Digital Rights Ireland* [56]–[59], [66]–[67]). See: Case C-473/12 *Institut professionnel des agents immobiliers (IPI) v Geoffrey Englebert, Immo 9 SPRL, Grégory Francotte* [2014] OJ C9/13 (*IPI*) [39]; Case C-73/07 *Satakunnan Markkinapörssi and Satamedia* [2008] ECR I-9831 (*Satakunnan Markkinapörssi and Satamedia*); Joined Cases C-92/09 and C-93/09 *Volker und Markus Schecke GbR and Hartmut Eifert v Land Hessen* [2010] ECR I-11063 (*Volker und Markus Schecke and Eifert*).

[161] J Milaj, 'Invalidation of the data retention directive – Extending the proportionality test' (2015) 31 *Computer Law & Security Review* 604, 613: The 'limited to what is strictly necessary' test does not open the doors for an assessment of the means used for surveillance since its aim is different. In the way this test has been used so far by the Court, it does not assess the form of surveillance and the way it is done but aims to limit the impact of the interference with the life of the individual by evaluating the existing safeguarding measures. In comparison, the 'less restrictive alternative' criteria, as the name suggests, aims to show that the desired result cannot be achieved with other means that would interfere less with the rights of the individual'. *cf* J Milaj, 'Privacy, surveillance, and the proportionality principle: The need for a method of assessing privacy implications of technologies used for surveillance' (2016) 30 *International Review of Law, Computers & Technology* 115, 120. This handling of affairs is part of a more general attitude of CJEU reluctance to use the 'less restrictive alternative' test when judging Union measures and Union laws, and to make the Charter more malleable by treating rights in the Charter as only principles or by not referencing to the Charter at all. See section IV.A–B above.

[162] *cf* with T Harbo, 'The Function of the Proportionality Principle in EU Law' (2010) 16 *European Law Journal* 171.

[163] ECtHR, *Malone v the United Kingdom*, Application no 8691/79, judgment of 2 August 1984 [101]; ECtHR, *Segerstedt-Wiberg and others v Sweden*, Application no 62332/00, judgment of 6 June 2006 [88].

[164] ECtHR, *Breyer v Germany*, Application no 50001/12, judgment of 30 January 2020 [88] ('An interference will be considered "necessary in a democratic society" for a legitimate aim if it answers a 'pressing social need' and if it is proportionate to the legitimate aim pursued'). For a full analysis, see P De Hert and G Bouchagiar, 'Adding and removing elements of the proportionality and necessity test to achieve desired outcomes. Breyer and the necessity to end anonymity of cell phone users' (2021) 7 *European Data Protection Law Review* 304.

[165] J Christoffersen, *Fair Balance: Proportionality, Subsidiarity and Primarity in the European Convention on Human Rights* (Martinus Nijhoff, 2009) 114. Based on a detailed analysis of case law, Christoffersen concludes that the ECtHR can only be said to have rejected the idea of including in the proportionality requirement the obligation for states to choose the least restrictive alternative to achieve the aim pursued. See for a confirmation of this analysis, Van Drooghenbroeck and Delgrange (n 130) 42–61. These authors attach great value to *Glor* (2009) where the ECtHR confirmed explicitly – in their view for the first time – that for a measure to be considered proportionate and necessary in

will insist on the requirement that the objective of the measure is not only legitimate but also meets 'compelling social need'.[166]

At the level of domestic law and domestic courts, work is to be done to verify whether there is a commitment to a broad test and, if so, if this commitment is upheld.[167] Some authors find that the overall picture of the test in the practice of domestic courts is a messy blend of cases in which judges employ a loose form of structured proportionality analysis.[168] The same messiness, incidentally, is also present in systems without proportionality testing.[169] Non-commitment to a fixed structure of reasoning seems to be the rule in the life of the judiciary. Judges do not want to apply a given structure of reasoning; they do not only want to assess the reasonableness of legislative decision-making, but also the motivations behind it. When the Constitution provides no specific further guidance, they want practical

a democratic society, the existence of a measure that less seriously infringes the fundamental right in question and achieves the same end must be ruled out (ECtHR, *Glor v Switzerland*, judgment of 30 April 2009 [94]). However, Van Drooghenbroeck and Delgrange find that after *Glor* this stance has not followed through.

[166] ECtHR, *Dudgeon v United Kingdom* [50]–[52]: '50. A number of principles relevant to the assessment of the "necessity", "in a democratic society", of a measure taken in furtherance of an aim that is legitimate under the Convention have been stated by the Court in previous judgments. 51. Firstly, "necessary" in this context does not have the flexibility of such expressions as "useful", "reasonable", or "desirable", but implies the existence of a "pressing social need" for the interference in question (see the above-mentioned Handyside judgment, p.22, par. 48). 52. (…) 'not only the nature of the aim of the restriction but also the nature of the activities involved will affect the scope of the margin of appreciation. The present case concerns a most intimate aspect of private life. Accordingly, there must exist particularly serious reasons before interferences on the part of the public authorities can be legitimate for the purposes of paragraph 2 of Art 8'. *cf* 'A particularly striking feature of the Dudgeon, Norris and Modinos cases, on the one hand, and the Handyside and Müller decisions on the other, is how similar issues, for example, concerning the position in other countries, 'pressing social need', and proportionality, were handled in different ways. Although there need not be uniformity of outcome in cases such as these, greater uniformity in method and reasoning is desirable' (Greer (n 28) 29).

[167] Selective remarks in literature on the Belgian *Conseil d'État*, and the French *Constitutional Court*, suggest a loose approach, without a faithful lipreading of the structured test. *cf* Y Mossoux, 'Les principes du raisonnable et de proportionnalité' in PO De Broux, B Lombaert and F Tulkens (eds), *Actualité des principes généraux en droit administratif, social et fiscal* (Anthémis, 2015) 51, 63: 'Certains arrêts du Conseil d'État pourraient être analysés comme une marque de réticence du Conseil d'État envers le contrôle de la nécessité. Ainsi, en matière de sanctions administratives'.

[168] At least two scenarios of judicial testing of rights limitations can be distinguished. Either courts do not commit or engage to apply in all cases to the structured test. In this scenario, some legitimacy and rationality check or justification is mentioned, a necessity test with consideration of possible alternatives is often skipped and a very brief, superficial of loose balancing test concludes. Or – second scenario – they do commit to the full structured test, but in sensitive cases go through the steps superficially. So, the presence of a full test does not in itself guarantee more proper proportionality thinking. In terms of rule of law systems having judges with good judgment, the first scenario is most preferable.

[169] Tushnet (n 2) 275: 'A doctrine … is a way of dealing with problems across a range of problems – ideally, in the present context, across the range of all cases raising questions about a statute's constitutionality … The overall picture in each jurisdiction is, I believe, a messy blend of cases in which judges employ a loose form of structured proportionality analysis and an equally loose version of categorical reasoning in which seemingly relevant characteristics sometimes affect the court's approach and sometimes do not.' Paul Yowell equally refers to abundant evidence that courts do not follow a 'formulaic approach' to the proportionality test. See P Yowell, *Constitutional Rights and Constitutional Design. Moral and Empirical Reasoning in Judicial Review* (Hart, 2020) 33 with examples.

reasoning without many of the constraining features that otherwise characterise legal reasoning.[170]

Against the myth of judges bound by structured review, we need to insist on the separated realities of judges and academics, and a better understanding of the reality of judging.[171] Academics are too eager to lecture judges. Forcing courts to march through *all* the components of a test established by academics makes no sense. Judges should only spend time on the components that affect the outcome.[172] What 'really' matters in adjudication is delivering 'good judgments'.[173] All other things considered are of a secondary nature,[174] methodology included.[175] Even more trivial or absurd are academic accusations about judges that deny testing proportionality, but implicitly make use of it.[176]

[170] Yowell (n 170) 33–34 with reference to M Kumm, 'Political liberalism and the structure of rights: on the place and limits of the proportionality requirement' in G Pavlakos (ed), *Law, Rights and Discourse: The Legal Philosophy of Robert Alexy* (Hart, 2007) 130, 140.

[171] Some discretion for judges to test and review state actions is needed. This discretion will be there anyway. It will be self-authorised by the judges through a variety of means (from implicit, hidden, to explicit). It is useful to recall the many distinctions between the work of judges and academics (see section II.B, above). The ideal of one unique top-down imposed structured that does not follow from explicit primary or secondary law, might hurt judges' inclination not to depart from the legal materials and formulations of rights at hand too lightly. These texts and their differences will adopt their rights-limitation test accordingly. *cf* 'Judges apparently believe, often enough, that obvious variations in the nature of rights and the subjects of legislative regulation call for different analytic approaches. I have little doubt that these approaches can be shoehorned into a framework labeled 'proportionality', but my sense is that doing so obscures more than it illuminates – precisely because doing so substantially reduces the distinctive virtue of proportionality in promoting transparency' (Tushnet (n 2)).

[172] Tushnet (n 2) 274. Marching through the components makes no sense when a state measure makes obvious sense with one component of the structured proportionality test but appears to make little sense with respect to another. *cf* 'the Strasbourg institutions tend only to refer to the margin of appreciation when a decision is finely balanced. Where they have no doubt about accepting or rejecting the state's case, they tend to make no reference to it at all' (Greer (n 14) 14).

[173] *cf* 'we should seek judges with good judgment. And, I believe, when we put judgment at the center of our concern, the structure of doctrine retreats to a distant periphery. Judges with good judgment will reach the right result – will optimize appropriately – no matter whether the doctrine they apply is proportionality, case-specific balancing, categorical balancing, a complex set of categorical rules, or whatever other alternatives there might be. Judges with bad judgment will reach bad results along both dimensions of concern no matter what' (M Tushnet, 'Three Essays on Proportionality Doctrine' (2016) *Harvard Public Law Working Paper no 16-43* 52, available at ssrn.com/abstract=2818860 or http://dx.doi.org/10.2139/ssrn.2818860.

[174] 'I agree with one of the major premises of Christoffersen's thinking, that it is often hardly possible to demonstrate that a specific decision is uniquely correct. But it might be acceptable as the reasoned product of informed impartial choice. And so, the Court's task is, as the author puts it, 'doing fairness through a vision of reasonableness'. (See the foreword of Luzius Wildhaber, former president of the ECtHR, in J Christoffersen, *Fair Balance: Proportionality, Subsidiarity and Primarity in the European Convention on Human Rights* (Martinus Nijhoff, 2009) xiii.

[175] In his lecture on the relationship between judges and academics, Lord Burrows, insists on a passage in a book of Lord Goff stating that the desired result, not the methodology used, is what counts foremost for judges. It explains, Burrows continues, why in general, judges do not articulate and, it may be, do not seriously think about their own methodology (Burrows (n 29) 60).

[176] There is also nothing wrong with judges who formulate reasonings that can be partly connected with the structured test. There is nothing unique about the components of the structured proportionality test as a specific way of constitutionally reviewing rights limitations. The components are or should be simply elements of *any* reasoned evaluation of constitutionality. Principles such as

For Tushnet there is enough ground to doubt the existence of a true proportionality doctrine.[177] The distinctive virtue of proportionality doctrine, as highlighted in the previous section, is its structure, which promotes transparency about the considerations that the judges take into consideration when reviewing. That transparency is not delivered when the overall comparative picture is one of judges using loose forms or bits of the structured test.[178] A doctrine of proportionality applied by courts would only be the case if they follow the fully structured approach, which is rarely pretended as such by courts and even more rarely in practice.[179] Hints of proportionality analysis in cases not using its structured version may not in fact illustrate proportionality analysis at all.[180]

V. Normative Discussion: The Need for a Doctrine?

A. Undertheorising Categorical Logic (First Weaknesses of Proportionality Testing)

After having answered a descriptive question ('Is there a doctrine of proportionality in court?'), I now turn to a more normative question ('Should we have such a doctrine in court?'). To answer this question, myths surrounding proportionality testing must be punched through (see above) *and* weaknesses surrounded the test must be identified. Tushnet compared European proportionality testing and US-based categorical reasoning (characterised by a black-and-white, yes-or-no

choosing the right means to reach an end, the choosing the relatively best and the lesser evil, are long-established elements of any technical or academic formation. *cf* M Weber, *Wissenschaft als Beruf* (Reclam, 1995) 38. Using a component is not specific to proportionality testing but can point at any kind of reasoned analysis. *cf* Tushnet (n 2) 273: 'Noting the appearance of such components in a decision show that the court is engaged in reasoned analysis, not that it is engaged in a 'semblance' of proportionality'.

[177] Tushnet (n 2) 275.

[178] See the opening epigraph of this chapter.

[179] 'But, in my view, a doctrine of proportionality just is the fully structured approach its academic advocates describe. Without such a structure, we do not have a doctrine of proportionality – though we might well have completely acceptable reasoned explanations for results' (Tushnet (n 2) 274).

[180] In the context of ECtHR analysis Van Drooghenbroeck and Delgrange acknowledge albeit with a certain sadness that it is analytically more exact to distinguish between a full 'proportionality rule' and a 'proportionality test' – which does not necessarily check compliance all components depending on the extent of the margin of appreciation granted (Van Drooghenbroeck and Delgrange (n 130) 57). Tushnet's understanding usefully corrects Tor-Inge Harbo's more dogmatic understanding of what judges should do. Harbo argues that judges should do what they say they do, and that they should not do something else. For Harbo there seems to be only two options: either judges test proportionality (and then they *have to go through* the full structure) or they do not and then they undermine it by offering in reality a more arbitrary *Wednesbury* reasonableness test (Harbo (n 163) 158, 181). In the author's view, however, this all depends on the commitment of judges to a full structured test. In the name of a doctrine prohibiting judges to produce reasoned evaluations of constitutionality is hard to defend.

approach making balancing redundant)[181] and identified two pitfalls. A first pitfall is difficult to avoid, regardless of the method of review: it is making errors of judgement. This all-too-human, inevitable phenomenon can distort proportionality analyses but, sometimes, this is only understood later in time through experience. The second pitfall of proportionality analysis, at least in the dominant version proposed by Alexy, is its rejection of categorical thinking.[182] For Tushnet, an American academic, this is a difficult aspect of the European approach. We hear Dworkin's echo when Tushnet argues that adopting some categorical rules can be a means of achieving better results overall than proportionality would produce directly.[183] The outcome of Tushnet's analysis is a preference for categorical reasoning, with proportionality testing as a first approach for novel legal problems.[184]

There is a strong case for injecting categorical clarity in every legal system. If not, judges may walk on quicksand. Conceiving *all* rights as malleable principles always in need of balancing, as some proponents of proportionality testing do, is a dangerous option. Judges do deliver this categorical clarity in their judgment when

[181] Tushnet (n 2) 274–79. Tushnet's approach is partly normative developed to make the American review method more performative (in particular, the component of the availability of less restrictive alternatives should be part of any reasoned analysis of constitutionality, Tushnet writes), but at the same time avoiding turning fully structured proportionality testing into the new constitutional approach for the US legal system. Courts engaging in categorical reasoning identify only a handful of a statute's characteristics or the circumstances in which it is invoked. Categorical reasoning instructs the judge to disregard features of the statute or situation that non-lawyers would almost always think relevant to deciding whether application of the statute was well advised. See on the American model of review, A Miller, 'Proportionality Paradigm or Paradox? The Proportionality Principle in American and German Security Law Jurisprudence' in E Billis, N Knust and JP Rui (eds), *Proportionality in Crime Control and Criminal Justice* (Hart Publishing, 2021) 181–206.

[182] We recall that Alexy was able to position balancing as a dominant solution for conflicts between fundamental rights after having affirmed that all fundamental rights are mainly and foremost principles (understood as optimisation requirements) and not rules. See R Alexy, *A Theory of Constitutional Rights* (Oxford University Press 2002) 47–49. There is a clear link between Alexy's theory of rights as principles and his defence of a broad use of the proportionality principle: his rights are principles understood as optimisation requirements, which means that their application requires proportionality analysis (Harbo (n 163) 166). A good case for characterising at least some fundamental rights as rules, rather than as principles is given by C Pace, 'Robert Alexy's A Theory of Constitutional Rights critical review: key jurisprudential and political questions' (2012) 1 *Dinamia'Cet Working Paper*, 11, available at repositorio.iscte-iul.pt/bitstream/10071/3883/1/DINAMIA_WP_2012-01.pdf.

[183] Tushnet gives the example of a categorical rule that prohibits prior restraints on any demonstration as opposed to proportionally assessing by courts of possible risks of every single demonstration. 'All elements of that calculation are highly speculative in advance of the demonstration. In contrast, after the demonstration it is easier to determine how much social harm and social benefit actually occurred. The "no prior restraints" rule produces correct outcomes more often than would judicial consideration of the (obviously relevant) potential social harms and benefits' (277).

[184] Proportionality analysis would be the natural approach for novel problems dealt with by legislation, until judges have built up enough experience with evaluating this kind of legislation and can identify any systematic error of evaluation (if any). At this moment in time, categorical rules and exceptions to these rules can be developed that support the constitutional work of courts. See Tushnet (n 2) 277–78. A similar thesis was defended by Frederick Schauer in 2003, who provocatively held that as European constitutional law matures over time, it will develop the same rule-like structure that characterises the more mature American constitutional system. See F Schauer, 'The Convergence of Rules and Standards' (2003) *New Zealand Law Review* 303. See also Cohen-Eliya and Porat (n 134) 263–64.

needed.[185] Preferably, constitutions and rights declarations help the judges to find that clarity by distinguishing between fundamental and less fundamental interests. Differences in the formulation of limitation grounds can be one way to do that. Another option is explored in the CFR, which recognises constitutional *rights* with a more or less strong character, next to *principles* that are more malleable.[186] We saw however that the CJEU treats certain rights as principles and that proponents of the proportionality test ignore, to a certain degree, all strong formulations of rights to make balancing possible. Van der Sloot demonstrates how both the CJEU and the ECtHR avoid proper testing of rights limitations and prefer to present cases as if based on conflicting rights.[187] A principled deontological approach to rights is, step by step, being replaced with a utilitarian consequentialist approach that avoids thinking in fundamental and less fundamental terms: every principle is relative and can be measured, and when an act causes more good than harm, it is considered a good act.[188]

The remoteness with Dworkin's vision of rights shielding against utilitarian policies could not be more serious. In Europe this was quickly understood by Habermas. Taking away rights formulated as rules or watering down their deontological nature amounts to tearing down the firewall of the legal system based on fundamental rights.[189] Habermas's famous firewall objection to proportionality testing as a default constitutional setting is that the 'balancing approach deprives fundamental rights of their normative power': by means of balancing, rights are

[185] Granting less privacy protection to corporations than to individuals, for instance, is a categorical decision. In *Volker und Markus Schecke and Hartmut Eifert v Land Hessen* the CJEU, referring to the publication of personal data relating to beneficiaries of agricultural aid, held that 'legal persons can claim the protection of Articles 7 and 8 of the Charter in relation to such identification only in so far as the official title of the legal person identifies one or more natural persons. … [T]he right to respect for private life with regard to the processing of personal data, recognized by Articles 7 and 8 of the Charter, concerns any information relating to an identified or identifiable individual … However, when examining the proportionality of publishing information concerning legal persons who received aid, the CJEU reached a different conclusion, ruling that such publication did not go beyond the limits of the proportionality principle. It stated that 'the seriousness of the breach of the right to protection of personal data manifests itself in different ways for, on the one hand, legal persons and, on the other hand, natural persons' (CJEU, Joined cases C-92/09 and C-93/09, *Volker und Markus Schecke GbR and Hartmut Eifert v Land Hessen* [GC], 9 November 2010 [87]).

[186] The concept of absolute rights in Europe is one example of a tool allowing to inject categorical rules in the stage of the final balancing stage (Tushnet (n 2) 271). These rights can be recognised through textual analysis ('how are they formulated?'; 'are there exceptions to the right in the text?'). A bit more judicial interpretation is warranted when the categorical rule is based on the observation that a measure affects the essence of a right or a most intimate aspect of a right. *cf* ECtHR, *Dudgeon v United Kingdom* [52]: 'not only the nature of the aim of the restriction but also the nature of the activities involved will affect the scope of the margin of appreciation. The present case concerns a most intimate aspect of private life. Accordingly, there must exist particularly serious reasons before interferences on the part of the public authorities can be legitimate for the purposes of paragraph 2 of Article 8'.

[187] B van der Sloot, 'The Practical and Theoretical Problems with 'Balancing'' (2016) 23 *Maastricht Journal of European and Comparative Law* 439.

[188] ibid 457.

[189] Habermas maintains that 'a deontological understanding of legal norms and principles' is like 'a firewall erected in legal discourse'. See J Habermas, *Between Facts and Norms* (The MIT Press, 1996) 256–59. On the Habermas–Alexy debate, see also van der Sloot (n 190) 439–59.

downgraded to the level of goals, policies and values, losing their deontological character and their 'strict priority', their characterisation as 'normative points of view'.

B. Ignoring Hidden Categorical Logic (Second Weakness of Proportionality Testing)

Tushnet's problem with proportionality testing is not so much that it rejects categorical reasoning, but that it has no eye for the hidden categorical 'moments' in its inquiry: judges creating, de facto either openly or below the level of consciousness, categorical vetoes and preferences, perverting the proportionality testing they claim to apply.[190] The obvious example is national security measures.[191] This is indeed a more vicious phenomenon – at least for a doctrine that aspires to transparency.

As discussed above, proportionality testing does not only claim the virtue of transparency but also of its capacity to incorporate a great deal of context-sensitivity. This flexibility afforded by its endorsement of explicit consideration of all rationally relevant considerations allows judges using proportionality to address or adapt easily to the political environment in which they operate. Politics of the moment can affect, either openly or below the level of consciousness, the way in which relevant considerations are considered, Tushnet holds, adding with palpable pleasure that American-style categorical analysis can be more resistant to the politics of the moment.[192]

Hence, proportionality analysis can lead to under-protecting state interest and over-protecting individual rights by allowing judges to take into consideration a broad range of considerations, but the opposite is also true. By sneaking into the proportionality analysis categorical perceptions, not much is left of the original intent of the test.[193]

[190] Tushnet (n 2) 274–79. Tushnet insists on a shielded but de facto present coexistence of categorical analysis withing the context of proportionality testing. This secretive surfacing of simplicity happens particularly at the 'less restrictive alternatives' and/or the *stricto sensu* stage of the proportionality analysis. He points at the tendencies amongst judges to restrict the range of alternatives to be considered in the former stage as one that builds in categorical reasoning into the proportionality analysis.

[191] Tushnet (n 2) 277–78. Proportionality testing leading up to invalidation is hardly to be expected in this area. Courts, Tushnet observes, are components of the overall political system and only under some circumstances will they set themselves against claims by executive officials and legislatures that some acts threaten national security. Engaging in a proportionality analysis, 'judges might well treat protection of national security as a transcendent goal weighing extremely heavily in their thinking and worry that they are not in a position to contest the judgments made by specialists in national security in the executive or legislative branches'.

[192] Tushnet (n 2) 281.

[193] We recall the observations made by academics from Eric C Ip, a Hong Kong-based academic, that proportionality testing unlike ordinary substantive review standards such as *Wednesbury* unreasonableness (a famous English lenient test named after a 1948 case that spread through the common law system: a reasoning or decision is *Wednesbury* unreasonable (or irrational) if it is so unreasonable that no reasonable person acting reasonably could have made it), is transparent and in principle hostile to legal fictions that might justify disproportionate measures (Ip (n 137)).

Habermas and Tushnet's objections against proportionality review (treating rights as principles that can be balanced against others; ignoring hidden categorical moments that bring in the irrational) are not fictional. Even strong proponents of the proportionality test admitted its general failure during the COVID-19 pandemic.[194] Several taboos affected the proper application of the test by the courts worldwide.[195] The irrationality of these taboos (on the mortality question, on the age question, and on hospitals being overburdened) could have been challenged with solid Socratic questioning,[196] but judges proved not able to properly engage in correct balancing as required by the proportionality test. Instead, they gave openly or implicitly categorical preference to 'physical life' ('life') over 'living one's life' ('freedom').

Möller sees this as 'wrong' and contrary to what the proportionality test instructs us to do, namely, to balance the need to protect lives against the importance of maintaining as much freedom as possible, rather than giving unconditional priority to one of these values.[197]

Habermas's authoritative warning three decades ago, for the 'danger of irrational rulings' associated with proportionality testing, respectful of Dworkin's political conception of rights, was visionary for what happened with our legal system during the pandemic.[198] Proportionality testing lacks rational standards, Habermas argues. It therefore invites arbitrary balancing in which policies and politics trump rights. 'Weighing takes places either arbitrarily or unreflectively,

[194] Most lockdown measures taken by states, although *prima facie* disproportionate, were left untouched. Courts around the world watered down structured proportionality testing to leave these measures unaffected. Ip (n 137). See also S Thomson and EC Ip, 'COVID-19 Emergency Measures Are Hurting Democracy Globally' (2020) 110 *American Journal of Public Health* 1356. Examples from New Zealand, England and Australia show recourse to blunt, non-substantiated statements of the 'necessary, reasonable, and proportionate' nature or the 'unarguably proportionate' nature of COVID-19 emergency measures.

[195] Möller (n 128) 157–70.

[196] 'A taboo was quickly placed on one of the crucially important questions: the relevance of the age distribution of the people dying of Covid. Thus, it became publicly and politically impossible to openly and freely discuss whether the fact that the average age of people dying of Covid was in the low 80s was relevant in deciding what measures were justified. The reason given for this was that all lives were equally valuable and entitled to the same protection' (158); 'Nor was there much public discussion about the harms of lockdowns, for example in the media. Rather, the focus both on the part of the governments as well as the public was continually on the other side of the balance, namely on questions such as the Sars-Cov-2 incidence, hospitalizations, death rates, long Covid, etc. This created an imbalanced picture which will have led many to believe that the protection of people from the virus was the only relevant factor in assessing the justification and proportionality of lockdowns' (162); 'it is not clear why the protection of the health service should be given priority over all other considerations. The idea is certainly psychologically understandable … It is simply not clear why the avoidance of this particular evil (hospitals being overburdened) should be prioritized over all others, including, for example, the avoidance of the evil of inflicting considerable developmental damage or trauma on children that will presumably burden many of them for the rest of their lives' (166).

[197] Möller (n 128) 164.

[198] The danger of irrational ruling is one of Habermas's main objections to Alexy's theory of constitutional rights in addition to the firewall objection discussed above. See: Habermas (n 190) 256–59. See also Pace (n 183) 13.

according to customary standards and hierarchies' and this danger of irrational rulings only increases when the judicial is founded 'on a kind of moral realism or moral conventionalism'.[199]

C. Leaving Open Important 'Technical Questions' (Third Weakness of Proportionality Testing)

The foregoing analysis merely identifies the limits of what can be expected of the structured proportionality principle in courts. Its openness to a broad range of considerations allows judges to bring in openly or below the level of consciousness categorical preferences that are often state-friendly. In this light it is disturbing to note how many 'technicalities of the test' remain vague – 50 years after *Handyside* and *Dudgeon* – when compared with the US doctrine on testing and scrutiny.

Take the starting point of the test and the question of whether there are legitimate purposes served by a proposed rights limitation. *Is any state interest – including interest that are not unreasonable but no more – enough or do we need a compelling state interest to limit rights?*[200] Is the test really about the priority of rights or is it about balancing rights and state interest put on equal footing?

Who should prove what of the components of the test? The burden of proof when applying the test might be a trustworthy indicator for finding out what can be expected from it. Academic literature on the test is silent on the matter or suggests that the burden of proof lies on the shoulders of the state.[201] In European practice,

[199] Habermas (n 190) 259. See more in detail, Pace (n 183) 13. Habermas's critique is directed to Robert Alexy. This author, in his reply, argues that the balancing can be made more rational by assigning the values 'light', 'moderate' and 'serious' to evaluate the competing reasons and reaching rational judgments. Moreover, these values can be translated into numerical values, allowing users of his proportionality test to use mathematical formula ('weight formula') that are further enriched with three variables (the importance of the principles at stake, the abstract weight of those principles and the reliability of the empirical assumptions). See R Alexy, 'Discourse Theory and Fundamental Rights' in AJ Menendez and OE Eriksen (eds), *Arguing Fundamental Rights* (Springer, 2006) 15–29.

[200] As discussed above, the ECtHR selects the components of the proportionality tests case-by-case and amends its formulation of the components of the proportionality test when useful. The first proportionality component –whether the interference promote legitimate state interests – will usually be dealt with as 'promoting any legitimate state interest'. Only now and then is the semantic meaning of the term 'necessity' used in the Convention taken seriously and the component is reformulated as a requirement about the legitimacy of the state objective that must also meet a 'compelling social need'. Any state interest in most cases versus compelling state needs in some cases. It is perfectly possible that judges follow the structured proportionality test but formulate the components in such a state friendly way that the interference passes the test without difficulties.

[201] 'The doctrine of structured proportionality typically requires the state, when imposing measures restrictive of rights and freedoms, to pursue legitimate objectives; to prove that impugned measures are rationally related to those objectives; and to guarantee that the impugned measures are no more than necessary to achieve legitimate objectives' (Ip (n 137)). Various phrases have been used by the ECtHR over time to express the idea that the rights in the Convention should take priority, with the state carrying the burden of justifying the interference. For example, the grounds must be 'relevant and sufficient', the necessity for a restriction must be 'convincingly established', and the exceptions to Arts 8–11 should be narrowly construed.

however, it is not always clear which party has the burden of proving that the interference has been proportionate.[202] The result is confusion, and not on a minor detail. Vagueness on the burden of proof creates an ethos of sloppy European review – unable to choose between the 'priority to rights' or the balancing of equal interests.[203]

Another area of further clarification of the doctrine is about scrutiny. The US system is transparent about its categorical rule-reasoning *and* about the scrutiny levels.[204] From 1938 onwards, with *United States v Carolene Products Co*, the Supreme Court started developing a layered doctrine of testing rights limitations, with three levels of scrutiny (strict scrutiny; intermediate scrutiny; and rational basis review). These levels, developed over the years, not only determine the intensity of the scrutiny (compelling or important or normal legitimate objective; narrowly related to the objective or substantially related or rationally related) but also the burden of proof (the state in the first two cases of scrutiny; the challenger in the last).[205]

The levels of scrutiny in European proportionality literature are undertheorised or presented as 'closely connected' to proportionality.[206] Some overlap

[202] Greer (n 28) 15; Greer (n 14) 20.

[203] Greer (n 28) 15; Greer (n 14) 20.

[204] The outcome of the categorical analysis is either that a measure is constitutionally permissible or unconstitutional, or that a certain standard of review needs to be applied: mere reasonableness, intermediate scrutiny, and strict scrutiny. Strict scrutiny is very much like structured proportionality, as it requires legislation that restricts fundamental constitutional rights to promote compelling governmental interests; be substantially and directly related to promoting those interests; and be the least restrictive means that effectively promote them (Ip (n 137)).

[205] Yowell (n 170) 2024; B Snider, 'What Are The Levels of Scrutiny?' (FindLaw, 12 May 2020), available at www.findlaw.com/legalblogs/law-and-life/challenging-laws-3-levels-of-scrutiny-explained. The difference with the fuzzy margin of appreciation test of the ECtHR is striking. Not much seems to have changed since Van Dijk and Van Hoof in the 1990s concluded that the development of a 'model margin of appreciation test' in *Handyside*, and subsequent judgments have 'not provided clarity', and that it is 'still quite hazardous to try and foretell' whether in any given case the discretion national authorities are permitted will be wide or narrow (P Van Dijk and G Van Hoof, *Theory and practice of the European Convention on Human Rights* (Kluwer, 1990) 589). See also the summary of their analysis made by Greer (n 28) 16–17: 'Van Dijk and Van Hoof distinguish four different approaches to the doctrine in the Strasbourg case-law: cases in which (a) no margin of appreciation has been allowed at all and a fully-fledged review of state discretion has been conducted; (b) a narrow margin of appreciation has been permitted; (c) a reasonableness test has been applied and; (d) a "not unreasonable" test has been employed. As the authors argue, the difference between (a) and (b) is not always easy to determine because the Strasbourg organs sometimes refer to the state's margin of appreciation yet carry out a full review themselves, while the key difference between (c) and (d) lies in the burden of proof. Under the former, the "reasonableness test", the state must prove that its decisions were reasonable, whereas under the latter, the "not unreasonable test", the applicant has to prove that they were unreasonable, the benefit of any doubt being given to the state. The authors also claim that, although not all decisions neatly fit their hypothesis.'

[206] See Bjorge and Zglinski (n 99) 199. Bjorge and Zglinski – authors of an excellent study on proportionality in EU law – do pay attention to the issue of review, which they introduce as 'closely connected' to the theme of proportionality but conflate both concepts to a large degree. They equate 'lenient proportionality testing with light scrutiny review' and 'intensive proportionality scrutiny' with 'strict scrutiny'. Their rule of thumb is that the CJEU, which chooses its levels of scrutiny review, is lightly reviewing EU acts, but strictly reviewing Member States acts, although the CJEU in recent years seems

between proportionality questions and review standards cannot be denied,[207] but the two are analytically distinct. It is therefore perfectly possible for a judge to allow discretion but to apply the full test, or, to allow no discretion but to test via lenient proportionality. Asking judges to identify their level of scrutiny is asking them to go beyond 'neutral interpretation' and position themselves with agency-setting agenda; distinguishing between aspects of rights that are more important than other aspects of the same right. One would have expected this much from the ECtHR,[208] but its margin of appreciation test doctrine has never approached the level of clarity given by the Supreme Court.

The combination by the ECtHR of a vague margin test with an equally vague proportionality test is toxic for every ideal of certainty and predictability. Robert Spano, former president of the ECtHR, can be credited for having proposed some kind of integration of both test under the general label 'proportionality model', but the model has hardly any predictable qualities.[209]

A positive aspect of Spano's model is that it starts from what is written in the ECHR to distinguish between a *standard* test for the relative rights, and a *most strict* test for limitations of absolute rights.[210] Spano then departs from textual

to enrich its approach and is more willing to grant Member States more discretion in certain areas approaching the margin of appreciation–concept central to the case law of the ECtHR.

[207] This is the case when judges go beyond interpretation and draw normative lines about the importance of subsets of rights. *cf* 'the Federal Constitutional Court developed its tiered theory of freedom of occupation within its balancing considerations, a theory that relies on the distinction between the choice of occupation and the exercise of that occupation, alluded to in the text of the norm, which also distinguishes between the choice and the exercise of an occupation. It thus tries to effectuate the bindingness of Art 12 Basic Law with respect to the legislature via hermeneutically guided balancing considerations within its appropriateness test. In functional terms, the tier-based approach derived from the *Pharmacy Decision* is like various tests developed in the US for regulating limitations on freedom of expression. Thus, early proportionality jurisprudence foreshadowed a re-entry of hermeneutics into the rationality control established with the proportionality test' (Poscher (n 132) 65).

[208] This Court is overburdened by complaints and to survive must select. The Court also must deal with a political sensitive clientele (more than 40 states with different political regimes).

[209] Spano's proportionality model proposes three levels of scrutiny (presented as three proportionality tests) with a standard test for the relative rights, a stricter test for mass surveillance because of its risks for the rule of law, and the strictest test for limitations of absolute rights. More concretely, Spano distinguishes between 'the general proportionality criterion' (applied under the second paragraphs of Arts 8–11 ECHR), the 'absolute proportionality criterion' (to judge limitations of the right to life under Art 2 ECHR) and 'strict or intermediate proportionality criterion' to judge cases about mass surveillance (Spano (n 91) vi).

[210] Behind the framework we hear an echo of the important textual analysis done in *Handyside* taking precise textual formulations of ECHR-rights as a point of departure, in particular their use of adjectives and terms like 'necessary' (Art 8–11), 'indispensable' (Arts 2 and 6), 'absolutely necessary', 'strictly necessary' and 'to the extent strictly required by the exigencies of the situation' (Art 15), 'admissible', 'ordinary', 'useful' (Art 4 and Art 1 of Protocol no 1), 'reasonable' (Art 5) or 'desirable'. The ECtHR has however quickly abandoned this textual method to understanding rights limitations and levels of scrutiny in two ways. Firstly, it added to the textual analysis that it is up to the states to make the initial assessment of the reality of the pressing social need implied by the notion of 'necessity', thus undermining the strong sense of urgency implied by the term. Secondly, it dropped textual methods all together to embrace the catch-all concept of proportionality absent in the text of the ECHR (see above) as a 'one size fits all' solution. *cf* ECtHR, *Handyside* judgment of 7 December 1976 [48]: 'The Court notes at this juncture that, whilst the adjective "necessary", within the meaning of Article 10 par. 2, is

analysis underlying his model to add an '*intermediary*' or '*strict*' test for mass surveillance because of its risks for the rule of law.[211]

There is, however, a problem with Spano's proportionality model, one that could have been avoided by presenting one proportionality test and three levels of scrutiny (weak, intermediate, and strong). There is simply no reason to test proportionality differently according to the level of scrutiny recognised. Spano's formulation suggests that not all components of proportionality are looked at with the weaker testing, whereas it is perfectly conceivable to apply a full structured test without intensive scrutiny.[212]

Almost 50 years after *Handyside*, there are still too many disturbing shortcomings surrounding proportionality testing, be it in the hands of academics or of judges. The net result is a heavy rhetoric about a quasi-ideal standard that allows judges to uphold rights against state pressure when needed. However, in practice, demands of the state and the general interest, rather than rights, seem to form the starting point of the test.

VI. Proportionality in a Society Confused about its Priorities

A. Why Judges Like Academic Doctrines: Securing Legitimacy

We miss in European literature a more thoughtful approach of the work of the judiciary. In the past, academics were either worshipped (Germany) or not (rest of the world). The relationship between legal academic and judges is evolving worldwide. Both perspectives are important and the growing exposure of the non-German judiciary to the legal scholarship of 'their' academics has many benefits, granted that judges are not coerced into a bigger theoretical framework proposed by academics.[213]

not synonymous with "indispensable" (cf., in Articles 2 par. 2 and 6 par. 1, the words "absolutely necessary" and "strictly necessary" and, in Article 15 par. 1, the phrase "to the extent strictly required by the exigencies of the situation"), neither has it the flexibility of such expressions as "admissible", "ordinary" (cf. Article 4 par. 3), "useful" (cf. the French text of the first paragraph of Article 1 of Protocol No. 1), "reasonable" (cf. Articles 5 par. 3 and 6 par. 1) or "desirable". Nevertheless, it is for the national authorities to make the initial assessment of the reality of the pressing social need implied by the notion of "necessity" in this context.'

[211] The qualifier 'strict' is apparently taken from Art 15(1) ECHR, but in fact borrowed from the CJEU's *Digital Rights Ireland* judgment on mass surveillance. The ECtHR follows this example. In these cases, the standard ('general') proportionality test of the Arts 8–11 ECHR is replaced by 'strict or intermediate proportionality' test. See on this, S Parsa and JM Van Gyseghem, 'Surveillance de masse, liberté publique et état d'exception' in Parsa and Tulkens (n 42) 128–29.

[212] This remark betrays an academic concern, where my central thesis in this chapter is to point to the lack of commitment of judges (like Spano) to full structured tests proposed by academics.

[213] On the difference between 'practical legal scholarship' and the pursuit of theory and deeper theories of law, Burrows (n 29) 55 ff.

Academic proportionality advocates that pretend that strict proportionality testing (comparable with strict scrutiny review in the US) is the normal practice in court create a false image of European judicial review. Even the presence of the full structured proportionality test does not guarantee strict review. It is perfectly possible that judges follow the structured proportionality test but formulate the proportionality components in such a state-friendly way that the interference passes the test without difficulties.[214] The proportionality test is then de facto replaced by a lesser assessment scheme of scrutiny with the bottom end of the manifest inappropriate test.[215]

This practice of weak proportionality testing brings us back to Dworkin's 'trump' conception of rights versus a European paternalist tradition with its relativist conception of rights that had to be reconciled with 'the free and rational direction of public affairs' (Hegel) in a bureaucratic, expert-driven world (Meierhenrich and MacIntyre). We observed that the proportionality principle not only benefits the citizen, but also facilitates interaction between the legal sphere with other spheres in a controlled manner, enabling state actors (checked by the judiciary) to obtain and maintain social legitimacy. The role of the state is ubiquitous in the mindset of European judges hesitating between prioritising rights or balancing them with state interests that are considered fundamental.[216]

The introduction of the proportionality test indeed ended the era of absolute legalism but, at the same time, due to its malleability, it continued Europe's rich tradition of expert-driven paternalism. The result is a practice where reasonability tests are carried out most frequently, and more intensive testing is kept at limits. However, hints of structured proportionality testing are not avoided to position the expertise of the judges next to the expertise of the executive officials and experts appointed by legislatures to explain in court the rationale of state actions defended in the name of the public (legitimate, substantial or compelling) interest.

The role of presumed expertise in our bureaucratic society – one of the themes highlighted by MacIntyre – is key in understanding the attraction of the proportionality test for the judiciary.[217] The presentational aspect of the principle in the

[214] A simple proportionality question like 'does the measure pursue a legitimate interest?' is less simple in light of the possible formulations of that question: compelling legitimate interest? important legitimate interest? normal legitimate interest? (see previous section). Depending on the answer, proportionality testing will be lenient testing or strict testing.

[215] Harbo (n 163) 161, 181. Remember that the *Wednesbury reasonableness* test only allows for government decisions to be attacked if they are so unreasonable or irrational that no reasonable public body would make the decision.

[216] The last attitude seems to prevail in practice supported by judicial restraint to step on the seat of the legislator.

[217] B Joxerramon, 'Conform Interpretation as a Method for Balancing Autonomy and Heteronomy: Introduction' (2012) 1 *Oñati Socio-Legal Series* 5, available at ssrn.com/abstract=1991701. In modernity, justice becomes progressively removed from the local context where conflicts emerge and acquire meaning, to become a more distant and formal power, at best an administrative service in more democratic understandings. The judiciary becomes a professional group that will insist on impartiality and professionalism. Rituals are preserved or transformed to confirm the impression of distance and specialised knowledge (and power). Max Weber was full of praise for the (early) proportionality test

hands of the judiciary ('we are experts too, with our sophisticated tools'), is historically in line with mainstream formal German legal science of the late nineteenth century, led by Friedrich Carl von Savigny, defending an understanding of law with logical rule creating process based on the model of natural sciences.[218]

In the search for securing even more objective legitimacy, our judges are served by Alexy's dominant presentation of proportionality testing as a rational and objective form of legal reasoning, complete with weight formula and other quasi-arithmetic formulae to capture variables and context elements.[219] Others insist on the neutrality of the test. Jean-Marc Sauvé, vice-president of the French *Conseil d'État* therefore defends an understanding of the proportionality principle as a balancing act between equal interest, without any undertone of priority of rights. Proportionality is a double-headed Janus, defending both individual freedoms and the efficiency of the state. The proportionality is about the equilibrium between both, not about the priority of rights.[220] The principle is the necessary tool to complement the public interest, but should never disregard these interests.[221]

developed by the Prussian courts at the end of the nineteenth century with their insistence on the reasonable relationship between means and ends (the first subtest of proportionality). For Weber this formalistic analysis (which avoids more substantive scrutiny) was a win both for the state as a crucial means for ensuring a more effective governmental system and for maximising individual freedom, since it set clear limits on state actions. See M Weber, 'Diskussionerede zu dem Vortag von H. Kantorowicz Rechtwissenschaft und Soziologie' (1924) *Gesammelte Aufsätze zur Soziologie und Sozialpolitik* 477. See also Cohen-Eliya and Porat (n 134) 274.

[218] Cohen-Eliya and Porat (n 134) 275, 279, German scholars who influenced American balancing – von Jhering and the other *Freirecht* scholars – were in no way associated with the principle of proportionality in Germany and the *Rechtswissenschaft* defended by von Savigny.

[219] See R Alexy, 'On balancing and subsumption. A structural Comparison' (2003) 16 *Ratio Juris* 433. See for a complete analysis of proportionality testing of principles to secure formal and substantive legitimacy and its benefits (rationalisation of decisions, predictability of decisions), Harbo (n 163) 160–64. For a critique of Alexy's Weight Formula, see T Urbina, *A Critique of Proportionality and Balancing* (Cambridge University Press, 2017) ch 3.

[220] 'La proportionnalité est, par conséquent, un « mécanisme de pondération entre des principes juridiques de rang équivalent, simultanément applicables mais antinomiques », qui s'affirme naturellement à la fois comme le garant des libertés individuelles et celui d'autres buts légitimes, comme la sauvegarde de l'intérêt général et, notamment, la protection de l'ordre public ou l'efficacité de l'action publique. L'équilibre entre ces deux branches est affaire de proportion ou de juste milieu, pour paraphraser Aristotle' (Sauvé (n 121) 1).

[221] 'Le principe de proportionnalité est « le complément nécessaire de l'intérêt public ». Mais s'il « manifeste qu'un intérêt public en soi suffisant ne peut … se réaliser à n'importe quel prix … », il ne saurait se traduire par une remise en cause du principe même de la séparation des pouvoirs et du pouvoir d'appréciation des Gouvernements et des Parlements. Le principe de proportionnalité est indispensable à la garantie de l'État de droit, mais il ne saurait conduire à méconnaître les intérêts généraux dont l'État et les collectivités publiques ont la charge et qui sont, avec les libertés et les droits fondamentaux, les piliers du vivre-ensemble. Il est important de souligner que les cours européennes ont procédé, ces toutes dernières années, à une mise en balance plus attentive et prudente de l'ensemble de ces exigences. C'est une évolution qui mérite d'être à la fois saluée et confirmée' (Sauvé (n 121) 4).

B. Explicit Constitutional Generosity towards the Modern Regulatory State?

The foregoing is well understood by Tushnet, who grasps, like no other, the purpose and nature of all sorts of transactions between courts and other components of the political system.[222] Tushnet openly defends a system where the judiciary in today's regulatory state uses reasonability tests, unless the case for strict or intermediary scrutiny is made explicitly by the constitutional courts. Tushnet proposes a more selective and moderate limitation test, making possible 'only a modest degree of judicial intervention to prune the excesses of the modern regulatory state'.[223] Needed is 'a generous approach' when dealing with proportionality questions about legitimate purpose and less intrusive alternatives. The complexities of the modern regulatory state must make choices about welfare programmes, licensing of professions and minimum wages demands for it.[224] In particular, the 'less restrictive means' part of the test is in need for moderation or generosity towards the state.

Modest, rather than intensive judicial review, is the best answer to the democratic objection against judges invalidating laws,[225] and to the objection about regulatory complexity. How to test proportionality when most state interventions and laws have not one, but several objectives,[226] and are the result of vulnerable compromises in a landscape of pluralist politics?[227] The question about the function of the proportionality test in today's regulatory state is all the more compelling since judges make (predictable) systematic errors of judgement about rationally

[222] See section IV.E above, discussing Tushnet (n 2) 277–78.

[223] Tushnet (n 174) 15.

[224] 'Generosity with respect to an imputed public purpose of increasing social welfare means accepting the empirical claims of the regulations' proponents. To do otherwise would authorize judges to move rather intrusively into the larger structure of the modern regulatory state' (Tushnet (n 174) 11).

[225] 'Could the imputed public purposes be accomplished at least as well by some regulatory system that had a smaller adverse effect on the specific liberty in question? Here too a somewhat generous approach to answering the question seems appropriate, because it is almost always possible to devise *some* less restrictive alternative to almost any regulatory program. A less-than-generous approach would be inconsistent with the aim of the present inquiry, which is to devise a doctrine that will help prune the excesses of the modern regulatory state (while acknowledging that there will be reasonable disagreement about precisely what policies are excesses) without driving deep into the regulatory state' (Tushnet (n 174) 11).

[226] 'It seems to me, then, that the practice of proportionality analysis indicates that it lacks the resources for preventing skilled advocates from turning seemingly easy cases into hard one. Proportionality analysis might work reasonably well were it possible to identify a singular purpose for every challenged statute. But I have suggested, once we proliferate purposes – which, given my assumption that there is a wide range of permissible legislative purposes, seems to me possible in a high proportion of cases – the simplicity and transparency of proportionality analysis fades' (Tushnet (n 174) 40–41).

[227] 'Courts should do their best to avoid invalidation at that stage, because their normative judgments will have some effects on disruptive the ordinary operation of pluralist politics' (Tushnet (n 174) 14).

relevant considerations,[228] and lack full understanding of all the factors that drive the regulator to choose one solution over another.[229]

I do not necessarily agree with Tushnet's proposal for making judicial review more selective for the sake of state generosity,[230] but I welcome his openness on this point. What is interesting is his assumption that the modern regulatory state demands amendment of our rights-based legal system with priority for the individual.[231] Has complexity risen to such a Weberian degree that our rights-based social contract needs an update?

Tushnet's proposal is based on an analysis that captures well the reality of reluctance from the side of the courts to engage in strict scrutiny and/or structured proportionality testing by default. His concept of constitutional generosity

[228] Tushnet (n 2) 279.

[229] In his essay, Tushnet criticises judgments of the German Court that assumed too quickly that there was a better alternative for the measures proposed by the German state to regulate its economic markets or health-related matters. In its judgment *53 BVerfGE 135 (1980)* the German Court indeed overturned a ban on selling sweets because there was an alternative viz disclosure and warning via labels. Tushnet then demonstrates with behavioural economics that the judiciary alternative is not a valid alternative, highlighting the inadequate position of judges to make these kinds of assessments: 'A legislature might reasonably believe that these candies are mostly impulse purchases, made without much deliberation, often under time-pressure (while on the check-out line, for example), so that purchasers are (often enough) distracted at the moment of purchase. Under such conditions, disclosures will simply not be noticed (often enough), particularly in light of all the other things going on at the same time … Under these (realistically imaginable) circumstances, a flat prohibition is (at the very least) better than the disclosure alternative that the German Constitutional Court believed was less intrusive on other interests but equally effective with respect to the consumer interest' (Tushnet (n 174) 37).

[230] The point is not that Tushnet is right in his plea for constitutional generosity in review. That would require further analysis, for example, of Dworkin's refutation of the democracy argument against review (Dworkin (n 68)), and of Dworkin's distinction between principles and policies, and his view that judges should only adjudicate on basis of legal principles, not based on policy options, thus respecting the democratic nature of political decisions (Dworkin, *Taking Rights Seriously* (n 6) ch IV). Note that Tushnet is not unprepared for a discussion at this level of legal theory; 'The general question this analysis raises is whether (or, in my view more properly, to what extent) can proportionality analysis take into account – in a rationally defensible and transparent way – the costs associated with administering the alternatives proposed as equally effective (along one dimension, but not along the dimension of cost) to the challenged regulation. It seems to me that a rational doctrinal system would have to give them *some* weight' (44). See similarly A Altman, 'Legal realism, critical legal studies, and Dworkin' (1986) 15 *Philosophy and Public Affairs* 205. Note also that Tushnet cannot be accused of loyalty towards authoritarian regimes or rejecting strict scrutiny in all cases (see for instance his insistence on the importance of the less alternative means inquiry for *all* constitutional regimes). Concerns for democracy in complex regulatory landscapes and modesty about the added value of judicial review drives him to a clear delineation of more intense or deep forms of scrutiny in the name of generosity. Advocating a fully structured proportionality does not seem to further this constitutional generosity and seemingly impedes on the discretion of states when making policy (Tushnet (n 174) 12).

[231] Tushnet departs from the reality of judiciary review, which is one where judges must deal with a range of cases and fall back on 'a messy blend of cases in which judges employ a loose form of structured proportionality testing or equally loose other tests'. Although there is room for improvement, room should be left for state discretion, and strict review (whether categorical or based on proportionality) should be reserved for limited cases. The primacy of politics demands for 'authorizing a modest degree of judicial intervention only to prune the excesses of the modern regulatory state' (Tushnet (n 174) 15).

is also present in Judge Spano's presentation about the role of the ECtHR.[232] Awareness of the difficulties of modern governance nicely explains a string of cases where the ECtHR rejects the idea that failure to pass the necessity test automatically leads *ipso jure* to a violation of the proportionality test.[233] Judge Paul Lemmens in *Gülbahar Özer and Ysuf Özer v Turkey* (2018) advances textual and more principal arguments against giving too much weight to the less intrusive alternatives test. Failure by the regulator to adopt a less restrictive measure is *only* an element, among others, that *may* lead to the conclusion that the measure adopted was not necessary.[234] A similar resistance against 'a formulaic' application of the test is present in the Canadian Supreme Court's finding that it would be 'dangerously misleading' to consider the proportionality test to be 'rigid and technical'.[235]

A degree of clarity and of vision comparable to that of Tushnet is present in the work of Rivers and Tor-Inge Harbo. The former, writing in the British tradition of parliamentary sovereignty (or legislative supremacy), finds courts unsuitable for resolving 'polycentric' questions affecting many disparate interests, and highlights the special expertise of executive bodies concerning complex matters of fact and prognosis. 'The doctrine of proportionality needs structuring in such a way that, although applied by the judiciary, it is sensitive to the proper contribution of the other branches of government'.[236] A programme of constitutional generosity for Europe could not be better summarised.

Harbo is a Norwegian author with a strong penchant for German legal philosophy. In his writings, there is no trace of attachment to the idea that the law of human and constitutional rights should have a greater moral worth than other laws and interests. Confronted with Habermas's twofold criticism of Alexy,[237] he simply observes that Habermas's strong conception of rights (as trumps) is not the only one and should *not* guide Europeans.[238] Interestingly, his argument is

[232] Section IV.A mentioned the formulation of the ECtHR-specific proportionality principle by Robert Spano. His seemingly arbitrary reformulation of the principle (reasonable relationship; fair balance; essence of rights and margin of appreciation) is explicit on the importance of this last component.

[233] ECtHR, *James and others v United Kingdom*, judgment of 21 February 1986 [86]; *Animal Defenders International v United Kingdom*, judgment of 22 April 2013 [110]; ECtHR *Garib v the Netherlands*, judgment of 6 November 2017 [157]; ECtHR, *National Union of Rail, Maritime and Transport Workers v United Kingdom*, judgment of 8 April 2014 [103].

[234] Paul Lemmens, Concurring opinion appended to the ECtHR, *Gülbahar Özer and Ysuf Özer v Turkey* judgment of 29 May 2018. See also the concurring opinion of the same judge appended to ECtHR, *Saint-Paul Luxembourg SA v Luxembourg*, judgment of 18 April 2013. See Van Drooghenbroeck and Delgrange (n 130) 58.

[235] *R. v Keegstra*, 1990, 3 *SCR* 697, 735–36; Yowell (n 170) 33.

[236] J Rivers, 'Proportionality and Variable Intensity of Review' (2006) 65 *Cambridge Law Journal* 174, 175–76.

[237] See section V.A above. Habermas advanced an argument about proportionality testing downgrading rights by placing all sorts of interests on an equal footing, and about the danger of irrational, moral conventionalist-based balancing when testing proportionality.

[238] Not all Harbo's arguments convince, and some sound rather circular. He states, for example, that Alexy's theory about rights as (only) principles or optimisation requirements without any priority

that proportionality testing and a relativist concept of rights better fits Europe with its consensual decision-making mode aimed at realising a common good reaching beyond that of a calculus of consent, as opposed to the democratic decision-making process in the US characterised by the strong influence of lobby groups.[239]

Harbo's observation projects an idealistic image of European decision-making. Hence, the legislator can be given the benefit of the doubt. Judges are expected to limit themselves to the role of peacemaking or truce-keeping in a world without shared moral first principles,[240] which is open for the accommodation of the various political programmes of the legislator,[241] by balancing collective interest, collective rights, and individual rights without priority.

Harbo's article is not often dealt with in a substantive way that honours its theoretical depth.[242] Our objection to Harbo's work is the normative tone-setting, borrowed from Alexy (a philosopher, not a lawyer).[243] In constitutional-setting 'ought' discussions have an important role, but cutting constitutional analysis completely loose from the formulations used in constitutions and human rights declarations sounds like replacing legal analysis by political thinking.[244]

Proponents of proportionality have long neglected constitutional role-playing between the branches (institutional competences) and a general account of the separation of powers. Julian Rivers equally insists on complementing the proportionality test with clarity about review. He phrases the problem in terms of judicial

simply better fits the proportionality test. If you want the test, then drop Dworkin and adapt the relativist understanding of rights as proposed by Alexy, Harbo suggests. *cf* 'There is a clear link between Alexy's theory of rights as principles and the proportionality principle: since rights are principles and principles are optimization requirements this means that their application requires proportionality analysis' (Harbo (n 163) 167).

[239] Harbo (n 163) 170.

[240] MacIntyre (n 5) 253.

[241] Harbo (n 163) 168.

[242] It is possible to sympathise to a certain degree with Harbo's dissatisfaction with courts claiming to test proportionality, but *not doing it*, and only applying a limited test like the manifest inappropriate test. I follow Harbo in his plea for more clarity. Like the US Supreme Court, courts could identify the levels of scrutiny applied in certain areas, with a possibility for modulation. These levels should not only inform us about the intensity of the scrutiny (compelling or important or normal legitimate objective; narrowly related to the objective or substantially related or rationally related), but also the burden of proof (the state in the first two cases of scrutiny, the challenger in the last case).

[243] Harbo writes without caveats when he refers to Alexy's categorisation of rights as principles rather than rules 'regardless of their more or less precise formulation' (Harbo (n 163) 168 referring to Alexy (n 183) 388).

[244] Again, the key concern here is not to disregard the choices make by the constitutional drafters. The EU Charter, for example, distinguishes explicitly between rights and principles, and includes both. The ECHR formulates certain rights in an absolutist way, others in a more relativist way, each time carefully formulating the limitation ground. Brushing aside these choices completely based on philosophical theories about adjudication will find very few followers in court. On textualism and its importance for legal certainty, see K Lenaerts and JA Gutiérrez-Fons, 'To Say What the Law of the EU Is: Methods of Interpretation and the European Court of Justice' (2013) 9 *EUI Working Papers* 48.

deference and judicial restraint and proposes a system of variable intensity of review within proportionality.[245]

Judges should lay their self-defined scrutiny cards on the table. Clarifying scrutiny does not imply a duty for judges to always follow the structured proportionality test, as Harbo and Rivers seem to hold. In the case of absolute formulated rights, a proportionality test is simply not wanted and the classical test of applying the grounds of limitations (if any), or exceptions (if any) imposes itself. In other cases, the reasoned result is what counts. In all other cases some testing of proportionality can be used. It is feasible to test all components of the structured test in cases where low or light scrutiny is chosen, but there is nothing that stands in the way of judgement that only focuses on textual arguments (textualism) or other methods of interpretation and adjudication,[246] *and* if needed, on relevant components of the proportionality test in each case.[247]

This clarity about scrutiny intensity will inform us about the constitutional generosity that judges are willing to take as a starting point and will remedy confusing aspects of adjudication methods like proportionality.[248] People might disagree with Tushnet's generosity plea that is supposed to be needed because of the nature of today's regulatory state. In Europe, too much generosity might be the excuse to reconnect with a tradition of expert-driven, bureaucratic managerialism.

Tushnet's proposal raises at least the question of the relationship between the judiciary and the other branches when testing rights limitations proposed by the other branches. Proponents of proportionality testing have neglected this issue and many other important technical questions (What kind of interest? Who carries the burden of proof?). Bringing in the issue of levels of scrutiny will not only address some of the important open-standing 'technical questions' about the test, but also the issue of role-playing and respective institutional competences, so central to the preoccupations and concerns of the judiciary.

[245] 'It is argued that the correct intensity of review should be set by the seriousness of the rights-infringement in the case at hand. We should therefore conceive of two parallel principles in operation: a substantive principle of proportionality which requires the seriousness of any rights-infringement to be matched by the importance of a competing right or public interest, and a formal principle of intensity of review, which requires the seriousness of prima facie rights-infringement to be matched by decreasing judicial deference and restraint' (Rivers (n 237) 177).

[246] On alternative adjudicative methods, see Yowell (n 170) 35–39. On available methods of interpretation, see Lenaerts and Gutiérrez-Fons (n 245) 48.

[247] See section IV.E above. One caveat: the choice of the scrutiny level is partly informed by the formulation of a right. It seems to be logical to assume that the more absolute the formulation of a right, the more intense the level of scrutiny, but textualism is only one relevant element. Intensity of scrutiny in the practice of courts, is not fully determined by the abstract category of a right, but the specific individual interest claimed to be protected by the right. In US constitutionalism freedom of expression is a 'fundamental' right, but limitations of political speech are subjected by courts to high-intensity review, whereas commercial speech receives medium scrutiny and indecent speech only lower-level scrutiny. See Yowell (n 170) 28; Rivers (n 237) 174–207.

[248] 'The basic solution is to join the doctrine of proportionality to an equally general doctrine of variable intensity of review. The former structures the substantive inquiry into the justifiability of a limitation of the enjoyment of a right; the latter structures the formal allocation of responsibilities to the various powers of government for carrying out the substantive inquiry' (Rivers (n 237) 207).

VII. Conclusions

A. The Post-World War II Human Rights Narrative in Context

This chapter discussed the dominant narrative about rights development in Europe especially after World War II. By then Europe was ready to go beyond legalism. Substantive constitutional and human rights norms were introduced to evaluate and review laws and other state actions. Specific courts, also at the European level, were established to carry out this review. Germany was hailed as the constitutional forerunner in Europe, with very highly regarded courts and benchmarks like human dignity that have found their way in other national and European texts of constitutional order. Equally successful, at least at the symbolic level, was the introduction in the German *Grundgesetz* of the prohibition to affect the essence of a right, a message copied by other states and introduced in the EU Charter and now and then recalled by the ECtHR, although the 1950 Convention does not refer to it.

This narrative needs more context. Concerns for constitutions and human rights have undoubtedly driven European states towards a model of rule of law as constitutionalism, but these concerns were far from being the only trigger. The spread of constitutional review in Europe was, and is, also due to institutional–functional motives, like the growing turn to federalist forms of organisation in states. This historical clarification is only one element in a more mature assessment of dominant narrative. Another element is more empirical. How well are individual rights safeguarded by judicial review and the installment of constitutional courts in an increasing number of states? Although this contribution is approaching its final paragraphs, I find it tempting to recall some elements about this part of the discussion.

Constitutional and individual justice do not necessarily overlap. In the agenda of constitutional courts – set up to safeguard broad constitutional agendas – there is no time to review all citizens' complaints about rights violations. Hence, the existence of multiple methods of selecting cases applied by these courts.[249] This equally holds for the ECtHR, which rejects as inadmissible about 95 per cent of the applications it receives, an admissibility rate not dissimilar to that of national constitutional courts.[250] Not individual, but constitutional justice has de facto priority.[251]

[249] The right of individual petition, if recognised in a procedure before these courts, is a right to make a complaint, not a right to have it judged on its merits. See, S Greer and L Wildhaber, 'Revisiting the Debate about "constitutionalising" the European Court of Human Rights' (2012) 12 *Human Rights Law Review* 655, 675.

[250] ibid 665.

[251] 'in view of the changes of the past half century there is simply no realistic prospect of justice being systematically delivered to every applicant with a credible complaint about a Convention violation. And unless it is systematic, individual "justice" risks becoming arbitrary' (ibid 665).

Then, what happens in the not-so-frequent hypothesis that a case about rights violations does make it to these national and European courts designed to safeguard supreme norms? Although constitutional and human rights are said to have greater moral worth than ordinary statutory law, in practice, courts find it frequently justifiable that the right in question is infringed.[252] Elsewhere, I suggested that human rights are part of a secular religion, but in practice offer legal crowbars that only work occasionally.[253]

One explanation for the de facto stronger status of ordinary rights in the law of crime, contract and property as opposed to constitutional rights has to do with the abstract, more vague formulation of the latter.[254] The other explanation, the almost hidden elephant in the proportionality class, is the concern for institutional role-playing, with courts being generous in recognising the applicability of a right, but frugal in recognising its priority in a given case. In general, these courts apply a dynamic and extensive interpretation of fundamental rights and constitutional principles, but that does not necessarily lead to findings of unjustified violations. Even when everything points at problematic state interventions, courts often avoid declarations of unconstitutionality by using the technique of constitution-conforming interpretation.[255] The technique is also used by the CJEU, for instance

[252] 'Paradoxically, ordinary legal rights are treated as *stronger* than constitutional rights in this sense: they are defeasible by the general interest' (Yowell (n 170) 25).

[253] Gutwirth and De Hert (n 36) 420–62.

[254] Ordinary rights 'express, firm, relatively precise requirements … Courts *interpret* these rights, resolving disputes about their application to certain situations, in a way that is formally structured around protecting the right and stating its meaning. Constitutional rights are in most cases not interpreted in the same way. Invoking a constitutional right gives the court a platform for evaluating a law alleged to violate the right; the point of adjudication is not to *interpret* the constitutional right but to evaluate the law in question. This can be seen most clearly in the proportionality inquiry, which starts from the premise that it is frequently justifiable to infringe, or to interfere with, a constitutional right' (Yowell (n 170) 15).

[255] de Visser describes this 'not uncontroversial' technique of constitutional-conform interpretation as follows: formally speaking, a law under review is not declared unconstitutional, but constitutional courts 'include guidelines in their decisions for the interpretation under review that must be followed by administrative authorities and the regular courts when applying and enforcing the relevant legislative provisions. Constitution-conform interpretation may thus entail the judicial rewriting of the legislation in question, which technically speaking can take the form of adding in words or phrases, substituting a portion of the text, or removing particular expressions or complete sentences from the statute' (Visser (n 69) 293). See more generally Visser (n 69) 291–310. See also, Claes, Heringa, Sluis and Stremler (n 69) 4; A Stone Sweet, 'The politics of constitutional review in France and Europe' (2007) *International Journal of Constitutional Law* 69; S Sottiaux, 'Grondwetsconforme interpretatie. Garantie voor of aantasting van de scheiding der machten?' in A Alen and S Sottiaux (eds), *Leuvense Staatsrechtelijke standpunten 2* (Die Keure, 2010) 193–252); A Von Brünneck, 'Constitutional Review and Legislation in Western Democracies' in C Landfried (ed), *Constitutional Review and Legislation. An International Comparison* (Nomos, 1988) 219–53; T Moonen, *Het Grondwettelijk Hof en de interpretatie van de Grondwet. Een perspectief op argumenten en legitimiteit* (Doctoraat, Ghent University, 2014) 680. See for a historical-cultural as well as a philosophical-comparative perspective on conformity interpretation, J Bengoetxea, 'Conform Interpretation as a Method for Balancing Autonomy and Heteronomy: Introduction' (2011) 1 *Oñati Socio-Legal Series* (2012) 5, via available at ssrn.com/abstract=1991701: 'Conform interpretation is an important methodological and theoretical device in understanding this new predicament of justice and the judiciary; it helps define the limits of autonomy and discretion: sometimes it is possible to interpret state law in order to adapt it

in a case about the Directive on *Copyright in the Digital Services Market*.[256] What if platforms 'over-block' content to make sure that their copyright duties imposed by this Directive are respected? The CJEU sees the problem of over-blocking when use is made of automatic filtering as prescribed by the Directive. However, it does *not* invalidate the Directive, but only adds a long list of guarantees against over-blocking in its interpretative reading of the Directive.[257] Legislative supremacy respected? A rights-triumph? Platforms will now have to apply a European Directive, while not ignoring the additional detail in a European judgment.

The picture about the post-World War II turn to the priority of rights and preserving the Constitution through the judiciary is only telling half of the truth, Hans-Heinrich Vogel writes. The other half is cautiousness, judicial restraint to step on the seat of the legislator, and reluctance to give priority to rights.[258]

to supranational standards with no need for the legislator to step in. … But conform interpretation can also be seen as a socio-legal practice that helps structure the legal profession and bring in a new form of uniformity, coherence, harmony in a diplomatic, smooth or non-aggressive manner, avoiding power clashes' (4).

[256] The case was brought before the Court due to fundamental right concerns (in particular, freedom of expression and information) raised by online platforms' content moderation practices of prior automatic filtering. Directive (EU) 2019/790 of the European Parliament and of the Council of 17 April 2019 on copyright and related rights in the Digital Single Market and amending Directives 96/9/EC and 2001/29/EC, OJ L 130, 17.5.2019, 92–125. See G Frosio, 'Platform Responsibility in the Digital Services Act: Constitutionalising, Regulating and Governing Private Ordering' (2022) *Queen's University Belfast Law Research Paper*, available at ssrn.com/abstract=4236510 (forthcoming in A Savin and J Trzaskowski (eds), *Research Handbook on EU Internet Law* (Edward Elgar, 2023)).

[257] CJEU, judgment of the Court (Grand Chamber) of 26 April 2022, *Republic of Poland v European Parliament and Council of the European Union*, available at eur-lex.europa.eu/legal-content/EN/TXT/?uri=CELEX%3A62019CJ0401. One of the criticised obligations is Art 17 CDSM, which mandates that providers are primarily liable for user uploads on their platforms, for which they will need to obtain authorisation by copyright holders. Should they be unable to obtain it, they can avoid liability if they comply with certain obligations, including those stipulated in Art 17(4)(b)–(c). This establishes preventive measures to monitor and block user uploads, requiring the providers to proactively ensure the unavailability of once notified works, as well as to prevent their future uploads. These provisions have been challenged in an action for annulment by the Republic of Poland, which alleged a violation of Art 11 CFR, maintaining that the de facto preventive monitoring measures on online content-sharing service providers via prior automatic filtering, without providing safeguards to the right to freedom of expression and information, infringe upon the latter inasmuch as they neither respect the essence of the right, nor are proportionate. The CJEU ruled that the liability regime mandated by Art 17 of the CDSM indeed limits freedom of expression and information. However, such limitation appears compatible with the principle of proportionality flowing from Art 52(1) of the Charter, as it is mandated by law, it is necessary in light of the protection of copyright, and it genuinely meets the EU's objectives of general interest, thereby striking a fair balance between the right to conduct a business in Art 16 CFR, Art 11 and intellectual property rights in Art 17(2), also due to the *ex ante* and ex post safeguards to fundamental rights in place. Nevertheless, the Court added multiple safeguards to users' fundamental rights in its proportionality *stricto sensu* analysis of Art 17 CDSM in respect of the avoidance of over-blocking. It clarified, for instance, that upload filters can only be employed if they are able to recognise, and not automatically block, lawful uploads, otherwise this fair balance between fundamental rights would not be respected. So, Art 17 of the CDSM was not declared to be violating primary law. Hence Poland lost the case, but considering the total rewriting of the said provision following the judgment, it can also be said to have won e.

[258] HH Vogel, 'Constitutional Review and Democracy – Constitutional Courts and the Legislative Process', report for the European Commission For Democracy Through Law (Venice Commission), 15 July 2003 (11), available at www.venice.coe.int/webforms/documents/default.

Conclusions about the glorious history of the rule of law and the protection of rights can only gain analytical power if they are of a cautious tone and recognise this judicial cautiousness.

B. The Priority of Rights in Europe and its Proportionality Test

The *Rechtsstaat* tradition in continental Europe differs from the Anglo-Saxon *rule of law* tradition and was historically inferior in ranking rights and citizens on top.[259] After World War II, the whole of Europe moved closely towards the idea of the rule of law, defined as constitutionalism, with the adoption of substantive standards and judicial review of administrative and legislative acts by the domestic and the European judiciary as two highlights. On the continent, the term *Rechtsstaat* was given a new definition, to make it quasi-identical to the concept of the rule of law. But sociological insights teach us that change is never entirely change, but is constructed on legal, mental and symbolical heritage.

Meierhenrich's work on the multilayered history of the *Rechtsstaat* emphasises that the entrenchment of morals in the 1949 German *Grundgesetz* and the substantive alignment of the *Rechtsstaat* with the rule of law, 'did not alter the centrality of the state – its phenomenological significance – in Germany's social imaginary'.[260]

How does the triumphal narrative about the proportionality test, devised by the German judiciary and exported to the rest of the world, fit in this cautious picture? Proportionality is said to be superior to other adjudication methods like traditional reasonableness test. These traditional tests are state-friendly, ad hoc, vague and not guided by a framework of questions that states need to answer to.[261] Compared to US categorical balancing it is more sensitive to facts and elements of context, and more transparent. Both the US test and the proportionality test are about balancing, but the balancing done in the framework of the final subtest of proportionality is preceded by two subtests (suitability and necessity) that are said to be more objective and informative for proper balancing.

aspx?pdffile=CDL-JU(2003)025-e: 'But these provisions for control of the constitutionality of legislation in the United States and Germany are telling only half of the truth. The courts of both the United States and Germany are rather cautious, when the possibility arises, that a decision of Congress of the United States or of the Federal Parliament of Germany concerning a statute or an international treaty may be unconstitutional. They observe a doctrine of judicial restraint, which means that their judges can give parliamentary decisions the benefit of doubt and can avoid declaring them unconstitutional in certain situations. Partly unconstitutional provisions of enacted statutes may, for example, sometimes be saved by interpretative measures, which restrict possible applications to what is constitutionally acceptable for the court. I may add that the courts of the United States and Germany definitely are not the only ones to observe judicial restraint when acts or other decisions of parliament are in question. I think you can find similar reluctance more and less explicit in every constitutional jurisdiction of the Western Hemisphere.'

[259] The reality of the reign of the rule of law in the UK since the 17th century is equally the object of discussion, by virtue of its move to parliamentary sovereignty.

[260] Meierhenrich (n 44) 53.

[261] ibid.

So, proportionality is about justification and interrogating state actions based on a structured transparent inquiry. It benefits the individual and contributes to a culture of justification in a liberal constitutional state: it allows the individual to call upon the democratically elected legislature to justify the need to infringe on fundamental rights. The proportionality requirement forces the majority to present this justification to an appropriate and independent constitutional institution.

Proportionality as a test for rights limitation does indeed allow the judiciary to limit or invalidate limitations made possible by laws. In this function it pronounces the priority of right over legalism. On the other hand, it stresses the malleability of rights and their social function that are asked to accommodate utility and the priority of state interest. This two-fold Janus-like, dichotomic nature 'reflects a balancing act moored in European legal tradition whose symbolism outperforms its utility as a judicial tool'.[262]

The twofold function of proportionality as we understand it resides here: it is both a tool to temper legalism on substantive grounds, and a technical device for lawyers to meet the terms, lifeworld and self-perception of modern state managers with their aura of expertise, neutrality and objectivity. It not only suggests a predictable methodology or structure, but equally a thorough understanding of how state logic works and how it can be assessed and balanced with logic of rights. Proportionality not only benefits the citizen, but also the state, through its strong legitimising effects. Although proportionality testing in court – with courts carrying out their own assessment – can cause irritations with other social systems (like politics, the army and the police), it can seal actions of state organs with green light, serving as complementary evidence of the rationality the system's bureaucratic structure.

My analysis furthermore highlighted the reality of adjudication: a standard formula for the proportionality test in Europe is simply absent, and so is the structured proportionality test desired by many academics in the slipstream of German constitutionalism. Courts like the ECtHR simply refuse to embrace one standard. A structured proportionality test desired by many academics in the slipstream of German constitutionalism is as such absent. As a rule of thumb one can observe that the higher the number of elements of the structured proportionality test involved, the stricter the scrutiny that the ECtHR wishes to engage in.[263] If fewer elements are included, all that remains is a simple balancing exercise allowing only some sort of low-level scrutiny. This loose approach to proportionality is not

[262] *cf* Tridimas and Gentile (n 26) 794. These authors focus on another Janus concept, that of essence as 'the limits to limits'. The analysis in this chapter uses and adapts their formulation to characterise the very similar; Janus-like character of proportionality.

[263] Recall that the possible elements of the Strasbourg's necessity test can be 'pressing social need' (not always mentioned by the Court), 'sufficient and relevant reasons' (only applied when testing is stricter), 'least harmful means' (very seldom used) and proportionality of the measure to the legitimate aim pursued. The last element serves as a baseline of the Strasbourg proportionality test that – whenever the Court finds it appropriate – is complemented with elements, such as 'pressing social need' and 'relevant and sufficient reasons'; as well as, rarely, with the 'least harmful means'.

unique. Courts all over the world have rejected explicitly or implicitly a formulaic approach to proportionality or any other elaborated method of adjudication.

Most academic literature is affirmative about the existence of a fully matured doctrine on proportionality. But the formulation of the components and the test in general is often more normative than descriptive. When discussing judgments with loose proportionality testing, scholars speak of 'sidestepping' away of the structured proportionality test by courts.[264]

This way of presenting things might not be the right way. The myths surrounding the test prevent a clear vision. I addressed several of these myths, such as proportionality, as more protective of rights than US categorical balancing.

For Habermas, proportionality deprives us of the necessary firewall of strong rights against political crazes of the day and, lacking stable reference points, invites irrational judicial judgement. It is a broad test, and the components invite reasoned analysis. But its openness to a broad range of considerations allows judges to bring in openly or below the level of consciousness categorical preferences that are often state-friendly, but not faithful to the idea of balancing that is respectful of all interests at stake. Categoric reasoning is extruded but brought back in via back doors in a 'wrongly' way.[265] Examples are case law on national security and on the pandemic, where balancing was replaced by over or implicit categorical preference to 'physical life' ('life') over 'living one's life' ('freedom').

Poorly rooted, easily captured, one is amazed to note how many 'technical' questions about the test (burden of proof; nature of the interest to limit rights; relationship with levels of scrutiny) remain vague.

Apart from the principled objections against certain formulations of the test (by Alexy), the biggest weakness of the test resides in its vagueness over the separation of powers and the proper role of the judiciary next to the other branches. This matter is high on the judges' minds but absent in the presentation of the proportionality doctrine by scholars who insist on the predictability of the test and praise its neutrality.

In the last sections, I discussed proposals for an explicit recognition of constitutional generosity in review, with only limited and selective interventions of the judiciary. This explicit embrace of generosity towards the other branches is rare in academic work, but probably alive in the mindset of our judges. The advantage of the concept might be its insistence on the context of judicial review amidst branches that claim more democratic legitimacy and more expertise in policymaking. However, I presented this plea for generosity without embracing it. It might be a dangerous one in continental Europe characterised by paternalism and bureaucratic managerialism.

Rather, I insisted on the need to complement theories on methods of adjudication, with a doctrine of levels of scrutiny as has been developed in US constitutionalism. Theories on methods of adjudication like the doctrine of

[264] Ip (n 137).
[265] Möller (n 128) 164.

proportionality should be complemented with a doctrine of variable intensity of review. The former structures the substantive inquiry into the justifiability of a limitation of the enjoyment of a right; the latter structures the formal allocation of responsibilities to the various powers of government for carrying out the substantive inquiry.[266]

With a doctrine on levels of scrutiny, important technical answers with regard to proportionality testing (like the burden of proof and the nature of interest that are balanced) can be answered. The ECtHR is not far from this combination of doctrines, with its concept of 'margin of appreciation',[267] but this doctrine is too vague compared with the Supreme Court's doctrine on levels of scrutiny. Attempts like the one by European Judge Spano to clarify the ECtHR method through a combination of a vague margin test with a vague proportionality-test were discussed,[268] but deemed unsatisfactory and confusing. Tushnet's question – whether constitutionalism should authorise a far-reaching degree of judicial intervention or a modest degree only to prune the excesses of the modern regulatory state[269] – should best be understood when doctrines on adjudication methods like proportionality *and* on levels of scrutiny have reached a level of maturity. Unfortunately for Europe, having the malleability of the proportionality test in the hands of the judiciary has not only allowed them to act as neutral experts averse to politics, but also to skillfully avoid any development of importance towards maturity by clarifying scrutiny levels that define the relation between legal review and politics. In practice, the proportionality test allowed the same judiciary in many cases to uphold state interest, while at the same time promising that tomorrow, with new factors being considered, rights *might* triumph, keeping the secular belief in the power of constitutional and human rights somewhat alive.

A clean slate should begin freeing the judges from realising agendas on adjudication set by scholars and avoiding rhetoric adherence to a fully structured test. This test does indeed contain many rationally relevant considerations, but

[266] Rivers (n 237) 207. The distinction is not always easy, but relevant. Rivers rightly observes that both doctrines are guided by the seriousness of the limitation of rights in the case in question. 'Where there is a minor limitation of a less important right, the gain to the public interest need not be large, and courts will ordinarily accept the appropriate executive body's assessment of the degree to which the public interest is furthered and admit a range of possible policy choices. By contrast, where the limitation of rights is substantial and the right is important, the gain to the public interest must also be substantial. In these cases, review will also be more intense: the executive will have to demonstrate that its assessments of the public interest are as reliable as they can be and persuade the court that the cost to rights really is worth it. In the case of the most serious limitations of rights, the court's constitutional duty is to ensure to its own satisfaction that the decision is correct all things considered.'

[267] On the prima facie conflicting image of the ECtHR as an international court with strong expressive powers, which is expected to be at the same time cautious and leading the development of human rights standards in Europe and beyond, see A Margariab, 'Honner v France: Damage Prevention and/or Damage Control?' *Strasbourg Observers* (12 January 2021), available at strasbourgobservers.com/2021/01/12/honner-v-france-damage-prevention-and-or-damage-control.

[268] Section V.C, above.

[269] Tushnet (n 174) 15.

addressing them all in every judgment sounds like an invitation to mimicry.[270] The question of least intrusive alternatives, for example, is a most relevant component brought under the academic proportionality test. It fits the toolbox of the judiciary, but cannot be always answered easily by the non-expert judge. Other questions can then carry more weight to reach an acceptable outcome. This chapter is written with cold feelings for the structured proportionality test and its benefits. Transparency by judges about the level of scrutiny was advocated, much less the transparency about the number of components of proportionality that should be checked in each case.

Apart from being transparent about the level of scrutiny, the best outcome would be to concentrate on a duty of reasoned assessment (using hints of proportionality or not), not forgetting that the legal formulation of human rights matter as much as the formulation of ordinary rights and can be a useful element in that reasoning. Judges in constitutional courts or with powers of constitutional review should, equally, not be misled by the proportionality promise of neutrality. Judging other branches *is political* or at least has political implications.[271]

When fundamental texts require judges to look at 'the necessity in a democratic society', they are called to speak out on political concepts. Courts should not shift away from trying to estimate what society would consider reasonable or necessary, to substituting a doctrinally constructed determination of reasonableness.[272]

A fixed constitutional settlement, with or without proportionality, is neither proposed nor desired. Judging and speaking out on other branches is, of its nature, relational:

> [D]ecisions are made according to perceptions of relative roles in the structure of public authority, and since political right functions to maintain the power of the system, power should not be said to reside in any specific locus; it is generated through the relationship itself. This relational dimension gives the system its dynamic quality. But it also means that there can be no fixed constitutional settlement. Constitutions are constantly evolving in the light of political necessities and, because of this evolutionary impetus, the meaning and impact of legal concepts and doctrines will similarly change.[273]

[270] Imagine that European from now would run through all proportionality questions and address all four components combined – legitimacy, rationality, necessity, balancing components. In the current climate with 'technical matters' such as the burden of proof and the nature of state interest left unclarified (section V.C), it is reasonable to expect very little improvements in terms of rights protection. Concerns that militate for a structured test like foreseeability and legal certainty would not be served.

[271] See the analysis of the political role and the bottom-up approach of judges, compared to the top-down approach of academics in section II.B above.

[272] On a similar 'troubling trend' in US law, see Anonymous, 'Fourth Circuit Holds that Government Acquisition of Historical Cell-Site Location Information Is Not a Search' (2017) 130 *Harvard Law Review* 1273.

[273] M Loughlin, *Foundations of Public Law* (Oxford University Press, 2010) 12. See equally Zalar (n 102) 332.

4

Proportionality of Goals or Means? The Politics of Data Governance in the Shade of Constitutional Norms

PRZEMYSŁAW PAŁKA[1]

I. Introduction

Designing data policy is a difficult task. Its difficulty stems not only from the need to reconcile several competing objectives and legal values but,[2] more importantly, from the need to answer the fundamental question: in what society do we want to live?

The answer to this question will include two components: a substantive one – 'Who should be allowed or required to do what with what data, and under what conditions?'[3] – and a procedural one – 'Who should be, institutionally, empowered to answer these substantive questions?'[4] For example: should individuals

[1] Assistant Professor, Faculty of Law and Administration, Jagiellonian University in Krakow, Poland; Affiliated Fellow, Information Society Project, Yale Law School, the United States. The research leading to these results has received funding from the Norwegian Financial Mechanism 2014–2021, project no 2020/37/K/HS5/02769, titled 'Private Law of Data: Concepts, Practices, Principles & Politics'. For helpful feedback on the earlier versions of this chapter, I would like to thank Filipe Brito Bastos, Jan Czarnocki, Nik Guggenberger, Paulina Jabłońska, Daniel Kwiatkowski, Maciej Próchnicki, Mauro Arturo Rivera León, Thomas Streinz, Karolina Śliwa, Bohdan Widła and Katarzyna Wiśniewska. All errors, obviously, remain solely mine.

[2] For an overview of the EU data law's trajectory, see T Streinz, 'The Evolution of European Data Law' in P Craig and G de Búrca (eds), *The Evolution of EU Law*, 3rd edn (Oxford University Press, 2021); recently I have analysed in detail how the EU's data law is guided by almost exactly opposite principles when personal data is concerned (data minimisation, purpose limitation, secrecy, individual rights) and when non-personal data is concerned (data maximisation, freedom of use, access, public good). See P Pałka, 'Harmed While Anonymous: Beyond the Personal/Non-Personal Distinction in Data Governance' (2023) 2023 *Technology and Regulation* 22.

[3] Salome Viljoen calls the totality of norms answering these questions 'data governance law'; see S Viljoen, 'A Relational Theory of Data Governance' (2021) 131 *Yale Law Journal* 573; I have attempted to theorise the same body as 'data management law': P Pałka, 'Data Management Law for the 2020s: The Lost Origins and the New Needs' (2020) 68 *Buffalo Law Review* 559.

[4] For a classic discussion, see DJ Solove, 'Introduction: Privacy Self-Management and the Consent Dilemma' (2012) 126 *Harvard Law Review* 1880.

have the power to consent to processing of their data that can lead to the generation of group-wide insights?[5] Should online companies be required to share with their customers the profits made of user-generated data?[6] How many of such questions should be answered by lawmakers, and which are better left to the markets? How competitive, horizontally and vertically, do we want such markets to be? The world we currently live in has been constructed on one – contingent and quite possibly suboptimal – set of answers given by the law.

The proportionality principle can seem like a useful tool when embarking on the difficult task of designing data policy. In one obvious sense, it is indispensable; all laws must comply with constitutional norms.[7] Designed to help assess whether measures advancing certain (legitimate) goals are not excessively limiting other interests or rights, proportionality principle serves as an important check in many situations.[8] For example, the principle is essential when scrutinising norms empowering public authorities, like police or social services, to collect and use information about the individuals. Similarly, proportionality is crucial when assessing rules with potential to limit fundamental rights like free expression or privacy. Put simply, and somewhat trivially: the proportionality principle is a helpful tool for limiting the reach of lawmakers who want to do *too much*.

However, as I argue in this chapter, proportionality principle can also serve as an *excuse* for the lawmakers willing to do *too little*. Let me call this 'proportionality-washing'. In situations where the goal of legislation would be to limit the power or affect economic interests of huge corporations (or local incumbents), lawmakers might hesitate when proposing significant changes or succumb to the pressure of omnipresent lobbyists.[9] In such cases, lawmakers who need to justify the limited scope of legislative intervention might find an unexpected ally in the proportionality principle. The principle, at its heart a technocratic, seemingly neutral and apolitical exercise,[10] presents a perfect opportunity to say 'maybe we would want

[5] Given the problem of externalities. See A Solow-Niederman, 'Information Privacy and the Inference Economy' (2022) 117 *Northwestern University Law Review* 357.

[6] As advocated by, among others, Jaron Lanier; see J Lanier, 'Opinion | Jaron Lanier Fixes the Internet' *The New York Times* (23 September 2019), available at www.nytimes.com/interactive/2019/09/23/opinion/data-privacy-jaron-lanier.html.

[7] Note that the principle of proportionality is both a general principle in theory of law, see for example, A Barak, *Proportionality: Constitutional Rights and Their Limitations* (Cambridge University Press, 2012); E Engle, 'The General Principle of Proportionality and Aristotle' in L Huppes-Cluysenaer and NMMS Coelho (eds), *Aristotle and The Philosophy of Law: Theory, Practice and Justice* (Springer Netherlands, 2013); concretised by the EU positive law: T-I Harbo, *The Function of Proportionality Analysis in European Law* (Brill, 2015).

[8] Proportionality is a general principle of the EU law; see T-I Harbo, 'The Function of the Proportionality Principle in EU Law' (2010) 16 *European Law Journal* 158, 159. In this sense, even though the Charter test and the Art 5.4 TEU test might seem like 'different proportionality principles', they are however just aspects of the same general principle.

[9] On the phenomenon in general, see I De Bruycker and J Beyers, 'Lobbying Strategies and Success: Inside and Outside Lobbying in European Union Legislative Politics' (2019) 11 *European Political Science Review* 57; on the practices deployed most recently by the so-called 'big tech', see A Tarrant and T Cowen, 'Big Tech Lobbying in the EU' (2022) 93 *The Political Quarterly* 218.

[10] And for these reasons criticised, see eg, FJ Urbina, 'A Critique of Proportionality' (2012) 57 *American Journal of Jurisprudence* 49.

to do more but doing so would be unlawful.' Proportionality might help disguise, in a move familiar to law and technology scholars, political choices as technocratic ones.[11]

Furthermore, I argue that focusing on the proportionality test too early in the policymaking process might limit the creativity and imagination of the lawmakers.[12] Let us call this the 'proportionality mindset'. The principle can help assess whether the measures are proportionate towards the goals pursued but will help little in choosing the goals in the first place. It might help determining what goals are legitimate but cannot help come up with the list of all goals available or determining which ones are optimal. And in an area so complex as data policy, this is an impediment. One might end up pursuing minimalist and suboptimal policy goals not only as a result of lack of political will or courage, but also due to lack of regulatory imagination.

A recent example of a lawmaker missing the opportunity to introduce meaningful changes can be found in the EU's data policy. When comparing the European Strategy for Data[13] with the two legislative instruments concretising it – the Data Governance Act (DGA)[14] and the Data Act (DA)[15] – one is struck by the disconnect between the extremely ambitious aspirations of the former and rather modest changes introduced by the latter. The Union claims that it wants to transform the world, but then acts in a way that will shake the status quo a little but not too much. Of course, proportionality principle is not the only reason for this state of affairs or the only strategy the European Commission deployed in its explanatory memoranda, but it epitomises a certain technocratic, minimalist mindset detectable in the proposals and ultimate texts of the data regulations. Further, in adopting these regulations, based on Article 114 TFEU, the EU has preempted legislative action by the Member States.[16] In its explanatory memoranda, the Commission has hardly proven that the data legislation is proportionate under Article 5.4 TEU, ie, 'necessary'. As I argue in this chapter, this is a proportionality paradox of the EU data policy: the Union did too little while doing too much.

[11] For a classic text on the matter, see L Winner, 'Do Artifacts Have Politics?' (1980) 109 *Daedalus* 121.

[12] On the indispensable role of imagination when designing regulations of technology, see L Robb and K Tranter, 'Hype and Cultural Imaginary in Law and Technology' in B Brożek et al (eds), *Research Handbook on Law and Technology* (Edward Elgar Publishing, 2023) 128–40; and P Pałka and B Brożek, 'How Not to Get Bored, or Some Thoughts on the Methodology of Law and Technology' in ibid 82–98.

[13] Communication from the Commission to the European Parliament, the Council, the European Economic and Social committee and the Committee of the Regions: A European strategy for data, Brussels, 19.2.2020, COM(2020) 66 final.

[14] Regulation (EU) 2022/868 of the European Parliament and of the Council of 30 May 2022 on European data governance and amending Regulation (EU) 2018/1724 (Data Governance Act) [2022] OJ L 152.

[15] Regulation (EU) 2023/2854 of the European Parliament and of the Council of 13 December 2023 on harmonised rules on fair access to and use of data and amending Regulation (EU) 2017/2394 and Directive (EU) 2020/1828 (Data Act) [2023] OJ L, 2023/2854.

[16] P Craig and G de Burca, *EU Law: Text, Cases, and Materials*, 5th edn (Oxford University Press, 2011) 84.

One important caveat: we live in a time when it's difficult to criticise the EU's policies without coming across as anti-European, or to object to specific regulations without being labelled an anti-regulation libertarian. It is not my intention to be either of these. On the contrary, I believe especially that the proponents of the European project should speak out when the EU makes mistakes, and the believers in regulation should be able to critique the concrete regulations. That is my intention in this chapter.

This chapter's critique of the EU's data policy builds upon the assumption that the lawmakers' goals could have been different and far more ambitious. Crucially, however, this assumption pertains not just to the specific provisions – eg, the fact that objective scope of the user rights established by the DA could have been wider or accompanied by fewer limitations – but also to the adopted regulatory paradigm. To endow this assumption with more gravity, one should substantiate the claim that the goals could have been more ambitious. And to do that one needs to see how our existing sociotechnical world is contingent, how it could be different and why, even though we're used to it, it is really *weird*. Let me begin with that.

II. On the Contingency and Weirdness of Our (Data) World

We are used to living in the world as it is. When using technology for daily purposes – sending emails, shopping online, or scrolling social media – we are not actively encouraged to appreciate the contingency of our sociotechnological reality.[17] This also pertains, as I argue in this chapter, to the way various actors collect and deploy data, and the way the law facilitates these practices.[18] To see how and why the goals of the EU's data policy could have been different (and far more ambitious), let us first ponder the nonessentialist character of the existing technological world.

First, notice how certain electronic services seem to be 'naturally' interoperable with one another, while others are not.[19] For example, email is an interoperable service: one can easily send messages from one's university account to someone else using Gmail, Yahoo!, or any other provider. Similarly, one can access websites using a variety of browsers: Chrome, Safari, Firefox, etc.[20] One

[17] On why understanding 'technology' as sociotechnological practices rather than merely qualities of inventions offers superior theoretical insights, see JM Balkin, 'The Path of Robotics Law' (2015) 6 *California Law Review Circuit* 45, 47–49.

[18] On the law's facilitative role in this regard, see JE Cohen, *Between Truth and Power: The Legal Constructions of Informational Capitalism* (Oxford University Press, 2019) 8.

[19] On the concept of interoperability, see W Kerber and H Schweitzer, 'Interoperability in the Digital Economy' (2017) 8 *Journal of Intellectual Property, Information Technology and E-Commerce Law*, available at www.jipitec.eu/issues/jipitec-8-1-2017/4531.

[20] And the occasional notification stating that 'the browser you are using is not supported, pleased download XYZ' serves as an exception confirming the rule.

can call or text someone using an Android phone on a contract with Verizon from an iPhone on a contract with T-Mobile.[21] One can download software on one's PC or MacBook from essentially any website on the internet.

At the same time, one cannot react to posts on X (formerly Twitter) in any other way than by using Elon Musk's service. One cannot join a Facebook group without having a Facebook account.[22] One cannot download an app on one's iPhone from any other source than Apple's official App Store. Just like the interoperable nature of the 'early' internet was not necessary, neither is the siloed version we live in today.[23] The existence of services like Bluesky or Mastodon[24] – even if not (yet) particularly successful – proves that the lack of interoperability in social media is a contingent business decision, not a technological necessity; there is nothing 'natural' here. The law allowed such business decisions to be taken and the incremental move towards some interoperability required by the EU's Digital Markets Act (DMA) showcases that it can also intervene.

Of course, the law always could have intervened. Lawrence Lessig made that point 25 years ago. He argued that different regulatory modalities – law, social norms, economics and code/architecture – not only guide human behaviour but also affect one another.[25] A quarter of a century ago, Lessig demonstrated that whether access to a service is easy or difficult, or whether data about one's use of the service is recorded or not (and who precisely has access to that data), is the service provider's technical decision.[26] This decision might be constrained or guided by the law but, if it is not, it will be influenced by the provider's interests, most certainly economic ones.[27]

Which leads me to the second contingent feature of our sociotechnical world: omnipresent and seamless data collection. Currently, various entities record in the form of data whatever we do online (and, with the rise of the Internet of Things (IoT), increasingly offline).[28] We all know this – and it may feel trivial – but

[21] Which is a relatively new phenomenon Wu, *The Curse of Bigness: Antitrust in the New Gilded Age*, Illustrated edn (Columbia Global Reports, 2018) 93–101.

[22] I explore this problem in more detail in P Palka, 'The World of Fifty (Interoperable) Facebooks' (2020) 51 *Seton Hall Law Review* 1193.

[23] Predicted and discussed already in J Zittrain, *The Future of the Internet--And How to Stop It*, Illustrated edn (Yale University Press, 2009).

[24] See P Sawers, 'Standard Protocol: In a Post-Twitter World, Mastodon and Bluesky Need to Get on the Same Page' (*TechCrunch*, 6 July 2023), available at techcrunch.com/2023/07/06/mastodon-bluesky-protocol-twitter-elon-musk.

[25] L Lessig, 'The Law of the Horse: What Cyberlaw Might Teach' (1999) 113 *Harvard Law Review* 501, 507–15.

[26] L Lessig, *Code and Other Laws of Cyberspace* (Basic Books, 1999) 26–27.

[27] Lessig (n 25) 511, 537.

[28] Some scholars have for some time questioned the descriptive and explanatory power of the online/offline distinction. See L Floridi (ed), *The Onlife Manifesto: Being Human in a Hyperconnected Era* (Springer, 2015). For great descriptions of how the IoT functions, and analyses of what its emergence signifies for private and privacy law, see JAT Fairfield, *Owned: Property, Privacy, and the New Digital Serfdom* (Cambridge University Press, 2017); A Tamò-Larrieux, *Designing for Privacy and Its Legal Framework: Data Protection by Design and Default for the Internet of Things*, 1st edn (Springer, 2018); K Kryla-Cudna, 'Consumer Contracts and the Internet of Things' in V Mak et al, *Research Handbook*

the important point is that the world did not have to function this way. It is incorrect to say that our actions 'leave a digital trail or footprint'. Such a statement brings to one's mind an image of shoes leaving a print on fresh snow or mud, something physically impossible to avoid. But having a 'digital footprint' was possible to avoid. Providers did *not want* to avoid it, however, and the law did not make them do so.

Very importantly – note that I'm speaking of 'data' in general, not just 'personal data' – the phenomenon of extensive data collection can (and, in my opinion, should) be analysed from a much wider point of view than that of privacy or data protection law.[29] As I have argued elsewhere, the often-overlooked feature of corporate data collection (what distinguishes corporations from various public actors) is the partial incentive alignment with the users, where both companies and individuals have an interest in keeping private information private and limiting their uses to the seamless ones.[30] Put simply: Alphabet, Meta and X want to make money out of the data they gather and, if the users do not feel secure or comfortable with this, they will simply make less money.

How does one make money out of data? One can use it to deliver personalised ads.[31] Or, one can use it to create new products, eg, by training machine learning algorithms for machine-translation, facial recognition, operating self-driving cars, or any other computable task.[32] Eric Posner and Glen Weyl refer to this phenomenon as 'data labor':[33] in a hypothetical world in which corporations cannot (for technical or legal reasons) train AI systems using data generated by users (like tagging faces on Facebook, ie, providing training data for facial recognition algorithms, or rating translations, ie, providing feedback to translation algorithms) they would have to hire and pay people to do this work. This could be quite expensive. And yet, we live in the world in which training systems using data generated by users seems a perfectly acceptable practice.

in Data Science and Law (Edward Elgar Publishing, 2018) 83–107; R Crootof, 'The Internet of Torts: Expanding Civil Liability Standards to Address Corporate Remote Interference' (2019) 69 *Duke Law Journal* 583.

[29] Other scholars have made this point before; see eg O Ben-Shahar, 'Data Pollution' (2019) 11 *Journal of Legal Analysis* 104.

[30] Pałka (n 2) 29–30.

[31] This phenomenon has been widely discussed by scholars, usually from the perspective of values like autonomy and the corresponding problem of potential manipulation; see E Mik, 'The Erosion of Autonomy in Online Consumer Transactions' (2016) 8 *Law, Innovation and Technology* 1; D Susser, B Roessler and H Nissenbaum, 'Online Manipulation: Hidden Influences in a Digital World' (2019) 4 *Georgetown Law Technology Review* 1; S Zuboff, *The Age of Surveillance Capitalism: The Fight for a Human Future at the New Frontier of Power*, 1st edn (PublicAffairs, 2019); However, there is growing empirical evidence suggesting that online ads might be less effective (and thereby less manipulative) than their opponents and proponents like to claim; see T Hwang, *Subprime Attention Crisis: Advertising and the Time Bomb at the Heart of the Internet* (FSG Originals, 2020).

[32] For a lawyer-friendly introduction and examples, see A Porębski, 'Machine Learning and Law' in B Brożek et al (eds), *Research Handbook on Law and Technology* (Edward Elgar Publishing, 2023) 451–55.

[33] EA Posner and EG Weyl, *Radical Markets: Uprooting Capitalism and Democracy for a Just Society* (Princeton University Press, 2018) 205–49.

It is a lawful practice. Importantly, it emerged neither in violation of the law nor somehow 'next to' the law; the law co-created it.[34] First, information is, by design, not subject to IP protection, meaning that whoever captures it can use it without having to ask for permission.[35] The matter becomes more complicated with personal information, of course, but the American model of 'notice and choice' (under which most of the significant companies have emerged) places the bar rather low, where users don't even need to actively consent but should merely be notified.[36] In the EU, the GDPR *seems* to tame these practices but, arguably, merely increases the costs of compliance: as long as the purpose of processing is lawful, a legalising basis has been secured and data subjects have been informed, corporate data collection is permissible.[37] This led Julie Cohen to propose the concept of 'biopolitical public domain',[38] meant to capture the reality in which an individual is free to profit a piece of information they have collected. We can argue, of course, to what extent specific practices are substantively complaint with the GDPR and where the law's toleration of them is not a result of underenforcement.[39] However, as long as data is anonymised – and anonymous data is all one needs for training machine learning algorithms or statistical analysis – privacy laws do not attempt to get involved.[40]

Maybe all this data collection (and subsequent usage for profit) strikes us as 'normal' or 'natural' because services like Google, Facebook,or X are 'free' to use. Of course, we know it's not 'free-free'; the EU consumer law and some scholars hold that consumers 'pay' precisely with their data,[41] while others focus on attention.[42] However, one must admit that not having euros or dollars disappear monthly from one's bank account is a pleasant arrangement. To some, this might

[34] For an account of how the law co-creates our sociotechnical reality, see K Pistor, *The Code of Capital: How the Law Creates Wealth and Inequality* (Princeton University Press, 2019).

[35] P Bernt Hugenholtz, 'Against "Data Property"' in H Ullrich et al. (eds) *Kritika: Essays on Intellectual Property* (Edward Elgar Publishing, 2018); I Cofone, 'Beyond Data Ownership' (2021) 43 *Cardozo Law Review* 501.

[36] R Calo, 'Against Notice Skepticism in Privacy (and Elsewhere)' (2011) 87 *Notre Dame Law Review* 1027; JR Reidenberg et al, 'Privacy Harms and the Effectiveness of the Notice and Choice Framework' (2015) 11 *I/S: A Journal of Law and Policy for the Information Society* 485.

[37] Note that the recent drama around the Meta case concerned precisely the presence or absence of the legalising basis. Also, generally on the GDPR's ineffectiveness, see AE Waldman, *Industry Unbound: The Inside Story of Privacy, Data, and Corporate Power* (Cambridge University Press, 2021).

[38] Cohen (n 18) 48.

[39] G Gentile and O Lynskey, 'DEFICIENT BY DESIGN? THE TRANSNATIONAL ENFORCEMENT OF THE GDPR' (2022) 71 *International & Comparative Law Quarterly* 799; F Brito Bastos and P Pałka, 'Is Centralised General Data Protection Regulation Enforcement a Constitutional Necessity?' [2023] *European Constitutional Law Review* 1.

[40] As 'personal data' limits the objective scope of application, see eg, PM Schwartz and DJ Solove, 'The PII Problem: Privacy and a New Concept of Personally Identifiable Information' (2011) 86 *New York University Law Review* 1814.

[41] A Metzger, 'Data as Counter-Performance: What Rights and Duties for Parties Have' (2017) 8 *Journal of Intellectual Property, Information Technology and Electronic Commerce Law* 2; A De Franceschi, 'Personal Data as Counter-Performance' in R Senigaglia, C Irti and A Bernes (eds), *Privacy and Data Protection in Software Services* (Springer, 2022).

[42] T Wu, 'Blind Spot: The Attention Economy and the Law' (2019) 82 *Antitrust Law Journal* 771.

seem like a good deal and a very egalitarian one, for that matter. In our unequal societies, not everyone can afford healthy food, dental care, or private education[43] but everyone – as long as they have a device with an internet access[44] – can access the wisdom (and the folly) of Google search and YouTube, or communicate with folks from all over the world.

And yet, the arrangement where corporations collect all the data they can, and use it for profit, and don't charge users for their services, *is weird*, should one pause to think about it. Imagine going back to 1974 and telling people there about this world. Some of the most innovative consumer services do not charge their users money yet collect all the information they can to train algorithms and serve personalised ads. A person not familiar with this world might ask: 'Well, how much would the corporations charge for using the service if they were not allowed to make money this way?' and, conversely, 'How much would the corporations have to pay the people for generating all this data?' What is the surplus and who get to keep it?

Notice how the reverse is not true. While corporations get to keep, analyse and profit from all data they can factually capture (with some hurdles regarding personal data), users of online services are often legally prohibited from doing the same.[45] This prohibition often applies regardless of the intended use and covers not only for-profit deployment of data scraped from public websites but also scraping for research or journalistic purposes.[46] The exception introduced by the Digital Services Act (DSA), ie, right access to access for vetted researchers only confirms the rule. The fact that companies are freer to capture data about individuals' private behaviour than individuals are to observe public behaviour of companies would no doubt seem strange to those in 1974. And yet, we're so used to this.

This leads me to the third contingent feature of our sociotechnological reality, namely the prevalence of the (quasi-)monopolies. All these services, also due to the lack of mandated interoperability, are offered by just a handful of multibillion dollar companies. A most basic economic knowledge is sufficient to know that the monopolist extracts the surplus. For a long while we were unable to pinpoint that extraction, as the services indeed seemed 'free'. And, especially in the US, after Robert Bork's thought transformed antitrust,[47] the lack of monetary payment made it difficult to measure the market share or to prove the abuse of a dominant position. But the law – historically quite intolerant of monopolies – did not have to allow this concentration to happen. Yet it did.

[43] D Markovits, *The Meritocracy Trap: How America's Foundational Myth Feeds Inequality, Dismantles the Middle Class, and Devours the Elite*, Illustrated edn (Penguin Press, 2019) 12–45.

[44] In the EU, 92% of residents have internet access, the highest percentages being Luxemburg (99.3%) and the Netherlands (99.2%), and the lowest Bulgaria (80.4%) and Croatia (83.4%). Source: ec.europa.eu/eurostat/statistics-explained/index.php?title=Digital_economy_and_society_statistics_-_households_and_individuals.

[45] For a marvellous account of the development of the so-called 'cyber trespass' laws in the US, see TE Kadri, 'Platforms as Blackacres' (2021) 68 *UCLA Law Review* 1184, 1194–221.

[46] ibid 1187–91.

[47] RH Bork, *Antitrust Paradox*, 1st edn (Free Press, 1978); Wu (n 21) 102–18.

The sociotechnological world we live in, including the legally facilitated data collection and for-profit usage by a handful of giant companies, is contingent and weird. It is not random; we can know the reasons why it turned out the way it did. But it did not have to be the way it is. And, when we look to the future, we should remember it could be very different. Now, how exactly the sociotechnical world we live in *should* look like is a more difficult question.

III. On why the EU's Goals Could have been More Ambitious

It is not automatically obvious what the goals of the data law's reform should be. At least two possible worlds are conceivable; two worlds that can hardly coexist. Let us note that from merely knowing that (i) the world does not have to be the way it is,[48] and that (ii) there is something wrong with it from the standpoint of privacy, competition, surplus distribution, etc, we cannot deduce the exact goal of legal reform. Political decisions must be made. These decisions are obviously constrained by constitutional law stipulating both what aim the law must and must not pursue. However, between these two extremes lies the space of legislative freedom, subject to political and not legal reasoning. This is illustrated in Figure 4.1 below.

Figure 4.1 Space for legislative freedom

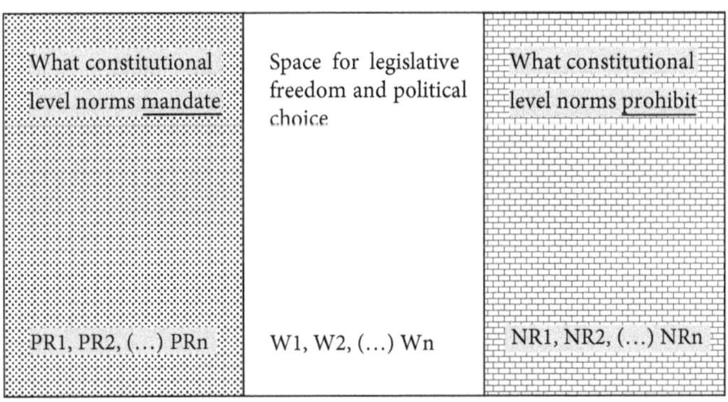

Constitutional level norms, either national constitutions or the EU Treaties, create positive constraints (PR) and negative constraints (NR) for the lawmaker. To know these, one needs to engage in legal (technocratic) thinking.[49] However,

[48] As both the code and the social practices can be modified through the law, Lessig (n 25).
[49] F Schauer, *Thinking Like a Lawyer: A New Introduction to Legal Reasoning*, reprint edn (Harvard University Press, 2012).

between those two extremes exist several conceivable worlds (W) that are both factually possible and legally permissible. For example, in Poland it is currently prohibited to drink beer in public parks. Polish lawmakers are free to lift the ban or to keep it. Neither world is factually impossible nor constitutionally impermissible. The Polish Constitution does not require that drinking in public be prohibited nor that it is allowed. It is a political choice.

In the realm of data law, several factually possible and legally permissible worlds also exist. Let us imagine two such worlds. On the one hand, we could strive for a world of much less data collection. As large swaths of data currently collected and processed are personal data,[50] and the GDPR (concretising the fundamental right to personal data protection)[51] envisions the principles of data minimisation and purpose limitation, our goal could be a radical decrease in 'commercial surveillance'. Although scholars point out that the GDPR merely scratches the surface here, the EU does close to nothing about this.[52]

On the other hand, we could strive for a world of the same (or an even higher) level of data collection, characterised however by a much broader access to data and/or much fairer distribution of surplus. This seems to be the direction pursued by the DGA and the DA,[53] which however note that the goals of personal data protection should be simultaneously upheld.[54] And yet, once we move from the level of stated goals to the specific provisions of these regulations, it is difficult not to become disappointed.

In its Data Strategy, the EU holds that it 'can become a leading role model for a society empowered by data'[55] and that 'Europe aims to capture the benefits of better use of data, including greater productivity and competitive markets, but also improvements in health and well-being, environment, transparent governance and convenient public services.'[56] The Strategy notes that 'Data is the lifeblood of economic development'[57] and 'will also fuel the wide implementation of transformative practices'[58] yet underscores its commitment to 'European values and fundamental rights and the conviction that the human being is and should remain at the centre.'[59] A certain tension runs throughout the document, ie, the realization

[50] N Purtova, 'The Law of Everything. Broad Concept of Personal Data and Future of EU Data Protection Law' (2018) 10 *Law, Innovation and Technology* 40.

[51] G González Fuster, *The Emergence of Personal Data Protection as a Fundamental Right of the EU*, vol 16 (Springer International Publishing, 2014).

[52] With the sole exception of the attempt to harmonise the procedures. On why this won't help much, see Bastos and Pałka (n 39) 17–20.

[53] Recitals 2 and 3 DGA; recitals 1, 2, 4, 5 DA.

[54] Recitals 4, 7 DGA; recitals 7 and 8 DA.

[55] EU Data Strategy (n 13) 1.

[56] ibid.

[57] ibid 2.

[58] ibid 3. On the analysis and critique of various metaphors used for talking about data, see A Fisher and T Streinz, 'Confronting Data Inequality' (2021) 60 *Columbia Journal of Transnational Law* 829, 837–42; JM Nolin, 'Data as Oil, Infrastructure or Asset? Three Metaphors of Data as Economic Value' (2019) 18 *Journal of Information, Communication and Ethics in Society* 28; C Puschmann and J Burgess, 'Metaphors of Big Data' (2014) 8 *International Journal of Communication* 1690.

[59] ibid 4, British spelling original.

that economic goals require wide access to data whereas protection of fundamental rights might require constraints,[60] yet the document's tone suggests an optimism that properly thought-through regulation can advance these objectives simultaneously. The Strategy sets forth to combat problems like data concentration in the hands of just few companies,[61] lack of data availability,[62] low data quality,[63] or limited access to data infrastructures.[64]

In short: the EU's 2020 Strategy for Data envisions a world where the Union is a leading role model, harnessing all the benefits of a data-rich society, while combatting all the potential problems to individual's fundamental rights and collective interests. Clearly, those are ambitious aspirations. These aspirations are to be realized by several policy initiatives, including two equally ambitiously named regulations: the DGA and the DA. However, the names are possibly the only ambitious features of these instruments.

The DGA centers around four issues: (i) conditions for reuse of certain categories of data held by public sector bodies; (ii) regulation of 'data intermediation services'; (iii) a voluntary framework for entities willing to engage in the so-called 'data altruism'; (iv) establishment of the European Data Innovation Board.[65] Will these be meaningful steps in realising the ambitions of the Data Strategy? In theory, they could be, yet a closer look at the specific provisions raises doubts.

Regarding the first issue, the DGA 'does not create any obligation on public sector bodies to allow the re-use of data'.[66] So what *does* it do? It relies on other national, or Union, laws mandating reuse and limits itself to a prohibition of exclusive reuse arrangements (though with far-reaching exceptions),[67] and creation of a series of information obligations,[68] general rules for fairness in conditions for access, and some technical specifications on implementations.[69] These are important moves, without a doubt, but moves of a third-order importance. The real game concerning reuse takes place elsewhere in national or Union laws, and the DGA only tightens regulations on the margins. The remaining three issues are equally underwhelming: it is difficult to imagine how a market for new data intermediation services should emerge *after* it has been regulated, why anyone would want to engage in data altruism free-willingly (given all the new constraints created, and close to zero incentives), or how a newly created board, with no funding abilities, will bolster innovation. The entire DGA reads like a list of marginally good ideas,

[60] I explore this tension elsewhere: Pałka (n 2).
[61] EU Data Strategy (n 13) 3.
[62] ibid 6.
[63] ibid 8.
[64] ibid 9.
[65] Art 1.1 DGA.
[66] Art 1.2 DGA.
[67] Art 4 DGA.
[68] Which, as has been shown, usually fail as a regulatory instrument; see O Ben-Shahar and CE Schneider, *More Than You Wanted to Know: The Failure of Mandated Disclosure* (Princeton University Press, 2014).
[69] Art 5 DGA.

accompanied by exceptions, whose job is to improve things on the margins as conveniently as possible. So not disproportionate.

This shape of the DGA is especially saddening and disappointing given its title, echoing vivid academic debates held under the 'data governance' label.[70] For several years now, scholars aware of the shortcomings of the individual-focused models of data law have been calling for collective approaches to deciding who should be allowed to do what with data, and under what conditions.[71] 'Data governance', understood as in these contributions, would cover answers to difficult questions like: when should individual consent legalise data use, and when should some collective mechanism step in? What should be the legal character of the collective mechanism: top-down regulation by legislatures, administrative regulations, or some type of collective bargaining?[72] How to deal with externalities stemming from data processing?[73] These are complicated and politically loaded questions, answers to which are likely to cause disagreement. Yet, those are questions central to 'data governance'. Meanwhile, the shies away from any of these, and deals with non-controversial issues like information obligations,[74] harmonisation of procedures that must exist anyway, regulation of non-existent industries, voluntary frameworks, and creation of new advisory bodies.

The DA goes a little further.[75] It creates a right 'of users to access and use data generated by the use of products or related services'.[76] This is a meaningful change. In practice, users of products making up the IoT – smart cars, toothbrushes, fridges, washing machines, vacuum cleaners, etc – would have a right to access data generated by their use of the product (free of charge)[77] and request that it be shared with other companies (against remuneration).[78] The idea is to allow third parties to monitor the lifecycle of products and develop markets for related services. Also purely legally, this constitutes a visible change in the regulatory landscape, as the Act limits rights under the Union's Database Directive[79] and

[70] For an overview and discussion, see A Pericles Lima Monteiro, 'Privacy at a Crossroads' in B Brożek et al (eds), *Research Handbook on Law and Technology* (Edward Elgar Publishing, 2023).

[71] For an early discussion of the pros and cons of both individual and collective approaches to data governance, see Solove (n 4); for a then-heterodox, now prescient, reply, see JE Cohen, 'What Privacy Is For' (2012) 126 *Harvard Law Review* 1904; for a comprehensive argument for collective data governance model, see Cohen (n 18); for a vision of how data governance could occur through democratic frames, see Viljoen (n 3); for the discussion of collective governance mechanisms given the inference character of the data economy, see Solow-Niederman (n 5); for my own modest attempt at wrestling with these issues, see Pałka (n 3).

[72] On the idea of how the last one could look, see J Lanier and EG Weyl, 'A Blueprint for a Better Digital Society' (2018) *Harvard Business Review* 18.

[73] See Ben-Shahar (n 29).

[74] Famously uncontroversial and ineffective; Ben-Shahar and Schneider (n 68).

[75] See Bohdan Widła's chapter in this tome.

[76] Art 4 DA.

[77] ibid.

[78] Art 5 DA.

[79] Art 35 DA. For a criticial discussion, see also Bohdan Widła's chapter in this volume and M Husovec and E Derclaye, 'Why the Sui Generis Database Clause in the Data Act Is Counter-Productive and How to Improve It?' (8 March 2022), available at papers.ssrn.com/abstract=4052390.

extends the unfair terms logic to some B2B contracts on making data available.[80] However, the Act also features some important exceptions. For example, users are barred from using the obtained data 'to develop a product that competes with the product from which the data originate'.[81] The same prohibition applies to corporations with whom the user has their data shared.[82] Hence, we want to boost competition, but not too much. So not disproportionate.

Most importantly, however, the DA limits users' right to access the data generated by physical devices and does not apply to data generated by using online services. Hence, a user can request to access or share data generated by their use of Rumba vacuums, but not by their use of Google. They can have a third party monitor data about their use of electric toothbrushes, to help control their dental health, but cannot request Meta to share, in real time, data about their use of Facebook and Instagram to help monitor their mental health.[83] Of course, IoT devices generate a lot of data of some economic value. But much more intricate data is generated by individuals' smartphones or, more precisely, services on these smartphones. And this data is out of the DA's scope.

How to explain the discrepancy between the ambitious proclaimed goals of the EU's data policy and the modest goals actually pursued by the legislation? Why, given what the EU *could* be doing – forcefully rendering services interoperable, encouraging new modes for collective data governance, empowering users to directly profit from the data they help generate for online services or, conversely, significantly limiting data collection – it is doing so little? The explanations, of course, will be multifaceted. Certainly, they will combine the political pressures of various lobbying groups[84] and, possibly, reluctance regarding the prospects of drastically changing the sociotechnical reality without sufficient legitimacy. However, I would claim that an undertheorised reason is precisely the lack of regulatory imagination of various actors engaged in the lawmaking process (the proportionality mindset). To know what the goals could be, one needs to *imagine* other possible worlds. And this is not a technocratic exercise. Yet, one can find comfort in claiming that the stipulation of the minimalist goals was a result of precisely such reasoning, legal and seemingly apolitical (proportionality washing).

The proportionality principle is a fundamental tool for taming the excesses of the lawmakers who want to do too much. Yet, when used as an epistemic tool constraining the lawmakers' imagination and the justificatory tool making them confident in the results, it can unexpectedly lead lawmakers to do too little. And when the EU lawmakers proceed this way, we can witness a paradoxical outcome: of doing too much while doing too little.

[80] Art 13 DA.

[81] Art 4.4 DA.

[82] Art 6.2.(e) DA.

[83] One can, of course, attempt to claim that the GDPR's data portability right is sufficient here. However, notice how it does not create a mechanism for facilitating the *real time* transfer to a third party, only the right of the data subject to acquire the data once per request.

[84] On the phenomenon in general, see Bruycker and Beyers (n 9); on strategies adopted by the so-called 'big tech', see Tarrant and Cowen (n 9).

IV. On the Proportionality Paradoxes in EU Data Policy

Let us return to Figure 4.1 above to visually illustrate the concepts I've been using thus far: proportionality-washing and proportionality mindset. Remember how the space for legislative freedom, where choices are motivated politically and not legally, is constrained by what the constitutional level norms require on the one hand and prohibit on the other. However, when proportionality-washing occurs, lawmakers falsely claim (in good or bad faith) that certain choices they are making are mandated by the law, whereas others are not available. in Figure 4.2 below, these would be 'W1' and 'Wn,' respectively.

Figure 4.2 Proportionality-washing and proportionality mindset

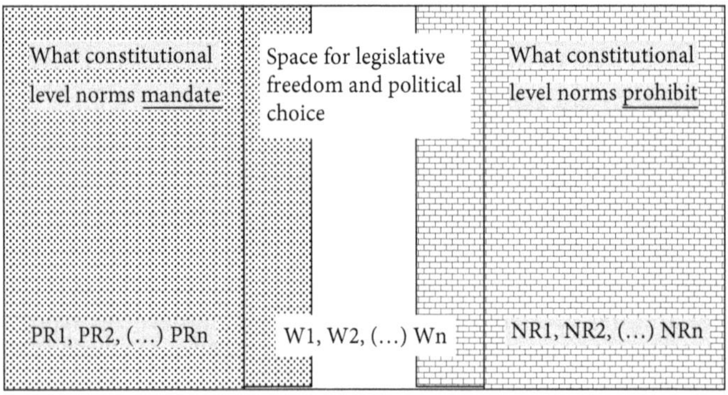

Notice also the '(...)', indicating that there exists an indefinite number of possible worlds that the lawmakers could be trying to achieve. In a sense, this set will be infinite, if we image making very slight changes to the specifics (eg increasing the highest possible fine by one cent). However, if we remain on a general level here, eg, imagine that there exists a W3 where individuals are compensated for the use of data they help generate, and a W4 where they do not (disregarding the specifics), we can assume that number is finite. In this example, imagine that there exist 10 possible worlds that are constitutionally permissible that the EU could be instituting with its legislation. 'Proportionality mindset', limiting the imagination of the lawmakers, would shorten the list of all possible worlds considered from 10 to less; in our picture there is only W2 (as W1 and Wn were eliminated by proportionality-washing).

By way of a concrete example, imagine a world (W3) in which individuals *are* compensated for the use of data they help generate by using products or services.[85] In this world, whenever a corporation captures data it later uses for training machine learning algorithms (eg data on how people drive their Teslas,[86] or fix

[85] As argued for by Lanier (n 6).

[86] M Harris, 'The Radical Scope of Tesla's Data Hoard' *IEEE Spectrum* (3 August 2022), available at spectrum.ieee.org/tesla-autopilot-data-scope.

automated translations, or react to content by labelling it enraging or saddening) it must: (i) estimate how much it would have to pay a human generating such data as a job; and (ii) pay the money out to the individual. Of course, the company would be free to start charging users (more) for their services to offset the loss, or to refrain from such data collection. Suddenly, we would have much more information about the market available, not necessarily in the form of disclosures[87] but discernable from corporate action.[88] We would have a better idea about the size of the surplus kept by the corporations. We would encourage competition in this regard. Such a world is physically possible and, arguably, neither unconstitutional nor required by the Treaties or national constitutions. It exists out there, in the space for legislative freedom and political choice.

Yet, the EU did not even come close to pondering the pros and cons of such a solution, neither in the DA proposal, nor the DGA proposal, ie, the instruments suggesting that if such measures were to be adopted, they should find their home in these acts precisely. Of course, the EU did not have to consider such a possibility (though it could have). However, it also did not have to preclude the Member States from considering such possibilities (and it arguably did). Why is that?

The legal basis for the DGA and DA is Article 114 TFEU. As this is an area of shared competence, once the Union has acted, the Member States' action becomes preempted.[89] Of course, this does not mean that Germany or France cannot do anything in the area of data law, but their action becomes much more constrained. For example, the Member States cannot broaden the objective scope of DA to online services. Or, given that the access to the data should be given 'for free', they will have very hard time now requiring remuneration *for the users*. But why would the Member States even want to legislate here?

This takes us close to a very contentious issue in the EU law – one that clearly sets it apart from American though – ie, the question of how much and how soon to harmonise state legislation. In the US, the dominant view is that of 'laboratories of democracy'.[90] The idea could be, at the risk of simplicity, reconstructed as follows: it is (sometimes) *good* for state laws to be different. For example, if California adopts online privacy protections of some sort, Illinois of another, and Texas does not, in a decade we will be able to observe the effects of each and choose policy measures (in other states or at the federal level) based on the documented experiences. This is good because, especially when dealing with new types of problems, we do *not know* what the exact effects of a regulation will be, we do

[87] Which we know don't work very well; see Ben-Shahar and Schneider (n 68).

[88] For a classic discussion of how the price mechanism is a source of information, see FA Hayek, 'The Use of Knowledge in Society' (1945) 35 *The American Economic Review* 519; For my contemporaty take, see P Pałka, 'Algorithmic Central Planning: Between Efficiency and Freedom' (2020) 83 *Law and Contemporary Problems* 125.

[89] Craig and Burca (n 16) 84.

[90] For a reconstruction of this commonly held idea, and its critique, see CW Tyler and HK Gerken, 'The Myth of the Laboratories of Democracy' (2022) 122 *Columbia Law Review* 2187.

not know what the optimal measures are, and so pre-empting states' action too soon might lead us to suboptimal, and very difficult to change, federal legislation.

In the EU, the thinking seems to be exactly the opposite. What we fear is 'fragmentation' and legal uncertainty, standing in the way of completing the Single Market.[91] Oftentimes this fear is warranted as the EU, unlike the US, does not yet have a fully fledged internal market, national laws are written in different languages, and legal differences indeed might stand in the way of economic integration. But in the case of data policy, the question is if the EU has jumped the gun. Notice how, in the case of the GDPR, the regulation followed almost two decades of experience with irective 95/46, which in turn harmonised re-existing national laws.[92]

With DA and DGA the EU has decided to adopt a regulation without first passing directives and with a very limited Member State legislative action preceding the adoption. In its explanatory memorandum for the DA, the European Commission wrote:

> Given the cross-border nature of the use of data and the many areas of impact of the Data Act, the issues this proposal deals with *cannot* be effectively addressed at Member State level. Fragmentation arising out of differences between national rules should be avoided, as it would lead to higher transactional costs, lack of transparency, legal uncertainty and undesirable forum shopping. … A regulation *is necessary in light of the goal of comprehensive harmonisation* pursued by the proposal, in order to ensure legal certainty and transparency for economic operators … and to provide legal and natural persons in all Member States with the same level of legally enforceable rights and obligations, to ensure consistent enforcement in all Member States, as well as effective cooperation between the competent authorities of different Member States.[93]

Notice how the language of this passage is a clear example of proportionality-washing. In the EC's narrative, the choice of the goal, and of the instrument, seems inevitable, almost deduced from the Treaties. But this is not the case. First, it is not true that Member States already adopted diverging regulations on data access. In reality, there was no lack of transparency or legal uncertainty in this regard. The Union acted preemptively, to ensure that such problems would not arise. But on what basis did the European Community decide that if Germany, Portugal and Poland adopt legislation aiming to create W3, and France, Greece and Latvia different legislation, this must lead to legal uncertainty or lack of transparency? Second, what is the Treaty basis for ensuring the same rights in access to data generated by IoT devices? These are not fundamental rights, but policy instruments.[94] Third,

[91] On the overview of idea of integration through law, see L Azoulai, "Integration through Law' and Us' (2016) 14 *International Journal of Constitutional Law* 449.

[92] Streinz (n 2) 904 ('before there was European data protection law, there was data protection law in Europe').

[93] DA Proposal 7–8. Emphasis added.

[94] See Konrad Gliściński's chapter in this volume.

where does the goal of 'comprehensive harmonisation' of rules on access to data come from? Certainly not the Treaties! And nowhere in the explanatory memorandum does the Commission actually demonstrate that full harmonisation is necessary to construct the single market.

Let me restate the caveat I made in the introduction: please do not read this critique as an objection to Union regulation in general, or any stance taken in the 'EU versus Member States' debate, or an opposition to data regulation as such. My only point is that the specific regulations adopted by the EU are far from optimal and yet, while adopting them, the EU has pre-empted Member State legislative action which could be a vehicle for regulatory experimentation. With the DA and DGA adopted, the EU's data law has become fixed.

By engaging in proportionality-washing the EU lawmakers did much less than they could have and, arguably, should have. They stopped the Member States from experimenting in the area of data policy. And they have done so without ever proving that this action was necessary to achieve the objectives of the Treaties. Article TEU states 'Under the principle of proportionality, the content and form of Union action shall not exceed what is necessary to achieve the objectives of the Treaties.'

In this sense, the EU has done too much – pre-empted Member State action where it was not necessary – by doing too little, ie, not introducing any meaningful changes to the European data governance laws. And that is the paradox of proportionality in the EU data policy.

V. Conclusion

The argument of this chapter has been that the proportionality principle, albeit a great tool for taming the excesses of the lawmaker who wants to do too much, might also serve as an excuse for the lawmaker who wishes to do too little. This has been the case regarding the EU's data policy. The EU has missed the chance to introduce meaningful changes to its data law, failed to engage in proper exercise in regulatory imagination, and has closed the doors for the Member States willing to do so. It did too much while doing too little.

The overall lesson from the analysis provided above could be that proportionality analysis is necessary for creating good legislation but absolutely insufficient. In certain cases, engaging in legal and technocratic thinking too soon might make good policymaking more difficult. There is no legal tool or legal method that can replace creative thinking in attempting to change the world for the better. Although, when faced with difficult tasks like that of creating a data policy, one might be tempted to find comfort in known legalistic approaches, one should resist that temptation.

At the time of writing (autumn 2023), the EU's digital law introduced by the 2019–2024 von der Leyen Commission seems close to completion. With the DMA, the DSA, the DGA and the DA on the books, and political agreement reached over the AI Act, a certain window of legislative opportunity in the EU has closed. Now, legions of lawyers will continue developing the doctrine based on these laws. Although developing doctrine is an important task as, most certainly, new problems and judgments have arisen, I would urge the reader to remain critical. The EU's most recent data policy is contingent. It did not have to be the way it is, and itis most certainly suboptimal. When a new legislative round opens, and new acts are proposed and discussed, let us remember that. And let us use the lessons learned from the unimpressive data policy concretising an ambitious strategy, to do (at least a little bit) better the next time.

5

Between Rights, Interests and Risk – The Role of Proportionality Balancing in EU Digital Law

JAN CZARNOCKI

I. Introduction

In this chapter, I argue that EU digital law[1] faces two challenges that may jeopardise its objectives: rights and economic interests protection. I claim that the proportionality principle is necessary to simultaneously achieve these objectives and address the diagnosed challenges. The first challenge is complexity, related to rapid legislative inflation contributing to a lack of a clear sense of the rights and obligations of parties in a given case. The second is indeterminacy, which stems from EU digital law usually pursuing those two structurally conflicting objectives, to which a similar degree of legitimacy is given – protection of rights and economic interests. These two objectives simultaneously appear throughout the majority of EU digital laws.[2]

The proportionality principle is used to solve both these challenges and, therefore, should be central to the digital law discourse. As a judicial methodology, the principle aids in cutting through complexity, indeterminacy and reconciling rights protection and economic interests in a given case. The principle also helps to clarify the role of the risk-based approach when rights and

[1] By 'EU digital law' I understand the totality of the EU laws whose purposes is to regulate broadly understood digital technologies. For the useful overview of the current state of EU digital law, see 'A dataset on the EU legislation for the digital world' (Bruegel, 16 November 20231), available at www.bruegel.org/dataset/dataset-eu-legislation-digital-world.

[2] See section III.B. Structural duality is surely not something unique to EU digital law. Various other strands of law pursue seemingly contradictory objectives. Yet, given the simultaneous proportionality and risk reliance of these laws, the impact on legal practice is different, as explained in section III.

interests are balanced.[3] However, burdened with numerous shortcomings, the principle is capable of achieving only this much. The fundamental political conflicts regarding right and wrong in the digital milieu will persist, as the principle's application rarely provides generalisable answers to contentious issues.[4] The risk-based approach's pervasiveness in digital regulation further complicates the picture.

The principle is criticised by numerous scholars for its arbitrariness when applied.[5] However, I argue that imperfections of proportionality are its feature rather than a bug. There is nothing wrong with proportionality's imperfection and related judges' discretion, provided that arguments and reasons for a decision are transparent, decision-makers are accountable, and decisions themselves can be challenged. Virtue ethics and rhetorical perspective on law, and Alexy's law's ideal dimension argument, help to explain and understand why.[6]

I argue that simultaneously acknowledging the vital role of the proportionality principle and being conscious of its imperfections is the only feasible way forward to reconcile rights and interests, other than rigid and casuistic regulation through rules. Moreover, the principle benefits legal discourse as it helps unveil real social tensions underneath the particular legal case and the extra-legal factors guiding its solution. The example can be value judgements and discretion by the courts or interests pursued by economic actors covered by the mixture of risk-based and rights rhetorics.

To illustrate the above points, in section II, I describe the proportionality principle and review its criticism. Further, in the section III, I explain what I mean by the rising complexity of EU digital law and what challenges it poses. Next, I describe why EU digital law faces an indeterminacy challenge due to a duality of the objectives it pursues – that is, both protection of rights and economic interests. Further, I describe various incarnations of the proportionality principle as appearing in EU digital law. I will briefly discuss the interrelation between the proportionality principle and the risk-based approach and how the principle was applied in a few chosen landmark cases. I further explain why the proportionality principle is embedded in these laws due to EU digital law objectives' duality and must be applied whenever a conflict emerges. Only then, in section IV, will I describe how the criticism of proportionality can be countered with Robert Alexy's theory of law as a rational discourse and his law's ideal dimension argument. I conclude in section V by proposing that seeing proportionality as a legal virtue is the way to the principle's effective and pragmatic application in EU digital law.

[3] For the overview of the risk-based approach in the GDPR, DSA and AI Act, see generally G De Gregorio and P Dunn, 'The European Risk-Based Approaches: Connecting Constitutional Dots in the Digital Age' (2022) 59 *Common Market Law Review*, available at kluwerlawonline.com/journalarticle/Common+Market+Law+Review/59.2/COLA2022032.

[4] Principle is applied case-by-case, for more see es R Alexy, *A Theory of Constitutional* Rights, 1st edn (Oxford University Press, 2010).

[5] For the overview of the criticism of the proportionality principle, see section III.C.

[6] See section IV.

II. Proportionality Principle in the EU Digital Law and its Discontents

A. Constitutional Role of Proportionality Balancing

The proportionality principle is a constitutional principle that provides a legal methodology to determine whether a limitation to the right introduced by law can be reconciled with, eg, a constitution or another higher-level act (in the case of the EU, these are the EU Treaties).[7] The principle is present in most modern Western constitutions and is an important standard in international and European human rights law.[8] It is also a general principle of the EU law.[9] The proportionality principle can be found in numerous limitation clauses, whose role is to define the scope of permitted limitations to the right.[10] Usually, a limitation clause states that a certain right needs to be necessary and proportionate, and pursue the public interest acceptable in a democratic society. Limitation clauses often also state that the limitation to the right cannot breach the essence of a subject right in order to be proportionate.[11]

To evaluate whether a law is proportionate, that is, whether a limitation to a right is reconcilable with the constitution of a democratic society, the proportionality principle usually envisions a four-step test.[12] According to Alexy and Barak's conceptualisation of the principle, the first step is to evaluate whether a subject measure pursues a legitimate goal or proper purpose, which justifies a limitation to the right. The second step is to investigate a rational connection or suitability of a measure to achieve a legitimate goal or purpose. That means that a measure must be fit to pursue an envisioned goal. There must be a reasonable expectation that the measure will achieve its purpose. The third step is to inquire whether a measure chosen is not excessive or whether the least harmful one for a right was chosen. It means whether a measure is necessary. The third part of the test demands assessing whether other, less restrictive measures could have been chosen. The last part of the proportionality test is *stricto sensu* proportionality balancing, which means that a measure's benefits must be balanced against a detriment to a right. A negative impact on a right cannot be disproportionate to a benefit achieved by a measure. This step requires essentially a value judgement

[7] For the general theory of the principle and its structure, see esp Alexy (n 4), and A Barak, *Proportionality: Constitutional Rights and Their Limitations* (Cambridge University Press 2012).

[8] For the general overview of how the principle is present in the Western constitutional and international law, see Barak (ibid) ch 8.

[9] Consolidated version of the Treaty on European Union (TEU), Title I – Common Provisions, Article 5 (ex Article 5 TEC), OJ C 202, 7.6.2016, p 18.

[10] See, eg, Art 52 Charter of Fundamental Rights of the European Union, 2000, C 364/1 (CFEU). For the general overview of the character of limitation clauses see: Barak (n 7) ch 5.

[11] Art 52 of the CFEU.

[12] See n 7.

about the relative weights of competing rights and interests.[13] Proportionality is also a facet of the subsidiarity principle, which demands that what can be regulated and governed by an authority at a lower level of an institutional hierarchy should remain so.[14]

The proportionality principle played an important role in resolving landmark digital law cases.[15] The following cases showcase how proportionality resolves conflicts between competing rights and interests. In *Volker und Markus Schecke and Eifert* the CJEU decided that publication on a freely accessible website of information naming beneficiaries of EU funds and amounts received is disproportionate in pursuing general interest against the privacy of the beneficiaries of the funds.[16] Limitations to rights should be applied only as strictly necessary, which was not the case when such data was indiscriminately disclosed, even if taxpayers' interest in transparency as to public funds was at stake.[17] In *Digital Rights Ireland* the CJEU invalidated the Data Retention Directive,[18] which allowed for the retention of electronic communication data by service providers for the purposes of national security and the fight against terrorism. The CJEU stated that the EU legislature adopted the measure that exceeds what proportionality demands, specifically because of the lack of strict necessity of indiscriminate time and space data retention of not predetermined categories of individuals.[19]

The examples above show that courts often resort to proportionality balancing in order to weigh and compare often incommensurable values that are very difficult to reconcile against each other, such as rights to privacy against the public interest in access to information. The difficulty lies in both mentioned rights pursuing the objective of a democratic society – a priority needs to be given only to one in a given case, with potential additional safeguards for another. Proportionality then also demands nuance and respect for all values at stake to the extent possible. Such respect is to be achieved through following proportionality as a procedure to arrive at a just (and proportionate) outcome.

[13] See R Alexy, *Law's Ideal Dimension* (Oxford University Press, 2021) ch 11. There, the author explains his methodology for weighting conflicting rights and interests.

[14] Art 5 of TEU.

[15] See esp Digital Rights Ireland Ltd v Minister for Communications, Marine and Natural Resources and Others, Kärntner Landesregierung and Others [2014] ECLI:EU:C:2014:238 (Joined Cases C-293/12 and C-594/12); Google Spain SL, Google Inc v Agencia Española de Protección de Datos (AEPD), Mario Costeja González [2014] ECLI:EU:C:2014:317 (Case C-131/12); Maximillian Schrems v Data Protection Commissioner [2015] ECLI:EU:C:2015:650 (Case C-362/14); Bodil Lindqvist v Åklagarkammaren i Jönköping [2003] ECLI:EU:C:2003:596 (Case C-101/01); Volker und Markus Schecke GbR and Hartmut Eifert v Land Hessen [2010] ECLI:EU:C:2010:662 (Joined Cases C-92/09 and C-93/09).

[16] *Volker und Markus Schecke GbR and Hartmut Eifert v Land Hessen* [2010] ECLI:EU:C:2010:662 (Joined Cases C-92/09 and C-93/09) [77], [79], [85], [86].

[17] ibid [65].

[18] Directive 2006/24/EC of the European Parliament and of the Council of 15 March 2006 on the retention of data generated or processed in connection with the provision of publicly available electronic communications services or of public communications networks and amending Directive 2002/58/EC, OJ 2006 L105/54 (Data Retention Directive).

[19] *Digital Rights Ireland* [65], [57] and [59].

B. Proportionality as a Way to Resolve Conflicts in the Digital Milieu

However, the proportionality principle is not only a constitutional methodology to balance rights and interests and invalidate unconstitutional laws (or stating that their application would violate the treaty order, in case of the EU law). It can also be found at the sub-constitutional, secondary law level as a way to resolve conflicts or rights and interests where more than one law applies, such as conflicts between rights to privacy and data protection, intellectual property, or freedom of expression.[20] There is also an internal proportionality of particular laws, where conflict of rights and interests need to be reconciled internally or with a recourse to a fundamental rights doctrine.[21] For instance, although the GDPR focuses on rights to privacy and data protection, it also provides numerous norms demanding proportionality balancing that is internal to data protection law, but with respect to other rights and interests. Examples of such internal balancing are rights and interests such as freedom of expression[22] or scientific research.[23] All these incarnations of the proportionality principle can be found across EU digital law, with underlining rights provided in the CFEU and Treaties and their proportionality limitation clauses.[24] Fundamental rights and Treaty law are an umbrella aiming to unify and integrate the EU law and its interpretation downstream. The proportionality test is used as a reconciliation tool between rights.

There is another level of abstraction[25] at which three other types of proportionality balancing are present in the EU digital law: 1) proportionality in the form of rules established by the legislator; 2) proportionality balancing through principles to be yet reconciled; and 3) risk-based approach and risk management as a form of private rights and interests-balancing, with the digital rights serving as a trump to challenge the balance established by a private party.

In the first case, the legislator establishes the balance of rights and interests that is a predefined balance in a given case. For instance, data rights, when evoked, enforce a pre-established balance between the interests and rights of a data subject

[20] Respectively, Promusicae v Telefónica de España SAU [2008] ECLI:EU:C:2008:54 (Case C-275/06) and GC and Others v Commission nationale de l'informatique et des libertés (CNIL) (C-136/17) [2019] ECLI:EU:C:2019:773.

[21] For the in-depth analysis of internal proportionality balancing in the GDPR, and how the GDPR internally reconciles the right to data protection with other rights, see J Ausloos, *The Right to Erasure in EU Data Protection Law* (Oxford University Press, 2020).

[22] Art 85 of Regulation (EU) 2016/679 of the European Parliament and of the Council of 27 April 2016 on the protection of natural persons with regard to the processing of personal data and on the free movement of such data, and repealing Directive 95/46/EC (General Data Protection Regulation) OJ L 119/1 (GDPR).

[23] Art 89 of he GDPR.

[24] Art 5 TEU and Art 52 CFEU.

[25] For the description of the method of levels of abstraction (LoA), see L Floridi, *The Philosophy of Information* (Oxford University Press, 2011) ch 3.

and a controller.[26] Also, the proposed Artificial Intelligence Act's (AI Act) list of prohibited AI practices codifies a balance in which such prohibited uses are not proportionate to many rights protected by law and thus outlawed.[27] The balance is established by virtue of a democratic legitimacy vested in the legislator. Thus, a rule prohibiting certain behaviour provides an already established balance of rights and interests, which is legitimate in a democratic society. What a lawyer needs to do in such a case is a clear, traditional, syllogistic mode of legal thinking and practice – subsumption of an abstract legal norm (eg prohibiting sensitive data processing[28]) to facts in a given case.[29]

In the second case, that of applying principles, the balance needs to be established by their proper application against other applicable principles. Conflicting principles need to be balanced.[30] As an effect of the balancing exercise in a particular case, a rule emerges, which can be analogously utilised further. In such a situation, the balance can be established by the party initiating regulated activity, then challenged by other subject parties, and finally adjudicated by a court. Additionally, the law can, in an abstract way, give priority to certain rights and interests, providing an abstract guideline for setting up a balance.[31]

To exemplify two above-mentioned types of proportionality balancing (pre-established by the rules and to be established through principles application), when data protection law is applied, it often needs to be reconciled against other rights protected by the CFEU or other secondary laws, such as those protecting copyright or freedom of expression. The objective of privacy and data protection also needs to be reconciled internally against exceptions provided in the GDPR.[32] The examples of complex proportionality balancing, where numerous rights were to be reconciled and at stake, were *Google vs Spain*[33] and *Promusicae*.[34] In the first case, still based on the legacy Data Protection Directive,[35] the Court needed to

[26] Chs 2, 3 and 4 GDPR.

[27] Art 5 European Commission, Proposal for a Regulation of the European Parliament and of the Council laying down harmonised rules on Artificial Intelligence (Artificial Intelligence Act) and amending certain Union legislative acts, COM(2021) 206 final, 2021/0106 (COD) (proposed AI Act – EU Commission version).

[28] Art 9 GDPR.

[29] On the difference between subsumption and balancing, see R Alexy, 'On Balancing and Subsumption. A Structural Comparison' (2003) 16 *Ratio Juris* 433.

[30] See n 7.

[31] For example 'EDPS Guidelines on Assessing the Proportionality of Measures That Limit the Fundamental Rights to Privacy and to the Protection of Personal Data' (European Data Protection Supervisor, 25 February 2019), available at edps.europa.eu/data-protection/our-work/publications/guidelines/edps-guidelines-assessing-proportionality-measures_en.

[32] Arts 85, 86, 87, 88 and 89 GDPR.

[33] Google Spain SL and Google Inc v Agencia Española de Protección de Datos (AEPD) and Mario Costeja González (C-131/12) [2014] ECLI:EU:C:2014:317.

[34] Productores de Música de España (Promusicae) v Telefónica de España SAU (C-275/06) [2008] ECLI:EU:C:2008:54.

[35] Directive 95/46/EC of the European Parliament and of the Council of 24 October 1995 on the protection of individuals with regard to the processing of personal data and on the free movement of such data, OJ 1995 L 281/31 (Data Protection Directive).

reconcile the right to privacy with a public interest in access to information. It also needed to decide on the scope of responsibility of search engine providers for the personal data they process. Beyond others, the outcome is the famous rule and right then transposed into the GDPR, the right to be forgotten.[36] Through this right, the CJEU established a permanent balance in personal data privacy against public interest in access to information. Now, by default, the right to be forgotten entitles the deletion of data by a controller if no other persistent legitimate interest (to be proven) exists at the time of a request for deletion.

In the second case, *Promusicae*, the CJEU left it to the Member States to establish a balance between data protection and intellectual property rights in their national laws. The CJEU stated that the Data Protection Directive does not demand enactment of the laws transposing the Directive in a way that requires internet services providers to disclose personal data of potential infringers to those that pursue civil lawsuits to protect their intellectual property. Thus, the CJEU left the issue for further balancing to the Member States legislatures or their courts. The CJEU thus stated that it is not within the EU's competencies to establish a balance and prioritise copyright or privacy and data protection.

Returning to the three proportionality types listed above, the third instance is that of risk-based approach and risk management as a form of private rights and interests balancing. This instance needs to be analysed separately, as it poses particular challenges. I differentiate this type of balancing even though it relates to both rules' application with a predetermined balance and principles application with a balance to be yet determined. The risk-based approach balancing is analysed in more depth in section III.D. Still, here, it must be noted that this instance of proportionality balancing introduces a subjective private perspective on balance in a given case. Such a private perspective is supplied by risk analysis, which ought to determine the balance of rights and interests in view of a risk posed by a regulated activity (such as data processing in the GDPR or development and deployment of AI systems in the proposed AI Act).

Therefore, from a holistic perspective, the proportionality principle is a tangible judicial tool for balancing rights and interests, conflict reconciliation, and the meta principle of law. That is because it is the law's nature to coordinate human action and resolve conflicts.[37] Thus, as a judicial tool, proportionality is necessary to connect various rights and interests. It determines their relationship and interdependency when subject rights and interests appear together in real life. In this way and at the same time, the proportionality principle is a meta value and a virtue of the legal system.[38] That means that proportionality recognises the pluralism of conflicting rights and demands their best possible reconciliation in a given case.

[36] Art 17 GDPR.

[37] Such contention can be both supported by realistic or pragmatic theories of law, and positivist ones such as those in O Wendell Holmes, 'The Path of the Law' (1897) 10 *Harvard Law Review* 457; HLA Hart, *The Concept of Law* (Oxford University Press, 1961).

[38] This view is especially pronounced in Alexy (n 13).

C. Criticism of the Proportionality Principle

The theory of proportionality is well developed and elaborate, but the principle is still a subject of ongoing and comprehensive scholarly analysis[39] and relentless criticism.[40] The main argument against proportionality is that, at the conceptual level, it relativises the rights and strips them out of absolute qualities needed to safeguard the rights underlining content properly.[41] The principle is also criticised for aiming to compare and weigh against each other incommensurable values.[42] Further, proportionality prioritises utilitarian ethics, which allows for the sacrifice of important values if benefits for other values can be obtained. In fact, the majority of criticism is motivated by this utilitarian provenance.[43] Moreover, the use of proportionality by courts is commonly criticised as a way to merely justify and legitimise judges' decisions, but without an actual and substantial balancing that, in theory, the proportionality method demands.[44]

Therefore, Fontanelli, when analysing the principle, concludes that we face a mythology of proportionality principle rather than a coherent and rational doctrine.[45] He states that applying fundamental rights to digital activities is more a question of setting new policies rather than subsuming new facts under existing standards.[46] In the same article, Fontanelli provides a synopsis of various arguments raised against proportionality balancing and adds numerous important arguments about the principle's insufficiencies in the digital milieu. His essential contention is that the principle has been used as a policy-setting tool that adjusted existing rules and principles to the idiosyncrasies of the digital realm.

In this way, Fontanelli argues that proportionality methodology is a way to set up policies by courts and to downgrade certain fundamental rights depending on the socio-technological circumstances. For example, in his view, the Lindqvist

[39] For example: T-I Harbo, 'The Function of the Proportionality Principle in EU Law' (2010) 16 *European Law Journal* 158; E Engle, 'The History of the General Principle of Proportionality: An Overview' (2012) 10 *Dartmouth Law Journal* 1; CB Tranberg, 'Proportionality and Data Protection in the Case Law of the European Court of Justice' (2011) 1 *International Data Privacy Law* 239; K Moller, 'Proportionality: Challenging the Critics' (2012) 10 *International Journal of Constitutional Law* 709.

[40] eg, F Fontanelli, 'The Mythology of Proportionality in Judgments of the Court of Justice of the European Union on Internet and Fundamental Rights' (2016) 36 *Oxford Journal of Legal Studies* 630; L Dalla Corte, 'On Proportionality in the Data Protection Jurisprudence of the CJEU' (2022) 12 *International Data Privacy Law* 259; FJ Urbina, 'A Critique of Proportionality' (2012) 57 *American Journal of Jurisprudence* 49.

[41] Habermas states that 'In the proportionality test, values must be brought into a transitive order with other values from case to case. Because there are no rational standards for this, weighing takes place either arbitrarily or unreflectively, according to customary standards and hierarchies': J Habermas, *Between Facts and Norms: Contributions to a Discourse Theory of Law and Democracy* (William Rehg trans, MIT Press, 1996) 259.

[42] This argument underpins Fontanelli (n 40).

[43] Such as in Urbina (n 40).

[44] See n 41.

[45] 'The language of proportionality has become a mythology, a shorthand for legitimacy,' states Fontanelli (n 40) 631.

[46] ibid 638.

case[47] legitimised the factual diminution of a right to privacy and data protection caused by the emergence of the internet.[48] As Fontanelli explains, the internet lowers the level of privacy protection by default, and CJEU sanctioned it by not treating sharing personal data online as a transfer of data. In this way, the CJEU precluded the application of the international data transfer regime but also avoided an absurd result from the perspective of internet development. Another example of how the CJEU rewound traditional rules from the analogue world to adjust them to the digital milieu is the concept of intermediary liability.[49] To prioritise economic growth and innovation, a traditional editorial liability for the content has been waived for the sake of unconstrained information sharing. Through the proportionality principle, it is as if the CJEU argued why a given level of fundamental right protection needs to be lowered due to how socio-technological reality changes.

Because establishing the balance between rights and interests online is different from those in the real, Fontanelli states that:

> There is a potential problem every time regulation of internet behaviour purports to rest on a seemingly neutral balancing of values, because the sheer scale of massive behaviour online makes it impossible to strike a balance that is acceptable to all people whose fundamental rights are affected.[50]

Therefore, according to this author, proportionality is usually used by the CJEU as a window dressing for pragmatic or policy-based arguments. He suggests that proportionality should be abandoned when certain conditions commonplace in the digital milieu prevail. Rules dedicated to digital spaces should be used, since 'the three-step proportionality test is helpless to arbitrate fundamental rights implications in internet dispute'[51] and that it is 'an inadequate heuristic device to resolve legal disputes in which fundamental rights are affected by internet activities'.[52] Therefore, according to the author, proportionality balancing is too disconnected from the realities of the digital milieu.

He continues and states that the inadequacy of proportionality as a measure to regulate human affairs online stems from idiosyncrasies of human affairs in the digital arena.[53] Optimisation according to proportionality and weights assigned to competing values is impossible and only serves to 'infuse legitimacy by way of a recurrent mythology, rather than through authoritative reasoning'.[54] Usually, this

[47] *Bodil Lindqvist v Åklagarkammaren i Jönköping* [2003] ECLI:EU:C:2003:596 (Case C-101/01).

[48] Fontanelli (n 40) 639.

[49] Now regulated through the DSA. See: European Parliament and Council of the European Union, Regulation (EU) 2022/2065 of the European Parliament and of the Council of 19 October 2022 on a Single Market For Digital Services and amending Directive 2000/31/EC (Digital Services Act) [2022] OJ L 277/1.

[50] Fontanelli (n 40) 649.

[51] ibid 633.

[52] ibid 631.

[53] ibid 660.

[54] ibid.

is an effect of unscrupulous proportionality reasoning provided by courts, which falls short of appropriate necessity and proportionality *sensu stricto* assessment – alternative measures for regulation are not explored. Furthermore, in the CJEU proportionality judgments, argumentation relies on

> fuzzy and truncated reasoning (intensity of infringements is not measured; alternative measures are not explored and compared with the status quo; the interests of various groups are contrasted 'impressionistically' and not analytically; the reasoning shifts uncontrollably and inadvertently from the interest of the parties to the dispute to the interest of society at large, etc).[55]

Because, according to Fontanelli, in this way, proportionality leads to bad outcomes; it is worse than nothing.[56] Fontanelli calls for laws specific to the digital milieu that are properly connected to it from a regulatory perspective (designed to solve issues specific to the digital milieu). Instead of omnipresent proportionality balancing and covert policymaking by courts concealed by legitimising proportionality use, he suggests using rules more native and thus adjusted to the digital milieu.

His call seems to be addressed since recent years provided a wave of new digital laws – often conceptualised as the digital constitutionalism movement,[57] or what I call an emerging EU digital law. However, to Fontanelli's possible disappointment, the proportionality principle is still structurally ingrained in these new laws. Before analysing how proportionality is present in EU digital law, I investigate the reasons for its presence therein – that is, a need to reconcile rights and interests, which, on the other hand, causes EU digital law's complexity and indeterminacy, which, again, in my view can be only solved through proportionality principle.

III. Complexity and Indeterminacy of the EU Digital Law – Between Rights, Interests and Risk

A. Inherent Complexity of EU Digital Law

The EU is at the forefront of digital regulation.[58] The number of new laws and regulations makes it tough for even an expert in digital law to be up to date on recent legislative initiatives.[59] Practising lawyers without a focus on digital issues may

[55] ibid.

[56] ibid.

[57] For the overview of digital constitutionalism, see G De Gregorio, *Digital Constitutionalism in Europe – Reframing Rights and Powers in the Algorithmic Society* (Cambridge University Press, 2022).

[58] European Commission, 'Communication from the Commission to the European Parliament, the Council, the European Economic and Social Committee and the Committee of the Regions – A European strategy for data' COM(2020) 66 final, available at eur-lex.europa.eu/legal-content/EN/TXT/?uri=CELEX:52020DC0066.

[59] For the overview of the emerging corpus of EU digital law, see K Zenner, JS Marcus and K Sekut, 'A Dataset on EU Legislation for the Digital World' (Bruegel, 5 July 2023), available at www.bruegel.org/dataset/dataset-eu-legislation-digital-world.

not be even aware of new but very significant developments, such as the Digital Services and Market Acts (DSA and DMA),[60] the proposal for the AI Act,[61] or the corpus of the digital consumer protection law.[62] Clear and consistent application of data protection law is still a challenge a few years after the introduction of the GDPR.[63]

All these laws are applied in numerous jurisdictions with varying political priorities and legal cultures. On top of new legislative developments are guidelines by authorities and court decisions that impact how the law is interpreted.[64] Furthermore, a high level of technical expertise is required to understand digital law, which needs to be updated constantly, along with the dynamically evolving technological field, as showcased by the sudden and unfolding revolution of ChatGPT. There is a dynamically growing body of digital legal scholarship that aims to bring rationality and coherence to the interpretation of these new laws. The magnitude of this scholarship and interest paid to the field is a testimony to the imperfection of enacted laws and court decisions. The imperfections are necessarily caused by the sheer volume of information that needs to be digested to draft a wise law or strike a proper verdict. Thus, digital lawyer faces a bramble bush of new legal norms to be applied to a constantly changing technical landscape, and balanced against various public and private rights and interests.[65]

I argue that numerous new concepts, principles and rules pose a challenge to the traditional paradigm of rule to the fact subsumption based on syllogistic logic.[66] In the digital milieu it is often tough to arrive at an authoritative and unambiguous rule to fact application. That is because of a gap between technical and legal understanding of the concepts, as well as a lack of clarity regarding their scope,[67] and finally, because of a lack of clarity regarding legislative intentions.

[60] Regulation (EU) 2022/1925 of the European Parliament and of the Council of 14 September 2022 on contestable and fair markets in the digital sector and amending Directives (EU) 2019/1937 and (EU) 2020/1828 (Digital Markets Act) (Text with EEA relevance) PE/17/2022/REV/1, OJ L 265, 12.10.2022 (DMA).

[61] Proposed AI Act EU Commission version.

[62] For example: Directive 2011/83/EU on Consumer Rights [2011] OJ L304/64, Directive 2005/29/EC on Unfair Commercial Practices [2005] OJ L149/22, Directive 1999/44/EC on Consumer Sales and Guarantees [1999] OJ L171/12, Directive 97/7/EC on Distance Selling of Consumer Financial Services [1997] OJ L144/19, Directive 93/13/EEC on Unfair Terms in Consumer Contracts [1993] OJ L95/29.

[63] Testimony to this fact is a recent EDPS conference in June 2022, titled 'Effective enforcement in the digital world'; see: 'Home' (EDPS Conference 2022, 16 June 2022), available at www.edpsconference2022.eu/en.html.

[64] Especially influential in this regard are European Data Protection Board guidelines, that clarify data protection rules and principles.

[65] For Llewellyn the bramble bush is a metaphor for a complexity and indeterminacy of the legal system. KN Llewellyn, *The Bramble Bush: The Classic Lectures on the Law and Law School* (Oxford University Press, 2008).

[66] For an overview of the modes of legal reasoning theory, see in general N MacCormick, *Legal Reasoning and Legal Theory* (Clarendon Press, 1994).

[67] CA Jasserand, 'Avoiding terminological confusion between the notions of "biometrics" and "biometric data": an investigation into the meanings of the terms from a European data protection and a scientific perspective' (2016) 6 *International Data Privacy Law* 63.

Depending on the interest pursued, I believe that compelling arguments can often be forged to solve a case in two or more rational but contradictory ways.

An example is a core concept of personal data.[68] The concept impacts a variety of digital laws, such as the GDPR, the Law Enforcement Directive (LED Directive), the ePrivacy Directive, the Data Governance Act (DGA),[69] and the soon-to-be-enacted Data Act (DA).[70] Its reach also impacts how privacy and data protection laws are applied beyond the EU.[71] However, the concept remains uncertain due to its novelty as well as its technical, social, philosophical and also physical meaning, which all overlap and need to be transposed into a legal meaning. There does not exist yet a definitive consensus as to how the concept of personal data should be interpreted.[72]

Another example of a challenge to traditional legal syllogism is numerous new principles appearing quite suddenly in the new digital laws. What distinguishes the following principles from those that can be found eg in the GDPR, such as purpose limitation and storage limitation,[73] is the lack of any preceding tradition and doctrine of their application.[74] An example is the AI principles as proposed by the amendments added by the European Parliament, such as 'human agency and oversight', 'technical robustness and safety', 'privacy and data governance', 'transparency', 'diversity, non-discrimination and fairness', or 'social and environmental well-being'.[75] As much as these concepts have been present for some time in the expert and academic discourse,[76] they have never been before a source of rights and duties. Therefore, their application and meaning (understood as their practical

[68] Art 4(1) GDPR states that '"personal data" means any information relating to an identified or identifiable natural person ("data subject"); an identifiable natural person is one who can be identified, directly or indirectly, in particular by reference to an identifier such as a name, an identification number, location data, an online identifier or to one or more factors specific to the physical, physiological, genetic, mental, economic, cultural or social identity of that natural person'.

[69] Regulation (EU) 2022/868 of the European Parliament and of the Council of 30 May 2022 on European data governance and amending Regulation (EU) 2018/1724 (Data Governance Act) (Text with EEA relevance), PE/85/2021/REV/1, OJ L 152, 3.6.2022.

[70] Proposal for a regulation of the European Parliament and of the Council on harmonized rules on fair access to and use of data (Data Act), COM/2022/68 final (Data Act). See also P Pałka, 'Harmed While Anonymous: Beyond the Personal/Non-Personal Distinction in Data Governance' (2023) *Technology and Regulation* 22.

[71] See in depth discussion in PM Schwartz and DJ Solove, 'The PII Problem: Privacy and a New Concept of Personally Identifiable Information' (5 December 2011), available at papers.ssrn.com/sol3/papers.cfm?abstract_id=1909366.

[72] See the overview debate on personal data either as context-dependent, or an absolute concept in N Purtova, 'The Law of Everything. Broad Concept of Personal Data and Future of EU Data Protection Law' (2018) 10 *Law, Innovation and Technology* 40.

[73] Art 5 GDPR.

[74] Data protection doctrine is already almost 40 years old and can be dated back to as early as the Council of Europe Convention for the Protection of Individuals with regard to Automatic Processing of Personal Data from 1981. See www.coe.int/en/web/data-protection/convention108-and-protocol.

[75] Art 4a proposed AI Act: General principles applicable to all AI systems in the version of the EU Parliament. See www.europarl.europa.eu/doceo/document/TA-9-2023-0236_EN.html.

[76] For example in the work of the High-level expert group on artificial intelligence. See digital-strategy.ec.europa.eu/en/policies/expert-group-ai.

consequences[77]) is extremely uncertain. It is easily conceivable that depending on a political and ideological priority, they can be given any subjective meaning by adjusting the degree of their intensity accordingly (that is, the scope of prohibited or allowed behaviour), depending solely on political priorities in a given time and space.

On top of this, there is a gap between legal and technical communities' understanding of concepts, which has already caused numerous problems in eg the realm of biometric technologies, such as facial recognition.[78] Legal and technical experts are engaged in a debate to rationalise the GDPR's definition of biometric data, which clearly has not foreseen and considered the consequences of this definition's literal meaning. This impact includes a blurry level of rights protection but also uncertainty regarding the legitimate use of biometric data through biometric technologies. Biometric technologies, although very impactful for a democratic society, are a narrow example of the complexity problem. Another example of a broader impact is the definition of automated decision-making and a requirement for their human oversight, that can be found in the Article 22 of the GDPR. It is still contested what is the precise meaning of the right not to be subject to automated decision-making, and to what it entitles a data subject, or whether such right's existance is feasible at all.[79]

B. Complexity and Risk-based Approach

What contributes to this possibility and further exacerbates the complexity problem is risk-based approach, which is widely implemented throughout EU digital law.[80] Examples can be the GDPR, the AI Act, the DSA and the DMA, which all have risk-based regulatory elements.[81] According to the risk-based approach, for a set of facts, the law does not prescribe determined behaviour but determines regulated behaviour as risky (such as personal data-processing) and demands that the action is taken or not according to the level of risk it poses, with safeguards undertaken to mitigate the risk. Therefore, the party undertaking the behaviour must foremostly assess the risk according to the guidelines and criteria provided by law and other relevant fields of knowledge (such as technical expertise and risk management). The subject party then decides whether to undertake

[77] According to Charles Peirce, a meaning of an idea or concept is nothing other than its practical consequences. See pragmatic maxim in CS Peirce, 'How to Make Our Ideas Clear' (1878) 12 *Popular Science Monthly* 286.

[78] See n 74.

[79] Wachter and Mittelstadt argue that such a right effectively does not exist. See S Wachter, B Mittelstadt and L Floridi, 'Why a Right to Explanation of Automated Decision-Making Does Not Exist in the General Data Protection Regulation' (2017) 7 *International Data Privacy Law* 76.

[80] For the comprehensive analysis of risk-based approach in data protection, see generally R Gellert, *The Risk-Based Approach to Data Protection* (Oxford, 2020; online edn, Oxford Academic, 22 October 2020), available at doi-org.kuleuven.e-bronnen.be/10.1093/oso/9780198837718.001.0001.

[81] De Gregorio and Dunn (n 3).

the action if the level of risk can be mitigated, or whether to abandon it. If the action is taken, certain risk management measures need to be introduced, corresponding to the level of risk, to diminish the risk to the acceptable level. In this way, law based on the risk-based approach neither allows nor prohibits a certain behaviour, unlike classical rule-based laws.

Risk-based law provides a set of rules and principles according to which risk is to be evaluated. The risk-based approach assumes that compliance with rules and principles will diminish risk to an acceptable level,[82] ie the level where the probability of negative occurrence is diminished to an acceptable degree (depending on the context). Therefore, in risk-based regulations, it is often not a question of whether something is legal or not, but whether, in a particular context, it is legitimate and justified to undertake certain risks. The decision to undertake a risk is usually a privilege of the initiating party, perhaps to be reviewed by relevant courts and authorities based on facts and necessary documentation accompanying the risk assessment and mitigation process.

Consequently, and from a practical perspective, a legal decision often boils down to a business decision whether to undertake risk and accept a potential collateral punishment (usually in the form of a fee) if the risk materialises. That means that risk-based approach is essentially agnostic regarding certain actions' moral and ethical dimensions, reducing them to utilitarian considerations. Such an approach is hailed as much more effective for the goals that other more 'moral or ethical' approaches might pursue (eg right- or rule-based approaches[83]). Sunstein argues that numerous solutions to various problems that are at face value immoral, due to their risk management-focus and utilitarian approach, are more effective in eg environment protection. Ultimately, even though seemingly immoral, these risk-based solutions contribute better (based on the observable outcomes) to the moral goals of which lack of it is accused.[84] Due to the popularity of risk management regulation in previous decades, it was copied to data protection. The goal is to not overtly constrain or prohibit legitimate economic activities.

The existence of the risk-based approach adds to the complexity and uncertainty of legal interpretation, as this approach again deviates from the traditional syllogistic logic of facts to predefined rules subsumption. Such syllogism is what people were used to – either I can do something or not. Thus, I argue that what the risk-based approach leaves a layman interpreting a digital law with – once we leave the armchair, academic ivory tower perspective – is an ambiguous, and

[82] For the clarification of the role of risk-based approach in data protection see 'Article 29 Data Protection Working Party Statement on the Role of a Risk-Based Approach in Data Protection Legal Frameworks' (2014), available at ec.europa.eu/justice/article-29/documentation/opinion-recommendation/files/2014/wp218_en.pdf.

[83] About the relationship between rights and risk based approach see generally R Gellert, 'We Have Always Managed Risks in Data Protection Law: Understanding the Similarities and Differences between the Rights-Based and the Risk-Based Approaches to Data Protection' (2016) 2 *European Data Protection Law Review* 481.

[84] See generally C Sunstein, 'Moral Heuristics' (2003) *Law & Economics Working Papers*, available at chicagounbound.uchicago.edu/law_and_economics/326.

morally agnostic mountain of conflicting rules, that seems to be totally subjective, unless interpreted by a skilled lawyer equipped with a very specialised theoretical, technical and experiential toolkit. Even demanding to meet such a Herculean[85] benchmark of craft from judges is a very high expectation.

Still, to avoid unreconcilable indeterminacy, it is necessary to use both these regulatory and judicial tools: a risk-based approach and proportionality balancing. Otherwise, EU digital law would not be able to achieve simultaneously the two competing objectives that it pursues, ie rights protection while respecting the pursuit of various interests (with a priority on economic ones).

C. Indeterminacy of the EU Digital Law Objectives – Rights and Interests as Equal Priorities

What further contributes to the complexity and underpins the EU digital law is its indeterminacy as to its objectives due to lack of clarity as to their practical importance and priority. The key digital laws lack a definitive objective that does not need to be balanced against a competing one. Although incarnating in different linguistic frames throughout different laws, it is possible to contend that two simultaneous goals lead almost every EU digital law. That is, on the one hand, fundamental rights protection and, on the other, economic growth within a free market paradigm (this statement is exemplified further below). Therefore, at the meta or political level, each digital law aims to strike a balance between these often conflicting goals. These two objectives are given a similar degree of recognition (therefore, to some extent, a similar degree of legitimacy).

The first reason for this situation is that from a political and pragmatic perspective, the Single Market is no less, if not more important objective of the European Union,[86] than fundamental rights protection. Only after establishing a moderately well-functioning Single Market, a political ambition appeared for further integration through a unifying ideology of fundamental rights.[87] Fundamental rights then supplied EU law interpretation rather than the other way.[88]

What sets the digital laws apart from other laws where both problems occur (that of pursuing contradicting goals simultaneously) is the fact that crucial EU

[85] In Dworkin's theory of law as integrity, Hercules is an ideal judge who knows the legal system and its objective perfectly and can always strike a proper verdict. See generally R Dworkin, *Law's Empire* (Belknap Press, 1988).

[86] L van Middelaar, *The Passage to Europe: How a Continent Became a Union*, Reprint edn (Yale University Press, 2014), available at www.amazon.com/Passage-Europe-Continent-Became-Union/dp/0300205333. This book provides the in-depth history behind European integration and forces driving it. After the Second World War trauma, peace was a priority to be achieved through economic integration and interdependency. Even now, although rights are the dominant rhetoric, what underpinned the process of European integration were rights related to pursuing the build-up of the Single Market.

[87] In the form of the CFEU, and also to some extent ECHR before it.

[88] Source – rights were present in the CJEU case law, but not in the law as such.

digital laws are premised on the risk-based approach, often exercised by powerful actors. These actors, possessing data power, can exert disproportionate influence over opinion formation and choices.[89] Therefore, structural favoring of their interests through risk based approach enabled decisions (eg as to whether process data or not) and simultaneous equal priority for economic interest pursuit, may mean a strong legitimizing argument for such actors conduct.

Hence, I argue that, in principle, rights protection and economic interests are irreconcilable *in abstracto*, because digital laws usually give comparable legitimacy to claims and arguments based on rights protection and economic interests. Obviously, that rights should prevail in a democratic society is self explainable and normatively reinforced by the CFEU. Still, freedom to conduct a business is also a right. More importantly, from a pragmatic, historical, and political perspective, a drive to build the EU Single Market was a cardinal and is still an ongoing objective of the EU. Peace and growth are achieved through the Single Market, and hence, a higher level of rights protection is possible. Rights protection beyond the Member States emerged as a pan-European priority only after the success of the Single Market.[90] Therefore, although, in principle, not equal in normative weight to rights, economic interests should not be easily brushed off as a legal argument justifying various practices in the digital milieu. They are furnished with legitimacy and lawfulness by the EU digital law to the extent that they are regulated and constrained by rights.

The second reason is that, under a literal reading, the goals of fundamental rights protection and respect for economic interests are usually mentioned one after the other, and in the same, opening provisions of the EU digital laws. These first provisions create an interpretative frame for the following norms.[91] This pattern of the duality of the objectives is present throughout all major EU digital laws.

The General Data Protection Regulation (GDPR) is one of the main EU digital laws since it governs the ways and means of personal data-processing, which is omnipresent online and often inevitable. Therefore, the GDPR's impact is manifold. Article 1 states that GDPR 'lays down rules relating to the protection of natural persons with regard to the processing of personal data and rules relating to the free movement of personal data', that it 'protects fundamental rights and freedoms of natural persons and in particular their right to the protection of personal data', and finally that 'The free movement of personal data within the Union shall be neither restricted nor prohibited for reasons connected with the protection of natural persons with regard to the processing of personal data'.[92]

[89] For the overview of data power, see O Lynskey, 'Grappling with "Data Power": Normative Nudges from Data Protection and Privacy' (2019) 20 *Theoretical Inquiries in Law* 189.

[90] The Lisbon Treaty and accompanying CFEU were only adopted in 2009, whereas the Single Market is more then 70 years old.

[91] Through establishing an objective to which these laws strive. Teleological interpretation, very popular in EU law, dictates that law is to be interpreted according to the objectives it aims to achieve.

[92] Art 1 GDPR.

Therefore, although the processing of personal data is regulated and lawful only if data protection rules and principles are respected, the processing of personal data is allowed at the basic level, despite often inherent risks related.[93] This is a pragmatic contention that without personal data processing, the development of the digital economy is impossible. However, the tension is underlined and persists between rights protection and economic interest.

The ePrivacy Directive sets out the rules for confidentiality of communication and end-to-end devices. In Article 1 it states that the Directive

> provides for the harmonisation of the national provisions required to ensure an equivalent level of protection of fundamental rights and freedoms, and in particular the right to privacy and confidentiality, with respect to the processing of personal data in the electronic communication sector and to ensure the free movement of such data and of electronic communication equipment and services in the Community.[94]

These objectives essentially repeat the objectives of the GDPR and the underlining logic – protect privacy (confidentiality of communication) – but do not constrain the flow of data itself (which is necessary for economic activity).

The DGA lays down 'conditions for the reuse, within the Union, of certain categories of data held by public sector bodies'.[95] The majority of the Act's provisions are *lex specialis* to the GDPR,[96] which means that due to the objective of the reuse of data, including personal data, the DGA further extends the GDPR's regulatory objective of free movement of data. However, the DGA states at the same time that it does not lower in any way the level of rights protection associated with personal data, especially rights to privacy and data protection. Regardless, the structure of the Act is designed to encourage data processing and sharing while respecting rights to privacy and data protection.[97] The law thus proclaims that it is in itself possible to reconcile these two goals.

Before providing further examples, the contradiction within the objectives pursued by the corpus of these data protection or data laws must be noted. The risk of unwanted events in case of personal data processing (such as harm, or the leakage of data) is usually directly proportional to the amount and quality of the data processed. Simultaneously, the degree of economic benefit (depending on the nature of the organisation that processes data) is usually directly proportional to the quantity and quality of the data processed (as well as the technical and organisational capacity to process it). Therefore, the categorical statement that it is possible to protect rights and privacy and data protection while deriving economic

[93] Processing personal data is treated as inherently risky, and therefore there is a need for the right to data protection. About sources and history of EU data protection law see O Lynskey, *The Foundations of EU Data Protection Law* (Oxford University Press, 2015).

[94] Art 1 Directive 2002/58/EC of the European Parliament and of the Council of 12 July 2002 concerning the processing of personal data and the protection of privacy in the electronic communications sector (Directive on privacy and electronic communications) OJ L 201/37.

[95] Art 1 DGA.

[96] Recital 4 DGA.

[97] Recital 6 DGA.

benefits is a contradiction if understood at face value and in a maximalistic way. Therefore, as will be discussed further, there is a need for nuance and balancing through the proportionality principle.

Article 1 of the Digital Single Market Copyright Directive (Copyright Directive) states that it

> lays down rules which aim to harmonise further Union law applicable to copyright and related rights in the framework of the internal market, taking into account, in particular, digital and cross-border uses of protected content. It also lays down rules on exceptions and limitations to copyright and related rights, on the facilitation of licences, as well as rules which aim to ensure a well-functioning marketplace for the exploitation of works and other subject matter.[98]

Therefore, the Directive aims to adjust copyright rules to the digital markets. A functioning market, that is an ability to pursue an economic interest, is a persistent and important policy objective. Rights (copyright in this case) here are also not treated in an absolutistic way and are balanced against a policy of economic interest protection of those with stakes in others' copyright.

Article 1.1 DMA, a landmark digital competition protection law, states that:

> The purpose of this Regulation is to contribute to the proper functioning of the internal market by laying down harmonised rules ensuring for all businesses, contestable and fair markets in the digital sector across the Union where gatekeepers are present, to the benefit of business users and end users.[99]

Here, as well, market efficiency and equal opportunity to pursue an economic interest is the main goal, as well as users' welfare, achieved through the rules of the Act. However, the provision mentions opposition between the interest of the gatekeepers, on the one hand, and business owners, on the other. By bringing a balance into this relationship, users are to benefit.[100] As a competition law, the Act aims to prevent monopolisation of the digital market and thus enhance consumer welfare.[101] Still, this objective is balanced against the economic interests of powerful gatekeepers. In this case, the economic interest of the weaker parties in the digital marketplace can be understood as their economic rights according to CFEU, such as to conduct a business, which can be constrained if equal access to the market is not safeguarded by the law.

Artifical intelligence regulation follows a similar logic, though it is less explicitly verbalised where the objectives of the draft AI Act are expressed.[102] Article 1 of the draft AI Act states that the Act

[98] Art 1 Directive (EU) 2019/790 of the European Parliament and of the Council of 17 April 2019 on copyright and related rights in the Digital Single Market and amending Directives 96/9/EC and 2001/29/EC (Text with EEA relevance) OJ L 130, 17.5.2019, pp 92–125 (Copyright Directive).

[99] Art 1.1 DMA.

[100] Recital 2 DMA.

[101] ibid.

[102] For the overview of the up-to-date versions of the proposal for AI Act by the EU Commission and amendments by the Council and the EU Parliament, see www.europarl.europa.eu/news/en/headlines/society/20230601STO93804/eu-ai-act-first-regulation-on-artificial-intelligence.

> lays down: (a) harmonised rules for the placing on the market, the putting into service and the use of artificial intelligence systems ('AI systems') in the Union; (b) prohibitions of certain artificial intelligence practices; (c) specific requirements for high-risk AI systems and obligations for operators of such systems; (d) harmonised transparency rules for AI systems intended to interact with natural persons, emotion recognition systems and biometric categorisation systems, and AI systems used to generate or manipulate image, audio or video content; (e) rules on market monitoring and surveillance.

Since the objective of AI systems is usually to pursue an economic interest, the AI Act facilitates their provision in a way that minimises risks to fundamental rights. It also prohibits certain AI use cases, assuming that they cannot be reconciled with rights protection through risk management procedures (on which the draft AI Act heavily relies).[103] Still, the marketplace is a priority, and the draft AI Act allows for placing on a market risky AI systems, provided that the risk is properly managed.

Finally, the DSA, which is a new EU standard for content provision and moderation online, aims to

> contribute to the proper functioning of the internal market for intermediary services by setting out harmonised rules for a safe, predictable and trusted online environment that facilitates innovation and in which fundamental rights enshrined in the Charter, including the principle of consumer protection, are effectively protected.[104]

Therefore, through setting up rules and regulating the intermediary services, safety, predictability, and trust in markets are established. This is achieved by extension of the exemption of liability of intermediary services, provided that they comply with the DSA.[105] Again, a priority is to set the stage for the pursuit of economic interests devoid of practices that would undermine safety and trust in the marketplace.

EU consumer protection law is more one-sided, the interest of the customer being a principal policy goal. There is an assumption that, in principle, a party providing a service or a product is usually in a stronger contractual position than a customer. Therefore, these laws aim to bring a proportional balance by outweighing the initial advantage possessed by the providers of products and services.[106] However, as such, the consumer protection law also aims to facilitate an enhanced market exchange and economic interest pursuit by favouring the interests of the

[103] All versions of the AI Act demand the introduction of elaborate risk management programmes for developers and users of high-risk AI systems. For an in-depth analysis of licencing schemes for high-risk AI systems, see G Malgieri and F Pasquale, 'Licensing High-Risk Artificial Intelligence: Toward Ex Ante Justification for a Disruptive Technology' (2024) 52 *Computer Law & Security Review* 105899, available at www.sciencedirect.com/science/article/pii/S0267364923001097.

[104] Art 1 DSA.

[105] Ch II DSA.

[106] See generally S Weatherill, *EU Consumer Law and Policy*, 2nd edn (Edward Elgar Publishing, 2014).

consumer and their rights in cases where there is a possibility for their abuse (such as manipulation or unequal contractual strength, which both affects rights and economic interests of a consumer).

Therefore, along with complexity, indeterminacy is a structural feature ingrained in the EU digital law. That also means that a conflict of rights and interests necessarily emerges. If the EU digital law does not decisively prioritise rights or economic interests, then such conflicts need to be resolved case-by-case. What EU digital law provides, then, is a regulatory roadmap to guide risky behaviour and to solve potential disputes through the proportionality principle.

D. Indeterminacy of the EU Digital Law Rules Due to Risk-based Approach

In many of the EU digital laws, behaviour subject to regulation (eg, processing personal data or supplying AI systems) and any potential emerging conflicts are designed to be guided and solved in three principal ways. The first way is the rules, which prohibit certain behaviours. The second is principles, which are optimisation requirements that need to be applied and reconciled against each other through the proportionality principle. The third is meta-regulation through a risk-based approach. This way signifies an assessment of the risk by the legally entitled party that sets up an initial balance of rights and interests, undertakes regulated action and adjusts risk management measures depending on the severity of the risk.

Regulation through principles and risk is what dominates EU digital law. Examples of the pervasiveness of principles are data protection principles, such as purpose limitation, or storage limitation.[107] These principles define the legality of any personal data-processing. The risk-based approach is present eg in the GDPR, the draft AI Act, the DSA and the DMA.[108] Principles provide an abstract guideline for the behaviour. What they require needs to be evaluated once they are applied in a given case. Rules only emerge when principles are applied to a given case and are reconciled against other principles. Rules are legal norms providing direct rights and correlated duties. A newly emerged rule in such a way can be analogously applied in a similar case later.[109]

Direct rules are rare in EU digital law. However, principles application, which creates rules, is moderated by the risk-based approach, demanding risk assessment-based conduct. Moderation by risk impacts principles and rules in a way that relativises rules application in a traditional way – in their role of prohibitions or authorisations for certain behaviour. The risk-based approach adds

[107] Art 5 GDPR.
[108] For an overview of the topic, see generally De Gregorio and Dunn (n 3).
[109] For the general theory of the principle and its structure see esp Alexy (n 4).

that even if the rule is derived from the principle, it can still be further relativised by the context and risk assessment of the party conducting a certain behaviour. Such a party, having applicable principles and rules to a behaviour, can still ask itself whether it can nonetheless undertake certain action given the technical and organisational context (or any other relevant context), even though the behaviour is risky (except when there is a clear-cut prohibition, such as behavioural categorisation without prior notice or social credit scoring.[110])

'Risky' here means that certain behaviour can negatively impact the rights and interests of the parties with an interest in a behaviour (such as in the case of personal data processing of a data subject). However, the party can decide that the likelihood of a negative impact is negligible; there are safeguards in place, and so it can undertake the risk. The verdict can also be negative – the risk is too severe, and there are no safeguards, so the behaviour should be ceased. Both outcomes could stem from the same rule emerging from the principle application, but moderation through risk changes the final outcome.

An example could collecting data online for the purpose of training AI models, which triggers the application of the GDPR, the draft AI Act and the Copyright Directive. This example shows how, depending on the context, the same rules can prohibit or allow the collection of certain data. To legitimise data collection, which may include personal data and copyrighted material, exemption for data mining for research purposes from the Copyright Directive can be used,[111] and exemption to process personal data for scientific research purposes in the GDPR.[112] Although the dataset can include sensitive data, such processing can also be justified.[113]

The contentious issue here is the definition of 'research', which is ambiguous as to whether research is an activity only for public interest or also when used directly for commercial purposes.[114] A hefty argument can be used that private entities conduct the most important AI research; thus, that is how progress is made in the field. Therefore, such activities should be recognised as research falling under exemptions from the GDPR and Copyright Directive.

Furthermore, the draft AI Act will regulate how such a dataset should be composed and documented to mitigate risks – the legality of the AI system will be dependent on the effects directly stemming from the quality of the dataset.[115] In this situation, if we assume that the organisation conducting the research and training of AI has appropriate technical and organisational safeguards to minimise risks such as data leakage (risking privacy and copyright infringements by

[110] Title II proposed AI Act.
[111] Art 4 Copyright Directive.
[112] Art 89 GDPR.
[113] Art 9.2(j) GDPR.
[114] For instance Recital 159 GDPR indicates that research for commercial purposes is also considered as falling under Art 89 GDPR, since it states that research should be understood broadly, also encompassing private research.
[115] Art 10 proposed AI Act.

access to data by unauthorised), and has a properly composed dataset (which is an organisational and administrative burden able to be undertaken by big or very specialised institutions), then the rules from the GDPR, Copyright Directive and draft AI Act allow the collection of data and the training AI system. Otherwise, if the organisation cannot technically and organisationally cope with the risk, the same rules can prohibit it since the risk to rights (eg data leakage) is too severe. Nevertheless, whether the subject party can undertake the risk is a highly subjective matter, not predefined by the legal text.

Such relativism and risk dependency do not apply to all rules. Some of the new ones are lessons from a few years' application of older digital laws. Therefore, there is a tendency to append new digital laws with clear-cut rules that are supplying the older digital laws and are in effect their new *lex specialis*. However, principle-based and risk-based regulation still prevails for the defined subject matter of these new laws. An example can be both the DSA and the draft AI Act, which prohibit dark pattern interfaces,[116] targeting ads to minors,[117] facial recognition systems and manipulative AI.[118] These prohibitions are clear rules that amend the GDPR, resolving ambiguities within it that were recognised after it came into force. After all, these rules counter privacy infringements – not necessarily an explicit goal of the DSA and the draft AI Act. The actual subject matter of the DSA and draft AI Act is respectively providing a broad frame for content governance online and putting on the market AI systems according to the risk. At the same time, both these laws still heavily rely on the interplay between principles and risk-based regulation.

To summarise, it is the pursuance of economic interests that usually causes risks to fundamental rights in a digital milieu.[119] At the same time, most EU digital laws legitimise economic interests by constraining them through the above-mentioned regulations, which also protect rights. In this way an abstract *ex ante* balance is the aim. However, every time a factual conflict of interest emerges, parties with legal claims want to protect their rights or pursue their economic interests further. Therefore, the balance needs to be achieved case-by-case and considering the facts. However, the fact of ingrained competition of objectives in EU digital law causes uncertainty since it is rare that certain rights or interests are given determined priority *in abstracto*. The benefit of this indeterminacy is flexibility and adjustability to new technologies. Still, at the same time, addresses of the law do not have clear-cut authorisations and prohibitions. A legislator tells them to decide by themselves what to do, using the guidelines and methods of risk management and proportionality judicial thinking. Given the ingrained conflict

[116] Recital 67 and Art 25 DSA.
[117] Art 28 DSA.
[118] Title II proposed AI Act.
[119] For an excellent overview of the challenges to rights caused by economic activities see A Mantelero, 'Human Rights Impact Assessment and AI' in *Beyond Data* Information Technology and Law Series, vol 36. (TMC Asser Press, 2022) ch I.

of rights and interests described in XYZ, the relevant and structurally present method to guide subject behaviour and dispute resolution is a consequence of the proportionality principle.

At the same time, however, criticism of proportionality, described in section II.C, cannot be ignored. For proportionality to properly fulfill its role, neither impossible expectations should be created, such as a necessity for the courts or other entitled parties to meticulously pass through each step of proportionality assessment, nor acceptance for relativism and over-extended judicial discretion. A pragmatic perspective is needed, explaining why proportionality is necessary and helpful, but also what are its limitations. I believe that seeing the principle from the perspective of Robert Alexy's theory of law and his law as ideal dimension argument provides a suitable normative framework for understanding proportionality as a legal virtue in EU digital law that allows us to strike a balance between rights protection and economic interests.

IV. Proportionality as a Virtue Excercised in a Rational, Legal Discourse

A. Law as a Rational Discourse and Law's Ideal Dimension – Robert Alexy's Theory of Law

It is impossible to ignore Robert Alexy's contribution to the contemporary theory of law. His work contributes to understanding constitutional rights in relation to the proportionality principle[120] and legal argumentation.[121] His work started an important discussion on the nature of rights and proportionality balancing, in which luminaries such as Habermas[122] and Barak[123] took part. What distinguishes Alexy's work is his effort to reconcile a normative, or ideal, validity claim-based perspective on law with legal practice based on rhetorics, legal argumentation, and interest pursuit. He simultaneously explains both theory and practice of law. A synthesis of his views is provided in his law's ideal dimension argument.[124]

[120] See n 7.

[121] See generally R Alexy, R Adler and N MacCormick, *A Theory of Legal Argumentation: The Theory of Rational Discourse as Theory of Legal Justification*, rev edn (Oxford University Press, 2010).

[122] For how the Alexy–Habermas debate can be seen from the perspective of ECtHR jurisprudence, see S Greer, '"Balancing" and the European Court of Human Rights: A Contribution to the Habermas-Alexy Debate' (2004) 63 *The Cambridge Law Journal* 412.

[123] R Alexy, 'Proportionality, constitutional law, and sub-constitutional law: A reply to Aharon Barak' (2018) 16 *International Journal of Constitutional Law* 871.

[124] Alexy (n 13).

To the question of what law is, Alexy states that law is everything that has been enacted in an appropriate and legitimate procedure,[125] except for those norms that cross Radbruch's extreme injustice threshold.[126] Alexy states that there needs to be an essential minimum moral integrity content of any law because it is in the nature of a concept of law that it appeals to a transcendent moral element.[127] However, only extremely unjust laws are not laws. The threshold of extreme injustice is evaluated through the famous Radbruch's formula. Alexy provides an example of laws expropriating Jews by Germans before and during the Second World War as those crossing the threshold of extreme injustice.[128] These laws were *ex tunc* invalid. Except for laws not passing Radbruch's formula test, all other laws are valid even though they might be unjust, because they were enacted in a legitimate procedure by the legitimate government. This last contention is how Alexy reconciles the law naturalism perspective with legal positivism or conventionalism, which are usually disinterested in the law's moral dimension (or only interested to a very limited extent).[129]

Alexy's further work also strives to constructively reconcile seemingly irreconcilable into an integral perspective. Alexy states that the nature of law is dual, resembling the Janus face, which looks simultaneously in two opposing directions.[130] The first direction is that of valid claims to the normative ideal. Law aspires to realise valid normative claims, such as claims to justice or legitimacy. Defining law solely on a factual and positive basis, without the law's moral claim (or law's ideal dimension) does not provide a full picture. The second direction is that of a positive and facts-based dimension. Law is simultaneously a practical social tool to reconcile conflicts and provide a coordination tool for people, with a threat of using legitimate force to coerce compliance with an established legal order. Both the ideal, moral dimension and the positive one are necessary parts of the concept of law.

Alexy also provides the theory of constitutional rights and of the proportionality principle. A constitution consists of principles and rules. Rights usually take the form of principles, rarely rules, except for categorical prohibitions, such as those of torture or slavery.[131] Whereas rules define in a determinate way the entitlements and duties of subject parties, delineating clearly allowed and prohibited behaviour, principles operate at a higher level of abstraction. Principles are optimisation requirements that demand that certain values they prescribe will

[125] According to the Hartian rule of recognition. See generally HLA Hart, *The Concept of Law*, 3rd edn (eds J Raz and PA Bulloch) (Oxford University Press, 2012.

[126] G Radbruch, 'Statutory Lawlessness and Supra-Statutory Law' (1946) 26 *Oxford Journal of Legal Studies* 1.

[127] Alexy (n 13) ch 3.

[128] ibid ch 8.

[129] ibid ch 1.

[130] See n 13.

[131] Arts 3 and 4 European Convention on Human Rights, Art 4 and 5 CFEU. These are categorical prohibitions which are not subject to limitation clauses and proportionality balancing.

be realised to the furthest possible extent.[132] In this way, rights as principles are social aspirations that must be implemented. However, principles are in constant tension with other principles forming a constitution. Since a constitution defines an abstract order that must be realised in practice, principles are optimisation requirements, demanding the realisation of their content as much as possible when in conflict with another principle. Therefore, principles also define the extent to which certain rights can be limited. The proportionality principle is the precise way in which principles are to be optimised against each other and reconciled. Therefore, it is through proportionality balancing in a given case that the content of a right is determined. A rule is an effect of a proportionality principle applied to a conflicting principle. A rule is a permanent balance of rights in a given case that then can be analogously transcribed to solve other similar cases.

Although providing an elaborate methodology for proportionality balancing (presented in section II.A), Alexy acknowledges a practical dimension through which the law's objectives are realised. Therefore, he argues, notwithstanding his theories above, that law has an inherently discursive nature and is a part of social practice.[133] That means that what is law is established through a social discussion governed by rules, ascribing procedures for valid law enactment, and law's rational evaluation, with the use of argumentation. Alexy contends that in a society, people pursue their particular interests with the use of law, but what nevertheless unites everybody is shared ideal to which the realisation law as a system strives. Therefore, law is a special form of discourse and a rational one.[134]

Therefore, although people, while engaged in a legal discourse, pursue their political, ideological or economic interests, they need to justify their pursuits in a form appropriate for a legal discourse. Justification of interest pursuit needs to be formed as a rational, legal argument, where a necessary element is a validity claim to a certain value furthered by a legal system as a whole. For example, pursuing economic interest can be justified with recourse to the right to freedom to conduct a business or other liberties. Therefore, although particularisms collide, it is possible to reconcile them by evaluating the arguments justifying those interests. The strongest arguments are most rationally justifiable given the ideals a law wants to achieve (or from the point of particular law objectives). The courts adjudicate based on the rhetorical arguments presented by the parties. Moreover, courts themselves need to explain and justify their verdicts, evoking values to which the legal system aspires.

The practice of the proportionality principle follows the same rules.[135] Proportionality is an important concept in law as an ideal realised through rational,

[132] See n 7.
[133] Alexy (n 13) ch 17.
[134] Alexy (n 13) ch 19.
[135] Alexy says that '[proportionality is] an argument form of rational legal discourse. As such, it is indispensable in order to introduce "order into legal thought". It makes clear which points are decisive and how these points are related to one another': Alexy (n 4) 64.

legal discourse. Parties pursue their case and justify the priority of their rights and interests, necessarily arguing against the priority of competing rights and interests. However, such arguments need to be justified, which means that an inherent legitimacy of other competing rights and interests is acknowledged. A court must decide which arguments are more rational to better realise a legal system's objectives. This perspective shows that proportionality as a judicial mode of thinking is therefore omnipresent in the legal practice, as any party subject to a dispute needs to use legal arguments against competing ones. Although there are numerous instances where clear rules are applicable and elaborate proportionality balancing is unnecessary, in numerous cases, a contention persists as to which norm and how to apply it. Such contention is a necessary outcome of the very nature of legal practice – applying abstract norms to the real world. The gap between norm and reality is a cause of uncertainty that is bridged when law is applied. The final verdict on how norm should be applied to a fact is sanctioned by democratic legitimacy vested in courts.

That is a way in which theory meets practice. However, Alexy goes even so far as to state that usually, at a constitutional level, once there is uncertainty regarding the precise content of a right or principle and purely legal argumentation is exhausted, legal discourse becomes nothing other than a practical discourse. In such a discourse, what takes place is the weighing against each other of moral, ethical, political and interest-based arguments. As an effect, judges, when deciding to use the proportionality principle – that is, when a conflict of rights and interests arises, with arguments supporting contradictory claims – need to also decide on a certain values' priority. Their decision is covered by the veil of objective legal argument. The extent to which such proportionality judgement is correct is measured by the degree to which it is just and to the degree that such judgements further the legal system's objectives.

B. Proportionality as a Legal Virtue

I argue that the clearer the objective of a given law, the more certainly principles and rules are applied. Consequently, an easier and more determined application of proportionality balancing is needed. The reason is that the goal towards which a particular law strives is clearly defined in such cases. Therefore, teleological interpretation of the legal text can be used to aid textual and systemic interpretation methods in case of doubt. However, suppose the subject law's objectives are undetermined, or dual and contradictory, as with the various EU digital laws. In that case, there is more uncertainty, and the broader necessity for discretion exists when balancing rights and interests with proportionality principle's use.

I assume that given EU digital law's structural dependence on two contradictory objectives, proportionality balancing is inevitable and necessary, and occurs very often when EU digital law is applied. I propose that combining Alexy's various strands of legal theory, with virtue ethics perspective,[136] can provide a better understanding of this principle's role and its better, more pragmatic application, but with the view to the ideal of proportionality. Virtue ethics emphasises practice as a dimension in which morality and ethics is realised.[137] Only through applying principles and rules to a real problem does one have an understanding of the moral and ethical principles. However, in order to achieve an appropriate outcome in practice, one needs to know which good one's action strives for. In the case of legal practice, this can be Dworkinian ideal of law as an integrity,[138] or the Rawlsian ideal of justice as fairness.[139] All these legal ideals can be interpreted as leading to a good social and individual life.

However, virtue ethics demands that in order to be able to differentiate between good and bad, and to choose a good action leading toward a certain good, one needs to develop certain traits of character, which are necessary to choose a sound course of action and persist in it. Therefore, character virtues are necessary for moral and ethical conduct. In legal practice, these virtues for a person interpreting law can be wisdom, knowledge, courage, justice or moderation. Similarly, one can speak about the virtues of a legal system, such as those envisioned by Fuller,[140] like generality, non-retroactivity, stability, clarity or consistency. I add proportionality to the list of lawyers' and legal system's virtues. Proportionality as a legal virtue is an ability to strike the best possible balance of rights and interests in a given case, in a particular time, space and social context, with the view to the reasonably foreseeable consequences of such a decision.

From this perspective, I interpret numerous criticism of the proportionality principle as a failure of lawyers, decision-makers and judges to properly exercise virtues that are demanded while conducting proportionality balancing. One such virtue is meticulousness and care, with which in theory, the judge should pass through each step of the proportionality balancing test. From this point of view, it is not a failure of the concept of proportionality but a failure of how it has been put into practice. Given its dual objectives, such a contention assumes that the principle's use is inevitable in EU digital law.

Moreover, the other criticism related to proportionality's application can be interpreted as an accusation for failing to properly exercise the *virtue* of proportionality while applying the *principle* of proportionality. The claim of failure is usually evoked when a court fails to establish a proper balance, gives priority

[136] Whose father is Aristotle. See Aristotle, WD Ross and L Brown, *The Nicomachean Ethics* (Oxford University Press, 2009).

[137] See ibid, Introduction.

[138] In Dworkin's theory of law as integrity, Hercules is an ideal judge who knows the legal system and its objectives perfectly and can always strike a proper verdict. See generally Dworkin (n 85).

[139] See generally J Rawls, *A Theory of Justice* (Belknap Press, 2005).

[140] See generally LL Fuller, *The Morality of Law: Revised Edition* (Yale University Press, 1969).

only to one right or interest, or uses proportionality simply as a rhetorical tool to justify policy choice without acknowledging the fact with the use of proper arguments – I assume that such arguments are possible to construct when a court faces necessary policy choice.

V. Inevitability of the Proportionality Balancing in the EU Digital Law

This links to Alexy's rhetorical or argumentative perspective on law. From such a perspective proportionality is a methodology to arrive at a certain decision in a certain case. Therefore, I argue that what should be criticised is the way the proportionality principle is exercised, rather than the concept per se. If proper attention is given to developing virtues necessary for the principle exercise, then the judgements in proportionality use will be better. What changes if this proposal is accepted is that it is necessary to start to be more critical of the way judges judge and how they justify their decisions based on the proportionality principle – that is also how they exercise the virtue of proportionality. Similarly, given the prevalence of the risk-based approach and, in consequence, numerous private parties deciding on proportionality of given introduced measures, the focus of the criticism should be on the way they exercise their virtues when applying the proportionality principle, along with on the arguments they use, including those to justify risks taken.

The rhetorical perspective explains the imperfections of the proportionality principle and helps to understand its necessity as a judicial tool. Thus, I argue that proportionality is an imperfect but necessary rhetorical tool to limit courts' and authorities' (but also private parties') discretion, streamlining their reasons for action into a legal language with recourse to valid legal claims. Proportionality forces them to disclose discretionary arguments and frame them into legal language, especially when irreconcilable conflict emerges, such as between rights and economic interests. Therefore, the party using the proportionality principle needs to necessarily give recourse to the rights and interests of the party against which it does something (even if it is just lip service). This recognition provided by proportionality balancing is important, as it acknowledges the existence of a conflict and conflicting reasons – reconciled only in a particular case. I thus argue that proportionality is the legitimate tool to provide a provisionary balance, but avoiding overregulation by cutting the Gordian knot of already complex and uncertain digital law. After all, an imperfect but working solution is better than no solution.[141]

[141] Nirvana fallacy is comparing a realistic solution with an idealised one, and discounting or even dismissing the realistic solution as a result of comparing to a 'perfect world' or impossible standard, ignoring the fact that improvements are often good enough. See www.logicallyfallacious.com/logicalfallacies/Nirvana-Fallacy.

However, proportionality is subject to criticism for that very reason – that it is rarely used meticulously by judges and that numerous steps of proportionality methodology are skipped, or cherry-picked to justify a decision. I believe that as much as we should not resign from the ideal of the proportionality principle as described by Alexy, we need to also accept the pragmatics of legal decision-making, which is short of perfect. Proportionality offers a method to justify rights limitation in a way closest to the Fuller's rule of law virtues and ideal, since it forces us to disclose the substantial arguments behind the decision (both by lawmaker, the judge, or any other party conducting proportionality test).

I believe there is a need for pragmatic demystification of proportionality in digital law, while affirming the practice and the principle's use. That is because proportionality helps to focus the attention of judges, politicians, legal scholars and subject parties on their role and power, especially in the digital milieu. The role of the party that conducts the proportionality test, or risk assessment, is often equivalent to the role of a judge giving priority to this or that right or interest. This contention is especially important given the popularity of risk-based approach in EU digital law, which privileges the judgement of a party undertaking certain regulated behaviour (such as data processing), by allowing it to set up an initial balance (eg to decide whether to process personal data or not in a given case). This initial balance is rarely challenged, except for the influence caused by strategic litigation. That is why the proportionality principle plays an essential role in EU digital law not only at the adjudication level but also in everyday law interpretation. Such use of proportionality as a methodology to resolve conflicts between rights and interests in the digital milieu is the closest it is pragmatically possible to get to the ideal of coherent and rational EU digital law.

6

Proportionality in the Proposed Artificial Intelligence Liability Directive and the Revised Product Liability Directive

LI SHU

I. Introduction

In 2021, the Commission published a proposal for harmonising the risk regulations for AI systems ('draft AI Act').[1] The goal of the draft AI Act is to ensure that the AI systems that are placed on the market must be safe and respect fundamental rights. All AI systems will be subject to different levels of regulatory requirements, which are proportionate to their risk profiles. It should be underlined that although the draft AI Act provides a comprehensive regulatory framework to reduce the risk of various AI systems, it cannot guarantee that a harmful event will not occur in reality. Once a person suffers a kind of harm caused by AI systems, we need to ensure that an ex post mechanism is properly in place. From this angle, the significance of the liability regime should not be underestimated.[2]

Traditionally, whenever a person is harmed by a defective product, they may choose to claim against the producer on the basis of strict product liability. Alternatively, if the product was not defective when it was placed on the market, the victim may rely on fault-based civil liability to claim against the device's owner or deployer. The effectiveness of this conventional paradigm is challenged by the growing deployment of digital technologies, particularly AI systems, which

[1] Commission, 'Proposal for a Regulation of the European Parliament and of the Council Laying down Harmonised Rules on Artificial Intelligence (Artificial Intelligence Act) and Amending Certain Union Legislative Acts', COM(2021) 206 final. The final text of the AI Act has been approved by the European Parliament on 13 March 2024. The final version is available at www.europarl.europa.eu/doceo/document/TA-9-2024-03-13-TOC_EN.html.

[2] See S Lohsse, R Schulze and D Staudenmayer, 'Liability for Artificial Intelligence' in S Lohsse, R Schulze and D Staudenmayer (eds), *Liability for Artificial Intelligence and the Internet of Things* (Nomos Verlagsgesellschaft mbH & Co KG, 2019) 14.

further disadvantage consumers when they file claims for damage in any scenario. On the one hand, many AI-empowered systems may fall outside the scope of the current Product Liability Directive ('1985 PLD'[3]).[4] For instance, intangible goods like software are not defined as 'products'. On the other hand, the features of AI systems (eg complexity, non-transparency and autonomy) will increase the burden of proof that a victim has to bear, especially where they have to rely on a fault-based liability to receive compensation.[5] In light of this, it is imperative to ensure that victims will not be treated differently while seeking justice simply because they are harmed by AI systems.[6]

Therefore, it is of great importance to close the gap between the existing liability regime and the new challenges caused by new technologies like AI. The Commission identified in a report that neither the 1985 PLD nor the fault-based rules scattered in domestic provisions are effective to incentivise relevant parties to behave properly or sufficient to compensate victims.[7] The Expert Group on Liability and New Technologies to some extent took the first step in light of making a proposal for adapting the current liability regime to AI and other digital technologies.[8] The Expert Group suggested that producers and operators (ie, deployers and keepers) should be subject to strict liability, if the product provided or operated by them could cause significant harm.[9] The Expert Group also made it clear that the definition of 'product' should not be restricted to tangible goods. Intangible goods, such as software that can generate safety issues, should also be included.[10] In December 2020, the European Parliament delivered a Resolution[11] regarding the civil liability for AI. A lot of substantial suggestions laid down in the Report by the Expert Group were further developed in the Resolution. For example, a distinction based on the risk profile of AI systems (ie high-risk AI systems and other AI systems) was proposed as the criterion to determine the liability for operators: operators of high-risk AI systems would be subject to strict liability, while operators of other AI systems would be subject to fault-based rules.[12] The Resolution enquired about the possibility of replacing the fragmented liability

[3] Council Directive 85/374/EEC of 25 July 1985 on the approximation of the laws, regulations and administrative provisions of the Member States concerning liability for defective products. OJ L 210, 7.8.1985, 29–33.

[4] See eg, B Koch, 'Product Liability 2.0 – Mere Update or New Version?' in Lohsse, Schulze and Staudenmayer (n 2) 105.

[5] See eg, C Wendehorst, 'Strict Liability for AI and other Emerging Technologies' (2020) 11 *Journal of European Tort Law* 150, 156.

[6] ibid 174.

[7] Commission, 'Report on the safety and liability implications of Artificial Intelligence, the Internet of Things and robotics', COM(2020) 64 final.

[8] European Expert Group on Liability and New Technologies – New Technologies Formation (EG-NTF), 'Report: Liability for Artificial Intelligence and Other Emerging Digital Technologies' (2019).

[9] ibid 39.

[10] ibid 42.

[11] European Parliament, 'Resolution of 20 October 2020 with recommendations to the Commission on a civil liability regime for artificial intelligence' (2020/2014(INL)).

[12] ibid Art 4.

framework among EU Member States with a harmonised liability regime for operators of AI. This approach, however, received a lot of criticism due to its ambiguity (eg the definition of 'operator') as well as its far-reaching effect and the potential distortion of the balance between consumer protection and business innovation.[13]

On 28 September 2022, the European Commission published two proposals for the purpose of adapting the liability regime to digitalisation. One is the revised Product Liability Directive. This Commission's proposal[14] was adopted by the European Parliament on 12 March 2024 ('revised PLD'[15]). The other is the AI Liability Directive (AILD[16]). The proposal for the AILD is currently still under discussion. This chapter aims to provide an explanation of these two proposals with a critical analysis of how they enshrine the principle of proportionality. In particular, it examines whether the two proposals pursue a legitimate goal in general and whether the concrete rules are suitable and necessary means to achieve the goal.[17] Section II analyses how the principle of proportionality is reflected in the AILD. Section III discusses how policymakers attempt to adapt the existing 1985 PLD proportionately to the challenges resulting from digitalisation. A critical analysis is provided in section IV, which considers the problems that may prevent the two directives from properly achieving the goal of proportionality.

II. Proportionality in the AILD

In order to claim damage under tort law, a victim is generally required to prove the fault of the defendant who caused that damage. Strict liability can only apply when it is expressly provided for by law. Strict liability is considered a double-edged sword: on the one hand, it plays a role in providing tortfeasors with an additional incentive to control their activities and easing the burden of proof undertaken by victims; on the other hand, strict liability may deter innovative activities. Therefore, strict liability should be reasonably limited only to ultra-hazardous activities.[18]

[13] See for example, S Li, M Faure and K Havu, 'Liability Rules for AI-Related Harm: Law and Economics Lessons for a European Approach; (2022) 13 *European Journal of Risk Regulation* 618; A Bertolini and F Episcopo, 'The Expert Group's Report on Liability for Artificial Intelligence and Other Emerging Digital Technologies: A Critical Assessment' (2021) 12 *European Journal of Risk Regulation* 1.

[14] Commission, 'Proposal for a Directive of the European Parliament and of the Council on liability for defective products', COM(2022) 495 final.

[15] European Parliament, Legislative resolution of 12 March 2024 on the proposal for a directive of the European Parliament and of the Council on liability for defective products, COM(2022)0495 – C9-0322/2022–2022/0302(COD) ('revised PLD').

[16] Commission, 'Proposal for a Directive of the European Parliament and of the Council on adapting non-contractual civil liability rules to artificial intelligence (AI Liability Directive)', COM(2022) 496 final.

[17] W Sauter, 'Proportionality in EU law: a balancing act?' (2013) 15 *Cambridge Yearbook of European legal studies* 439, 448.

[18] BA Koch, 'Strict liability' in F Busnelli et al (eds), *Principles of European Tort Law* (Springer, 2005) 104.

The applicability of strict liability may extend over time as new risks are identified. Remarkably, strict liability evolves respectively in each country, determined by their own social and economic conditions.[19] In this regard, although different countries could learn from each other, their liability regimes would be significantly divergent concerning not only substantive issues, such as the applicable scenarios of strict liability and the definition of key concepts (eg damage), but also the procedural issues, such as the burden of proof. The increasing application of AI raises the concern to every Member States as whether the current liability regime is suitable for the damage caused by AI. What is more, concerning the transboundary externalities that the output of an AI system can generate, a policymaking-related issue emerges as whether the EU needs to develop a harmonised liability regime that applies to all Member States to address the damage caused by AI. The response to the last issue, like any other motion for harmonisation, should take into account local preferences, and the measures must be suitable and necessary.[20] The AILD was proposed against this background. The following discussion shows how policymakers were attempting to make rules within the AILD proportionate to necessity. Later, in section IV, some counterarguments regarding the proportionality of the AILD are provided.

A. Proportionality in Light of the Extent of Harmonisation

The first issue that policymakers need to address lies in the scope of harmonisation. That is, whether the directive aims to harmonise substantive issues (eg the scope of strict liability and the concept of fault) and/or procedural ones (eg burden of proof). The appropriate response to this issue is the key to reflect the legitimate goals that the directive pursues.

The AILD indicates in its Explanatory Memorandum that three options were proposed for examination.[21] Option 1 only concentrates on procedural issues by easing the burden of proof undertaken by the victims, when they have to rely on fault-based rules to claim their damage that an AI system caused. In this sense, the harmonised liability framework will not endeavour to harmonise any substantive issues. Option 2 is a bit more ambitious. Its idea is that in addition to the uptake of the procedural measures laid down by Option 1, the proposed directive should also address the issue of harmonising liability rules by clarifying the circumstances (in accordance with the risk profile of AI systems) where strict liability shall apply. In other words, Option 2 is similar to the approach given by the Resolution issued by the European Parliament in 2020. Option 3 offers a middle way by suggesting

[19] M Martín-Casals, 'The Principles of European Tort Law (PETL) at the Beginning of a Second Decade' in P Giliker (ed), *Research Handbook on EU Tort Law* (Edward Elgar Publishing, 2017) 361.

[20] D Leczykiewicz, 'Compensatory Remedies in EU law: the Relationship between EU Law and National law' in P Giliker (ed), *Research Handbook on EU Tort Law* (Edward Elgar Publishing, 2017) 63.

[21] Explanatory Memorandum, 9, AILD.

achieving Option 1 and Option 2 in a staged approach: in the first stage, the directive should only provide limited harmonisation for procedural issues; later in the second stage, upon a positive assessment, further harmonisation for substantive issues may be introduced.

The Impact Assessment that comes with the AILD implies that Option 3 is a suitable strategy.[22] Therefore, no substantive matters will be harmonised at this stage. In other words, the liability for any developer and deployer of a specific AI application will still be subject to existing liability regimes, which are largely reshaped by national laws. Since the proposed AILD will only focus on procedural issues, the following question that policymakers need to address is what kind of concrete measures shall be developed to alleviate the burden of proof sustained by victims. A variety of measures are on the table, ranging from the reversal of the proof burden to mere information disclosure. Policymakers ultimately considered that evidence disclosure and rebuttable presumption of causal link would be proportionate, because such measures will strike a better balance between innovation and consumer protection.[23] The following two subsections will pay closer attention to these concrete measures.

B. Proportionality in the Disclosure of Evidence

In the era of AI, victims may have limited access to understand the performance of an AI system, since the data may be kept by the providers and deployers respectively. Without access to such data, it would be extremely difficult for victims to prove the fault that providers and deployers made in the process of developing or controlling the AI system. Concerning this information asymmetry, the draft AI Act has already required the providers of high-risk AI systems to store relevant information properly.[24] Correspondingly, from an ex post perspective, when harm occurs, the law should ensure that victims can access such information in a fair manner. Against this background, the AILD attempts to address the issue of evidence disclosure in its Article 3. The disclosure of evidence, nevertheless, must be consistent with the principle of proportionality.

On the one hand, the rule concerning evidence disclosure must ensure that victims can access relevant information in a smooth manner. The AILD not only allows the claimant that is already in litigation to request the disclosure of evidence, but it also allows the *potential* claimant that has not yet brought a case before the court to do so.[25] The result of their failure to disclose and preserve evidence

[22] Commission, 'Impact Assessment Report accompanying the document Proposal for a Directive of the European Parliament and of the Council on adapting non-contractual civil liability rules to artificial intelligence', SWD(2022) 319 final, 60.
[23] Explanatory Memorandum, 9, AILD.
[24] See eg Arts 11–13 and Art 52 draft AI Act.
[25] Art 2(7) AILD.

would be a presumption of non-compliance with a relevant duty of care.[26] This presumption of non-compliance does not necessarily lead to a presumption of fault per se – whether they are equivalent depends on the national law. This last issue reflects the fact that the AILD will not touch upon substantive issues (eg the concept of fault), so as to keep its unnecessary influence on national legal tradition to minimum.

On the other hand, the disclosure of evidence shall not place too much burden onto the providers and deployers of AI systems. Firstly, evidence disclosure will only apply to the providers and deployers of *high-risk* AI systems. This restriction demonstrates the policymakers' determination to limit measures to what is necessary. Since AI systems without high risk are not required to establish a risk management system or to keep recording, it is reasonable that their providers do not bear an extra burden to provide such information from an ex post perspective. This is proportionate to the regulatory requirement that is placed on these parties. Secondly, a request by a (potential) claimant does not necessarily result in the disclosure of evidence. It is the national court that has to decide whether or not to order a disclosure. Some requirements must be satisfied before the court issues an order. Noticeably, according to the AILD, the court should limit the disclosure to *necessity* and *proportionality*.[27] For all potential claimants, and claimants who have the need of evidence disclosure, they must prove that they have undertaken all *proportionate* attempts in order to collect such evidence, but have failed.[28] If the request for disclosure is from a claimant to a *third party* (ie a party that sits outside the current legal procedure) other than the defendant, the claimant must further prove that they have 'undertaken all proportionate attempts at gathering the relevant evidence from the defendant'. There will be even more stringent measures for *potential claimants*, if they want to request evidence disclosure from *a third party*. In this scenario, they must prove that they have already asked the relevant third party that holds the relevant evidence but were refused, and also present *sufficient facts and evidence* to support the plausibility of a claim for damage. Therefore, the AILD intends to limit its measures to necessary by differentiating the concrete scenarios of evidence disclosure.

It should be remembered that a national court must examine the legitimate interests of all parties while deciding whether or not to issue an evidence disclosure. For example, the court shall consider whether a disclosure can have a negative impact on private interests such as intellectual property and trade secrets as well as public interests such as national security.[29] If the disclosed trade secret has been identified as confidential, courts shall take necessary measures to preserve confidentiality.[30] What is more, to keep the measures proportionate, the defendant is endowed with the possibility of rebutting the presumption of non-compliance.[31]

[26] Art 3(5) para 1 AILD.
[27] Art 3(4), para 1 AILD.
[28] Art 3(2) AILD.
[29] Art 3(4), para 2 AILD.
[30] Art 3(4), para 3 AILD.
[31] Art 3(5), para 2 AILD.

C. Proportionality in Rebuttable Presumption of Causal Link

The second measure that the AILD establishes for the sake of alleviating the proof burden is a rebuttable presumption of causal link for fault-based claims.[32] Different from the rules proposed for evidence disclosure, which applies to only high-risk AI systems, the rebuttable presumption of causal link applies to *all* AI systems regardless of their risk profiles. The possible interpretation of this difference would be that AI systems, regardless of whether they are high-risk or not, can be opaque when it comes to explaining the causal link between their output/failure and the fault of relevant parties.

It is noted that certain conditions must be met before a causal link (between the fault and the output of the AI system) in fault-based rules can be presumed.[33] According to the AILD, there are three conditions that must be met in order to establish a presumption of causal link. First, the fault of the defendant must be established. According to the AILD, however, the threshold of fault for a presuming the causal link is lowered. Specifically, the fault can be sufficiently established if the defendant failed to disclose evidence as ordered by the court according to Article 3(5), or if the defendant failed to comply with a duty of care laid down in Union or national law.[34] Second, it must be *reasonably likely* that the fault has an influence on the output or failure produced by the AI system. Third, the claimant has demonstrated that the output or the failure of the AI system gave rise to the damage.

The aforementioned conditions for a presumption of causation will therefore in principle apply to all types of AI systems as long as the claim is on a fault basis. Nevertheless, the AILD further reshapes the applicability of the presumption concerning the risk level of AI systems. In specific, for the damage caused by high-risk AI systems, the national court shall not apply the presumption based on the aforementioned three requirements, if the defendant demonstrates that the claimant has reasonable access to sufficient evidence and expertise to prove the causal link. In comparison, for the damage caused by AI systems without a high risk, the presumption of causal link can *only* be made if the national court considers it 'excessively difficult' for the claimant to prove the causal link.

III. Proportionality in the Revised PLD

Product liability defines the liability rules in cases where damage was caused by defective products. In 1985, the Product Liability Directive (PLD) was established, which set up harmonised rules that Member States should respect. In particular, the producer of a defective product would be liable when their defective product

[32] Art 1(1)(b) AILD.
[33] Art 4(1) AILD.
[34] Art 4(1)(a) AILD.

caused damage. The effectiveness of the 1985 PLD, however, has been challenged due to emerging technologies driven by AI, 3D printing and cloud computing.[35] Against this background, it is necessary to specify how to adapt the current PLD to the transformations led by digital technologies and circular economy. It should be noted that the PLD is a directive with maximum, rather than minimum, harmonisation. A minimum harmonisation may enable Member States to set up more stringent rules to enhance consumer protection, but it can meanwhile hamper innovative activities.[36] Therefore, as the Explanatory Memorandum in the Commission's proposal states, the revised PLD should strike a balance between the interests of industry and consumers in the digital age.[37] The following section provides a critical analysis of how the revised PLD attempts to achieve this balance.

A. Proportionality in Defining the 'Product', 'Damage' and 'Defectiveness'

Several concepts, such as product, damage and defectiveness, are crucial in outlining the scope of product liability. This section discusses how the proposal for the revised PLD is intended to adapt its key concepts for the purpose of striking a balance between innovation and consumer protection.

Firstly, the revised PLD substantially extends the definition of *product*. According to the current 1985 PLD, the scope of product is limited to 'movables'.[38] This definition, however, is considered outdated in the digital age, since intangible goods like software can also raise safety concerns.[39] The revised PLD attempts to address this gap. First of all, it clarifies that software per se is a product in its own right. Specifically, the PLD numerates in its recital that operating systems, computer programs, applications and AI systems are software.[40] What is more, digital services that are integrated into or interconnected with a product will be considered a component of the product, on the condition that their absence would prevent products from performing their functions.[41] The damage caused by services is traditionally addressed on a fault basis. By recognising the related service as a component of the overall product, it enables consumers in certain circumstances to claim their damage directly against the service providers based

[35] See eg, G Wagner, 'Liability Rules for the Digital Age: Aiming for the Brussles Effect' (2022) 13 *Journal of European Tort Law* 191; S Li and L Visscher, 'Product liability in the Context of 3D printing: A Law and Economics Approach' (2020) 3 *Aansprakelijkheid, Verzekering en Schade* 1.

[36] J-S Borghetti, 'Taking EU Product Liability Law Seriously: How Can the Product Liability Directive Effectively Contribute to Consumer Protection?' (2023), available at papers.ssrn.com/abstract=4502351.

[37] Explanatory Memorandum, 6, Commission's proposal for the revised PLD.

[38] Art 2 Council Directive 85/374/EEC.

[39] TS Cabral, 'Liability and Artificial Intelligence in the EU: Assessing the Adequacy of the Current Product Liability Directive' (2020) 27 *Maastricht Journal of European and Comparative Law* 615.

[40] Recital 13 revised PLD.

[41] Recital 17 revised PLD.

on tort liability, even if there is no contractual relationship. However, the revised PLD made it clear that a related service would be considered a component only if it is within the control of the manufacturer of the overall product. In the case that it is not authorised by the manufacturer, the related service is out of its control, so it is unfair to require the manufacturer to bear the liability caused by such as service. Moreover, digital data or information per se is not defined as a product according to the revised PLD.[42] In contrast, a digital manufacturing file that represents a digital version of a product (eg the digital file used for 3D printing) will be considered a product. Finally, free and open-source software supplied outside the course of commercial activity will be excluded from the concept of product. This reflects how the revised PLD attempts to strike a balance between consumer protection and innovation.[43] Therefore, while the reshaped definition of product tremendously empowers consumers, it attempts to provide more legal certainty for industry.

Secondly, the revised PLD reshapes the concept of *tort damage* that can be compensated through a claim based on product liability. 'Tort damage' refers to the compensable harm defined by law. According to the current 1985 PLD, the scope of tort damage is strictly limited to the *material damage* resulting from personal injury, death and property loss of less than 500 euros.[44] In contrast, the compensation for the material damage to other legal interests and the non-material damage would be left to the legal framework, which will be further clarified under national laws.[45] In general, the revised PLD reshapes the protected interests in three aspects.[46] First, the material damage of medically recognised harm to psychological health that results from personal injury or property loss will be considered compensable tort damage in the revised PLD.[47] In this regard, the scope of protected legal rights and interests has been slightly extended to psychological wellbeing. This change is consistent with technological development: safety not only includes physical wellbeing but also mental health. What is more, the proprietary aspect of data will be considered a protected interest under the revised PLD.[48] Whether data is a kind of property is a controversial issue on which Member States have not yet reached an agreement.[49] In this regard, conceiving data as a protected interest under liability law is a compromise to compensate for the losses resulting from unsafe products. Moreover, the revised PLD removes the threshold of

[42] Recital 13 revised PLD.

[43] Recital 14 revised PLD.

[44] Art 9 Council Directive 85/374/EEC.

[45] S Li, 'Compensation for non-material damage under Article 82 GDPR: A review of Case C-300/21' (2023) 30 *Maastricht Journal of European and Comparative Law* 335; S Li and B Schütte, 'The proposal for a revised Product Liability Directive: The emperor's new clothes?' (2023) 30 *Maastricht Journal of European and Comparative Law* 573.

[46] Art 6(1) revised PLD.

[47] Art 6(1)(a) revised PLD.

[48] Art 6(1)(c) revised PLD.

[49] See eg, N Purtova, *Property Rights in Personal Data: A European Perspective* (Kluwer Law International, 2012).

500 euros for the loss of property. This is proportionate to the social and economic conditions of Member States. 500 euros is not a small loss for victims in certain states, so the removal of this threshold could better protect consumers.

Thirdly, the revised PLD reconfigures the criteria for assessing *defectiveness*. The current 1985 PLD adopts a consumer expectation test to decide whether a product is defective or not. In particular, consumers' expectations of the presentation and potential use of the product are key factors of evaluating defectiveness.[50] A product will not be considered defective solely because a better product is subsequently placed in circulation.[51] The revised PLD pertains to the consumer expectation test, but it introduces new factors that should be considered when evaluating the defectiveness. For example, considering the fact that many products now employ learning-based systems to optimise the performance of products after circulation, the failure to *update* such systems after sale can lead to damage. In this regard, the evaluation of defectiveness will no longer be constrained to the time when a product is placed on the market. Instead, its assessment will be a continuous process as long as the provider still takes control of the product.[52] In addition, the failure to adopt proper safety-relevant cybersecurity measures may contribute to defectiveness according to the revised PLD.[53]

To briefly summarise, this section shows how the revised PLD attempts to adapt key concepts, such as product, damage and defectiveness, to the new challenges. Such changes will have profound influence on the applicability of the PLD in the digital age, reflecting the ambition of EU policymakers to rebalance technological development and consumer protection. Nevertheless, the concrete measures that the revised PLD has proposed may still deviate from the principle of proportionality. These issues will be raised and discussed in section IV.

B. Proportionality in Allocating the Liability for Economic Operators

According to the 1985 PLD, 'producer' is the party that is subject to strict product liability.[54] 'Producer' refers to a number of parties, including the manufacturer of a finished product or a component part, the producer of raw materials, the importer and any person who presents themselves as such.[55] What is more, the supplier will be recognised as the producer if none of the previous actors can be identified by the victim.[56] In this regard, the current 1985 PLD distinguishes strict liability and

[50] Art 6(1) Council Directive 85/374/EEC.
[51] Art 6(2) Council Directive 85/374/EEC.
[52] Art 7(1)(c) and (e) revised PLD.
[53] Art 7(1)(f) revised PLD.
[54] Art 1 Council Directive 85/374/EEC.
[55] Art 3(1) and (2) Council Directive 85/374/EEC.
[56] Art 3(3) Council Directive 85/374/EEC.

fault-based rules in accordance with the position and role that an actor takes along the supply chain. Actors from the upstream of the supply chain are subject to strict liability due to their substantial impact on the function of a product. In comparison, actors residing downstream are in principle subject to fault-based liability, since they normally cannot directly influence the functionality of a product.

This logic of allocating liability among different actors along the supply chain reflects how legislators strive to protect vulnerable consumers, and it has been largely maintained in the proposal for revising the PLD. The revised PLD replaces 'producer' with 'economic operator'. This change is consistent with other regulations, such as the draft AI Act.[57] The revised PLD further extends the scope of liable persons, making sure that consumers will not be unfairly disadvantaged considering the complex supply chain in the digital age.[58]

Firstly, the 'manufacturer' shall be liable for the damage caused by defective products. The 'component manufacturer' shall be liable for the damage caused by defective components. It is noteworthy that, since the definition of 'product' has been expanded to software and digital files, the scope of manufacturers is becoming broader accordingly. Actors like software developers and AI system providers will be defined as economic operators.

Secondly, considering that the manufacturer of a defective product may reside outside the EU, the revised PLD makes it clear that the importer as well as the authorised representative of the manufacturer will be liable in this situation.[59] In a case where neither of them can be identified, the fulfilment service provider shall be liable for the damage caused by a defective product.[60] The scope of the fulfilment service provider, however, should be reasonably restricted to avoid excessive liability. According to Article 4(13) of the revised PLD, it refers to

> any natural or legal person offering, in the course of commercial activity, at least two of the following services: warehousing, packaging, addressing and dispatching of a product, without having ownership of the product, with the exception of postal services as defined in Article 2, point (1), of Directive 97/67/EC of the European Parliament and of the Council.

Thirdly, if the victim is unable to identify any of the aforementioned economic operators, the distributor of the defective product shall be recognised as an economic operator unless it could disclose the identity of the above-mentioned parties.[61] In the digital age, consumers are increasingly relying on online platforms to acquire products that are manufactured outside the EU. In that case, an injured person may not have the chance to identify an importer or local representative of the manufacturer. Taking this challenge into consideration, to better protect

[57] Art 3(8) draft AI Act.
[58] Art 8 revised PLD.
[59] Art 8(1)(c) revised PLD.
[60] ibid.
[61] Art 8(3) revised PLD.

consumers, the revised PLD recognises the provider of the online platform as an economic operator, *given that* an average consumer believes that the defective product was provided by the online platform.[62]

Last but not least, the revised PLD adapts the scope of economic operators to the challenges that circular economy brings about. Any person who makes a significant modification to a product after it has been released onto the market and outside the control of the original producers will be regarded as a new manufacturer. They will be held accountable under the same legal standard (ie strict product liability) as other predetermined manufacturers in this situation.[63] A substantial modification can be explained as an upgrade that changes the original intended functions of a product. In comparison, carrying out necessary repairs to restore the function of a product will not be defined as a substantial modification.[64]

To summarise, the revised PLD significantly extends the scope of liable parties, making sure that consumers could have a fair chance to find a liable person, when they suffered damage caused by defective products.

C. Proportionality in Evidence Disclosure, Presumption of Defectiveness and Presumption of Causal Link

In a product liability claim, the claimant has to prove that (1) the product is defective, (2) there is damage, and (3) the damage is caused by the defective product.[65] Although fault is no longer an element to be proved, the proof of the three above-mentioned elements can still be a huge burden for a claimant. Against this background, besides refiguring the scope of the product, another goal of the revised PLD is to set up concrete rules to ensure that victims can have smooth access to justice to claim their damage.

During the public consultation phase, two options were proposed concerning the measures to ease the burden of proof in the revised PLD.[66] One option aims to enable victims to require the disclosure of relevant evidence from defendants and to presume the defectiveness and causal link. The other option is more drastic, aiming at *reversing* the burden of proof from victims to producers. According to this second option, it will be the producers that have to prove that their products were not defective or did not cause the damage. Ultimately, policymakers considered that the first option would be a strategy that is proportionate to the necessity, while the second option is too far-reaching and could deter innovative activities.

[62] Art 8(4) revised PLD.
[63] Art 8(2) revised PLD.
[64] Recital 39 revised PLD.
[65] Art 10(1) revised PLD.
[66] Commission, 'Impact Assessment Report accompanying the document Proposal for a Directive of the European Parliament and of the Council on liability for defective products', SWD(2022) 316 final, 31.

Regarding the disclosure of evidence, similar to the AILD, the revised PLD also requires the claimant to present sufficient facts and evidence to support the plausibility of their claim.[67] In addition, consideration must be given to other parties' interests, including trade secrets. Apart from that, there are some significant differences between the AILD and the revised PLD concerning the rules on evidence disclosure. Firstly, under the revised PLD the only party who may ask for the disclosure of evidence is the claimant. The potential claimant, in contrast, cannot demand evidence disclosure. Secondly, unlike the AILD, which limits the disclosure of evidence to the damage caused by a *high-risk* AI system, the disclosure of evidence can apply indifferently to all products under the revised PLD. Therefore, compared with the AILD, fewer people are eligible to demand a disclosure of evidence based on the revised PLD, but the range of products that the disclosure of evidence applies to is significantly broader. Thirdly, the consequence of failing to disclose evidence under the AILD will lead to a presumption that the defendant is at fault. In contrast, according to the revised PLD, the failure to properly disclose evidence may lead to a presumption of the defectiveness of the product.[68]

The revised PLD also outlines the scenarios under which a causal link shall be presumed. According to the revised PLD, a causal link can be presumed, 'where it has been established that the product is defective and the damage caused is of a kind typically consistent with the defect in question'.[69] The extent to which the damage claimed by the injured person is typically consistent with the defect in question will thereby be a matter left to the discretion of national courts.

The revised PLD indicates that in the cases where the conditions of presuming the defectiveness or causal link is not met, the presumption can still be made if two conditions are satisfied. Firstly, the national court judges that the claimant faces technical or scientific complexity to prove the defectiveness or causal link or both.[70] Based on that, secondly, the claimant can at least demonstrate that 'the product contributed to the damage' and 'it is likely that the product was defective or that its defectiveness is a likely cause of the damage, or both'. Proportionally, the defendant can void the presumption by contesting either of the two conditions aforementioned.

IV. Discussion: Rethinking Proportionality within the AILD and the PLD

The analysis so far summarises the measures that policymakers have established within the two proposals that concern proportionality. This section argues that

[67] Art 9(2) revised PLD.

[68] According to Art 10(2) besides (a) the failure of disclosing evidence, another two conditions, which are (b) the failure of compliance with mandatory safety requirements and (c) that the damage was caused by obvious malfunction during normal use, can be used to presume the defectiveness of the product.

[69] Art 10(2)(a) revised PLD.

[70] Art 10(3) revised PLD.

the expected proportionality may not be achieved due to the uncertainties existing in the proposals.

A. Rethinking Proportionality in the PLD

The key to proportionality within the revised PLD is adapting current rules to the challenges of digitalisation with a concern for balancing the interests between consumers and industry. The discussion in this section indicates that while the revised PLD pursues a legitimate goal, some concrete definitions and measures might be unsuitable, which could distort the principle of proportionality.

First, despite the fact that classifying software as a product can significantly increase the level of consumer protection, making sure that they could be compensated even if the product is intangible, the definition of software is missing in the revised PLD. In the digital era, the distinction between software and digital services becomes blurry. Therefore, it is necessary to provide a clear guideline to stakeholders.

Second, defining software as a product could be a double-edged sword. On the one hand, as has been seen, software providers might be encouraged to develop safe software. On the other hand, it could significantly deter innovative activities. How to draw a line that can strike a balance is thereby a challenging issue. According to the revised PLD, as a failure to timely update software can lead to defectiveness and thus result in tort liability rather than contractual liability, the burden that a software developer undertakes to keep software safe throughout the lifecycle can be overwhelming.[71] In brief, while ensuring a swift safety update for software must be implemented for the sake of protecting consumers, imposing a non-contractual duty on software developers may unsuitable.

Third, it is controversial whether or not the measures of alleviating the burden of proof will ultimately benefit consumers. The PLD is by nature a maximum harmonised directive. This implies that Member States shall not introduce or maintain more, or less, stringent rules in their national laws than the directive.[72] As a consequence, those Member States that have already taken, or are preparing to introduce, stricter procedural rules (eg reversal burden of proof) will not be allowed. In this sense, from a federalism perspective, the procedural harmonisation may prevent the local preference from being realised.

B. Rethinking Proportionality in the AILD

In contrast with the PLD, the AILD is a brand-new directive, which targets the liability for the damage that is caused by AI systems. The key to proportionality

[71] P Hacker, 'The European AI liability directives – Critique of a half-hearted approach and lessons for the future' (2023) 51 *Computer Law and Security Review* 1, 28.

[72] Art 3 revised PLD.

is the degree to which the harmonisation shall be established. As analysed, policymakers agreed that it would be too far-reaching to provide harmonisation for substantive issues at this stage. Instead, the harmonisation shall be limited to procedural issues. The pullback from the contentious substantive issues reflects that policymakers have realised the different local social and economic conditions in each Member State and agreed that the proposed AILD should be proportionate to such a divergence. Different Member States developed their own liability rules in a simultaneous manner and thereby formed different understandings concerning concepts like fault and damage. Therefore, there is not yet a collective willingness among Member States to pursue harmonisation for the substantive issues.

What remains unclear within the current version of the AILD, however, is its added value. Given the difficulties that victims can meet when claiming the damage caused by an AI system, it is reasonable to predict that, even without a harmonisation motion, Member States would still attempt to lay down their own rules concerning the alleviation of the burden of proof. Since local preferences are the primary driving force behind this, a paternalistic top-down harmonisation for procedural harmonisation may not be required.[73]

What is worse is that it is still not exactly clear about the exact scenarios that the AILD is intended to apply to. Although the AILD indicates that it will only apply to the damage that is 'caused' by an AI system,[74] causation as a substantive term could be understood quite differently from one Member State to another. Accordingly, there can be significant differences regarding the admissibility and implementation of the AILD at the national level.

Even worse, the degree to which the proportionality laid down by the AILD can be properly implemented in practice remains unknown. As seen above, many conditions that are key to the presumption of causation and evidence disclosure will be ultimately interpreted by national courts. For instance, one condition of presuming the causal link is that it is 'reasonably likely' that the fault has influenced the output produced by the AI system. However, what constitutes a 'reasonably likely' remains a matter that is not addressed by the directive. Therefore, guidelines shall be offered to national courts to make sure that their interpretation is consistent with the principle of proportionality that the AILD aims to reflect.

V. Conclusion

The recently proposed AILD and PLD show how EU policymakers are attempting to adapt the liability regime to deal with the challenges of digitalisation. This chapter discussed the major rules of the two proposals through the lens of the

[73] This dates back to the fundamental argument about why harmonisation serves as the starting point of legislation and what factors may justify a movement to harmonsation. See M Faure, 'Product Liability and Product Safety in Europe: Harmonization or Differentitation' (2000) 53 *Kyklos* 467.

[74] Recital 15 AILD.

principle of proportionality. By restricting the scope of harmonisation to procedural issues, the AILD is not intended to provide a far-reaching proposal that touches upon the substantive issues concerning liability. The revised PLD takes the principle of proportionality into account by carefully striking the balance between consumer protection and industrial innovation. This chapter critically showed that even though the two proposals marked an important step to adapt liability rules to the challenges raised by digitalisation with a concern about proportionality, the current provisions contain some uncertainties that can further distort the effectiveness of proportionality. These uncertainties come not only from the blurry definition of key concepts (eg software) but also from the reliance on the discretion of national courts. Therefore, further measures shall be taken. On the one hand, the two directives should further crystalise the key concepts within the two directives. On the other hand, extra guidelines shall be further developed to ensure that national courts can make decisions that are consistent with the principle of proportionality.

7

The Principle of Proportionality in Relations between Users and Providers of Digital Services

ALEKSANDRA GLISZCZYŃSKA-GRABIAS, MICHAŁ JABŁOŃSKI
AND KRZYSZTOF KOŹMIŃSKI

I. Proportionality in the Digital Age? Introductory Remarks

Given the broad scope of issues related to digital services, this chapter is limited to selected matters serving to frame a discussion about proportionality. Thus, we have decided to focus on the correct legislative approach – as we see it, based on our academic and practical experiences – for regulating relations between users and providers of digital services. PSD3[1] and the Payment Services Regulation[2] serve as background for a proportionality analysis from the perspective of consumer protection and regulation of social media platforms within the context of human rights (particularly freedom of speech).

It seems to us – which is the hypothesis verified in the chapter – that one of the sources of the problem in ensuring the implementation of the principle of proportionality in shaping legal relations between providers and users of digital services is the competition of various, difficult-to-reconcile principles and values of the legal system. On the one hand, it is easy to point to examples of over-regulation and obvious, disproportionate privileges given to consumers, clients or users, which pose a threat to entrepreneurs, market efficiency, free competition and the economy in general. At the same time, on the other hand, we see areas where freedom of speech, freedom of expression and exchange of views lead to threats to human rights and the protection of citizens against disinformation or political

[1] Proposal for a Directive of the European Parliament and of the Council on payment services and electronic money services in the Internal Market amending Directive 98/26/EC and repealing Directives 2015/2366/EU and 2009/110/EC.

[2] Proposal for a Regulation of the European Parliament and of the Council on payment services in the internal market and amending Regulation (EU) No 1093/2010.

propaganda. There are also justified questions as to whether self-regulation or no regulation is a good solution. As a consequence, the multitude of challenges facing the legislator makes it difficult to properly 'balance' interests, rights and reasons, which poses a threat to the principle of proportionality.

The principle of proportionality is, on the one hand, a foundational pillar of European Union law and, on the other hand, a fundamental principle of Member States' legal systems (being enshrined, inter alia, in Article 31(3) of the Constitution of the Republic of Poland). Proportionality prescribes that legal measures should be adequate (proportional) in relation to the desired target or outcome, thus appropriate and necessary to achieve its objectives.[3] In other words, legislative acts, as well as decisions on enforcement thereof must meet the following criteria commonly termed a 'proportionality test': adequacy (ie whether a given restrictive regulation is suitable for attaining the proclaimed general interest objective) and necessity (ie whether it goes beyond what is required to achieve said objective).[4] Furthermore, according to the jurisprudence of European courts, the proportionality test entails three phases of scrutiny: suitability, necessity, proportionality (in the strict sense).[5]

Furthermore, the principle of proportionality has other dimensions, as it delimits the respective powers of the EU and the Member States. Moreover, within contract law, proportionality balances the rights and obligations of contracting parties.[6] It also seeks to determine an outcome of conflicts between principles and values in the process of their application. In this way, proportionality emanates as a practical embodiment of Aristotle's idea of the golden mean, requiring the avoidance of extreme solutions.[7] Finally, proportionality is germane to the process of regulatory impact assessment (both *ex ante* and ex post).[8]

The focus of our analysis is proportionality against the backdrop of the digital age, a notion that is not strictly defined, yet intuitively understood. In most legal studies it means[9] an era of increased and widespread use of modern technologies, including multimedia communication tools, the internet, big data, cybersecurity,

[3] T Tridimas, 'The Principle of Proportionality' in R Schütze and Prof T Tridimas (eds), *Oxford Principles Of European Union Law: The European Union Legal Order: Volume I* (Oxford Academic Press, 2018).

[4] N Reich, *The Principle of Proportionality. In General Principles of EU Civil Law* (Intersentia, 2013) 155–88.

[5] G Scaccia, 'Proportionality and the Balancing of Rights in the Case-law of European Courts' (2019) federalismi.it, 6, available at www.federalismi.it/nv14/articolo-documento.cfm?Artid=38092.

[6] C Cauffman, 'The Principle of Proportionality and European Contract Law' (2013) 5 *Maastricht European Private Law Institute*, Working Paper 3.

[7] A Śledzińska-Simon, *Analiza proporcjonalności ograniczeń konstytucyjnych praw i wolności. Teoria i praktyka* (Wydawnictwo Uniwersytetu Wrocławskiego, 2019) 23–25.

[8] S Kasiewicz, *PSD 2: krytyczny przystanek na drodze do nowej ery bankowości* (Szkoła Główna Handlowa, 2018) 80.

[9] eg, T-E Synodinou, P Jougleux and C Markou, *EU Internet Law in the Digital Era: Regulation and Enforcement* (Springer, 2019); S Merill and W Raduchel (eds), *Copyright in the Digital Era. Building Evidence for Policy* (The National Academies Press, 2019); M Katsh, *Law in a Digital World* (Oxford University Press, 1995).

3D printing, software and AI technologies as well as the entire 'digital culture' of life, all of which, in turn, bring about new rights, obligations and crimes. Without doubt, this dynamically changing reality affects the law, generating significant consequences for its practice, theory and teaching.[10]

The chapter first provides a handful of observations on the evolution and impact of European consumer law on the national legal systems of the EU Member States. Next, it describes the tendency to strengthen consumer protection in the area of payment services, with particular emphasis on the currently projected amendment to the provisions of the PSD2 directive. This, will showcase the controversies, shortcomings and pitfalls of the legal framework, based on the discussion of some draft regulations promoting a far-reaching model of consumer protection, flouting common sense. In this critique, we rely on our previous publications questioning the excessive reach of consumer protection in the provisions of statutory law, which often reflect a burgeoning and radically pro-consumer case law.[11] The last section focuses on abuses of human rights protection (mainly freedom of speech) in the area of social media platforms, either through regulatory measures or judicial actions.

II. Consumer Rights Revolution and Related Changes in the Legal System

According to Benöhr, 'recent years have seen a progressive convergence of fundamental rights and consumer protection in EU law'.[12] Consumer law is differentiated as a separate field of law from the law of obligations, economic or administrative law.[13] Moreover, consumer rights are increasingly linked to human rights, and as such are found in the catalogue of first, second and third generation of human rights.[14] This link is even more evident in the so-called digital era, due to the development of modern technologies, which sometimes interferes with 'digital

[10] R Sherwin, N Feingenson and S Christina, 'Law in the Digital Age: How Visual Communication Technologies are Transforming the Practice, Theory, and Teaching of Law' (2006) *NYLS Legal Studies Research Paper* 227.

[11] See, inter alia, M Jabłoński and K Koźmiński, *Bankowe kredyty waloryzowane do kursu walut obcych w orzecznictwie sądowym* (Wolters Kluwer Polska, 2018); M Jabłoński and K Koźmiński (eds), *Procesy frankowe w Polsce po wyroku TSUE w sprawie C-260/18* (Wydawnictwa Drugie, 2018); K Koźmiński, 'Bank loans denominated and indexed to foreign currency – a Polish, Ukrainian or Europe-wide problem?' (2017) *Studia Iuridica* 117; K Koźmiński, 'Trwała bezskuteczność klauzuli abuzywnej. Glosa do uchwały (7) Sądu Najwyższego z 7 maja 2021 r. (III CZP 6/21)' (2022) *Monitor Prawa Bankowego* 51.

[12] I Benöhr, 'The Evolution of Consumer Protection and Human Rights' in I Benöhr (ed), 'EU Consumer Law and Human Rights' (Oxford Academic, 2013) ch 3.

[13] G Howells, I Ramsay and T Wilhelmsson, 'Consumer law in its international dimension' in G Howells, I Ramsay, T Wihelmsson and D Kraft (eds), *Handbook of Research on International Consumer Law* (Edward-Elgar, 2010) ch 1.

[14] M. Malczyńska-Biały, 'Consumer Protection in Chosen Systems of Human Rights' (2018) 4 *Polityka i Społeczeństwo* 112.

human rights' and may impact individual freedoms (including the right to privacy, personal data, etc).[15]

Malczyńska-Biały emphasises that

> consumer rights can be divided into four basic categories: the right to safety, the right to be informed, the right to choose and the right to be heard, which means in practice that: consumers ought to be protected against hazardous products … unfair market practices, advertisements, labels and misleading information. Consumers should be well-informed while making a choice of products and services.[16]

According to this approach, from the beginning of the 1960s, regulations aimed at enhancing consumer protection and thus modifying traditional institutions and principles of contract law, have been ushered in in many Anglo-Saxon and Western European countries.[17] As Micklitz, Sibony and Esposito noted:

> For decades consumer law has been the stepchild of the legal discipline, neither public nor private law, not classic but postmodern, not 'legal enough', 'too political' … Times are changing. We are perhaps reaching the point at which the world comes to understand the real value of consumer law.[18]

Currently, European consumer law is composed of numerous directives relating to narrow and selected issues, envisaging several hundred provisions, often general, enigmatic, inconsistent with each other and causing doubts as to their compatibility with the principles of legislative technique.[19]

Furthermore, what follows from the increased importance and expansion of consumer law is a 'radical change in civil law' requiring a 'new system of thinking' and engendering 'far-reaching effects of these legal changes'.[20] The magnitude of these changes is recognised by scholars who emphasise, for example, that consumer protection is currently at the heart of many banking regulations aimed at balancing the relationship between the bank and the client.[21] However, it is warranted to note, that several practical problems, negatively affecting the effectiveness of regulations, arise, as 'in the European Union there is no single,

[15] C Nyst and T Falchetta, 'The right to privacy in the digital age' (2017) 9 *Journal of Human Rights Practice* 104; see also C Goodwin, 'Privacy: Recognition of a Consumer Right' (1991) 10 *Journal of Public Policy & Marketing* 149.

[16] Malczyńska-Biały (n 14) 113.

[17] D Harland, 'Some International Dimensions of Consumer Law and Policy' (1987) 29 *Journal of the Indian Law Institute* 451.

[18] H-W Micklitz, A-L Sibony and F Esposito, 'The bright and adventurous of consumer law research' in H-W Micklitz, A-L Sibony and F Esposito (eds), *Research Methods in Consumer Law. A Handbook* (Edward-Elgar, 2018) ch 1. See also H-W Micklitz and T Wilhelmsson, 'Looking Back to Look Forward' in H-W Micklitz (ed), *The Making of Consumer Law and Policy in Europe* (Oxford University Press, 2021) ch 12.

[19] H Schulte-Nölke and L Tichy, 'Introduction' in H Schulte-Nölke and L Tichy (eds), *Perspectives for European Consumer Law Towards a Directive on Consumer Rights and Beyond* (Sellier, 2010).

[20] M Lutter, 'Polskie ustawodawstwo w ochronie konsumentów oraz inwestorów rynku kapitałowego' (2001) *Prawo Papierów Wartościowych* 5–6.

[21] I H-Y Chiu and J Wilson, *Banking Law and Regulation* (Oxford University Press, 2018) 9.

compact code of consumer protection, containing provisions including all EU directives concerning very diverse issues'.[22] European consumer law is fragmented and co-exists on two levels of consumer protection governance (EU and Member States).[23] Contemporary consumer law is therefore rather a patchwork of a myriad of distinct legal concepts. Consequently the current regulatory framework seems to offer solutions to the symptoms, rather than to the causes.[24]

Finally, consumer law is challenging existing legislative techniques, traced back to the Enlightenment. Notably the concept that each area of law should be codified in bespoke provisions within separate statutes as so-called *leges generales*. To the contrary, contemporary consumer law is an assortment of private and public law regulations, with its sources derived from individual provisions of civil codes, special laws (ie so-called *leges speciales*), as well as landmark judgments of national and supranational courts (especially the CJEU).[25] In this context, the rise of consumer protection is sometimes considered as a twilight of traditionally understood codification of laws.[26]

Notwithstanding the above, instances of abuse of consumer protection cannot be underestimated. Prevoiusly mentionedcase law of the CJEU, along with the dynamically evolving understanding of the notion of consumer, information obligations and unfair contract terms laws have sparked in Poland a string of actions and judgments seeking to challenge loan agreements concluded in the first decade of the twenty-first century, including those preceding Poland's accession to the EU. For instance, even though indexed/denominated mortgage loan agreements (in Poland, most prevalently linked to the Swiss franc exchange rate) had been historically deemed legally permissible and more favourable for borrowers (as such, they enjoyed great popularity), a worse economic environment after 2015 precipitated attempts to undermine them. Against this background, it is a defensible corollary that:

> The ECJ case law on Swiss franc mortgages is a prime example of the dynamic interpretation of EU law aimed at addressing challenges that could not have been envisaged at the time of drafting. (…) the Member States where the problem at issue arose (Poland,

[22] S Smyczek, *Consumer Protection Standards in Europe* (Placet, 2019) 279.

[23] C Poncibo, 'Some Thoughts on the Methodological Approach to EC Consumer Law Reform' (2009) *Loyola Consumer Law Review* 353.

[24] MG Porcedda, 'Patching the patchwork: appraising the EU regulatory framework on cyber security breaches' (2018) 34 *Computer Law & Security Review* 1077.

[25] This was a recent occurrence in Poland, when a judgment of the CJEU (based upon the relatively general Directive 93/13, duly transposed into Polish domestic law) radically changed the methodology utilised by Polish common courts to dispose of cases regarding loans indexed/denominated to a foreign currency between banks and consumers. For a critique of this approach, see J Rudnicki, 'Wyrok TSUE w sprawie Dziubak a trendy i zjawiska kształtujące współczesne prawo prywatne' in M Jabłoński and K Koźmiński (eds) *Procesy frankowe w Polsce po wyroku TSUE w sprawie C-260/18* (Wydawnictwa Drugie, 2020) 98–99.

[26] See F Zoll, 'The Sense of the Consumer Code at the End of the Concept of the Consumer' in M Novotná (ed), *Zásady európskeho súkromného práva v aplikačnej praxi: Spotrebiteľský kódex: áno či nie?* (Prague, 2018) 13–14.

Hungary, Romania, Croatia and, Slovakia) were not even EU Member States at the time when the directive was adopted (1993).[27]

Such 'dynamic interpretation' led courts to accept the inference that long-term (20–30 years) legal relationships may be terminated by the consumer when it is no longer economically profitable for them. This necessarily means a degradation of the founding principles of contract law such as *pacta sunt servanda*, and the undermining of constitutional principles, including *nullum poena sine lege* through *de facto* 'punishing' businesses exclusively based on an activist judicial interpretation. What had previously been seemingly inconceivable came into effect: the business should ultimately incur a loss by providing, in effect, a completely unprofitable or even complimentary service due to the consumer's objection – all of this despite the dubious character of the notions of information asymmetry and the weaker bargaining position of the consumer (said to be allegedly less aware of their rights or interests), and the complete 'detachment' of law from economic reality.[28]

It needs to be emphasised that the balanced consumer model still remains an unsolved conundrum. EU law does not lean on or otherwise spell out the concept of an average consumer, nor does it formulate a single, abstract consumer concept – the consumer pattern is not static but rather dynamic, as it is predicated upon and fluctuates according to the relevant socio-economic conditions. Whether the body of consumer law has an inherently dynamic character is invariably subject to permanent transformations, including changes in legislation and court decisions.[29] As faith in the rationality of financial market participants has been lost, and with the requirement to fulfill information obligations and develop financial awareness now denounced as insufficient, the consumer protection paradigm has undergone a change, too.[30]

Paradoxically, consumer law – contrary to the interests of the average consumer – is also considered over-regulated, excessively convoluted and, consequently, 'more expensive' and less effective.[31] Regardless of controversies over consumer rights being classified as human rights,[32] consumer protection may end

[27] R Mańko, 'Unfair terms in Swiss franc loans. Overview of European Court of Justice case law' (March 2021), available at www.europarl.europa.eu/RegData/etudes/BRIE/2021/689361/EPRS_BRI(2021)689361_EN.pdf.

[28] H Eidenmüller et al, 'Towards a Revision of the Consumer-acquis' (2011) *Common Market Law Review* 1077.

[29] J Dybiński, 'Pojęcie konsumenta na rynku kapitałowym w prawie polskim i unijnym' (2018) 27 *Kwartalnik Prawa Prywatnego* 505.

[30] D Cyman, 'Kierunki zmian ochrony konsumenta usług finansowych w Unii Europejskiej' (2016) *Annales Universitatis Mariae Curie-Skłodowska*, section 4.

[31] See, inter alia, S Becher, 'Unintended Consequences and the Design of Consumer Protection Legislation' (2018) 93 *Tulane Law Review* 105; E Mišćenić, 'Croatian Consumer Protection Law: From Legal Approximation to Legal Fragmentation (Part II)' (2018) 23 *Studia Iuridica Toruniensia* 177.

[32] See S Deutch, 'Are Consumer Rights Human Rights?' (1994) 32 *Osgoode Hall Law Journal* 537; M Cranston, 'Human Rights, Real and Supposed', in D Raphael (ed), *Political Theory and the Rights of Man* (Indiana University Press, 1967) 172; H Hannum, 'Reinvigorating Human Rights for the Twenty-First Century' (2016) 16 *Human Rights Law Review* 409, 413.

up facing dilemmas analogous to those human rights have had to grapple with. For the latter, often viewed sceptically as being 'on the verge of becoming a victim of their own success',[33] have had to combat worries[34] that the frivolous proliferation of new rights can also be an obstacle against the reinvigoration of human rights in the twenty-first century. As is the case with inflation in the field of monetary policy, human rights inflation leads to the apparent ubiquity of individual rights coupled with the undesirable effects of trivialising the same, as well as weakening their effectiveness, rank and importance.[35] Consumer rights find themselves, it appears, in a similar situation, as their multiplication does not give rise to an obvious improvement of consumers' security. On the contrary, businesses resort to limiting the scope of services offered and/or increase their prices in order to minimise the legal risks associated with consumer law. This, in turn, narrows the range of products and services available to consumers. Jurisdictions that unconditionally prioritise consumer protection over innovation (intrinsically co-existent with risk) can be considered less attractive for global players considering factors such as competitiveness and technological development. That consumers from such countries demand access to the same scope of goods as their counterparts elsewhere may prove a formidable challenge.

The list of recognised consumer rights is consistently and constantly expanding,[36] leading to the juridisation of an increasingly broader sphere of relations with businesses, thus spearheading the process of 'internationalization'.[37] To some extent, this is justified by the fact that the national legal systems of EU Member States differ, sometimes significantly, in terms of regulations in the area of consumer law.[38] This gradual uniformisation can be assessed either positively – as it propels an increase in the level of consumer protection, or negatively – as a fleeting fashion, the final cost of which will be paid by consumers themselves in the form of a higher price of the services provided.[39]

[33] Hannum (ibid).

[34] JT Theilen, 'The inflation of human rights: A deconstruction' (2021) 34 *Leiden Journal of International Law* 831: 'worries that we might have too many rights are often raised by pointing to concerns about the so-called "inflation" of human rights … the concern that 'positing too many rights' will lead 'to the devaluation of the currency of rights'.

[35] S Trechsel, *Inflation in the Field of Human Rights* (Nijmegen 1998); T Kerikmäe, *Protecting Human Rights in the EU Controversies and Challenges of the Charter of Fundamental Rights* (Berlin-Heidelberg, 2013); C Jones, 'The Human Right to Subsistence' (2013) 30 *Journal of Applied Philosophy* 57; D Clément, 'Human rights or social justice? The problem of rights inflation' (2017) 22 *The International Journal of Human Rights* 155; EA Posner, *The Twilight of Human Rights Law* (Oxford University Press, 2014); M Ignatieff, *Human Rights as Politics and Idolatry* (Princeton University Press, 2001) x.

[36] C Żuławska, 'O prawach konsumenta w okresie przemian' (1994–1995) 22–23 *Roczniki Nauk Społecznych* 375.

[37] M Durovic, 'International Consumer Law: What Is It All About?' (2020) 43 *Journal of Consumer Policy* 125.

[38] MH Austgulen, 'Understanding National Preferences in EU Consumer Policy: A Regime Approach' (2020) 43 *Journal of Consumer Policy* 767.

[39] O Ben-Shahar and O Bar-Gill, 'Regulatory Techniques in Consumer Protection: A Critique of European Consumer Contract Law' (2013) 50 *Common Market Law Review* 110.

III. Payment Services Regulation Change: Are We Going Too Far?

One of the aims of consumer protection in digital finance is to ensure payment security. Currently, this is the centrepiece of so-called PSD2[40] (the so-called PSD1 directive preceded its provisions), whose main objective is 'opening the payment services market to new technologically better equipped operators and actors'.[41] Despite PSD2 having been in force for only a few years, on 28 June, the European Commission published a draft of new regulations constituting a regulatory package in the areas of payment services, the digital euro and open finance. The legislative proposal incorporates the draft PSD3 directive (which is intended to replace the PSD2 directive), as well as the Payment Services Regulation (PSR).

We analyse specific provisions of PSD2 and of the proposed PSD3 and PSR, which define the situation of a customer (including a consumer) who makes transactions under the conditions of error or fraud. According to Article 64 of the PSD2, a payment transaction is considered to be authorised only if the payer has given consent to execute the payment transaction. However, due to various technical issues and glitches, the activity of fraudsters and diverse socio-technical methods used thereby (including manipulation of the payer by means of, inter alia, phone calls from fraudsters impersonating bank employees, spoofing, text messages sent from purported family members asking for a transfer of funds), the establishment of the payer's consent may prove contentious. In practice, on the one hand, the payer would argue they are a victim of a crime (fraud), manipulation, or an error, and therefore their informed consent is wanting, while on the other hand, the payment service provider (eg bank) would contend that the payment was properly authorised through the legally approved authentication method which, to add insult to injury, was accepted by the consumer themselves. Therefore, it would appear open for service providers to claim that they cannot be held liable for such a transaction. These matters are regulated mainly by Articles 72–74 of the PSD2.

Under the PSD2, the payment service provider is liable for unauthorised transactions, and the payer's liability is carved out as an exception. In the event of an unauthorised payment transaction, the payment service provider should immediately refund the amount of the transaction to the payer, and only then will it assess whether the refund was justified. The PSD2 limits the amount of the payer's liability for unauthorised transactions to the equivalent of 50 euros (Article 74 of the PSD2). It should be noted that

[40] Directive (EU) 2015/2366 of the European Parliament and of the Council of 25 November 2015 on payment services in the internal market, amending Directives 2002/65/EC, 2009/110/EC and 2013/36/EU and Regulation (EU) No 1093/2010, and repealing Directive 2007/64/EC. Official Journal of the European Union L 337/35.

[41] V Santoro, 'Foreword' in B Beroš, and G Gimigliano (eds), *The Payment Services Directive II A Commentary* (Edward Elgar, 2021) XXII.

> the rules allocating liability for unauthorized payment transactions in PSD2 resemble the rules incorporated in PSD1. However, looking more closely to these rules, it immediately becomes clear that several changes were made, which will have an important impact on the payer's protection. More specifically, the payer's protection is increased.[42]

Therefore, there is no doubt that historically – comparing the legal situation of the payer (consumer) in the light of PSD1 and PSD2, respectively – consumer protection is expanding, and this is happening at the expense of businesses, to whom the financial cost of erroneous payment transactions is effectively 'passed on'.

The justification for the PSD2's solutions is an assumption that a businesses, as a professional entity, can enhance security procedures and improve technical measures to minimise the risk of fraud and prevent payment errors. Moreover, the regulation is underpinned by the belief that professional financial market players can cover and recuperate possible consumer losses, from which that group should be shielded:

> Allocating a greater portion of losses to financial institutions could reduce the frequency of online financial fraud, provide some compensation for its victims and distribute the cost of fraud more effectively among those who benefit from financial services. It would also urge financial institutions to develop more secure solutions, without the need for regulators to decide precisely what institutions should do in this respect. … larger parts of loss after online financial fraud should be allocated from consumers to financial institutions.[43]

The above notwithstanding, individual provisions of the PSD2 are imprecise, which causes interpretation disputes as to the scope of liability in the event of a loss of funds (including doubts as to the understanding of the term 'gross liability') – especially in the context of phishing or spoofing. Phishing can be defined as

> a social engineering technique consisting in sending messages using e-mail containing content encouraging to click on a link included in the message; an example may be a message from a bank describing that the user's account has been compromised by breaking the password and in order to confirm this situation'[44] Spoofing is 'a social engineering attack technique in which the attacker impersonates an organization or financial entity, creates a counterfeit domain of a real company to provide WWW and e-mail services that are used to obtain the payer's confidential data.[45]

It is beyond the scope of this chapter to scrutinise individual cases, including those documented in judicial decisions available, but it should be noted that the provisions of the PSD2 have been inconsistently applied in practice in the

[42] R Steennot, 'Reduced payer's liability for unauthorized payment transactions under the second Payment Services Directive (PSD2)' (2018) 34 *Computer Law & Security Review* 954.

[43] M Eidsand Kjørven, 'Who Pays When Things Go Wrong? Online Financial Fraud and Consumer Protection in Scandinavia and Europe' (2020) 31 *European Business Law Review* 107.

[44] P Milik and G Pilarski, 'Cyberattacks and the bank's liability for unauthorized payment transactions in the online banking system – theory and practice' (2023) 9 *Cybersecurity and Law* 113.

[45] ibid.

Member States. For example, in Poland, service providers are usually exonerated from financial liability towards the consumer in the event of transactions forged with the help of phishing tactics where the payer's behaviour could reasonably be qualified as grossly negligent. Even so, there is no uniform, entrenched jurisprudence on how to recognise and qualify gross negligence in the context of payment services.

A markedly different approach is proposed in the PDS3 and the PSR. For the PSR stipulates that victims of 'spoofing' fraud can be entitled to claim damages from their payment service providers in the full amount of the fraudulent transaction, provided that they filed a police report and notified their providers of a breach without undue delay. Even though the content of the draft PSR demonstrates that the provider's liability shall not be unconditional and be subject to limitations, if these regulations come into force, the financial risk will in practice be plainly transferred to the business (payment service provider), thus burdening the same with effectively unlimited liability for fraudsters' actions and payer errors.[46]

Although the provisions of the PSR endorse the general concept of 'gross negligence' (which exempts the payment service provider from the obligation to return funds), the wording of Article 59 of the PSR dispels any doubts that the EU lawmaker significantly expands the scope of consumer protection by mandating refunds also when the payer (consumer) falls victim to spoofing.

Does that proposal meet the proportionality test and does it generate more benefits than costs? The answer to a question so formulated is, naturally, not straightforward, but several notes should be made in this connection. First of all, while it is true that consumers do not act rationally at all times and fraudsters use various new manipulation techniques to mislead the payer, it is likely that 'shifting' the responsibility and costs onto the service provider will hamper the consumer's vigilance. Secondly, it is likely that the excessively pro-consumer PSR regulation will incentivise non-professional individuals to engage in moral hazard. Both of these potential predicaments are highlighted in the PSR (recital 79). Thirdly, it is reasonable to assume that professional market participants (payment service providers who are entrepreneurs) will attempt to adapt to the new PSR requirements by not only improving systems and preventive actions to protect against spoofing, but also by imposing additional/increased fees for their services. Finally, we are not at all convinced that the protection of the payer (consumer) should

[46] 'However, payment service providers have more means than consumers to put an end to these fraud cases, through adequate prevention and robust technical safeguards developed with electronic communications services providers such as mobile network operators, internet platforms etc. Cases of bank employee impersonation fraud affect the good repute of the bank, of the banking sector as a whole and may cause significant financial damages to Union consumers, affecting their trust in electronic payments and in the banking system. A good-faith consumer who has been the victim of such 'spoofing' fraud where fraudsters pretend to be employees of a customer's payment service provider and misuse the payment service provider's name, mail address or telephone number should therefore be entitled to a refund of the full amount of the fraudulent payment transaction from the payment service provider, unless the payer has acted fraudulently or with "gross negligence"' (PSR, recital 80).

go so far that businesses should entirely bear the financial consequences of their mistakes in connection with an attempted spoofing.

IV. Proportionality in Digital Law: The Case of Social Media Platforms and the Human Rights Lawfare

The legislator's interference in the relations of digital market services also raises another issue in relation to proportionality, which falls within the provenance of human, or rather, fundamental rights.

We would like to focus here, in this particular context, on the matter of social media platforms.[47] Evidently, technological progress made in the last 30 years poses challenges for constitutionalism and relations between citizens, government and other private actors (like Big Tech companies), and nowhere is this more conspicuous than in the field of social media.[48] Social media platforms have become novel, contemporary *agoras*,[49] where people's ideas, views and beliefs are spread more easily and faster than any other time before, thus impacting profoundly the constitutional and political system.[50] Historically, an individual needed to have access to newspapers or other media to exercise freedom of speech fully and exert any influence upon the wider groups within a society. Currently, creating an account on a social media platform demands only rudimentary knowledge of the underlying mechanics and attendant consequences. Meanwhile, these media may become a conduit for propaganda, steering public debate with no recourse needed to print media. It is the platforms' terms of service which delineate the boundaries of public discourse.[51]

[47] Alternatively called social media networks; see A Strowel and W Vergote, 'Digital Platforms: To Regulate or Not To Regulate? Message to Regulators: Fix the Economics First, Then Focus on the Right Regulation' (European Commission, 2016) 5, available at ec.europa.eu/information_society/newsroom/image/document/2016-7/uclouvain_et_universit_saint_louis_14044.pdf.

[48] To imagine the scale of this fundamental shift, let us quote Mark Zuckerberg, an icon of new internet media and CEO of Facebook: 'If Facebook were a country, it would be the eighth most populated in the world, just ahead of Japan, Russia and Nigeria'. C Kennedy, 'Why Do People Join Facebook?' (Small Business), available at smallbusiness.chron.com/people-join-facebook-26657.html. See also K Forst, 'Facebook we współczesnym świecie komunikacji społecznej' in K Doktorowicz (ed), *Media społecznościowe: dialog w cyberprzestrzeni* (Wydawnictwo Uniwersytetu Śląskiego, 2017) 37–55. This statement, published on Zuckerberg's blog, marked the surpassing by Facebook of 150 million users. Nowadays, Facebook can boast more than three billion users, and so the impact of the platform has multiplied 20 times. N Helberger, 'The Political Power of Platforms: How Current Attempts to Regulate Misinformation Amplify Opinion Power' (2020) 8 *Digital Journalism* 842.

[49] A Rozehnal, *Social Media – Digital Democratic Agora or Threat to Democracy?* cited by J Szinek, 'The Impact of Digital Platforms and Social Media on Freedom of Expression and Pluralism – in specific terms' (2022) 49 *Prawo w działaniu. Sprawy karne* 141; L Salter, *Conflicting Forms of Use: The Potential of and Limits to the Use of the Internet as a Public Sphere* (London Metropolitan University, 2007) 168.

[50] A Simoncini, 'The Constitutional Dimension of the Internet. Some Research Paths' (2016) 16 *EUI Working Paper Law* 12–13, M Bovens and E Loos, 'The digital constitutional state. Democracy and law in the information society' (2002) 7 *Information Polity* 185.

[51] B Cammaerts and R Mansell, 'Digital Platform Policy and Regulation: Toward a Radical Democratic Turn' (2020) 14 *International Journal of Communication* 139–40.

Owing to the transnational character of Facebook and similar digital media platforms, questions araise whether such entities should continue to be treated as merely private actors (even if wielding considerable power),[52] or whether we are witnessing the rise of a new category of stakeholders (governors).[53] Legal scholars point out that due to the impact of social media platforms on freedom of speech, political competition as well as people's beliefs and views, their significance in a modern society cannot be underestimated. More accurately, we are facing a new phenomenon: quasi-state[54] public actors with private origins[55] that bridge the gap in the traditionally understood public–private divide.[56] Particularly, relations between social media platforms like Facebook, YouTube or X (formerly Twitter) and their users, shaped by terms of service and user policies (of a theoretically private character), can be fraught with certain limitations[57] (discussed below) on the exercise of some fundamental rights, such as freedom of speech, participation in political campaigns and free dissemination of ideas. Decisions made by platforms against users (often a purely automated process handled by AI algorithms[58]) can be controversial and publicly reviewed, especially where important political figures, activists and political organisations and parties are involved.[59] The resulting backlashes sometimes lead to attempts to establish new platforms, hailed as being free from 'censorship' and 'political correctness'.[60] Most such initiatives have failed or achieved very limited impact.

[52] See ibid 141.

[53] LHM da Conceição, 'Digital Constitutionalism: The Intersection of National Politics and Transnational Platform Governance' (The Digital Constitutionist) 3, available at digi-con.org/digital-constitutionalism-the-intersection-of-national-politics-and-transnational-platform-governance; M Zalnieriute and S Milan, 'Internet Architecture and Human Rights: Beyond the Human Rights Gap' (2019) 1 *Policy & Internet* 8.

[54] See M Susi, 'Digital Human Rights Proportionality During Global Crisis' in MC Kettemann, K Lachmayer (ed), *Pandemocracy in Europe: Power, Parliaments and People in Times of COVID-19* (Hart Publishing, 2021) 290; O Pollicino, 'Digital Private Powers Exercising Public Functions: The Constitutional Paradox in the Digital Age and its Possible Solutions', available at www.echr.coe.int/documents/d/echr/Intervention_20210415_Pollicino_Rule_of_Law_ENG.

[55] P Popiel, 'Digital Platforms as Policy Actors' in T Flew and FR Martin, *Digital Platform Regulation. Global Perspectives on Internet Governance* (Palgrave Global Media Policy and Business, 2022) 131–44. See also a description of the DSA package: 'some large platforms control important ecosystems in the digital economy. They have emerged as gatekeepers in digital markets, with the power to act as private rule-makers', at digital-strategy.ec.europa.eu/en/policies/digital-services-act-package.

[56] E Marique and Y Marique, 'Power Beyond the Public-Private Divide on Digital Platforms After *laissez-faire*. Time for Organised Checks and Balances?' in E Bani et al (eds), *Public and Private Law and the Challenges of New Technologies and Digital Markets. Volume I. Regulatory Challenges* (CH Beck, 2020) 131–35.

[57] B Wagner, *The international and transnational politics of Freedom of Expression* (European University Institute, 2013) 115–46.

[58] Marique and Marique (n 56) 136. See also Facebook, 'How does Facebook use artificial intelligence to moderate content? How does artificial intelligence make decisions about content?', available at www.facebook.com/help/1584908458516247.

[59] K Brylak-Hudyma, 'Projekt ustawy o wolności słowa w internetowych serwisach społecznościowych – remedium na walkę z bezprawnymi treściami?' (2022) 4 *Prawo mediów elektronicznych* 23.

[60] For example, truthsocial.com and parler.com; in Poland, albicla.com and banbye.com.

Needless to say, these 'acts' of platforms (formally falling under the performance of contractual rights and obligations) could weigh heavily on an individual's right to express their views and social or political statements.[61] Still, as law usually does not consider such 'acts' as *acta de iure imperii*, there is no overt judicial review avenue available. Thus, there is a dearth, it could be contended, of procedural guarantees for the safeguarding of some of the fundamental rights in modern society. On the other hand, remedies accessible within a platform–user relationship, in contrast to state-afforded instruments, could assume a more prominent role and prove more effective in practice where freedom of speech oversteps its boundaries and encroaches upon other rights and freedoms (eg in cases of slander, libel and hate speech against a specific group of people like ethnic, religious or sexual minorities). This is especially so, considering that state measures are usually belated, culminate with a protracted and non-effective court procedure with an outcome that need not provide an adequate and efficacious remedy – many jurisdictions struggle to ensure the enforcement of court orders or judgments against content published on social media platforms, mainly because platforms are not parties to the court proceedings and, as such, cannot be obliged to comply with any such order[62] – and hardly accessible – n most jurisdictions the plaintiff is obliged to indicate the name and the details of the defendant in a lawsuit, otherwise the claim is dismissed *a limine* or returned to the plaintiff; this is why access to state-provided legal remedies in such cases is usually dependent on cooperation between the justice system and social media platforms.

Thus, legal scholars stress the significance of internal platforms' regulations, policies and bylaws[63] in governing the exercise of rights by individuals, as well as in preventing hate speech and infringements of personal rights.[64] However, there is a plethora of examples of coordinated so-called social media mobs that ultimately bring about a huge number of user complaints against other users, the site or platform, or content. Algorithms will occasionally suspend or even ban a user or content once satisfied that a certain threshold of submitted complaints has been surpassed. Any such decision may have the targeted user sustain significant economic, social and political losses, considering that the actions of the social media 'mob' cannot always be viewed as justified.[65]

The relationship between a social media platform and its user can encroach upon freedom of speech or the right to privacy[66] in manifold ways. More precisely,

[61] A Lee, *International human rights law in digital space: An examination of the need for new legal measures for the protection of rights online* (Geneva, 2020) 87.

[62] A Alubaidi, 'Challenges to Implementing the International Digital Law to Protect Digital Rights' (2023) 5 *Journal of Law and Sustainable Development* 14.

[63] Forst (n 48) 43.

[64] G De Gregorio, *Digital Constitutionalism in Europe. Reframing Rights and Powers in the Algorithmic Society* (Cambridge University Press, 2022) 81–82.

[65] D Trottier, 'Confronting the digital mob: Press coverage of online justice seeking' (2020) 6 *European Journal of Communication* 597.

[66] See D Joyce, 'Privacy in the Digital Era: Human Rights Online?' (2015) 9 *Melbourne Journal of International Law* 1.

the crucial question faced by social media platforms is not simply whether to ban certain content. The measures to which platforms can resort is considerably more sophisticated; they can be grouped into the general categories:

- marking of content (usually in the case of political content);
- suspension of a user, the user's site or particular content;
- demonetisation of published content or the entirety of the user's site;
- algorithmic limitations on the reach of particular content, including by restricting reach and limiting display of content to certain targeted groups (sometimes called 'algorithmic censorship');[67]
- ban of a user, the user's site or particular content.

All these measures are derived from platforms' respective terms of service and user policies which are, *de iure*, an integral part of the contract between the platform and its user (customer), even if some contractual clauses in certain jurisdictions mirror obligations imposed on a platform by a regulator. Thus, as much as such terms of service and user policies qualify as contracts of adhesion,[68] they are ultimately private covenants and *de iure*, not a manifestation of the exercise of state power even if it so happens that practical consequences of such terms of service seem akin to those stemming from public administrative measures.[69] On the other hand, as mentioned, states restrict or attempt to restrict (not always successfully) certain content on social media platforms for a variety of reasons, hence limiting digital freedom of speech. Some of these can be considered as justified in a modern democratic (free) society, such as prevention of hate speech or incitement to commit crimes.[70] Others may reflect a specific, autocratic or allegedly autocratic approach of a given government and should be deemed as at least controversial or even threatening the democracy and fundamental freedoms. Research[71] shows that such limitations usually attach to the reputation of a head of state or monarchy,[72] sedition,[73] protection of the security of the nation,[74] protection of

[67] J Cobbe, 'Algorithmic Censorship by Social Platforms: Power and Resistance' (2020) 34 *Philosophy & Technology* 739.

[68] About the concept of contracts of adhesion, see F Kessler, 'Contracts of adhesion-some thoughts about freedom of contract. Role of compulsion in economic transactions' (1943) *Columbia Law Review* 629, NK Duncan, 'Adhesion Contracts: A Twentieth Century Problem for a Nineteenth Century Code' (1974) 34 *Louisiana Law Review* 1081.

[69] Marique and Marique (n 56) 141.

[70] The Swedish Authority for Privacy Protection, The Ombudsman for Children in Sweden and The Swedish Media Council, 'The rights of children and young people on digital platforms' 10–11, D-A Ita, 'Emerging Challenges in the Protection of Digital Rights: Exploring the Intersection of International Human Rights Law and Technology' (2023) 6, available at academia.edu.

[71] D Sivaprakasam et al, 'Dictating the Internet: Curtailing free expression, opinion and information online in Southeast Asia' (International Commission of Jurists, 2019).

[72] eg, Thailand, Cambodia or Malaysia.

[73] eg, Malaysia, Brunei, Philippines.

[74] eg, Vietnam, Myanmar.

legal entities,[75] spread of 'disinformation'[76] or protection of historical remembrance.[77] The restrictions strike, on occasion, at the heart of citizens' right to express political views or voice criticism of the government. Others are controversial as they avail themselves of vague language and accord discretionary power to enforcement agencies, which may both precipitate instances of abuse of such restrictions and disproportionately restrict fundamental freedoms even where the rationale underlying a given restriction appears legitimate and reasonable.

The legislation discussed above can impose direct obligations or bans (sometimes of a penal character) on individuals and social media platforms alike. This can lead to an effective deprivation of access to a given platform for users from a given country or a conditional ban, based on the expectation that the platform provider would reflect the government's rules in the platform's policy. A recent Turkish statute is a case in point: it obliges social media platforms to establish authorised representatives in Turkey responsible for compliance with the platform's activity in Turkey and for implementing the authorities' orders. Pursuant to this law, the government-controlled Information and Communication Technologies Authority (Bilgi Teknolojileri ve İletişim Kurumu, BTK) can compel social media companies to comply with requests to take down online content and hand over user data (otherwise being subject to six-month bans on receiving advertising), and may impose mandatory 50 per cent bandwidth reductions, which could be increased to 90 per cent after 30 days for non-compliance with blocking or removal decisions.[78] This draconian law has put Big Tech companies between a rock and a hard place: they have to choose between complying with new rules that plausibly violate fundamental rights and freedoms or facing a significant drop in revenues.

The general picture that emerges is that restrictions on some individual rights and freedoms of users of social media platforms can be derived either from internal (self-governing[79]), contractual terms (Terms-of-service, ToS) governing the relation between a business and a customer or from governmental regulation. Moreover, the latter can impact users indirectly, through certain obligations imposed on social media platforms, later reflected in a policy toward customers.

On the other hand, social media platforms, by implementing measures discussed in section IV.D above, can purport to act not necessarily in their own interest, but often in the interest of another user, group of users (identifiable or non-identifiable), widely understood public interest[80] or on request by state authorities. This may place a social media platform in the role of a quasi-arbitrator in the event of a conflict of countervailing interests, including between different

[75] eg, Indonesia, Singapore.
[76] eg, Malaysia, Philippines.
[77] See eg 'Austrian laws against Holocaust denial' in *Austria. Country Reports on Human Rights Practices for 2015* (Bureau of Democracy, Human Rights and Labor, US Department of State) 6.
[78] The Law on Regulation of Broadcasts via Internet and Combating Crimes Committed by the Means of Such Publications, 04.05.2007, Official Gazette No 26530, see mbkaya.com/turkish-internet-law.
[79] De Gregorio (n 64) 85.
[80] See ibid 81.

users (or non-users) of the platform. All these relationships are also influenced by national and transnational policies which are liable to lead to a clash between expectations derived from state power (expounded below) and citizens' pressure on social media platforms to preserve human rights against an autocratic government. Thus, social media platforms face difficult choices in respect of particular content.[81] This interplay is demonstrated in Figure 7.1.[82]

Figure 7.1 Social media interplay

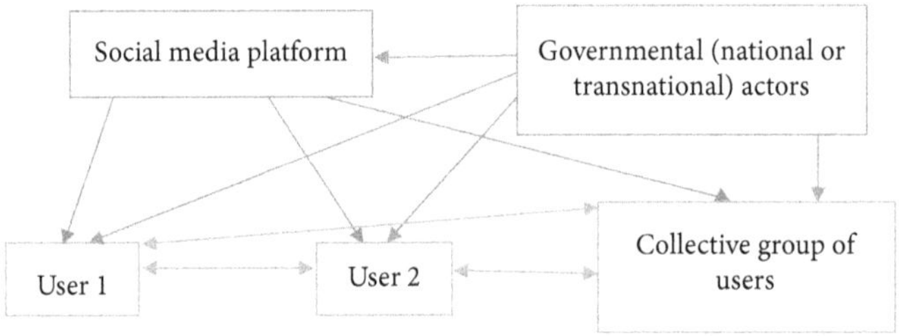

At any rate, the exercise of powers under the measures discussed at this juncture is always *de iure* a matter within the framework of a contractual relationship between a social media platform (as a business) and a user (as a customer). Contractual autonomy dictates that a social media platform can hold itself out and propose the provision of services to customers under certain conditions that can reflect national laws (needless to say), but also important social values, internal policy of the organisation and protection of rights of other users or third parties. Due to the significance of social media platforms for public debate, as well as for the preservation of civil standards of such a debate, exercising fundamental rights and freedoms and protection against hate, violence, incitement of crimes, platform operators in a free society shall be considered as having certain duties and responsibilities in this area. Thus, the exercising of certain contractual rights in a business-to-consumer relationship by a social media platform (eg by imposing a ban on the publication of content) need not necessarily equal an unwarranted limitation of constitutional freedoms; on the contrary, this could be treated as respecting constitutional standards and values within a contractual relationship.

Radical elements facing measures imposed by platforms against their socially unacceptable content (inter alia, hate speech against minorities) claim that these interventions are unconstitutional restrictions of freedom of speech and should be banned by state law. Sporadically, such views receive political support, as is borne out by recent Polish political practice. In response to calls of several far-right organisations in 2021, the Polish Government introduced a draft bill on the

[81] RF Jørgensen, 'What Platforms Mean When They Talk About Human Rights' (2017) 3 *Policy & Internet* 288–291.

[82] See also K Karppinen and O Puukko, 'Four Discourses of Digital Rights. Promises and Problems of Rights-Based Politics' (2020) 10 *Journal of Information Policy* 312.

protection of freedom of speech on social media platforms.[83] Under this draft regulation,[84] a Freedom of Speech Council was planned to be established as an authority 'that shall ensure that service providers respect the freedom to express opinions, obtain information, disseminate information, express religious, ideological and philosophical beliefs and freedom of communication' (Article 4). One of the objectives of the regulation in question was to 'fight with disinformation' through the endorsemet of so-called 'trusted flaggers' responsible for submitting notifications regarding disinformation to service providers. Every user of a social media platform or a trusted signalling entity would be able to ask the Freedom of Speech Council to reconsider any submission. Through quasi-judicial proceedings before the Council (albeit regulated by the administrative procedure), certain obligations could be imposed on social media platforms, including bans on certain content or republication orders in respect of content taken down by the platform itself. Evidently, this legislative initiative deeply interfered with the contractual autonomy of social media platforms and their users. The initial version of the bill envisaged that all internal decisions on banning content or user sites undertaken by the platform could be subject to a review by the Council. It is worth noting that the bill has never come into force and stalled at the governmental stage of the legislative process.[85]

Though the fight with disinformation and harmful, illegal content is underlaid by a legitimate objective, one which justifies legislative intervention in private relationships between platforms and users, it is prudent to dispute the proportionality of wider regulatory measures aimed at safeguarding the right of users to disseminate content otherwise not illegal, even if in contravention of a given platform's policy and values shared by the organisation in issue. Putting this into context, the EU legal framework in this respect, based on the so-called Digital Services Act (DSA),[86] is founded on a different philosophy. Above all, it obliges service providers to present transparent terms and conditions to users. These shall include details on any restrictions that they impose in relation to the use of their service in respect of information provided by the recipients of the service, particularly information on any policies, procedures, measures and tools used for the purpose of content moderation, including algorithmic decision-making and human review, as well as the rules of procedure of their internal complaint handling system.[87] Secondly, the DSA accords to every individual and entity a right to notify the service provider of the presence on their service of specific information that the individual or entity

[83] Draft of Law on protection of freedom of speech in social media platforms, UD293, available at legislacja.rcl.gov.pl/projekt/12351757/katalog/12819479#12819479. See also K Izdebski, 'Czy należy się spieszyć z uchwaleniem ustawy o ochronie wolności słowa w Internecie?' (Fundacja im Stefana Batorego, 2022).

[84] See version dated 20 May 2022.

[85] www.gov.pl/web/sprawiedliwosc/ochrona-wolnosci-slowa-w-internecie.

[86] Regulation (EU) 2022/2065 of the European Parliament and of the Council of 19 October 2022 on a Single Market For Digital Services and amending Directive 2000/31/EC (Digital Services Act).

[87] Art 14 DSA.

considers to be illegal content.[88] Such a notification initiates a procedure that can lead to the imposition of certain restrictive measures against particular information or a statement (or a refusal to do so). Users are authorised to lodge complaints against such measures, as well as against measures (prescribed in Article 20 DSA) taken by the platform itself in relation to content that is either (i) illegal or (ii) incompatible with its terms and conditions. However, measures prescribed in the Act do not restrict the autonomy of the platform as a private entity as it permits prohibitions or limitations of access to content on the basis of a given platform's own policy, provided that the latter was presented to the user and the platform afforded the user accessible and transparent remedies against such a decision. Thus, in this respect, the DSA focuses on procedural guarantees[89] and preserves a balance between self-regulation and the public interest.

Calling for a regulatory framework for social media platforms seems to be just and reasonable to some extent,[90] due to the increasing role and impact of such platforms on modern societies and political processes.[91] For a similar reason, one cannot dispense with the idea that corporations, like social media outlets, should have some obligations in the area of human rights protection[92] in the digital era and that the principle of the rule of law should be observed in relationships between platforms and users.[93] However, as services provided by platforms are still private in nature and as such are tendered on the basis of a contract, legislative and judicial attempts to this effect need to be circumspect[94] and wary of preserving an adequate balance between private and public interest.[95] Despite popular sentiment, freedom of speech does not entail the right to demand access to a particular forum for the dissemination of certain views, especially if such a forum is operated

[88] Art 16 DSA.

[89] AP Heldt, 'EU Digital Services Act: The White Hope of Intermediary Regulation' in Flew and Martin (n 55) 74–75. Regarding the importance of procedural guarantees for preserving human rights standards on digital platforms, see E Celeste et al, *The Content Governance Dilemma. Digital Constitutionalism, Social Media and the Search for a Global Standard* (Palgrave Macmillan, 2023) 78–89, 'Safeguarding freedom of expression and access to information: guidelines for a multistakeholder approach in the context of regulating digital platforms' (UNESCO, 2023).

[90] D Joyce, 'Internet Freedom and Human Rights' (2015) 2 *The European Journal of International Law* 505, Helberger (n 48) 847–54.

[91] C Bradley and R Wingfield, *A Rights-Respecting Model of Online Content Regulation by Platforms* (Global Partners Digital, 2018).

[92] 'Digital Technologies and Human Rights: a Legal Framework' Briefing paper (The International Commission of Jurists, May 2022) 22–23, Karppinen and Puukko (n 82) 320, M Zalnieriute, 'The Necessity for Binding Human Rights Obligations for Private Actors in the Digital Age: A Submission on New and Emerging Digital Technologies and Human Rights' (2019) *UNSW Law Research Paper* 19–81.

[93] Y Razmetaeva, Y Barabash and D Lukianov, 'The Concept of Human Rights in the Digital Era: Changes and Consequences for Judicial Practice' (2022) 3 *Access to Justice in Eastern Europe* 48–49, Jørgensen (n 81) 281–82, LHM da Conceição, 'Digital Constitutionalism – The Need For a Democratic Perspective' in J de Campos Amorim et al (eds), *Desafios Do Legaltech* (Porto Instituto Iberoamericano de Estudos Jurídicos – IBEROJUR, 2020) 205.

[94] Joyce (n 90) 497.

[95] B Botero and R Griffin, *Social media platforms and challenges for democracy, rule of law and fundamental rights* (European Parliament's Committee on Civil Liberties, Justice and Home Affairs, 2023)

by a private entrepreneur. That standard is confirmed by the European Court of Human Rights, and is enshrined in Article 10 of the European Convention on Human Rights.[96] For freedom of speech, 'notwithstanding the acknowledged importance of freedom of expression, does not bestow any freedom of forum for the exercise of that right'.[97]

In this context, any calls by a particular group of users, sometimes heeded and cheered on by politicians, to restrict the autonomy of social media platforms and preclude them from banning, under internal policies, content other than illegal content that is irreconcilable with values important for the platform, should be assessed as unbalanced. Moreover, attempts to ground such demands (usually coming from radical, anti-democratic groups) in fundamental, constitutional rights such as freedom of speech, even where hate speech or content defying human dignity is concerned,[98] can be put under the umbrella of 'lawfare', that is combating the enemy (in this case, a democratic society and values of liberal democracy) by using, misusing, and abusing the legal system.[99] To grant such an unconstrained right to disseminate statements, views and opinions on private social media platforms without regard for their objections can be viewed as abuse of human rights protection, an unnecessary intrusion into private relations, and one that is flatly in contravention of the proportionality principle.

Furthermore, it is argued that there is no reason to treat exercising freedom of speech on social media platforms differently than with respect to traditional forums of expression. As individuals' expectations to present their opinions and views in traditional, private media (eg in newspapers) are not protected, the same approach is defensible towards digital media, including social media platforms.[100] To sum up, two areas of potential regulation can be identified, provided that the intensity of potential regulatory intervention varies according to the requirements of proportionality. First, there is a legitimate public interest in regulating the dissemination through social media platforms (and imposing corresponding obligations on providers) of illegal content, hate speech, content impinging upon personal and intellectual property rights, spreading fake news and harmful interference with the

126, L Cooke, 'Regulating the Internet: policy and practice with reference to the control of Internet access and content' (Loughborough University, 2004), "French Court Strikes Down Most of Online Hate Speech Law' *New York Times* (18 June 2020) 62, available at www.nytimes.com/2020/06/18/world/europe/france-internet-hate-speech-regulation.html 62, T Pajuste (ed), 'Specific Threats to Human Rights Protection from the Digital Reality. International Responses and Recommendations to Core Threats from the Digitalised World' (EU COST Action – CA19143 – Global Digital Human Rights Network, 2022) 71.

[96] www.echr.coe.int/documents/d/echr/convention_ENG.

[97] Judgment of ECHR of 6 May 2003, *Appleby and Others v The United Kingdom*, no 44306/98.

[98] Joyce (n 90) 501.

[99] See SW Tiefenbrun, 'Semiotic Definition of "Lawfare"' (2011) *Case Western Reserve Journal of International Law* 1.

[100] IN Duy, 'The Limits to Free Speech on Social Media: On Two Recent Decisions of the Supreme Court of Norway' (2020) 3 *Nordic Journal of Human Rights* 244, Y Shany, 'Digital Rights and the Outer Limits of International Human Rights Law' (2023) 3 *German Law Journal* 4.

electoral process (the latter needs to be distinguished, however, from presenting ideas, views and participation in a public debate). Second, as to other content that can be, inter alia, contrary to the values of social media owners or their terms of service, a degree of autonomy accorded to social media platforms and their users (within the bounds of freedom of cntract) needs to be preserved, although it is reasonable to posit a legal framework providing for the contours of procedural guarantees with respect to powers exercised by the platforms. Above all, legislative intervention should supplement self-regulation in this area rather than replace it.[101]

V. Closing Remarks

This chapter shows that advancements in both consumer and human rights protection cannot be ignored in the context of digital services regulation. Nevertheless, it is important to question whether relations between digital services providers and users necessitate special, bespoke treatment. In particular, statutory measures that shift the majority of the burden onto one of the contracting parties and restrict the contractual freedom thereof seem excessive if we consider that threats to users in the digital era land not too far from those manifesting in offline reality. For example, fraud and other crimes exploiting the imprudence or naivety of victims, or targeting vulnerable groups, rely on the same psychological mechanisms in both real and digital worlds. Where the exercise of freedom of speech and the right to privacy is concerned, the content and objective of the underlying prerogatives remains immutable, albeit we now have to deal with newly emerging forums. The novelty of this lies, first, in the measures of interpersonal communication utilised and the manner and method of spreading views and information as well as providing services but not in the essence of such human activities.

Also of note is the frequency and incidence of performed transactions, interactions, exchange of views and opinions, which is unprecedented in the digital world. Certainly, regulatory attention is indispensable on account of the extreme prevalence of the aforementioned issues. However, the consumer and human rights paradigms must be applied cautiously and diligently in the digital market as even in the non-digital sphere an excessively one-sided approach which exclusively prioritises with a broad brush the interests of only one actor is liable to spark controversy. Lastly, it is a cliché that digital services have in most respects positively changed our lives and standards of living, and societies expect that this situation will continue while respecting constitutional rights and freedoms. Consequently, while one ought not to forget about attendant risks, the area in question cannot end up overregulated in the EU as this would stifle innovation and hamper consumer access to digital services.

[101] N Gibbs (ed), *Democracy and Internet Governance Initiative. Towards Digital Platforms and Public Purpose* (Harvard Kennedy School, 2023) 31–32.

8

Regulating AdTech: Chasing Chimeras or the Art of the Possible?

VASILEIOS MICHAIL KARKATZOUNIS,
APOSTOLOS VORRAS AND LILIAN MITROU

I. Introduction

The advertising landscape has been profoundly affected by the emergence of modern technologies, such as artificial intelligence (AI), machine learning and big data analytics. The enormous amount of available digital data and enhanced and low-cost computing power create tremendous opportunities but also disrupt traditional business models, radically affecting the interaction between enterprises and consumers.

The increasing use and effectiveness of advertising technologies, commonly referred to as 'Adtech', in data analysis and transaction automation has helped online advertising to quickly overtake traditional types of advertising[1] and gradually shape a new reality. Today online advertising has become a vast market[2] and a key source of income for a wide range of services. It is also perceived as a critical factor for the growth and expansion of the internet's economy[3] and a key pillar of the internet's free access model[4] and openness, enhancing aspects such as economic accessibility, freedom of expression and access to information.[5]

[1] G Sartor, 'New aspects and challenges in consumer protection Digital services and artificial intelligence' (2020) Study for the committee on the Internal Market and Consumer Protection, Policy Department for Economic, Scientific and Quality of Life Policies, European Parliament, available at www.europarl.europa.eu/RegData/etudes/STUD/2020/648790/IPOL_STU(2020)648790_EN.pdf.

[2] According to the Interactive Advertising Bureau Europe (IAB Europe), the value of digital ad spending only in Europe amounts to 92 billion euros per year, an increase of 21.5 billion euros compared to 2020. Interactive Advertising Bureau Europe, 'AdEx Benchmark 2021 Report' (IAB Europe, 28 June 2022), available at iabeurope.eu/wp-content/uploads/2022/06/IAB-Europe_AdEx-Benchmark-2021_REPORT_V3.pdf.

[3] Interactive Advertising Bureau Europe, 'Europe Online: An Experience Driven by Advertising' (IAB Europe, 7 September 2017), available atiabeurope.eu/knowledgehub/policy/europe-online-an-experience-driven-by-advertising.

[4] J Estrada-Jiménez, J Parra-Arnau, Rodríguez-Hoyos and J Forné, 'Online advertising: Analysis of privacy threats and protection approaches' (2017) 100 *Computer Communications* 32, available at doi.org/10.1016/j.comcom.2016.12.016.

[5] Organisation for Economic Co-operation and Development, 'Economic and Social Benefits of Internet Openness' (OECD, 17 June 2016), available at doi.org/10.1787/5jlwqf2r97g5-en.

Although advertising has been an integral part of the online environment since the early days of the internet, over the last few years it has rapidly evolved into a highly automated and data-driven industry. Nowadays, the 'bedrock of the online advertising industry'[6] is real time bidding (RTB),[7] a remarkably fast application of programmatic advertising,[8] which has lately been under intense scrutiny.[9] RTB engages a vast number of stakeholders, such as demand and supply-side platforms, ad networks and data management platforms, which interoperate in complex and often non-transparent schemes, allowing advertisers to serve targeted material to relevant audiences. In a nutshell, when a person loads a page on a news website, for example, high-speed advertising auctions occur behind the scenes. During these auctions, personal information about the user's characteristics, behaviour and preferences are exchanged between several stakeholders, such as demand and supply-side platforms, ad networks and data management platforms, to find the ideal match for each ad.[10]

These forms of online behavioural advertising and the dominance of Big Tech companies in the Adtech sector have raised several important and complicated legal issues, mostly in the areas of competition, consumer protection, privacy and personal data protection. These issues have been exacerbated due to a transparency deficit that is attributed to the online advertising industry, both in terms of its internal operation, but also in terms of users' awareness regarding the data processing methods that have been deployed in online advertising. Notably, the Article 29 Working Party – now the European Data Protection Board[11] – warned more than a decade ago of the privacy implications of online behavioural advertising (OBA). In

[6] Homo Digitalis, 'Homo Digitalis files a complaint against Google and IAB Europe for their harmful practices of behavioural advertising' (10 December 2020), available at www.homodigitalis.gr/wp-content/uploads/2020/12/Adtech-QA-1.pdf.

[7] According to the Irish Council for Civil Liberties, RTB is an industry worth more than $117 billion, while 178 trillion RTB broadcasts about people in the US and Europe take place every year. Irish Council for Civil Liberties, 'The Biggest Data Breach – ICCL report on the scale of Real-Time Bidding data broadcasts in the U.S. and Europe' (ICCL, 2 May 2022), available at www.iccl.ie/wp-content/uploads/2022/05/Mass-data-breach-of-Europe-and-US-data-1.pdf.

[8] According to the IAB Europe, programmatic advertising is using transactional or workflow automation mechanisms embedded in an infrastructure that relies on a set of rules applied by software and algorithms, commonly known as 'ad tech'. IAB Europe (n 2).

[9] This paper focuses on RTB as the predominant method of programmatic advertising; however, most of the findings apply to many other forms of online advertising. This is mainly because of the complex nature of the ecosystem and the heavy reliance of modern forms of advertising on personal and behavioural data. It was estimated in 2017 that behavioural data underpins €10.6 billion of the €16 billion digital display advertising market in Europe today, used either to buy or sell ads. Interactive Advertising Bureau Europe, 'The Economic Value of Behavioural Targeting in Digital Advertising' (7 September 2017), available at iabeurope.eu/wp-content/uploads/2019/08/BehaviouralTargeting_FINAL.pdf.

[10] Information Commissioner's Office, 'Update report into AdTech and real-time bidding' (20 June 2019), available at ico.org.uk/media/about-the-ico/documents/2615156/adtech-real-time-bidding-report-201906-dl191220.pdf.

[11] Working Party on the Protection of Individuals with regard to the Processing of Personal Data established by Directive 95/46/EC which has been replaced by the European Data Protection Board, according to Art 94 of the General Data Protection Regulation.

its Opinion 2/2010,[12] the Working Party recognised the massive impact of online advertising on the economics of the digital ecosystem and raised flags on a series of issues, such as the 'growing practice between advertising networks to collaborate through a bidding system'.[13] In the wake of these technological and market developments, the key question is whether – and if so, how – such complicated and innovative relationships can or should be regulated, and how the 'black box' of ad tech can be converted into more transparent models.[14]

Data protection authorities, regulators and policymakers have been asked to find a balance between fostering innovation and the digital economy on one side and protecting the fundamental rights embedded in the data protection framework on the other side. The key word in this dilemma might as well be 'proportionality'.

This chapter discusses the interplay between regulation and the advertising technology ecosystem, addressing the way the proportionality principle[15] influences the – at least prima facie – the competing rights and interests of individuals and online marketing actors. First, proportionality is a key element for the identification of and response to privacy shortcomings in the current Adtech ecosystem. In defence of this approach, this chapter examines the recent decision of the Belgian Data Protection Authority regarding the Transparency & Consent Framework that challenged the practices and foundations of the entire industry. At the same time, the proportionality principle is crucial to understanding the reasoning behind regulatory initiatives to mitigate the risks for individuals and society in connection with targeted advertising, such as the Digital Services Act (DSA).[16] Finally, it allows for an assessment of the potential alternatives to the current status of Adtech.

II. Proportionality in Adtech: Lessons from the Belgian Data Protection Authority's decision on TCF

Proportionality is conceived as an embodiment of the notion of justice,[17] but also as a methodological tool that comprises three known subtests: adequacy (for

[12] Art 29 Working Party, 'Opinion 2/2010 on online behavioural advertising' (WP 171, 22 June 2010).

[13] Most major ad networks have a structural collaboration with many other, secondary networks, for example, Google Adsense and Yahoo! (n 5).

[14] The issue of transparency in online advertising is of critical importance not only for the exercise of users' rights and freedoms but also for advertisers and publishers.

[15] Both as a general principle of EU law and *in concreto* as applied by the European Data Protection Supervisor concerning the assessment of personal data processing. See indicatively EDPS, 'Guidelines on assessing the proportionality of measures that limit the fundamental rights to privacy and to the protection of personal data' (19 December 2019).

[16] DSA: Regulation (EU) 2022/2065 of the European Parliament and of the Council of 19 October 2022 on a Single Market for Digital Services and amending Directive 2000/31/EC (Digital Services Act), OJ 2022 L 277/1.

[17] A Barak, Proportionality: Constitutional Rights and Their Limitations (Cambridge University Press, 2012) 175.

achieving the goal); necessity (less intrusive/restrictive measure); and proportionality *stricto sensu* (disproportionate or excessive regarding the goal to be achieved). This tripartite construction has deep roots in the European legal tradition and is considered a condition for the legitimacy of a measure that interferes with fundamental rights.[18] As such, it plays a crucial role in every aspect of European law, including data protection.[19] The principle of proportionality is also an inherent element of the data protection legal regime, as it provides the foundation for the balancing of competing rights and interests as well as the power and information asymmetries in processing activities.[20] In this sense, proportionality is a key element for the identification and assessment of privacy and data protection issues in the current Adtech ecosystem, but also for performing the balancing test and striking a fair and functional balance.

In the context of Adtech, proportionality has been applied by supervisory authorities on very limited occasions. Perhaps the most relevant, comprehensive and insightful analysis has been provided by the Belgian Data Protection Authority in its decision on the Transparency & Consent Framework (TCF).[21] TCF is a cross-industry best practice standard, developed by the Interactive Advertising Bureau Europe (IAB Europe), which facilitates the capture of users' preferences in a structured and automated way, through consent management platforms: user preferences are collected and shared with the organisations participating in this scheme so that each one of them knows what the user has consented or objected to. It is easy to understand why this mechanism plays a pivotal role in the architecture of the RTB ecosystem and the offering of tailor-made advertisements.

Several complaints had been filed across the EU regarding the TCF, alleging that this mechanism breaches the principle of proportionality on various levels. In February 2022 the Belgian DPA found that TCF fails to comply with several provisions of the General Data Protection Regulation (GDPR)[22] and imposed a fine of 250.000 euros as well as certain corrective measures. This development is important, since, due to the nature and purpose of TCF, the Belgian DPA approached a series of data protection issues that affect users everywhere in Europe, through a broader lens than in the past.[23] Unsurprisingly, IAB Europe appealed this decision

[18] See eg Art 8(2) European Convention on Human Rights and Art 52(1) Charter of Fundamental Rights of the EU.

[19] L Dalla Corte, 'On proportionality in the data protection jurisprudence of the CJEU' (2022) 12 *International Data Privacy Law* 259, available at doi.org/10.1093/idpl/ipac014.

[20] ibid.

[21] Case DOS-2019-01377 *Autorité de protection des données v IAB Europe* [2022].

[22] EU General Data Protection Regulation (GDPR): Regulation (EU) 2016/679 of the European Parliament and of the Council of 27 April 2016 on the protection of natural persons with regard to the processing of personal data and on the free movement of such data, and repealing Directive 95/46/EC (General Data Protection Regulation), OJ 2016 L 119/1.

[23] See eg, the decision of Commission Nationale de l'Informatique et des Libertes against adtech company Vectaury, CNIL, Décision MED-2018-042 du 30 octobre 2018.

before the Market Court, a special section of the Court of Appeal of Brussels, which decided to refer preliminary questions to the Court of Justice of the European Union (CJEU), before ruling on the case.[24]

The questions referred to the CJEU[25] concern not only TCF but also RTB and may affect core issues of online behavioural advertising in general. On the one hand, they touch upon the very fundamental parts of the Belgian DPA's decision, which allow for the data protection rules to be applied in the first place, ie whether the TC String, a string of characters which captures the preferences of a user when he visits a website,[26] can be considered personal data and, accordingly whether IAB Europe can be considered a (joint) controller for the relevant data processing within the meaning of the GDPR. On the other hand, the case before the ECJ might as well open new horizons for the overall legitimacy of RTB since one of the questions links the TCF to the subsequent processing of data by third parties, such as targeted online advertising by publishers and vendors.

While the final assessment of the ECJ is expected to play a critical role in shaping the future of online advertising, the Belgian DPA's decision at first instance provides many impactful insights regarding proportionality under the prism of data protection principles, such as data minimisation, purpose limitation, lawfulness, transparency and security of processing.[27] First, the Belgian DPA did not find that the TCF per se breaches certain provisions of the GDPR that embed the proportionality principle, such as data minimisation[28] and purpose limitation,[29] for several reasons – perhaps most importantly because the scope of the allegations was limited to the TCF. Although the decision indeed focuses on TCF, the Belgian DPA established a clear link between TCF and OpentRTB, one of the most widely used protocols for RTB, which allows us to obtain useful insights into the conformity of the RTB ecosystem to the personal data framework.

In particular, the decision expressly states that 'the processing operations carried out on the basis of the OpenRTB protocol are not in accordance with the

[24] Autorité de protection des données, 'IAB Europe case: The Market Court refers preliminary questions to the Court of Justice of the EU' (BE DPA, 7 September 2022), available at www.dataprotectionauthority.be/citizen/iab-europe-case-the-market-court-refers-preliminary-questions-to-the-court-of-justice-of-the-eu.

[25] Irish Council for Civil Liberties, 'Landmark GDPR decision against "consent spam" to be heard at Europe's highest court' (ICCL, 7 September 2022), available at www.iccl.ie/news/landmark-gdpr-decision-against-consent-spam-to-be-heard-at-europes-highest-court.

[26] This concerns the capturing of consent (or not) to the processing of personal data for marketing and other purposes, whether to share personal data with third parties (adtech vendors) and the exercise or not of the right to object; *Autorité de protection* (n 21) 41.

[27] For an analysis of the decision see M Veale, M Nouwens, and C Santos, 'Impossible Asks: Can the Transparency and Consent Framework Ever Authorise Real-Time Bidding After the Belgian DPA Decision?' (2022) *Technology and Regulation* 12, available at doi.org/10.26116/techreg.2022.002.

[28] According to Art 5(c) GDPR personal data shall be 'adequate, relevant and limited to what is necessary in relation to the purposes for which they are processed'.

[29] According to Art 5(b) GDPR, personal data shall be 'collected for specified, explicit and legitimate purposes and not further processed in a manner that is incompatible with those purposes'.

basic principles of purpose limitation and data minimisation'.[30] The Belgian DPA noted that no safeguards are provided to ensure that the personal data collected and disseminated within the framework of the OpenRTB are limited to information that is strictly necessary for the intended purposes. As far as purpose limitation is concerned, the Belgian DPA pointed out that the purpose of processing the TC String must be distinguished from purposes related to OpenRTB, though it underlined that the TCF is offered with the aim of promoting the use of RTB. A clear example is the inventory of purposes that participating organisations may pursue within the context of the TCF, such as 'create a personalised ads profile' or 'measure ad performance'.[31] Regarding the data minimisation principle, the Belgian DPA acknowledged that larger quantities of personal data will be processed at a later stage of the RTB process, including special categories.[32] These incidental findings provide strong indications that data processing activities within the RTB are fundamentally disproportional since they violate two fundamental data protection principles that echo the structure of *lato sensu* proportionality reasoning.[33]

This argument could be further supported by the fact that the principle of proportionality is also reflected in other principles enshrined in Article 5(1) GDPR,[34] such as lawfulness and security, but also in specific data controllers' obligations, like data protection impact assessments (DPIA). Indeed, the Belgian DPA identified a series of GDPR infringements by IAB Europe regarding these issues, which are interconnected on various levels. For instance, the obligation to carry out a DPIA requires an evaluation of the processing's necessity and proportionality. The Belgian DPA took into consideration the large number of data subjects and organisations involved in the TCF, as well as the TCF's impact on the large-scale processing of personal data in the context of RTB[35] and found that IAB Europe failed to fulfill its obligation to conduct a DPIA.[36]

Furthermore, the security of processing in conjunction with data protection by design and by default seems to be highly influenced by proportionality reasoning, since it revolves around the idea of appropriate and effective measures, which depend on multiple factors, such as the purpose of processing and the risks posed to the rights and freedoms, and in certain cases the state of the art and the costs of implementation. As it has been noted in the literature[37] and indicated in the TCF

[30] *Autorité de protection des données v IAB Europe* (n 21) [495].

[31] ibid [337]–[338].

[32] The fact that special categories of data are processed within the context of RTB has been repeatedly pointed out by academics, NGOs and DPAs. See indicatively 'RTB evidence, selected evidence submitted to data protection authorities to demonstrate RTB's GDPR problems' (Brave), available at /brave.com/rtb-evidencel.

[33] Dalla Corte (n 19).

[34] Opinion of Advocate General Szpunar in *Latvijas Republikas Saeima*, Case C-439/19, 17 December 2020, ECLI:EU:C:2020:1054 [109].

[35] *Autorité de protection des données v IAB Europe* (n 21) [516].

[36] The view that marketers must also conduct DPIAs of RTB has also been supported. J Ryan, 'Why marketers must conduct GDPR Data Protection Impact Assessments of RTB' (Brave, 24 September 2019), available at brave.com/dpia.

[37] J Ryan and C Santos, 'An Unending Data Breach Immune to Audit? Can the TCF and RTB Be Reconciled with the GDPR?' (2022), available at papers.ssrn.com/sol3/papers.cfm?abstract_id=4064729.

decision,[38] the failure to ensure the security of processing in the RTB is considered a serious offence. At the same time, the absence of appropriate measures in accordance with the principle of data protection by design and by default leads to the ineffective exercise of data subjects' rights and the ineffective monitoring of the validity and integrity of the users' choices.

Moreover, the lawfulness of processing is also directly affected by the concept of proportionality. Legitimate interest might be the most indicative example since it can only be used as a legal basis for data processing when a test, which shares similar components with the traditional *lato sensu* proportionality test, is passed.[39] To meet the legitimate interest test's requirements, the processing must be suitable and necessary for the controller's purposes, and the balance between the controller's interest and the data subject's rights and freedoms must be in favour of the controller. In the case of OBA and RTB, this test seems quite challenging since it would be almost impossible to identify a legitimate interest, even less so to demonstrate that the processing is necessary to achieve such an interest and balance it against the individual's interests, rights and freedoms.[40] In the words of the UK's Information Commissioner's Office (ICO), the nature of the processing within RTB makes it impossible to meet the legitimate interest's lawful basis requirements.[41]

In practice, the context of data processing in RTB,[42] the inherent weaknesses in the applicability of other legal bases, such as contract[43] and legitimate interest,[44] and the relevant guidance from data protection authorities and academics[45] all point to the direction of consent being the sole appropriate legal basis for processing personal data for behavioural advertising purposes. Nevertheless, consent has been long abused as a legal basis for (personal) data-driven advertising.[46]

[38] *Autorité de protection des données v IAB Europe* (n 21) [478].

[39] Art 6(1)(f) GDPR; see also I Kamara and P de Hert, 'Understanding the Balancing Act behind the Legitimate Interest of the Controller Ground: A Pragmatic Approach' in E Selinger, J Polonetsky and O Tene (eds), *Cambridge Handbook of Consumer Privacy* (CUP, 2018).

[40] *Autorité de protection des données v IAB Europe* (n 21) [414]–[428]. See also Article 29 Working Party, 'Opinion 3/2013 on purpose limitation' (WP 203, 2 April 2013) and M Veale and F Zuiderveen Borgesius, 'Adtech and Real-Time Bidding under European Data Protection Law' (2022) 23 *German Law Journal*, available at doi:10.1017/glj.2022.

[41] ICO (n 10) 18.

[42] In 2013, the IAB referred to its RTB system as 'the Wild West of auctions'; see Interactive Advertising Bureau, 'Programmatic and automation – The publishers' perspective' (2013), available at www.iab.com/wp-content/uploads/2015/06/IAB_Digital_Simplified_Programmatic_Sept_2013.pdf. See Ryan and Santos (n 37) 18.

[43] According to a recent decision of the Data Protection Commission of Ireland, Meta is not entitled to rely on 'contract' as a legal basis in connection with the delivery of behavioural advertising as part of its Facebook service. See decision of the DPC in the matter of LB, a complainant, concerning a complaint directed against Meta Platforms Ireland Limited (formerly Facebook Ireland Limited) in respect of the Facebook Service [2023].

[44] See also the relevant analysis by AG Rantos on how the concept of necessity affects the assessment of legal bases for personalised advertising. Opinion of Advocate General Rantos in *Meta Platforms Inc v Bundeskartellamt*, Case C-252/21, 20 September 2022, ECLI:EU:C:2022:704 [53]–[66] and [70].

[45] F Zuiderveen Borgesius, 'Personal data processing for behavioural targeting: which legal basis?' (2015) 5 *International Data Privacy Law*, available at doi.org/10.1093/idpl/ipv011.

[46] G Sartor et al, 'Regulating targeted and behavioural advertising in digital services' (2021) Study for the Committee on Legal Affairs, Policy Department for Citizens' Rights and Constitutional Affairs,

The assumption that users' informational self-determination could be combined with the right to conduct a business with a win–win outcome has not passed the test of reality,[47] leading to an ongoing debate regarding the future of consent in online environments. Alternatives range from an absolute prohibition of behavioural advertising, regardless of users' consent, to examining the use of consent as a counter-performance with certain restrictions.[48]

Consent as a legal basis, but also lawfulness of processing, in general, are also dependent on another factor which is directly related to proportionality reasoning: transparency.[49] Transparency has been one of the key priorities for regulators regarding online advertising, notwithstanding its purpose. To this end, it came as no surprise that the focus of the Commission's proposal for a Regulation on political advertising,[50] although with a broader rationale,[51] has been on transparency and targeting. In practice, however, the privacy information that individuals have access to is too generic and vague to allow them to obtain useful knowledge on what happens to their data, especially in such complex and opaque systems such as OBA and RTB.[52]

In conclusion, the decision on the TCF sheds light on the interrelation between proportionality and data protection principles and obligations in the context of programmatic advertising. These aspects of proportionality should be taken into consideration by the CJEU to the effect that it is structurally difficult (if not impossible) to reconcile RTB with European data protection law as a matter of principle.[53]

III. A Proportional (?) Response: From Targeted Advertising to Targeted Regulation

In the wake of sweeping technological and legal developments, the ability of the current legal framework to address efficiently all implications deriving from RTB or/and similar tracking and targeting technologies has been called into question.

European Parliament, available at www.europarl.europa.eu/RegData/etudes/STUD/2021/694680/IPOL_STU(2021)694680_EN.pdf.

[47] ibid 13.

[48] ibid 109.

[49] Several approaches aim to enhance transparency and improve the position of users, including the diversification of the data protection regulatory toolbox and measures for the operationalisation of privacy, such as privacy-friendly defaults, standardisation of options and interfaces and codes of conducts for online advertising.

[50] Proposal for a regulation of the European Parliament and of the Council on the transparency and targeting of political advertising [2021] COM/2021/731.

[51] As noted in recital 4 of the Proposal, a high level of transparency is necessary, among others, to support an open and fair political debate and free and fair elections or referendums and to combat disinformation and unlawful interference including from abroad.

[52] Information Commissioner's Office, 'Adtech Phase 2: Key findings' (December 2019), available at ico.org.uk/media/about-the-ico/documents/2616754/fff2-info-gathering-201912.pdf.

[53] M Veale and F Zuiderveen Borgesius, 'Adtech and Real-Time Bidding under European Data Protection Law' (2022) 23 *German Law Journal*, available at doi:10.1017/glj.2022.

Such technologies are usually applied in ecosystems that are so based on big data and complicated techniques that it becomes almost impossible to identify, understand and rationalise their *modus operandi* and decision-making processes. Many targeted advertising mechanisms have been described as 'black boxes', namely systems whose inner workings and decisional logics remain fundamentally opaque to human understanding.[54] Therefore, the ability to look inside this black box becomes of utmost importance for regulators and policymakers, since it will allow them to identify risks and their potential impact on data subjects but also society in general, to allocate liabilities and to intervene where necessary.

Since online behavioural advertising systems, such as RTB, are heavily entwined with personalised tracking and cannot be properly understood without it,[55] data protection and privacy legislation are crucial for addressing the concerns for users' rights and freedoms. However, the key question remains: is the regulatory framework sufficient or there is a need for Adtech-specific or Adtech-oriented rules? The response to this question entails the consideration of the increasing overlap between privacy, consumer protection and competition rules,[56] but also the societal concerns that arise from advertising-driven business models.[57] In this context, OBA falls within the scope of two highly important EU legislative initiatives, namely the DSA and the Digital Markets Act (DMA).[58] The proportionality principle is essential to understanding and assessing the reasoning behind these initiatives that regulate data processing in the context of targeted and programmatic advertising.

The DSA includes rules and principles regarding, essentially, the way intermediaries participate in the publication and distribution of online content,[59] which complement existing frameworks such as the GDPR. The proportionality principle influences the DSA in two manifest ways; firstly, it introduces a layered approach to imposing obligations, depending partially on the societal impact and indirectly on the financial status of each platform.[60] For instance, to avoid disproportionate burdens, many impactful provisions regarding online advertising do not apply to providers that qualify as micro or small enterprises.[61] At the same

[54] A Vorras and L Mitrou, 'Unboxing the Black Box of Artificial Intelligence: Algorithmic Transparency and/or a Right to Functional Explainability' in TE Synodinou, P Jougleux, C Markou and T Prastitou-Merdi (eds), *EU Internet Law in the Digital Single Market* (Springer, 2021).

[55] Veale and Borgesius (n 52).

[56] Group of 7 (G7), 'Compendium of approaches to improving competition in digital markets' (2022), available at www.bundeskartellamt.de/SharedDocs/Publikation/EN/Others/G7_Compendium.pdf?__blob=publicationFile&v=4.

[57] Recital 79 DSA.

[58] DMA: Regulation (EU) 2022/1925 of the European Parliament and of the Council of 14 September 2022 on contestable and fair markets in the digital sector and amending Directives (EU) 2019/1937 and (EU) 2020/1828 (Digital Markets Act), OJ 2022 L 265/1.

[59] M Cappello, 'Unravelling the Digital Services Act package' (2021) IRIS Special, European Audiovisual Observatory, available at rm.coe.int/iris-special-2021-01en-dsa-package/1680a43e45.

[60] According to recital 76 DSA, 'Very large online platforms and very large online search engines may cause societal risks, different in scope and impact from those caused by smaller platforms'.

[61] Art 19 DSA.

time, the highest standard of additional due diligence obligations applies to 'very large online platforms' (VLOPs) and search engines, in a way deemed proportionate to their societal impact.[62] This regulatory choice reflects the interconnection between proportionality and the effort to mitigate asymmetries of information and economic power. Finally, the DSA introduces a wide definition of 'advertisement', which covers commercial and non-commercial, eg political purposes.[63] Moreover, it explicitly mentions programmatic advertising and the 'actors involved in its value chain' in the provision regarding codes of conduct.[64]

Secondly, the DSA contains provisions that employ proportionality reasoning, such as purpose limitation and data minimisation, to regulate personal data processing in the context of online advertising. To this extent, the DSA introduces two new restrictions concerning targeted online advertising. It prohibits it for minors when it is based on profiling[65] but also for any recipient of services when special categories of personal data are used for profiling.[66] At first sight, these new restrictions present a balanced and proportionate approach to regulating behavioural advertising. However, there are enforcement issues that need to be addressed, especially regarding the ability of platform providers to confirm the age of their users[67] and the extended scope of what can be considered special categories of personal data.[68]

Furthermore, the so-called 'dark patterns'[69] which constitute a very common practice in the context of behavioural advertising and RTB, eg in cookie banners, are also explicitly prohibited,[70] although such practices are probably already covered by the GDPR.[71] Finally, the DSA rules aim at enhancing transparency

[62] As noted in recital 41 DSA, 'it is important that the due diligence obligations are adapted to the type, size and nature of the intermediary service concerned', while recital 76 mentions that 'providers of such very large online platforms and very large online search engines should therefore bear the highest standard of due diligence obligations, proportionate to their societal impact'.

[63] Art 4(f) DSA.

[64] ibid Art 46.

[65] ibid Art 28(2).

[66] ibid Art 26(3).

[67] According to Art 28 DSA, the prohibition applies when providers of online platform are aware with reasonable certainty that the recipient of the service is a minor. See also M Harding McGill, 'Social platforms say it's hard to tell which users are kids' (Axios, 9 December 2021), available at www.axios.com/2021/12/09/instagram-tik-tok-age-verification-child-safety.

[68] For the expansion of the definition of special category data and the scope of Art 9 GDPR, see Case C-184/20 *OT v Vyriausioji tarnybinės etikos komisija* [2022] ECLI:EU:C:2022:601.

[69] According to recital 67 DSA 'Dark patterns on online interfaces of online platforms are practices that materially distort or impair, either purposefully or in effect, the ability of recipients of the service to make autonomous and informed choices or decisions. Those practices can be used to persuade the recipients of the service to engage in unwanted behaviours or into undesired decisions which have negative consequences for them'.

[70] Art 25(1) DSA.

[71] CM Gray, C Santos, N Bielova, M Toth and D Clifford, 'Dark Patterns and the Legal Requirements of Consent Banners: An Interaction Criticism Perspective' (2021) in Proceedings of the 2021 CHI Conference on Human Factors in Computing Systems, available at ssrn.com/abstract=3780377.

and accountability for every online platform in relation to advertising,[72] but even more for very large ones, which will have to maintain and provide access to ad repositories,[73] to assess their advertising systems for societal risks,[74] and to take measures to mitigate them.[75]

The DSA rules are complemented by the DMA, which tries to respond to economic concerns over the advertising models of gatekeepers, ie large undertakings providing core platform services. In line with the principle of proportionality, the DMA 'targets' companies based on criteria like their size and impact on the internal market, imposing a stricter set of rules in the context of providing core platform services. Online advertising is a core platform service[76] and therefore the DMA affects targeted advertising in multiple ways. Perhaps most importantly, the DMA addresses the common practice of gatekeepers accumulating large amounts of data from end users, and to that extent it includes (a) requirements for independently auditing techniques for profiling consumers[77] and (b) a prohibition on tracking end users outside of the core platform service for targeted advertising, without consent.[78]

After 'allowing' data-intensive and programmatic forms of advertising to become an industry standard for years, it has become increasingly challenging for EU institutions to enforce a radical transformation of the Adtech ecosystem. Thus, a regulatory paradigm shift in online advertising would require deep reflection on its impact in practice. Could, for instance, a small or medium enterprise (SME) or a news organisation that largely depends on advertising as a business model, deviate from the 'rules of the advertising game' which are mainly dictated by gatekeepers and VLOPs, and, if so, at what cost? In their effort to overcome the Collingridge paradox,[79] EU lawmakers have gradually resorted to the following regulatory choices: either to provide at an initial stage for technology-neutral legal frameworks, such as the GDPR, or to conceptualise new rules and regulations in response to market developments, at a later stage of the evolution process, such as the DSA and the DMA. Time will show whether these initiatives succeed in limiting Big Tech's influence, but also creating fertile ground for privacy-friendly advertising methods and ultimately convincing online platforms that respecting users' privacy can actually be a competitive advantage.

[72] Art 26 DSA.
[73] ibid Art 39.
[74] ibid Art 34.
[75] ibid Art 35.
[76] Art 2(2j) DMA.
[77] Art 15(11) DMA.
[78] ibid Art 5(2a).
[79] Collingridge presents a paradox regarding the need to control the evolution of a technology, based on the prediction of its potential impact, which is summarised in the following quote: 'When change is easy, the need for it cannot be foreseen; when the need for change is apparent, change has become expensive, difficult and time consuming'; D Collingridge, *The Social Control of Technology* (Frances Pinter, 1980).

IV. Proportionality and the Future of Adtech: Cookies, Prohibitions and Walls

Undoubtedly regulation is 'Janus-faced' in terms of innovation and technology:[80] it is perceived either as an obstacle or as a stimulus, in both cases establishing a mutual and dynamic interface. Any regulatory model, whether it is heavy-handed or even 'impeding' regulation on one end of the spectrum, or a minimal regulatory approach or deregulation on the other end, will substantially affect the innovative process. In this context, proportionate regulation of Adtech could set specific rules for the stakeholders and clarify obligations, enhance compliance with the law, increase transparency, provide legal certainty in the market, mitigate risks and reinforce the idea that individuals should remain in control of their information. However, a disproportionate regulation of AdTech could have an unpredictable impact on the fragile balance of the web economy – perhaps to the detriment also of users' interests.[81] Therefore, applying the principle of proportionality, in the light of fundamental rights and social impact assessment processes, while regulating, is a determinant both to the present and the future of Adtech.

The future developments in the field of Adtech include new legal tools but also technical measures and market initiatives which could intervene with fundamental rights, such as the freedom of expression and information or the freedom to conduct a business, manifested as freedom to exercise commercial activities, freedom of contract or free competition.[82] First, there seems to be a growing wave of support, both within the EU and overseas,[83] towards a prohibition of online behavioural advertising, or at least of its most 'privacy intrusive' forms, like RTB. In its Opinion on the Proposal for a Digital Services Act,[84] the European Data Protection Supervisor (EDPS) underlined the risks associated with online targeted advertising and supported the Resolution of the European Parliament, which stated that targeted advertising must be regulated more strictly in favour of less intrusive forms of advertising that do not require any tracking of user interaction with content.[85] Taking into consideration the societal harms, such as the political

[80] J Pelkmans and A Renda, 'Does EU regulation hinder or stimulate innovation?' (CEPS, 19 November 2014) 96, available at www.ceps.eu/ceps-publications/does-eu-regulation-hinder-or-stimulate-innovation.

[81] Y Lau, 'A Brief Primer on the Economics of Targeted Advertising' (2020) Bureau of Economics Federal Trade Commission, available at www.ftc.gov/system/files/documents/reports/brief-primer-economics-targeted-advertising/economic_issues_paper_-_economics_of_targeted_advertising.pdf.

[82] EU Agency for Fundamental Rights, 'Freedom to conduct a business: exploring the dimensions of a fundamental right' (FRA, 5 August 2015), available at fra.europa.eu/sites/default/files/fra_uploads/fra-2015-freedom-conduct-business_en.pdf.

[83] B Cyphers and A Schwartz, 'Ban Online Behavioral Advertising' (EFF, 21 March 2022), available at www.eff.org/deeplinks/2022/03/ban-online-behavioral-advertising.

[84] European Data Protection Supervisor, 'Opinion 1/2021 on the Proposal for a Digital Services Act' (10 February 2021).

[85] European Parliament, 'Resolution of 20 October 2020 with recommendations to the Commission on a Digital Services Act: adapting commercial and civil law rules for commercial entities operating online' (2020/2019 INL, 20 October 2020).

and ideological polarisation, disinformation and manipulation of users, which are closely connected to the advertising-driven business models of the 'attention economy', the EDPS went one step further and urged the legislators to consider a phase-out leading to a prohibition of targeted advertising based on pervasive tracking.

However, a complete ban on targeted advertising currently seems unlikely. In the words of Commissioner Jourová, 'I am not here to help the platforms to do business. But also, I don't think I am here to make it impossible – especially when the political parties and political actors need the online space'.[86] Such statements probably also reflect the needs and expectations of several business sectors, including SMEs.

This position may be further supported by the fact that certain categories of websites have limited options regarding their revenue models. Could, for example, overregulating Adtech lead to the rise of paywalls, meaning models based on subscription fees to gain access to content? What would be the chilling effects of commercialising users' consent for tracking?[87] If subscriptions are offered as an alternative to tracking, would that allow consent to be freely given and, even more importantly, would that mean that the level of data protection is dependent on a person's financial status[88] ?

Furthermore, the European Parliament's position that less intrusive forms of advertising, which do not require tracking, should be supported is well-intentioned, but it does not come without risks. Some of the first to respond to such calls were organisations with immense interests and key roles in the Adtech market,[89] like Google, which introduced the world to its privacy sandbox.[90] It aims to create technologies that protect people's privacy online and, in this context, it came up with alternative proposals for interest-based advertising, eg replacing third-party cookies[91] with technologies like Federated learning cohorts[92] or Topics.[93] Although blocking third-party cookies is not a

[86] S Fleming and J Espinoza, 'Brussels set for clash over online political advertising' *Financial Times* (8 August 2022), available at www.ft.com/content/b9f7da07-3ff6-4358-96a3-f833be3689d2.

[87] V Morel, C Santos, Y Lintao and S Human, 'Your Consent Is Worth 75 Euros A Year – Measurement and Lawfulness of Cookie Paywalls' in 'Proceedings of the 21st Workshop on Privacy in the Electronic Society' (2022), available at doi.org/10.1145/3559613.3563205.

[88] NOYB, 'News Sites: Readers need to 'buy back' their own data at an exorbitant price' (13 August 2021), available at noyb.eu/en/news-sites-readers-need-buy-back-their-own-data-exorbitant-price.

[89] For a further analysis of the positions held by Google and Facebook in the Adtech market see Competition and Markets Authority, 'Online platforms and digital advertising Market study final report' (1 July 2020), available at www.gov.uk/cma-cases/online-platforms-and-digital-advertising-market-study.

[90] privacysandbox.com/intl/en_us.

[91] J Schuh, 'Building a more private web: A path towards making third party cookies obsolete' (Chromium Blog, 14 January 2020), available at blog.chromium.org/2020/01/building-more-private-web-path-towards.html.

[92] C Bindra, 'Building a privacy-first future for web advertising' (Google, 25 January 2021), available at blog.google/products/ads-commerce/2021-01-privacy-sandbox.

[93] Google Ads Help, 'Topics: The new Privacy Sandbox proposal for interest-based advertising' (22 February 2022), available at support.google.com/google-ads/answer/11899856?hl=en.

new approach[94] and behavioural is not the only kind of targeted advertising,[95] the effectiveness and proportionality of these initiatives should be carefully examined. Serious concerns have already been voiced over the impact that such initiatives would have on the market in terms of competition, and whether, at the end of the day, competition and privacy considerations point to different policy directions.[96]

Besides the impact such initiatives could have on the market and consumers, the benefits they bring to users' privacy should also be assessed. Taking into account (a) that the legal issues regarding data protection, consumer protection and competition are complex, intertwining and in many occasions overlapping, (b) the origin of these market initiatives, and (c) the limited information available about the proposed solutions, one cannot help but wonder whether methods that appear to be less intrusive might in practice create ever more opaque systems based on highly accurate data modelling for user profiling, using machine learning technologies that only a close group of organisations possesses. Once more, the proportionality principle seems to be rather relevant and important, as it should be used to assess the proposed alternatives to the current status of behavioural advertising and the related market and state initiatives, vis a vis other rights and interests.

At the same time, with the ePrivacy Regulation[97] being long overdue, there is a tendency for European countries to adopt potentially impactful measures at a national level. Most notably, the German Government is drafting a Regulation on Cookie Consent Management Services,[98] which would enable certain software applications to allow users to generalise and sort their consent by category of devices or websites. Moreover, the UK Government intends to move from an opt-in regime to an opt-out regime for cookies as soon as effective browser-based or industry solutions exist to manage cookies and opt-out preferences.[99] Besides the practical and theoretical barriers related to such initiatives,[100] the continuous

[94] Mozilla Firefox has announced such a block since 2019 and Safari since 2020: blog.mozilla.org/en/products/firefox/todays-firefox-blocks-third-party-tracking-cookies-and-cryptomining-by-default and webkit.org/blog/10218/full-third-party-cookie-blocking-and-more.

[95] A commonly used example of Privacy Preserving Targeted Advertising is Adnostic: crypto.stanford.edu/adnostic.

[96] D Geradin, D Katsifis and T Karanikioti, 'Google as a de facto Privacy Regulator: Analyzing Chrome's Removal of Third-party Cookies from an Antitrust Perspective' (2020) TILEC Discussion Paper, available at dx.doi.org/10.2139/ssrn.3738107.

[97] Proposal for a regulation of the European Parliament and of the Council concerning the respect for private life and the protection of personal data in electronic communications and repealing Directive 2002/58/EC (Regulation on Privacy and Electronic Communications).

[98] L Lensdorf, K Van Quathem, A Oberschelp de Meneses and D Valat, 'The German Government is Drafting a Regulation on Cookie Consent Management' (12 September 2022), available at www.insideprivacy.com/eu-data-protection/the-german-government-is-drafting-a-regulation-on-cookie-consent-management-services.

[99] Department for Digital, Culture, Media and Sport, 'Consultation outcome Data: a new direction – government response to consultation Data: a new direction – government response to consultation' (2022), available at www.gov.uk/government/consultations/data-a-new-direction/outcome/data-a-new-direction-government-response-to-consultation.

[100] J Kühling and C Sauerborn, 'The meaningfulness of § 26 TTDSG, PIMS as a medicine against 'Cookie-Click-Fatigue'?' (2022) *Zeitschrift für Datenschutz* 531.

legal uncertainty regarding online advertising may lead to fragmented solutions that would not guarantee the same level of protection for users across Europe.

From a broader perspective, besides RTB and the impossible asks[101] to bring it into compliance with GDPR requirements, it is worth questioning whether using any form of online advertising based on the 'track–profile–target' model,[102] can ever be in line with the proportionality principle. Assessing whether the purpose in the context of advertising can be specific, explicit and legitimate seems a luxury at this point whereas it is not even certain who is setting the purpose and how the various roles in the processing chain are assigned.[103] These ambiguities often provide the opportunity for organisations that dominate such markets to push forward solutions that conveniently enhance their dominance under a privacy cloak. However, broader legal considerations remain largely unaddressed, since they are fundamentally connected to the fact that online platforms are engaged systematically in user profiling activities on an unprecedented level.[104] This widely discussed power asymmetry is underpinned by users' technical, economic and social constraints, leading to a vicious cycle where online platforms amplify the advantage of their infrastructural power.[105] The involved interests and risks are now on an autonomous, economic and political level and the balancing exercise is increasingly delicate.

Regulating Adtech through the lens of proportionality leads us to two fundamental conclusions – perhaps two sides of the same coin. On one hand, despite its pivotal role in the digital economy, online advertising, especially in the current, behavioural and programmatic form, poses great – if not insuperable – challenges to the protection of personal data. At the same time, data-driven personalization in Adtech triggers significant considerations that go far beyond data protection and undermine individual autonomy, the proper functioning of the economy and the integrity of political discourse.[106]

On the other hand, it is a fact that programmatic advertising has become an integral part of the online ecosystem's operating models, varying from 'VLOPs' and 'gatekeepers' SMEs and news websites. To this extent, any regulatory initiative or alternative model of advertising should be made after a due assessment of its benefits, implications and side-effects for users, society and the internet.

The future of regulating Adtech is built on an amalgam of empowering individual autonomy by enhancing practical aspects of consent and protecting individuals

[101] Veale, Nouwens, Santos (n 27).

[102] J Chen, Regulating Online Behavioural Advertising Through Data Protection Law (Edward Elgar Publishing, 2021).

[103] The Belgian DPA's decision adopts a 'joint controller approach' and the ECJ will have to answer the relevant question.

[104] 'The scale of data collection and the techniques used to influence users are factors to be considered when assessing the impact of the processing'. See Article 29 Working Party, 'Opinion 6/2014 on the notion of legitimate interests of the data controller under Article 7 of Directive 95/46/EC' (WP 217, 9 April 2014) 32.

[105] Chen (n 101) 79.

[106] ibid 85.

and society by introducing prohibitions.[107] In both scenarios, the principle of proportionality is of key importance. Since online behavioural advertising has proven to be more than a new form of advertising,[108] lawmakers will have to leave behind traditional models to rethink their approaches and explore further innovative, collaborative and outcome-based co-regulation and self-regulation models, to enhance proportionality and maintain a balance between fostering innovation, protecting individuals' rights, and addressing any potential unintended consequences. Ultimately, 'good' regulation for technology should derive from agile, contemporary, democratically legalised and auditable lawmaking mechanisms, based on broader considerations about how data governance can be used to promote desirable societal goals.[109]

V. Conclusion

There are numerous indications that we are going through very volatile times in IT regulation. Many of the existing and already proposed measures can prove to be very useful in increasing transparency and enhancing compliance for online advertising. However, one cannot help but question whether these measures will be sufficient, and if not, whether future regulatory initiatives will be proportional vis a vis other rights and interests. The conception that law can keep pace with technological development proves to be a 'chimera' in practice, especially as conventional lawmaking tools and methods seem on many occasions inappropriate to deal with the innovative and unclassified relationships deriving from technological developments.

As the EDPS notes, the current state of the internet is not set in stone – it is instead the product of human and political choices.[110] If it is time to change things and establish a clear framework for online targeted advertising, the proportionality principle might be more relevant than ever. Taking into consideration the multiple risks for individuals, society and the economy, the fragility of the digital ecosystem, the constant evolution of technology and the practical difficulties of implementation and regulatory oversight, the relentless question with regards to regulating Adtech in the EU remains: is it a chase of chimeras or the art of the possible?

[107] F Zuiderveen Borgesius, 'Consent to Behavioural Targeting in European Law – What are the Policy Implications of Insights from Behavioural Economics?' (2013) Amsterdam Law School Research Paper No 2013–43, Institute for Information Law Research Paper No 2013-02.

[108] Chen (n 101) 205.

[109] ibid 207.

[110] W Wiewiórowski, 'Online targeting for political advertising: stricter rules are necessary' (EDPS, 14 March 2022), available at edps.europa.eu/press-publications/press-news/blog/it-time-target-online-advertising_en.

9

The Data Act and the Balance of Interests between Device Purchasers and Manufacturers

BOHDAN WIDŁA

I. Introduction

On 23 February 2022, the European Commission unveiled the proposal for the Data Act (DA).[1] It aims to ensure 'fairness in the allocation of value from data among actors in the data economy and to foster access to and use of data'.[2] The main objective is to improve access to and the use of data generated by connected devices. Other declared aims include the facilitation of switching between cloud and edge services, and the development of interoperability standards for data to be reused between sectors of the economy.[3] After nearly two years of legislative proceedings, the DA finally entered into force on 11 January 2024, with most of its provisions starting to apply from 12 September 2025.[4] Numerous academic comments were made available prior to the adoption of the final text.[5] The debate focused mainly on the role of the DA in the development

[1] Proposal for a Regulation on harmonised rules on fair access to and use of data, COM/2022/68 final ('Data Act Proposal').

[2] ibid 2.

[3] ibid 3.

[4] Regulation (EU) 2023/2854 of the European Parliament and of the Council of 13 December 2023 on harmonised rules on fair access to and use of data and amending Regulation (EU) 2017/2394 and Directive (EU) 2020/1828 (Data Act) OJ L 2023/2854.

[5] See esp C Ducuing, T Margoni, and L Schirru (eds), 'White Paper on the Data Act Proposal', available at dx.doi.org/10.2139/ssrn.4259428; J Drexl et al, 'Position Statement of the Max Planck Institute for Innovation and Competition of 25 May 2022 on the Commission's Proposal of 23 February 2022 for a Regulation on Harmonised Rules on Fair Access to and Use of Data (Data Act)', available at dx.doi.org/10.2139/ssrn.4136484; S Geiregat, 'The Data Act: Start of a New Era for Data Ownership?', available at dx.doi.org/10.2139/ssrn.4214704; W Kerber, 'Governance of IoT Data: Why the EU Data Act Will not Fulfil Its Objectives' (2022) 72 *GRUR International* 120; D Gill, 'The Data Act Proposal and the Problem of Access to In-Vehicle Data and Resources', available at dx.doi.org/10.2139/ssrn.4115443; M Leistner and L Antoine, 'IPR and the Use of Open Data and Data Sharing Initiatives by Public and Private

of the European data economy. However, there is another angle from which the new regulation may be assessed: the elusive balance between the owners and manufacturers of connected devices, often equated with the so-called internet of things (IoT) devices.[6]

Among crucial aspects of control over a device is the legal and practical capability to repair it, perform maintenance or refurbish it. The shift in the balance of power is evident in the case of connected devices, pointedly described as the 'Internet of Things You Don't Own'.[7] While the scope of property rights in tangible items remains unchanged in theory, their influence is weakening, as they are losing a tug of war against mechanisms such as copyright protection of computer programs, trade secrets' statutory protection, contractual or even purely factual control over services necessary to use the device and, last but not least, over data generated by the use of devices. In the section discussing fundamental rights, the explanatory memorandum to the Data Act Proposal refers to 'the right to use and dispose of lawfully acquired possessions', which is to be reinforced with the 'right to access data generated from the use of an Internet of Things object'.[8] This phrase echoes Article 17(1) of the EU Charter of Fundamental Rights,[9] which uses similar wording to describe the right to property. According to the drafters, the right to data access may cause device owners to 'benefit from a better user experience and a wider range of, for example, repair and maintenance services'.[10] The European Commission even chose to wave the banner of access to repair in the proposal's promotional materials.[11]

This chapter seeks to evaluate the effect that the DA will have on the interests of device manufacturers and purchasers. I focus on issues relevant to particular commercial relationships between such parties, not on the bigger picture of the data economy. Against what does the right to property need reinforcement to make this goal achievable? Does the DA provide meaningful reinforcement of the owners' rights? What fundamental rights, other than the right to property, will be affected by this measure? And crucially, will the restrictions on such rights, introduced by the DA, pass the proportionality test, as required by Article 52(1) of the EU Charter of Fundamental Rights? I argue that due to the narrow scope and numerous safeguards introduced during the legislative proceedings, the DA not only fails to tip the scales significantly in favour of device purchasers but also entrenches some existing practices favourable to manufacturers.

Actors', available at www.europarl.europa.eu/thinktank/en/document/IPOL_STU(2022)732266; A Metzger and H Schweitzer, 'Shaping Markets: A Critical Evaluation of the Draft Data Act' [2023] 1 *Zeitschrift für Europäisches Privatrecht* 42.

[6] For an overview of the notion of IoT and the regulatory challenges, see G Noto La Diega, *Internet of Things and the Law. Legal Strategies for Consumer-Centric Smart Technologies (Routledge*, 2023) 11–40.

[7] A Perzanowski and J Schulz, *The End of Ownership* (MIT Press, 2016) 139.

[8] Data Act Proposal (n 1) 13.

[9] Charter of Fundamental Rights of the European Union [2012] OJ C 326/391.

[10] ibid.

[11] Data Act Factsheet, available at digital-strategy.ec.europa.eu/en/library/data-act-factsheet.

Section II describes the legal landscape in user–manufacturer relationships and the factors determining control over connected devices. Section III sets the stage for the analysis of the balancing of rights under the framework adopted by the Court of Justice of the European Union. Section IV is devoted to the subject matter and scope of the DA, with a particular focus on the notions of 'connected product', 'related service' and various definitions of data. Section V examines the principle of 'data accessibility by design' and the users' rights to access data generated from a product and to allow third parties to access such data. Section VI concludes.

II. The Balance of Power between Device Purchasers and Manufacturers versus the Scope of the Data Act

Before the massive digitisation of our lives, owning a tangible object was quite uncomplicated. Even taking into account the differences between the approaches to property rights in civil law and common law countries, the owner of a movable thing, broadly speaking, did not have to reckon with competing rights that could prevent him from lawfully using, analysing, modifying or repairing his property. Today, traditional personal property rights can be outbalanced by other rights that the manufacturers can secure and by purely factual mechanisms.

Firstly, a connected device is, by definition, equipped with computer programs. These are almost always protected by copyright under the Software Directive.[12] It grants the copyright owner exclusive rights to reproduce, modify and distribute a computer program.[13] Both the reproduction right and the modification right are broadly defined. The first was designed to give the right holder significant control over the use of a computer program. Whenever, in order to run a program, it is necessary to reproduce it at least temporarily, such actions require the rightholder's consent.[14] Since such reproduction is almost always necessary, the reproduction right effectively serves as a right to control the use of a program and, by extension, the device. The second right makes 'translation, adaptation, arrangement and any other alteration of a computer program' dependent on the authorisation of the rightholder.[15] Such authorisation usually has the form of a

[12] Directive 2009/24/EC of the European Parliament and of the Council of 23 April 2009 on the legal protection of computer programs [2009] OJ L111/16 (Software Directive). Patent protection may also apply.

[13] Art 4(1) Software Directive.

[14] Art 4(1)(a) Software Directive.

[15] Art 4(1)(b) Software Directive.

licence agreement, and these may be adhesion agreements offered on a 'take it or leave it' basis. As a result, whoever holds the copyright in the program necessary to use the device has significant control over the actions of the owner of its tangible shell. The Software Directive is not entirely blind to users' interests. Its Article 5(1) introduces an exception to the reproduction and modification right, allowing a lawful acquirer to act without authorisation when it is necessary to use the program 'in accordance with its intended purpose, including for error correction'. However, specific contractual provisions may override this exception. While the rightholder may not entirely prevent the user from correcting software errors, a contract may recognise the rightholder as solely responsible for such maintenance.[16] Additionally, the legislative history of Article 5(1) shows that its scope includes only removing errors, not other activities connected with maintenance, such as performing upgrades.[17]

Notably, the problem of copyright protection of software arises not only in connection with programs that form the core functionality of a device. Programs may also be used to deliberately limit the possibility of independent repair or other forms of tinkering with the device. Examples of the first group include software that detects spare parts and authenticates only those originating from the manufacturer or limits access to diagnostic data.[18] The second group includes eg software that prevents users from installing alternative firmware (eg by accepting only files with the manufacturer's digital signature) or operating systems.

Secondly, technical protection measures (TPMs) can be used either as part of the device or its software to further limit user capabilities, thus acting as the so-called 'digital locks'.[19] In the EU, the Software Directive requires the Member States to prohibit, among others, putting into circulation and possession for commercial purposes of means 'the sole intended purpose of which is to facilitate the unauthorised removal or circumvention' of TPMs.[20] While the acts of removal and circumvention are not prohibited by themselves,[21] doing so may require unauthorised reproduction or modification of a computer program, which results in copyright infringement.

Thirdly, access to data produced or processed by the device finally comes into play. Such data (eg, photographs) may be protected by various intellectual property rights, particularly copyright, whose threshold for protection is nowadays

[16] Case C-13/20 *Top System SA v Belgian State*, ECLI:EU:C:2021:811.

[17] W Blocher and MM Walter 'Computer Program Directive' in MM Walter and S von Lewinsky (eds), *European Copyright Law. A commentary* (OUP, 2010) 155.

[18] A Rosborough, 'Unscrewing the Future: The Right to Repair and Circumvention of Software TPMs in the EU' (2020) 11 *Journal of Intellectual Property, Information Technology and Electronic Commerce Law* 26, 31.

[19] ibid 27.

[20] Art 7(1)(c) Software Directive.

[21] Blocher and Walter (n 17) 205–06.

very low.[22] Additionally, the data may form a collection of independent elements arranged systematically or methodically and individually accessible. In that case, it is a database that can be covered by copyright or by a *sui generis* right introduced in the Database Directive.[23] The data can also contain trade secrets as defined in Article 2(1) of the Directive (EU) 2016/943.[24]

Finally, there is the question of technical dependencies. A device may function only when an external network service is available. Convenience is counterbalanced here with an almost complete lack of influence over the service's inner workings and availability. At least from the technical standpoint, nothing prevents the service provider from limiting its function or outright shutting it down. The device is either connected or 'bricked'. The same applies to access to data.

Against this landscape, the solutions proposed in the DA are narrow. Critically, the DA does not affect existing intellectual property rights, with a minor exception of the *sui generis* database right.[25] Such a solution is intended by design, as none of the examined policy options provided an alternative.[26] While the lack of access to data is an entry barrier for providers of aftermarket services, it is merely one of the factors usually advantageous to manufacturers.

III. The Proportionality Test: Balancing the Right to Property Against …?

The notion of proportionality has at least two distinct contexts. The first refers to the legal tools used to assess whether a given limitation of rights and freedoms is allowed. This aspect could be defined as constitutional[27] proportionality. Its origins can be traced to the German Federal Constitutional Court,[28] but it quickly migrated to other legal systems.[29] On the level of EU law, it is

[22] See, eg case C-145/10 *Eva-Maria Painer v Standard Verlags GmbH and Others* ECLI:EU:C:2011:798, [2011] ECR I-12533.

[23] Directive 96/9/EC of the European Parliament and of the Council of 11 March 1996 on the legal protection of databases [1996] OJ L 77/20.

[24] Directive (EU) 2016/943 of the European Parliament and of the Council of 8 June 2016 on the protection of undisclosed know-how and business information (trade secrets) against their unlawful acquisition, use and disclosure [2016] OJ L 157/1 (Trade Secret Directive).

[25] Art 43 DA.

[26] Impact Assessment report and support studies accompanying the Proposal for a Data Act, SWD(2022) 34 final, 29.

[27] F Bauer, 'Proportionality in Private Law: An Analytical Framework' in F Bauer and B Köhler (eds), *Proportionality in Private Law* (Mohr Siebeck, 2023) 23–24; R Markiewicz, 'Zasada proporcjonalności w prawie autorskim Unii Europejskiej' (Wolters Kluwer Polska, 2023) 38–39; M Husovec, 'How Will the European Patent Judges Understand Proportionality?' (2020) 60 *Jurimetrics* 383.

[28] Judgment of the Bundesverfassungsgericht of 11 June 1958, 1 BvR 596/56, 7 BVerfGE 377.

[29] For a detailed discussion, see A Barak (transl D Kalir), *Proportionality. Constitutional Rights and their Limitations* (Cambridge University Press, 2012) 181 ff.

now firmly entrenched in Article 5(1) and (4) of the Treaty on the European Union and, perhaps more importantly, in Article 52(1) of the EU Charter of Fundamental Rights. In the second aspect, proportionality is used as a tool that assists in achieving an equitable or optimised outcome.[30] For example, in intellectual property law, the principle of proportionality can be used to decide whether specific remedies, such as injunctions, should be available to the rightholder in a given case.[31]

In this chapter, proportionality will be applied in its constitutional aspect to identify whether the limitations imposed on rights and freedoms to reinforce the right to property can be justified according to the standard defined in Article 52(1) of the EU Charter of Fundamental Rights. The judgment in *Sky Österreich* shows that the CJEU approaches constitutional proportionality by following the well-established test, evaluating whether the controlled measure maintains the essence of the limited right, is appropriate to attain the legitimate objective, is necessary for it, and is proportionate in the strict sense.[32]

The new measures discussed in this chapter are expected to force manufacturers to change their design practices by allowing more data to be accessible and to respond to requests to make data available to users and third parties who provide services to users. An obvious alternative would be to use non-binding measures promoting data access. This policy option was considered by the European Commission but it was rejected as insufficient and, therefore, not proportional.[33] Assessing whether the eventually chosen option that shaped the DA fulfils the necessity and appropriateness criteria is difficult without substantial empirical analysis, which would go beyond the scope of this chapter. Assuming that these criteria are indeed fulfilled, as argued by the European Commission,[34] we can turn to the final and more normative part of the proportionality test. If several fundamental rights are at issue, they must be reconciled to achieve a 'fair balance between them'.[35]

Granting rights to access data generated by IoT devices is designed to reinforce the fundamental right to property (Article 17(1) of the EU Charter of Fundamental Rights). But the question is against what? As noted earlier, the DA does not cover most measures that device manufacturers can use to exercise control over data access. Nor will it create any new rights to data or to use data generated by IoT devices.[36] What is left are primarily the factual mechanisms that come down to the design of the devices and the technical ability to access data. From this point of

[30] Husovec (n 27); Markiewicz (n 27) 38–39.

[31] R Sikorski, 'Towards a More Orderly Application of Proportionality to Patent Injunctions in the European Union' (2022) 53 *Intrnational Review of Intellectual Property and Competition Law* 31, 42–46.

[32] Case C-283/11 *Sky Österreich GmbH v Österreichischer Rundfunk* ECLI:EU:C:2013:28 [47]–[59].

[33] Data Act Impact Assessment (n 26) 65.

[34] ibid 65–66.

[35] Case C-275/06 *Productores de Música de España (Promusicae) v Telefónica de España SAU* ECLI:EU:C:2008:54, [2008] ECR I-00271 [70].

[36] Recital 25 DA.

view, the decision to share or refuse to share data is essentially protected under the freedom of contract, which is part of the freedom to conduct a business (Article 16 of the EU Charter of Fundamental Rights).[37]

Other factors are also at play. Despite the assurances in the impact assessment,[38] the protection of trade secrets became a hotly contested issue during the legislative process.[39] Which fundamental rights, if any, are affected here is not exactly clear. It is dubious that trade secrets, at least under EU law, are property in the strict sense.[40] Somewhat surprisingly, the CJEU recognises that trade secret protection has its roots in the right to respect for private and family life (Article 7 of the EU Charter of Fundamental Rights).[41] However, the DA deals with trade secrets mostly in the context of compulsory sharing of data. Again, this appears to interfere mainly with the freedom of contract.

IV. The Subject Matter and Scope of the Data Act

A. Users, Manufacturers and Data Holders

Article 2(12) DA defines a user as a natural or legal person that owns a connected product, to whom temporary rights to use that connected product have been contractually transferred, or receives related services. This definition covers most stakeholders, thus making the DA a far-reaching horizontal measure. The provisions concerning data access apply without meaningful differences in business-to-business and business-to-consumer relationships.[42] Thanks to the lack of distinction between professional users, the DA will support even powerful players who arguably have enough economic leverage to negotiate access to data. On the other side of the relationship, the DA distinguishes manufacturers from data holders. The crucial obligations concerning access to data are placed upon the latter, who, according to Article 2(13), are legal or natural persons with the right or obligation to use and make available data. Manufacturers may, and often will also, be data holders.

[37] *Sky Österreich* (n 32) [42].

[38] Data Act Impact Assessment (n 26) 29.

[39] Proposal for a Regulation of the European Parliament and of the Council on harmonised rules on fair access to and use of data (Data Act). Analysis of the final compromise text in view to agreement, 2022/0047(COD) 11284/23 2.

[40] Impact assessment accompanying the document proposal for a Directive of the European Parliament and of the Council on the protection of undisclosed know-how and business information (trade secrets) against their unlawful acquisition, use and disclosure (SWD/2013/0471 final), 248.

[41] Case C-450/06 *Varec SA v État belge*, ECLI:EU:C:2008:91, [2008] ECR I-00581 [48].

[42] However, Art 7(1) DA exempts microenterprises, small enterprises and, although for limited time, medium enterprises from the duties described in this chapter, provided that they do not have a larger partner or linked enterprise, and that they are not subcontracted to manufacture or design a connected product or to provide a related service.

B. The Connected Products

According to Article 2(5) DA, a connected product is an 'item that obtains, generates or collects data concerning its use or environment and that is able to communicate product data via an electronic communications service, physical connection or on-device access, and whose primary function is not the storing, processing or transmission of data on behalf of any party other than the user'. Recital 14 underscores the horizontal approach of the DA, mentioning that connected products can be found 'in all aspects of the economy and society'. The final text avoids the drawbacks of the proposal by removing the language that seemingly excluded many types of computing devices. According to the original proposal, a device would only fall within the scope of the DA if it transmitted data wirelessly and its 'primary function is not the storing and processing of data'. These reservations raised questions about the applicability of the new regulation to numerous omnipresent IoT devices, such as cameras or webcams. The latter also strengthened manufacturers by deferring to their decisions about the function of a device when it was placed on the market. The wording of Article 2(5) DA refers to devices 'whose primary function is not the storing, processing or transmission of data on behalf of any party other than the user'. Recital 16 suggests that this proviso excludes products such as 'servers or cloud infrastructure operated by their owners entirely on behalf of third parties'.

C. The Related Services

Turning an electronic device into a connected device requires not only hardware but also the software steering the device. Online services may also be necessary. If the data generated by the use of these were to fall beyond the scope of the DA, the regulation would become toothless. Such elements are covered by the definition of 'related services' (Article 2(6) DA). They are digital services, including software, connected with a product at the time of the purchase in such a way that their absence would prevent the product from performing one of its functions. It was quickly noted that this approach resembles the Consumer Sales Directive,[43] which refers to 'goods with digital elements'.[44] However, the latter notion is slightly broader because digital elements include both digital services and digital content. Moreover, it is questionable whether the definition requires the indispensability of the service for the proper functioning of the product. In the Consumer Sales Directive, the absence of digital content or service must prevent the goods from performing their functions. In the DA, it is sufficient if the absence of the service

[43] Directive (EU) 2019/771 of the European Parliament and of the Council of 20 May 2019 on certain aspects concerning contracts for the sale of goods, amending Regulation (EU) 2017/2394 and Directive 2009/22/EC, and repealing Directive 1999/44/EC [2019] OJ L 136/28 (Consumer Sales Directive).
[44] Geiregat (n 5) 19.

prevents the product from performing even one of its functions. The subtle shift from plural to singular bolsters the argument that the definition used in the DA should be interpreted broadly.[45]

D. What Data? Untangling the Web of Definitions

Although 'data' as such is defined broadly in Article 2(1) DA as 'any digital representation of acts, facts or information and any compilation of such acts, facts or information, including in the form of sound, visual or audio-visual recording', the actual scope of the regulation is limited by two factors. The first results from the controversial dichotomy between raw and derivative data. The second is introduced by additional notions: 'product data', 'related service data' and, most importantly, 'readily accessible data'.

Recital 15 confirms that unprocessed data and data 'pre-processed for the purpose of making it understandable and useable prior to further processing and analysis' fall within the scope of DA. However, it excludes 'information inferred or derived from such data, which is the outcome of additional investments into assigning values or insights from the data, in particular by means of proprietary, complex algorithms, including those that are a part of proprietary software'. This qualification has a substantial influence on the scope of the new regulation and, as such, should have been included in its normative part. Setting aside the questionable legislative technique, the substance of the exclusion deserves closer scrutiny.

The decision to remove derivative data from the scope of the definition was met with divergent reactions from manufacturers and academic commentators. During the public consultations on the Data Act Proposal, some industry representatives praised the exclusion, claiming that it is an 'enabler of innovation'[46] and that allowing access to such data would amount to free-riding.[47] Others warned that a broad interpretation would lead to an 'almost inexistent' protection of developers.[48] The academic response to the reasoning behind the exclusion was less enthusiastic. Some noted that data necessary to provide repair services, such as diagnostic codes, may qualify as derivative,[49] so placing them outside the scope of the DA would endanger one of its goals. Perhaps more importantly, the approach

[45] Geiregat (n 5) 20.
[46] 'Philips feedback to Data Act Proposal' 1, available at ec.europa.eu/info/law/better-regulation/have-your-say/initiatives/13045-Data-Act-amended-rules-on-the-legal-protection-of-databases/F3258758_en.
[47] 'Volkswagen Group Position Paper' 9, available at ec.europa.eu/info/law/better-regulation/have-your-say/initiatives/13045-Data-Act-amended-rules-on-the-legal-protection-of-databases/F3258521_en.
[48] 'BSA Recommendations on the EU Data Act' 4, available at ec.europa.eu/info/law/better-regulation/have-your-say/initiatives/13045-Data-Act-amended-rules-on-the-legal-protection-of-databases/F3258586_en.
[49] Gill (n 5) 11; Kerber (n 5) 126.

to distinguishing derivative data from raw data is questionable. Recital 15 uses 'proprietary, complex algorithms' as the key criterion and mentions that the data generated by those 'may be subject to intellectual property rights'. However, even if algorithms are protected by copyright as part of computer programs, such protection does not extend to the program's output. While patent protection of certain processes may extend to the information generated by that process, such situations would likely be very infrequent.[50] Consequently, the manufacturers have a clear incentive to overprocess data generated by the use of their products to circumvent the sharing obligations. Conflicts between intellectual property rights and data access rights may appear,[51] but they can and should be resolved on a case-by-case basis. The same argument applies to possible conflicts involving trade secrets, assuming that derivative data could be protected as such, which is very context-specific.[52]

The provisions of the DA dealing with data access rights do not refer to the broad notion of 'data' but to its subsets: 'product data', 'related service data', and 'readily accessible data'. These definitions seem to have been introduced in response to the criticism voiced by major manufacturers, who wanted to avoid obligations to make available data technically unavailable to themselves.[53] The product data are only those 'generated by the use of a connected product, that the manufacturer designed to be retrievable'. Strikingly, such a limitation does not appear in the definition of 'related service data', which represents 'the digitisation of user actions or events related to the connected product, recorded intentionally by the user or as a by-product of the user's action'.

Figure 9.1 The relationship between 'data', 'product data', 'related service data' and 'readily accessible data'

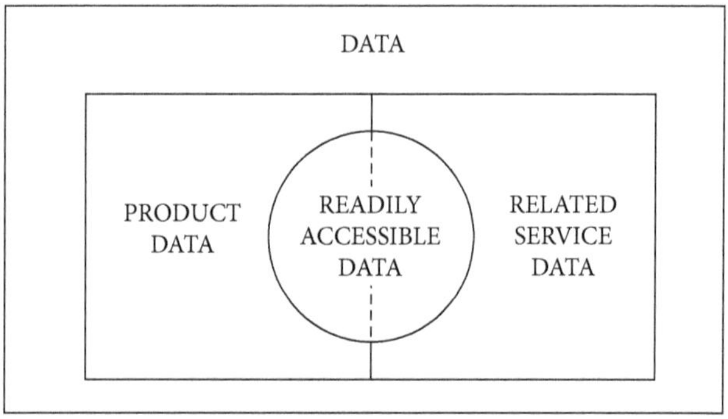

[50] Drexl et al (n 5) 13–14.

[51] Geiregat (n 5) 26.

[52] T Aplin et al, 'The Role of EU Trade Secrets Law in the Data Economy: An Empirical Analysis', (2023) 54 *International Review of Intellectual Property and Competition Law* 826, 843.

[53] Volkswagen Group (n 47) 7–8; 'BMW Group EU Data Act Position Paper' 3, available at ec.europa.eu/info/law/better-regulation/have-your-say/initiatives/13045-Data-Act-amended-rules-on-the-legal-protection-of-databases/F3258752_en.

However, crucial provisions of the DA (Articles 4 and 5 described below) apply only to more narrowly defined 'readily available data', which can be obtained from either the connected product or related service 'without disproportionate effort, going beyond a simple operation'. On the one hand, these provisos alleviate the legitimate fears that the DA could force the manufacturers into an impossible position of having to share data that they cannot access. On the other hand, however, they incentivise behaviour that may endanger the goals of the DA, namely designing the data to only be 'laboriously available' while retaining the technical capabilities to access it, thus gaming the scope of the new regulation. Perhaps anticipating this, Recital 20 suggests that further sectoral regulation can define the minimum levels of accessible product data.

V. Access to Data from the Perspective of the User–Manufacturer Relationship

A. Article 3 – Accessibility by Design, but to what Extent?

Article 3 DA sets requirements for designing and manufacturing products and providing related services. Product data and related service data must be accessible to the user 'by default, easily, securely, free of charge, in a comprehensive, structured, commonly used and machine-readable format', and, where relevant and technically feasible, directly. At first glance, it seems that if manufacturers implement this principle diligently, their advantage over users with respect to data access should diminish significantly. However, at least five issues persist.

Firstly, the principle only covers product data and related service data. As discussed earlier, the former notion especially essentially leaves it up to the manufacturers to choose the scope of data designed to be retrievable.

Secondly, Recital 22 mentions two ways of making data available. It may be available 'from an on-device data storage or from a remote server to which the data are communicated'. Both methods are treated as direct. As long as the server operates, the latter method may be more convenient and efficient for the users. However, it does not protect them from the arbitrary decisions to cease providing such services. As a result, a question appears of whether requirements stemming from Article 3 are constantly subject to evaluation or only when putting a product into the market. The wording of Article 3 points to the former option since it refers to design and manufacturing. Nowhere does it burden any market player with a duty to maintain remote servers allowing data access. Consequently, data accessibility by design comes with an asterisk, leaving considerable power in the hands of manufacturers.

Thirdly, a set of issues appears when one attempts to ascertain when direct access is 'relevant and technically feasible'. The technical feasibility test is essentially repeated twice: in the wording of Article 3(1) DA and, indirectly, in the definition of 'product data', which leaves only data designed to be accessible within the scope of Article 3(1). Consequently, product data can be divided into two categories: data directly accessible to the user and directly accessible only to other parties, such as data holders, including manufacturers. The design decisions of the latter will remain decisive. This reduces the chances that the principle of accessibility by design will significantly tip the balance towards device users.

Fourthly, another problem appears in connection with cybersecurity. IoT devices are notoriously vulnerable to attacks. The proposed Cyber Resilience Act[54] addresses these shortcomings by requiring that products with digital elements only be available on the market if they meet certain essential requirements.[55] These include protecting 'the confidentiality of stored, transmitted or otherwise processed data, personal or other, such as by encrypting relevant data at rest or in transit by the state of the art mechanisms'. Arguably, from the manufacturers' point of view, the most straightforward way of reconciling these seemingly contradictory provisions would be the strategy of erring on the side of caution. In other words, direct access to data is likely to be practically limited not only due to actual cybersecurity issues, but also under the pretext of plausible, albeit invented, problems. This conclusion is bolstered by the newly added Article 4(2), which allows users and data holders to contractually agree on restricting or prohibiting the access, use, or further sharing of data if it could undermine security requirements.

Finally, it is debatable whether purchasers can rely on Article 3 to argue that the sold goods do not conform with the sales contract.[56] The answer appears to be negative[57] as long as the manufacturer is not the seller. If the product is purchased directly from the manufacturer, the ability of the buyer to invoke Article 3 cannot be ruled out. The same applies to leases and other similar agreements. Ultimately, its application will depend on national law and specific contractual obligations.[58] However, the vague relevant-and-technically-feasible standard discussed above makes Article 3 ill-suited for application in particular contractual disputes. Whatever potential the principle in question may have to change the design practices of connected devices, it will most likely manifest itself thanks to its public enforceability[59] and not in disputes between private parties.

[54] Proposal for a Regulation of the European Parliament and of the Council on horizontal cybersecurity requirements for products with digital elements and amending Regulation (EU) 2019/1020 COM(2022) 454 final (CRA Proposal).

[55] Art 10(1) CRA Proposal.

[56] Drexl et al (n 5) 30–31.

[57] ibid 31.

[58] Leistner and Antoine (n 5) 85.

[59] Art 37 DA.

B. Article 4 – The User's Right to Access Data

According to Article 4 DA, readily available data must be made available to the user without undue delay, easily, securely and in a comprehensive, structured, commonly used and machine-readable format, free of charge and, where relevant and technically feasible, of the same quality as is available to the data holder, continuously and in real-time whenever it cannot be accessed directly from the product. This right is available only to the users, so its usefulness is necessarily limited by their technical capability to utilise the data. It is far likelier that it will be invoked against data holders by large businesses than by natural persons or small market players. Arguably, this is why the final wording of Article 4 makes it relatively easy for data holders, in particular manufacturers, to protect their interests by at least delaying access to the data. They can rely on three options.

Firstly, Article 4(2) DA allows users and data holders to contractually agree on restricting or prohibiting the access, use or further sharing of data from the product, should it undermine legally prescribed security requirements, thus resulting in serious adverse effects on the health, safety or security of human beings. Crucially, the data holder can refuse to share data while notifying the national regulatory authority.

Secondly, safeguards for trade secrets were added during the trilogues. Data holders are, in principle, obliged to share data even if it could result in disclosing trade secrets. In consequence, Article 4 amounts to a form of compulsory licence.[60] However, it is significantly watered down by Article 4(6) DA, which makes the disclosure of trade secrets conditional on whether the data holder and the user take all necessary measures prior to the disclosure to preserve their confidentiality, particularly concerning third parties. These technical and organisational measures are supposed to be proportionate. What this standard means will be defined by the practice of national regulatory authorities because if the data holder and the user fail to agree, the former may withhold or suspend data sharing while notifying the regulator. The data holder may also refuse to share data on a case-by-case basis if, despite the measures taken by the user, 'it is highly likely to suffer serious economic damage from the disclosure of trade secrets' (Article 4(8) DA). According to Recital 31, serious economic damage implies serious and irreparable economic losses, which is a rigorous standard. Again, such refusal must be notified to the national authority.

The risk of disclosure of trade secrets appears to be overblown. It is unlikely that the categories of data covered by the regulation (raw and pre-processed, but not derivative) can contain trade secrets.[61] However, the definition of the trade

[60] Drexl et al (n 5) 103.
[61] Aplin et al (n 52) 843–44.

secret remains vague.[62] Even if it can be challenging to prove the existence of trade secrets in court proceedings,[63] little prevents the data holders from 'tactically' claiming that the data contains such secrets[64] and obstructing access by escalating demands concerning the non-disclosure agreements and other protective measures. The new prohibition of unfair, unilaterally imposed contractual terms in business-to-business data sharing agreements[65] is unlikely to affect this. Obviously, the relevant provision applies only after the agreement has been concluded. More importantly, the only time it explicitly mentions trade secrets, it does so to protect the interests of data holders from too powerful users, by prohibiting terms allowing access and use of data in a manner significantly detrimental to the legitimate interests of the sharing party.[66]

In the case of alleged threats to cybersecurity and the protection of trade secrets, the user may either complain to the regulatory authority or seek court redress. In practice, however, even not entirely substantiated claims made by manufacturers can at least significantly delay access to data. As a result, the tangible usefulness of the users' right to access data is likely to depend on the efficiency of the competent national authorities.

Thirdly, although Recital 30 pays lip service to the freedom to 'use the data for any lawful purpose', the substantive part of the DA paints a less user-centric picture. Of particular note is the statutory non-compete obligation under Article 4(10), which prevents users from developing 'a product that competes with the product from which the data originate'. Other limitations include the prohibition of using the data to derive insights about the production methods. This clause is a disguised limit to reverse engineering. Although one can agree that some measure of protection of the manufacturers' interests is justified, the DA goes beyond the protection of trade secrets granted by the TSD. The latter allows observation, study, disassembly or testing of a publicly available or lawfully acquired product, except when otherwise contractually agreed.[67] However, non-compete provisions are not universally included in sales or non-disclosure agreements. In other words, when information has inherent commercial value because it is undisclosed, additional non-compete obligations still must be bargained for. The same applies to functions of computer programs, which lack copyright protection and, therefore, may be copied by competitors[68] unless a non-compete agreement is concluded.

[62] Art 2(1) Trade Secret Directive.

[63] Aplin et al (n 52) 840–45; SK Sandeen and T Aplin, 'Trade secrecy, factual secrecy and the hype surrounding AI' in R Abbott (ed), 'Research Handbook on Intellectual Property and Artificial Intelligence' (Elgar, 2022) 443–60.

[64] E De Noyette and T Margoni, 'The Data Act and the 2016 Trade Secrets Directive' in Ducuing, Margoni and Schirru (n 5) 82.

[65] Art 13 DA.

[66] Art 13(5)(b) DA.

[67] Art 3(1)(b) Trade Secret Directive.

[68] Case C-406/10 *SAS Institute Inc v World Programming Ltd* ECLI:EU:C:2012:259.

The DA essentially contains a statutory non-compete clause concerning otherwise unprotected data, which leads to a lack of systematic coherence.

The vagueness of the notion of a competing product also favours manufacturers. The scope of the non-compete obligation probably extends beyond products. Although related services are not explicitly mentioned in Article 4(10), they are an integral and essential part of products.[69] For example, replacing embedded software to improve a device's performance or functionality arguably leads to developing a new product. At the same time, the users will not be prohibited from developing competing aftermarket services (such as repair). As a result, the final wording of Article 4(10) is paradoxically not far from the version of the narrower access right advocated by the Max Planck Institute, ie 'purpose-bound' and designed only to overcome vendor lock-ins.[70]

C. Article 5 – Empowering Users or Legitimising the Dominance of Manufacturers?

According to Article 5 DA, the user may request that the data holder make the data available to a third party. However, more than a mere request is required for the data to be released. Access to data is contingent on separate agreements being concluded between the data holder and the prospective data recipient.

Firstly, Article 5(9)–(11) DA contain the same rules concerning the disclosure of trade secrets as those in Article 4(6)–(8), discussed above. Article 8(6), which reaffirms the lack of general duty to disclose trade secrets, also aids the manufacturers. Again, although the impact of these measures will eventually depend on the efficiency of national regulatory authorities who will resolve the complaints of the users, data holders will have the opportunity to at least delay access to data.

Secondly, some of the statutory constraints placed on the third party (ie, the data recipient) are stricter than those placed by the user. For example, while neither is allowed to use the data to develop a competing product,[71] the data recipients will also be constrained by obligations to limit the scope and purposes of use of the data and to delete the data as soon as it is no longer necessary.[72]

Thirdly, according to Article 8(1)–(2), in business-to-business relations, the data holder and the data recipient must agree to the 'arrangements for making the data available', which must be fair, reasonable and non-discriminatory (FRAND). The nature of the FRAND standard remains elusive in the area of standard-essential patents, and there is little hope that more clarity will appear within the framework

[69] Leistner and Antoine (n 5) 88–89.
[70] Drexl et al (n 5) 18–19.
[71] Arts 4(10) and 6(2)(e) DA.
[72] Art 6(1) DA.

of the DA.[73] From a broad perspective, the necessity of an agreement between the data holder and the data recipient makes the status of the right described in Article 5 questionable. Users are unlikely to be able to privately enforce granting data access to third parties. Although Article 10 establishes a dispute settlement mechanism, it is not mandatory. Once again, this places a considerable burden on the authorities competent to publicly enforce the DA.

Finally, Article 11 contains additional safeguards for the manufacturers' interests. There is little novelty in the first sentence of Article 11(1), which recognises that data holders may apply technical protection measures (TPMs). It merely restates the existing freedom to implement TPMs. It is the second sentence that warrants more attention. It prohibits using TPMs to 'hinder the user's right to effectively obtain a copy, retrieve, use or access data or provide data to third parties pursuant to Article 5 or any right of a third party under Union law or national legislation implementing Union law'. Although both Article 11(1) and Article 12(1) suggest that the provision concerning TPMs applies only in business-to-business relations and does not apply to data access under Articles 3 or 4, it is difficult to imagine effective protection measures that work only selectively against third parties and not against users.[74] Consequently, one should consider all forms of access to data when evaluating whether TPMs are excessive. The exact standard of evaluation will need to be refined by the courts. One possible avenue would be to apply the test developed by the CJEU in the case concerning protection measures used in video game consoles. To receive legal protection, TPMs designed to protect works 'must be suitable for achieving that objective and must not go beyond what is necessary for this purpose'.[75]

Whatever standard is eventually adopted, there remains the question of the consequences of applying excessive TPMs. Can the third party circumvent them? Absent a specific regime against TPM circumvention, similar to the one introduced in EU copyright by the InfoSoc Directive,[76] the answer may appear to be affirmative. However, criminal sanctions remain the elephant in the room.[77] Almost all EU Member States are parties to the Budapest Convention on Cybercrime,[78] which uses a very broad definition of 'computer system'.[79]

[73] See, eg C Ducuing and L Schirru, 'Making data available under FRAND terms' in Ducuing, Margoni and Schirru (n 5) 31–36.

[74] L Stähler, 'Article 11 of the Data Act – The regulation of unauthorised access to data' in Ducuing, Margoni and Schirru (n 5) 38.

[75] Case C-355/12 *Nintendo Co. Ltd, Nintendo of America Inc., Nintendo of Europe GmbH v PC Box Srl, 9Net Srl* ECLI:EU:C:2014:25 [31]–[34].

[76] Directive 2001/29/EC of the European Parliament and of the Council of 22 May 2001 on the harmonisation of certain aspects of copyright and related rights in the information society [2001] OJ L167/10 (InfoSoc Directive).

[77] Drexl et al (n 5) 44.

[78] Convention on Cybercrime of 23 November 2001 (Budapest Convention).

[79] 'any device or a group of interconnected or related devices, one or more of which, pursuant to a program, performs automatic processing of data'(Art 1(a) Budapest Convention).

A very similar definition is used by Directive 2013/40/EU.[80] Under either of them, a single IoT product can be a computer system. Both require penalising illegal access to computer systems.[81] The issue may come down to who is considered to be the owner or another right holder of the system capable of authorising the circumvention. If it is the data holder, an act of TPM circumvention may be qualified as criminally prohibited. Although this interpretation may appear far-fetched, the increasing reliance of connected devices on related services suggests that it is not inconceivable.

The provision that strengthens the position of manufacturers the most is Article 11(2). It provides data holders with remedies against data recipients who, in short, obtained the data illegitimately, used it for unauthorised purposes or disclosed it to another party without the data holder's authorisation. The remedies include the right to demand the destruction of the data and its copies and to demand the

> end the production, offering, placing on the market or use of goods, derivative data or services produced on the basis of knowledge obtained through such data, or the importation, export or storage of infringing goods for those purposes, and destroy any infringing goods.

These remedies resemble the corrective measures introduced in the TSD,[82] albeit with weaker limiting provisions. Article 11(2)(b) allows some room for balancing in a given case by requiring that measures imposed on the third party or data recipient 'would not be disproportionate in light of the interests of the data holder, the trade secret holder or the user'. However, it is far less specific than its counterpart in the TSD. To maintain the legal system's internal coherence, the data not covered either by intellectual property or the trade secret regime should not receive stronger protection. Therefore, factors listed in the TSD[83] should still be examined as part of the proportionality analysis under the DA. Nonetheless, the fact that the DA reaffirms the manufacturers' right to implement protection measures and grants them additional remedies amounts to the legitimisation of their factual control over product data.

VI. Conclusions

The DA defers numerous resolutions to the national regulatory authorities, which, among others, will handle complaints and impose financial penalties

[80] Article 2(a) Directive 2013/40/EU of the European Parliament and of the Council of 12 August 2013 on attacks against information systems and replacing Council Framework Decision 2005/222/JHA [2013] OJ L 218/8.

[81] Art 2 Budapest Convention and Art 3 Directive 2013/40/EU.

[82] Art 12(1)(b)–(d) Trade Secret Directive.

[83] Art 13(1) Trade Secret Directive.

(Article 37(5) DA). As a result, it is troublesome to conduct an abstract assessment of whether it properly balances the device owners' rights with manufacturers' freedoms. Due to the horizontal nature of the new regulation, it may benefit device users who hardly need any support. Simply speaking, a large business that uses connected devices produced by a large manufacturer can bargain for data access. In order to alleviate fears of imbalances in such relationships, measures protecting the interests of manufacturers were strengthened late in the legislative procedure. The new regulation became far less invasive to the manufacturers' fundamental freedoms. This affects mostly device users without strong market power, who would have benefitted the most from new data access rights.

For at least four reasons, it is unlikely that the DA will meaningfully shift the balance of interest towards the device purchasers. The first reason stems from the scope of the regulation, intentionally narrowed to only some factors and specifically avoiding almost all issues related to intellectual property rights. Even with respect to access to data, due to the exclusion of derivative data and limitations on the scope of data that is to be made accessible, the DA will affect only some purchaser–manufacturer relationships. Secondly, the principle of accessibility by design, although commendable as such, is introduced in a way that incentivises manufacturers to enable access only through remote servers, if at all. Thirdly, if the users receive access to data thanks to the new right described in Article 4, few are likely to have sufficient technical capabilities to benefit from that right. When a user needs to rely on external support, a separate right to third-party access can be invoked, leading to the final reason for scepticism. Whether a third party receives access to data is essentially contingent on an agreement with the data holder. The provisions concerning third-party access leave users with questionable power to enforce their rights while simultaneously legitimising the position of data holders. Perhaps some of these shortcomings may be addressed in subsequent sectoral regulations. However, one could expect a horizontal legislative solution to achieve its declared goal in some conceivable scenarios. At least in the context of the balance of power between device purchasers and manufacturers, the DA underdelivers. In other words, from the perspective of constitutional proportionality, it appears that the DA does not affect the manufacturers' rights strongly enough.

10

A Balancing Exercise: Applying the Principle of Proportionality to Determine the Effect of Withdrawal of Consent for Processing Personal Data in Biomedical Research

MARCU FLOREA AND JEANNE MIFSUD BONNICI

I. Introduction

The General Data Protection Regulation[1] (GDPR) provides that data subjects can withdraw their consent for the processing of personal data.[2] However, the consequences of withdrawal are not clearly delineated in the text of the Regulation. For other data subject rights, the GDPR clearly states the correlative duties: erase the data,[3] provide access to information,[4] and stop the processing.[5] This is not the case for the right to withdraw consent, as there is no clear indication of the correlative duties of data controllers.

Under a strict interpretation, a withdrawal of consent results in stopping all processing activities based on consent. This interpretation has the advantage of certainty and foreseeability and is an expression of informational self-determination. However, the text of the Regulation allows for a certain

[1] Regulation (EU) No 2016/679 of the European Parliament and of the Council of 27 April 2016 on the protection of natural persons with regard to the processing of personal data and on the free movement of such data, and repealing Directive 95/46/EC (General Data Protection Regulation, GDPR) [2016] OJ L119/1.

[2] Art 7(3) GDPR.

[3] Art 17 GDPR.

[4] Art 15 GDPR.

[5] Art 21 GDPR.

flexibility. The Article 29 Working Party (WP29),[6] the European Data Protection Board (EDPB),[7] and Modernised Convention 108[8] provide that processing personal data can continue after withdrawal, if it has a different legal basis. When health data are processed, there is a need to identify both a ground for lawfulness[9] and an exception to the prohibition to process special categories of data.[10]

However, it is not clear whether identifying these alternative grounds is sufficient. The text of the GDPR mentions the possibility of withdrawing consent at any time and without detriment. Therefore, it might come as a surprise for the data subjects to find out that the promised control is limited and that processing for certain purposes can continue after withdrawal, on the basis of a different ground for lawfulness. As stated by the ICO, 'it is inherently unfair to tell people they have a choice, but then continue the processing after they withdraw their consent.'[11]

The ECJ interpreted the right to withdraw consent as a request for erasure in a case concerning public telephone directories.[12] Notwithstanding that this construction is appropriate in certain contexts, this chapter argues that the scope of the right to withdraw consent can be the result of an agreement between the data controller and the data subjects. A withdrawal system can provide individuals with several choices of withdrawal, together with information regarding the consequences of these choices. However, this system can, at the same time, influence the choices of individuals towards a certain option. In designing it, it is important to draw a line between practices that enable data subjects to exercise their right and practices that obstruct them in doing so.

Assessing whether continuing the processing after withdrawal can continue, and designing a mechanism that enhances the right to withdraw consent should be the result of a balancing exercise.[13] The current chapter proposes a methodology based on the principle of proportionality for interpreting the right to withdraw consent.

[6] Article 29 Working Party, 'Guidelines on consent under Regulation 2016/679' (WP259 rev.01, 2018) 22.

[7] European Data Protection Board 'Guidelines 05/2020 on consent under Regulation 2016/679' (Version 1.1, 2020) 25.

[8] Explanatory Report of the Amending protocol to the Convention for the Protection of Individuals with Regard to the Processing of Personal Data (2018) 223 Council of Europe Treaty Series, para 45.

[9] Art 6 GDPR.

[10] Art 9 GDPR.

[11] Information Commissioner's Office 'How should we obtain, record and manage consent?', available at ico.org.uk/for-organisations/guide-to-data-protection/guide-to-the-general-data-protection-regulation-gdpr/consent/how-should-we-obtain-record-and-manage-consent/.

[12] *Proximus NV v Gegevensbeschermingsautoriteit* [2022] ECLI:EU:C:2022:833 (Case C-129/21).

[13] See M Florea, 'Withdrawal of consent for processing personal data in biomedical research' (2023) 13 *International Data Privacy Law* 107, where this argument has been developed on large.

II. *Evans* and Withdrawal of Consent as a Bright-line Rule

The European Court of Human Rights (ECtHR) interpreted the effects of withdrawal of consent on the right to privacy in *Evans v The United Kingdom*.[14] Even though consent for *in vitro* fertilisation treatment and consent for the processing of personal data are distinct concepts with separate legal regimes, we refer to this case because it offers two perspectives on the right to withdraw consent: that of a bright-line rule and that of a balancing exercise.

After the gametes of a couple undertaking *in vitro* fertilisation were collected and the embryos created, one of the donors decided to withdraw his consent for the treatment.[15] The other opposed this decision, arguing that withdrawal should not be constructed as a 'veto' right and that her specific condition (she could no longer become a genetic parent outside of this procedure) should be taken into account.[16]

UK law allowed withdrawal of consent up to the moment when the embryos were used, 'in providing treatment service' or 'for the purpose of any project of research'.[17] The applicant claimed that the regime for withdrawal interfered with her right to private and family life protected under Article 8 ECHR.[18] The Court rejected the claim and decided to uphold the primacy of the right to withdraw consent. The interests at stake were of a similar kind: the decision to become a mother versus the decision not to become a father. The Court considered that they could not be reconciled, as giving preference to one of them would frustrate the other.[19]

Besides the balancing of the private interests of the parties, the judgment included another consideration: the public interest in 'upholding the primacy of consent and promoting legal clarity and certainty'.[20] A clear rule was considered to avoid problems of arbitrariness and inconsistency that can result from balancing (incommensurable) interests on a case-by-case basis.[21] Against a background of fast-moving medical and scientific developments and in the absence of consensus, the ECtHR decided that the issue falls within the margin of appreciation of the states and found no violation of Article 8.[22]

However, in a separate opinion, the dissenting judges presented a different view: the measure, although provided for by law and having a legitimate

[14] *Evans v UK* ECHR 2007-I 353.
[15] ibid [18].
[16] ibid [19], [61].
[17] ibid [37].
[18] ibid [57].
[19] ibid [73].
[20] ibid [74].
[21] ibid [89].
[22] ibid [92].

aim, was not necessary and proportionate. The fact that the applicant was a woman who had lost her capacity to have biological children should have been taken into account and should have weighed more than the decision of her former partner.[23] The ruling of the court can represent the basis for questioning whether determining the effect of right to withdraw consent for processing personal data in biomedical research should be a bright-line rule or the result of a balancing exercise.

III. The Interests at Stake in Processing Personal Data for Biomedical Research

Deciding on the consequences of a withdrawal request involves resolving a tension between contrary interests. It can be argued that an inflexible construction of the right to withdraw consent for biomedical research can jeopardise the scientific integrity and verifiability of a research project and might affect the economic interests of the data controller who set up the study. Furthermore, if the study is intended to provide a benefit to society as a whole, it will also interfere with the public interest of completing the research and of maintaining the validity of the results. However, a very flexible approach, allowing the processing to continue freely after withdrawal might limit the autonomy of individuals.

This section will be divided into three parts, referring to the interests of the data subjects, the research entities, and the public interest. Before analysing these interests, it is important to note that this article focuses on withdrawal of consent for processing personal data. As clarified by the EDPB in the context of clinical trials,[24] withdrawal from participation in research has a separate regime, which is covered by sectoral laws,[25] international treaties[26] and soft law instruments,[27] and this regime will not be discussed here.

[23] ibid, joint dissenting opinion of judges Türmen, Tsatsa-Nikolovska, Spielmann, Ziemele [6], [13], [15].

[24] European Data Protection Board, 'Opinion 3/2019 concerning the Questions and Answers on the interplay between the Clinical Trials Regulation (CTR) and the General Data Protection regulation (GDPR) (art. 70.1.b))' (2019) 6.

[25] Art 28 Regulation (EU) No 536/2014 of the European Parliament and of the Council of 16 April 2014 on clinical trials on medicinal products for human use, and repealing Directive 2001/20/EC [2014] OJ L 158 1.

[26] Convention for the protection of Human Rights and Dignity of the Human Being with regard to the Application of Biology and Medicine 1997/1999 164 ETS (Oviedo Convention).

[27] 'The Nuremberg Code' (1947) in A Mitscherlich and F Mielke, *Doctors of infamy: the story of the Nazi medical crimes* (Henry Schuman, 1949); World Medical Association, 'Declaration of Helsinki: Ethical Principles for Medical Research Involving Human Subjects' (1964), available at www.wma.net/policies-post/wma-declaration-of-helsinki-ethical-principles-for-medical-research-involving-human-subjects.

A. Interests of Data Subjects

As shown by Broekstra and others, the reasons for withdrawal are related to both individual harm (negative experience during a visit, research organisation attracts negative news reports, time investment becomes too high, the research aim changes) and societal harm (research organisation becomes a for-profit organisation or starts collaboration with a commercial enterprise, research no longer contributes to healthcare).[28] From an ethical perspective, the value protected by the rules requiring consent and guaranteeing the right to revoke it is personal sovereignty. This value guarantees that the boundaries set by individuals allow them to control their lives and stop others from interfering with this freedom.[29]

Consent and personal sovereignty are related: individuals have a zone of personal inviolability that can only be invaded if they agree to this.[30] Research without consent might be ethically objectionable on the grounds that individuals are used merely as a means to scientific investigation.[31] Even in the absence of harm, this interference affects their autonomy and dignity, which is affirmed by protecting one's privacy.[32] A similar objection can be made concerning the continuation of processing after withdrawal. Although individuals agreed initially to the processing of their personal data, their preferences changed during the processing life cycle, and not acting upon them is a limitation of personal autonomy.

Individuals might experience harm in relation to the processing of their personal data. This can consist of physical, economic, reputational and psychological (emotional distress and disturbance), as well as autonomy harms, discrimination and relationship harms.[33] For example, in the case of data breaches, disclosure of health information to one's social circle can cause stigma or shame, and disclosure to insurance agencies, current or future employers or state agencies can result in discrimination.[34] While some of these harms can be mitigated by applying privacy-preserving technologies and by increasing security measures, autonomy harms (failure to inform, frustrated expectations, lack of control)[35] are not necessarily tied to the security of the processing activity. Even if there is no

[28] R Broekstra, *Values of Trust and Participation in Scientific Data Repositories* (PhD Thesis, University of Groningen 2021) 106, available at research.rug.nl/en/publications/values-of-trust-and-participation-in-scientific-data-repositories.

[29] F Miller, 'Consent to Clinical Research' in Miller and A Wertheimer (eds) *The Ethics of Consent: Theory and Practice* (Oxford University Press, 2010) 375.

[30] ibid 380.

[31] ibid 395.

[32] L Floridi, 'On Human Dignity as a Foundation for the Right to Privacy' (2016) 29 *Philosophy and Technology* 307, 308, 311.

[33] D Solove and D Citron, 'Privacy Harms' 102 *Boston University Law Review* 793, 831.

[34] L Gostin and J Hodge, 'Personal Privacy and Common Goods: A Framework for Balancing Under the National Health Information Privacy Rule' (2002) 86 *Minnesota Law Review* 1439, 1442.

[35] Solove and Citron (n 32) 845.

disclosure to third parties, participants in research might feel disrespected by the fact that their choices are not acted upon.[36]

B. Interests of Entities Conducting Research

Once the research has started, the entities conducting it have an interest in undertaking their activity in accordance with requirements regarding scientific integrity and verifiability. In the absence of such criteria, the research will not comply with the necessary standards and will not be accepted by the research community. The European Code of Conduct for Research Integrity[37] requires the secure preservation of all data and research materials for a reasonable period. The requirements are similar at national level in the Netherlands, where the Dutch Code for Integrity[38] requires that 'all data, software codes and research materials, published or unpublished, are managed and securely stored for the period appropriate to the discipline(s) and methodology concerned'.

The integrity policy of different universities or research centres might contain more specific requirements. For example, for the University of Groningen, subject to faculty-specific requirements and applicable laws, raw data and processed data must be saved for at least 10 years.[39]

In addition, the individuals involved in these activities are interested in completing their projects, in order to justify the resources invested from an economic perspective. Furthermore, the performance of researchers or research groups might be judged based on the outcomes of their research. An inconclusive study will definitely not be regarded as a success. The fact that data was altered because of withdrawal requests might be a mitigating factor, but the result will nevertheless be affected. Furthermore, the dataset will not be reusable for new projects, as per the FAIR principles, which require that data is Findable Accessible Interoperable and Reusable.[40]

C. Public Interest

Conducting biomedical research also has an important public purpose. The discovery of new knowledge can be used in improving diagnostic and care

[36] Gostin and Hoge (n 33) 1456.

[37] All European Academics 'The European Code of Conduct for Research Integrity' (2017), available at allea.org/code-of-conduct/.

[38] Netherlands Code of Conduct for Research Integrity (2018) 20, available at www.nwo.nl/en/netherlands-code-conduct-research-integrity.

[39] University of Groningen 'UG Research Data Policy' (2021) at 3.2, available at www.rug.nl/digital-competence-centre/ug-research-data-policy-2021.pdf.

[40] M Wilkinson et al, 'The FAIR Guiding Principles for scientific data management and stewardship' (2016) 3 Scientific Data, available at www.nature.com/articles/sdata201618.

procedures, in preventing disease or in the identification of risk factors for the life, health and well-being of the people. The quality of medical care depends on the accumulation and dissemination of scientific evidence. Other (future) patients can benefit from the findings, in the same way current treatments and diagnostic procedures are based on previous research. Findings resulting from research can be used in the public domain, included in news reports, considered by policymakers and used in innovation.[41]

The general government expenditure in the EU on healthcare amounted to almost eight per cent of GDP[42] in 2022, and improving the current state of knowledge in the field of health can have a positive impact on these costs. Research can expose inefficient practices or propose equally efficient ones for lower costs.[43] The social benefits of improved diagnostic and treatment procedures goes beyond material costs and improves the welfare of society. Furthermore, preserving raw data is also useful to test the integrity and reproducibility of the research[44] and to prevent academic fraud, such as data fabrication.[45]

Lastly, as emphasised in *Evans*, ensuring legal certainty and foreseeability is an important aspect related to the public interest. This will enable those affected by the regulation to shape their conduct and foresee the consequences of their behaviour. If the right to withdraw consent is fuzzy, blurry or indeterminate, it can be arbitrarily interpreted by data protection authorities and courts.

IV. Balancing and Proportionality

Having outlined the interests that are relevant for the stakeholders involved, the next question is how to reconcile them. The interests of individuals are protected under the GDPR by providing the right to withdraw consent. As the next section will briefly discuss,[46] the GDPR also allows for continuing the processing after withdrawal. This serves the interests of research entities and, in certain cases, the public interest. However, the GDPR does not provide a clear set of rules around continuing processing data activities after withdrawal of consent, and this leaves a space for legal interpretation, legislative intervention and for regulation by design.

[41] Y Yin et al. 'Public use and public funding of science' (2022) 6 *Nature Human Behavior* 1344.

[42] Eurostat, 'Government expenditure on health' (2022), available at ec.europa.eu/eurostat/statistics-explained/index.php?title=Government_expenditure_on_health.

[43] W Anderson, 'With the right kind of research, we can reduce health-care costs' (2014), available at theconversation.com/with-the-right-kind-of-research-we-can-reduce-health-care-costs-28898.

[44] T Miyakawa, 'No raw data, no science: another possible source of the reproducibility crisis' (2020) 13 *Molecular Brain* 2, available at https://doi.org/10.1186/s13041-020-0552-2.

[45] D Singh Chawla, '8% of researchers in Dutch survey have falsified or fabricated data' (2021) *Nature* (22 July 2021), available at www.nature.com/articles/d41586-021-02035-2.

[46] Florea (n 12) for a detailed discussion about the grounds on which processing can continue after withdrawal.

Following the approach of the ECJ in deciding on matters that involve a conflict of rights and interests in the field of data protection law,[47] this chapter proposes the elements for conducting a balancing exercise based on the human rights framework in order to determine the scope of the right to withdraw consent in the context of biomedical research. It has been argued that principle of proportionality can be used as a criterion for providing meaning to legislative norms.[48] The starting point of the balancing exercise is the fundamental right to protection of personal data under Article 8 of the Charter of Fundamental Rights of the European Union (EUCFR),[49] but reference will also be made to the European Convention on Human Rights (ECHR).[50]

In order to determine the scope of the right to withdraw consent, two scenarios showcasing the challenges in interpreting the right to withdraw consent will be analysed.

V. The Scenarios for Balancing

This section will describe two scenarios in which processing can continue after withdrawal of consent, focusing on the context of biomedical research. A first option is to continue the processing, based on an alternative legal basis. As further explained below, this option is available if there is a (sectoral) Union or Member State law supporting it. A second option is to develop a layered system, informing the data subjects about the (negative) effects of their withdrawal request on the rights and interests of others, providing them with the possibility and encouraging them to choose an option that reconciles the interests at stake.

A. Continuing the Processing after Withdrawal on the Basis of a Ground for Lawfulness

Due to the regime for processing special categories of data, there is a need to identify both a ground for lawfulness under Article 6 GDPR and an exception to the prohibition to process data concerning health, as per Article 9 GDPR. As far as the regime for special categories of data is concerned, collection of data can be based on explicit consent,[51] while subsequent processing operations can rely on

[47] L Dalla Corte, 'On Proportionality in the Data Protection Jurisprudence of the CJEU' (2022) 12 *International Data Privacy Law* 259; C Bagger Tranberg, 'Proportionality and Data Protection in the Case Law of the European Court of Justice' (2011) 1 *International Data Privacy Law* 239.

[48] A Barak, *Proportionality: Constitutional Rights and Their Limitations* (Cambridge University Press, 2012) 147.

[49] Charter of Fundamental Rights of the European Union [2010] OJ C83/389.

[50] Convention for the Protection of Human Rights and Fundamental Freedoms (1950).

[51] Art 9(2)(a) GDPR.

the exception concerning research or on the public interest in public health[52] or the exception for processing that is necessary for reasons of the public interest in the area of public health,[53] both of which depend on Union or Member State law. For example, the research entities could be under an obligation to report adverse effects to the relevant authority[54] or to store the master file of the research for 25 years, in the case of clinical trials.[55] Besides identifying an exception to Article 9 GDPR, the data controller must also rely on a ground for lawfulness in Article 6 GDPR.[56] As for the ground for lawfulness under Article 6 GDPR, if the said law expressly mentions the operations required (as in the examples mentioned above), the ground for lawfulness is Article 6(c) GDPR (compliance with a legal obligation). However, the law can regulate research without *requiring* a particular processing operation to be conducted. In such cases, the processing will, most likely, be based on Article 9(f) GDPR (legitimate interest).

In assessing the legitimate interest, research entities would have to undertake a balancing exercise and justify that the opposing interests outweigh the right of individuals whose data is processed.[57] This assessment is stricter compared to a standard test for assessing legitimate interest, because the data controllers must factor in the choice of the individuals and justify that the autonomy harms connected with the right to protection of personal data are balanced by the legitimate interest to continue processing.[58]

When individuals provide their consent, they will have to agree to a number of processing activities, some of them based on consent and others based on alternative legal grounds. This affects their right to withdraw consent, which is effective only in part. Although this is not a limitation of the right to withdraw consent from a formal perspective (some of the processing activities were never based on consent), the right to withdraw is, *de facto*, curtailed. In addition to this, the controller will have to justify why consent is used for a certain part of the processing life cycle, while the following operations rely on different legal grounds.

[52] Art 9(2)(j) GDPR.

[53] Art 9(2)(i) GDPR.

[54] European Commission Directorate-General for Health and Food Safety, 'Question and Answers on the interplay between the Clinical Trials Regulation and the General Data Protection Regulation' (2017) 7.

[55] Clinical Trials Regulation (n 24) Art 58.

[56] European Parliament, 'Resolution on the Commission evaluation report on the implementation of the General Data Protection Regulation two years after its application' (2021) OJ L119 1; Commission expert group on the Regulation (EU) 2016/679 and Directive (EU) 2016/680, 'Minutes of the Second Meeting' (2016), available at ec.europa.eu/transparency/expert-groups-register/core/api/front/expertGroupAddtitionalInfo/27803/download; and Information Commissioner's Office, 'Guide to the General Data Protection Regulation, Lawful basis for processing' (ICO), available at ico.org.uk/for-organisations/guide-to-data-protection/guide-to-the-general-data-protection-regulation-gdpr/lawful-basis-for-processing.

[57] Article 29 Working Party, 'Opinion 06/2014 on the notion of legitimate interests of the data controller under Article 7 of Directive 95/46/EC' (WP 217, 2014) 23–42.

[58] Florea (n 12) 110; J Ausloos, *The Right to Erasure in EU Data Protection Law* (Oxford University Press, 2020) 324, 332.

Although the GDPR does not permit nor forbid the separation between different processing activities or parts of the processing cycle, migrating from one legal basis to another might be considered unfair[59] or even deceitful.

B. Continuing the Processing after Withdrawal in the Absence of a Ground for Lawfulness

However, a Union or Member State law on which processing can rely does not always exist. Does this mean that processing can never continue after the moment when consent is withdrawn? In the view expressed in this chapter, this is not the case. The design of a layered withdrawal system can offer individuals the opportunity to file partial withdrawal requests and to select between various options: limiting further sharing of data, stopping future projects using the data, while allowing limited operations, such as the storage of the data, or finalising current projects, to continue.

To protect the individuals, the GDPR requires that it should not be harder to withdraw than it was to provide consent.[60] Furthermore, consent is free if the data subject is unable to withdraw without detriment.[61] This chapter explores whether and to what extent the GDPR allows the development of a system that, without denying the option to totally withdraw, influences the data subject to choose to exercise the right to withdrawal only in part.

In order to describe a lawful withdrawal system, we draw inspiration from the literature on nudging or libertarian paternalism. Contrary to manipulation, nudging[62] encourages choices that 'make choosers better off, as judged by themselves'.[63] It is therefore necessary to identity an optimal choice. We suggest that this option can be the result of a balancing exercise based on the principle of proportionality. We frame the action of continuing to process the personal data of an individual who intends to withdraw as a limitation of the right to protection of personal data and balance it against the benefits to other rights and interests at stake.

Providing information and designing a system that only favours the interests of research entities would be deceitful and not paternalistic. Conversely, if the information is presented in a manner that educates or creates awareness,[64] a withdrawal system can be lawful. Our analysis aims to identify the option the individuals are

[59] ICO (n 11).
[60] Art 7(3) GDPR.
[61] Recital 42 GDPR.
[62] R Thaler and C Sunstein, *Nudge: Improving Decisions About Health, Wealth, and Happiness* (Penguin Books, 2009) 5.
[63] ibid.
[64] A Ioannou et al, 'Privacy nudges for disclosure of personal information: A systematic literature review and meta-analysis' (2021) 16 *PLOS One* 14.

encouraged to choose. We argue that one of the essential distinctions between manipulation and nudging can be drawn by a balancing exercise inspired from the human rights framework.

The idea of embedding legal values in an information system can be traced back to the work of Lawrence Lessig who shows how law and technology can work together to shape the conduct of individuals.[65] Starting from this approach, the principle of proportionality can be employed to ensure that regulation by design is compliant with the GDPR.

Identifying a societally beneficial option is just the starting point for building a withdrawal system and its compliance with the law will depend on other characteristics of the interface necessary for its operation. For example, the data subject should have the opportunity to easily switch between different withdrawal options[66] and the information must be presented in a transparent manner and be easy to understand.

VI. The Suitability of the Limitation

A. What is the Purpose of the Limitation?

In analysing the options presented in sections V.A and V.B as limitations of the right to protection of personal data, the first step is to assess the suitability of the limitation. Suitability is understood as an optimisation requirement relative to factual possibilities.[67] It is a 'threshold requirement' and results in a binary judgement on whether the measure considered is fit for a specific purpose.[68] A first step in assessing suitability is to identify the purpose of the measure. Although this assessment depends on factual circumstances and is better suited to concrete cases, this section will pinpoint the aims that might be promoted by continuing the processing after the moment of withdrawal. The purpose of the limitation is tied to both the interests of entities conducting research and the public interest discussed in sections III.B. and III.C above. On a more practical level, these interests are of relevance in the cases presented below.

The first justification is to prevent 'strategic' withdrawal. For example, in the context of clinical trials, it is possible that interested parties encourage participants who have side effects or who do not react in a satisfactory manner to clinical trials to withdraw from the study in order to conceal any negative effects.[69]

[65] L Lessig, *Code: Version 2.0* (Basic Books, 2006) 123.

[66] S Cohen, 'Nudging and Informed Consent' (2013) 13 *The American Journal of Bioethics* 3.

[67] R Alexy, 'Constitutional Rights and Proportionality' (2014) 22 *Revus Online* 51, 52.

[68] Dalla Corte (n 46) 261.

[69] Office of the Commissioner, Office of Clinical Policy and Programs, Office of Clinical Policy, Office of Good Clinical Practice, 'Data Retention When Subjects Withdraw from FDA-Regulated Clinical Trials' (2008) 4, available at www.fda.gov/regulatory-information/search-fda-guidance-documents/data-retention-when-subjects-withdraw-fda-regulated-clinical-trials.

Furthermore, even in the absence of any external influence, withdrawal of consent can generate selective biases in the data.[70] Individuals with certain characteristics (demographics, level of education) might be more prone to withdraw their consent compared to the rest of the population. If, in these cases, withdrawal results in an obligation to delete the data, the reliability of the study might be affected.

The second justification is preventing academic fraud, for example in the form of data fabrication.[71] The third reason lies in the economic interests of the sponsors of the projects who invested resources in them. When the funds are provided from public sources, such as a national budget for research or the EU budget, these interests have a public dimension. Finally, conducting medical research is aimed at discovering new knowledge that can be used to improve the health and well-being of the people and stopping all processing activities after receiving a withdrawal request might hinder new discoveries.

B. Is the Purpose Worth Pursuing in the Legal System of the European Union?

Assuming that the purposes of continuing the processing are clear, the next step is assessing whether they are protected in the EU.[72] Some of the aims mentioned above fall under Article 13 CFREU (freedom of arts and sciences), while others are protected under Article 35 CFREU (right to healthcare).

Article 35 CFREU does not guarantee a right to health, only a right to healthcare 'under the conditions established by national laws and practices'. The connection between biomedical research and public healthcare is not immediately apparent. Even though the ultimate purpose of conducting biomedical research is to improve the level of knowledge in the medical field, this does not directly translate into better healthcare. Nevertheless, developing a proper climate for conducting biomedical research is essential for improving the level of healthcare in society and for contributing to health, understood as a social good.[73]

The freedom of arts and sciences is protected in Article 13 CFREU and the importance of scientific research is also affirmed in Article 179(1) TFEU.[74] The CFREU provides that scientific research shall be 'free of constraint'. It enables individuals to challenge existing knowledge by engaging is new discoveries.[75]

[70] Gostin and Hodge (n 33) 1447.

[71] Section III.B above.

[72] Dalla Corte (n 46) 261.

[73] T Hervey, 'The "Right to Health" in European Union Law' in T Hervey and J Kenner (eds), *Economic and Social Rights under the EU Charter of Fundamental Rights: A Legal Perspective* (Hart Publishing, 2006) 196.

[74] Consolidated version of the Treaty on the Functioning of the European Union [2016] OJ C202/1.

[75] D Sayers, 'Article 13' in S Peers et al (eds), *The EU Charter of Fundamental Rights: A Commentary* (Hart Publishing, 2021) 416.

Similar to the right to health, it is not clear if the freedom of arts and sciences is justiciable.[76]

The legal nature of both is rather unclear and falls either in the category of right or in that of principles.[77] Even when constructed as principles, they are binding on Member States when implementing EU law. This carries both positive and negative obligations[78] and these can be translated into ensuring that there is an appropriate environment for conducting biomedical research, which improves healthcare.

C. Is there a Logical Connection between the Limitation and the Purpose?

Finally, it is necessary to question whether there is a rational connection between the measure (ie, continuing to process personal data after withdrawal) and the objectives (protecting the right to healthcare and the freedom of arts and sciences).[79] To a certain extent, all research projects in the field of medicine are connected to both the right to health (because they aim at challenging or improving the current state of knowledge in the field) and the freedom of arts and sciences (because they involve conducting a scientific activity).

Individual projects can consist of applied or fundamental research. The former category is easier to analyse in connection with the objectives, as applied research promises tangible results. By contrast, fundamental research does not promise any immediate effects, but contributes to the development of knowledge. The remoteness of the connection between the measure and the purpose also depends on the urgency of the need. If the reason for conducting the research is a disease, the connection with public health needs depends on the transmissibility or the danger to life or quality of life.

VII. The Necessity of the Limitation

Similar to suitability, necessity requires optimisation relative to the factual possibilities,[80] and the assessment of this condition will depend on the concrete evidence supporting the efficiency and the level of intrusion of the measure.[81]

[76] ibid 426.
[77] T Hervey and J McHale, 'Article 35' in Peers et al (n 74) 1012, 1023.
[78] Art 52(5) CFREU and Sayers (n 74) 417.
[79] Dalla Corte (n 46) 261.
[80] Alexy (n 66) 56, 54.
[81] European Data Protection Supervisor, 'Assessing the necessity of measures that limit the fundamental right to the protection of personal data: A Toolkit' (2017) 16.

It is also a threshold requirement, with a binary outcome.[82] In the scenarios that are relevant to this chapter, there is a certain degree of interference with the will of the data subjects. In order to assess the level of interference, it is necessary to focus on the types of data and on the processing operations that are undertaken after the moment of withdrawal.

A separation can be made between different types of variables, based on their relevance for the particular study: general information (names, addresses, telephone numbers), variables of interest (demographics, geographical indicators) and substantive variables of interest for a particular study (symptoms, reactions to drugs, disease status).[83] Only data elements that are essential for completing the pending operations or for preserving the scientific integrity of the research should be processed. It can be argued that merely holding the data for verifiability and scientific integrity involves a different level of interference compared with making it accessible or actually using it in research.

Necessity also requires a comparison between the measures proposed (continuing the processing after the moment of withdrawal) and the alternative means. If these options are equally suitable and involve a less intensive interference, then the necessity test is failed.[84] Some of the aims could be achieved by processing data that were the subject of anonymisation techniques such as randomisation or generalisation.[85] Even if these techniques do not achieve anonymity[86] and the data subjects are still identifiable, the risks of (unlawful) disclosure of information will certainly be reduced.

Another option is to continue the research or to store the necessary information for verifiability in the form of synthetic data. The process of creating synthetic data is defined as the 'statistical process used to extract information from an actual data set collected from a set of respondents and is re-expressed as a collection of artificial or synthetic data sets'.[87] If the purposes can be achieved by processing synthetic data, then continuing the processing on the basis of the original, raw data seems unnecessary. If synthetic data affects the validity of the study and is not reliable in a specific case, the necessity requirement is checked. There are options for full or partial synthesis, depending on the variables that are synthesised.[88] Another option would be to re-collect (parts of) the data, in order to render the withdrawal irrelevant. Furthermore, the sample collected could be big enough to render potential withdrawal requests irrelevant. Both options would require additional resources and, in certain cases, might delay research

[82] Dalla Corte (n 46) 261.
[83] T Raghunathan, 'Synthetic Data' (2021) 8 *Annual Review of Statistics and its Application* 129, 131.
[84] EDPS Necessity (n 80) 17.
[85] Article 29 Working Party 'Opinion 05/2014 on Anonymisation Techniques' (WP216, 2014) 15–16.
[86] ibid 23.
[87] Raghunathan (n 82) 131.
[88] ibid 134.

projects. In addition, if the withdrawing agent has a particular characteristic that is difficult to find, re-collecting the data might be even more difficult.

VIII. The Proportionality of the Limitation

A. The Structure of Proportionality *Stricto Sensu*

Different from necessity and suitability, proportionality *stricto sensu* expresses 'optimization relative to legal possibilities'.[89] The degree of satisfaction of the right to health and the freedom of arts and sciences is balanced against the degree of dissatisfaction of the right to protection of personal data. This consists of a value judgement that involves balancing conflicting interest in cases when precedence is not given a priori to either of them.[90]

When rights collide, costs are inevitable;[91] but a fair allocation is possible by applying the principle of proportionality. Alexy elaborates, in connection with constitutional rights, a Weight Formula that can be integrated as part of the methodology proposed in this chapter.[92] The interference with the right to data protection should be assessed by relying on three parameters: (i) the intensity of the interference with the right to data protection; (ii) the abstract weight of this right; and (iii) the degree of reliability of the empirical assumptions concerning the intensity of the interference. These will then be balanced against the corresponding values of the opposing rights (ie, the right to health and the freedom of arts and sciences).

Each parameter shall be allocated a quantifier, for example light, moderate and serious or even numbers.[93] These quantifiers will be the result of judgements, justified by legal arguments.[94] A serious interference with the right to data protection justified by a low importance assigned to the other objectives will not satisfy the test. Establishing that a certain action is a serious interference involves making an assumption about the threats to the right to protection of personal data in accordance with standards that are not to be found in the Weight Formula.[95] This assessment depends on the facts and circumstances of each case and is the result of legal argumentation.[96]

[89] Alexy (n 66) 54.
[90] European Data Protection Supervisor, 'Guidelines on assessing the proportionality of measures that limit the fundamental rights to privacy and to the protection of personal data' (2019) 27.
[91] Alexy (n 66) 54.
[92] ibid.
[93] R Alexy, 'On Balancing and Subsumption. A Structural Comparison' 16 4 *Ratio Juris* 433, 440, 444.
[94] Alexy (n 66) 55.
[95] Alexy (n 92) 439.
[96] Alexy (n 66) 55.

B. The Intensity of the Interference with the Right to Protection of Personal Data

The case law of the ECtHR on the right to protection of private and family life shows that information concerning an individual's health constitutes a key element of private life.[97] Several ECtHR cases focus on the value of confidentiality, which is a vital principle in the legal system of the State parties to the ECHR and is also protected under Article 8.[98] Disclosure of health data may affect the employment situation or may expose individuals to opprobrium or ostracism.[99] The violation of the right to privacy is more intense if the information refers to certain health information, for example mental health[100] or HIV status.[101] A lack of confidence can disincentivise participation in research, as it affects the trust between the researchers and the data subjects. However, continuing the processing after withdrawal does not necessarily involve a breach of confidentiality. Data processed for biomedical research can be subject to privacy preserving technologies and this lowers the risk of unintended disclosure.

Nevertheless, the right to protection of personal data goes beyond privacy and involves an element of control over one's personal information.[102] By having a say in what data is disclosed about them, to whom and for what purposes, individuals can choose how to present themselves to society and this enables them to develop their personality freely. The right to withdraw consent can be considered one of the 'micro rights' that affirm individual control over the processing of personal data.[103] Besides this, consent and withdrawal can also help to reduce power and informational asymmetries between the participants and the entities conducting research.[104] The disparity of power results from the fact that the professionals have status and information superiority.[105]

Furthermore, in certain cases, once data is collected, the research can be conducted without any interaction between participants and data controllers. By giving consent, individuals operate a transfer of power to the research entities. Hence, they have an interest in maintaining a level of control in order to

[97] *Mockute v Lithuania* App no 66490/09 (ECtHR, 27 February 2018) [93]; *Kotilainen v Finland* App no 62439/12 (ECtHR, 17 September 2020) [83]; *Y v Turkey* App no 648/10 (ECtHR, 17 February 2015) [68]; *Z v Finland* App no 22009/93 (ECtHR, 25 February 1997) [95].

[98] ibid.

[99] *Z v Finland* (n 96) [96]; *Y v Turey* (n 96) [68].

[100] *Mockute v Lithuania* (n 96) [94].

[101] *Z v Finland* (n 96) [96]; *Y v Turkey* (n 96) [73].

[102] B van der Sloot, 'Privacy as Personality Right: Why the ECtHR's Focus on Ulterior Interests Might Prove Indispensable in the Age of "Big Data"' (2015) 31 *Utrecht Journal of International and European Law* 25, 41; V Mayer-Schönberger, 'Generational Development of Data Protection' in P Agre and M Rotenberg (eds) *Technology and Privacy: The New Landscape* (MIT Press, 1997) 232.

[103] O Lynskey, *The Foundations of EU Data Protection Law* (Oxford University Press, 2015) 181.

[104] O Lynskey, 'Deconstructing data protection: the "added-value" of a right to data protection in the EU legal order' (2014) 63 *International and Comparative Law Quarterly* 569, 592–97.

[105] Miller (n 28) 381.

prevent abuse. Concerning information asymmetry, the problem lies in that, at the moment of collection of the data, the research entities are better informed about what will happen with the data compared to the subjects of the research. During the processing life cycle, participants have the opportunity to gather more information about the processing of their personal data and this might influence their decisions to withdraw.[106]

Building a withdrawal system that influences the decisions of individuals, nudging them to choose an option that is societally desirable, interferes with individual control. Instead of having total withdrawal as the default choice, individuals are encouraged to understand the effects of their choice and exercise their right to withdraw to a limited extent.

C. The Intensity of the Interference with the Right to Health and with the Freedom of Sciences

The limitations to the right to protection of personal data should be balanced against the benefits to scientific research and knowledge-building. Seen from a different perspective, the benefits are actually the limitations for the right to health and for the freedom of sciences, had all processing activities ceased at the moment of withdrawal.[107] For example, withdrawal of consent might affect the research, rendering it unreliable and this might have a negative impact on the health of the population. The intensity of the interference can be measured by using the same triadic scale and classified as low, medium or high.

However, not all research projects have an equal impact on the right to healthcare, and their intensity depends on various factors. One of these factors is the availability of the results that can be disclosed to a large range of individuals and companies or might be restricted and only used by the entity that undertook the research or made it available to a limited range of individuals or entities, in exchange for economic value. In such cases, it is difficult to argue that the proceeds of the research are favoring common goods that can then have a positive effect on the right to healthcare.[108] When assessing the interest, it is important how much society gains from the results of scientific research. It is not always clear if the research serves the private interests (of individuals and groups) or the public interest (of society as a whole). If the results are openly available, the public interest is justified to a greater extent than in cases when they are available to a narrow group and in exchange for economic value.[109] Furthermore, not all research projects promise tangible results that have an application for human health. However,

[106] LA Bygrave and D Wiese Schartum, 'Consent, Proportionality and Collective Power' in S Gutwirth et al (eds), *Reinventing Data Protection?* (Springer, 2009) 164.
[107] Alexy (n 92) 441.
[108] Gostin and Hodge (n 33) 1440.
[109] ibid 1455.

creating an appropriate climate for scientific research is a necessary condition for exercising both the right to freedom of the arts and sciences in Article 13 CFREU and the right to healthcare in Article 35 CFREU.

D. The Result of the Balancing Exercise

Besides the intensity of the interference, the Weight Formula has two additional elements that influence the outcome: the abstract weight of the right, and the reliability of the empirical basis for the assessment. The CFREU does not provide a hierarchy of rights, so the abstract weight of the rights is hard to assess. However, considering the uncertain status of the right to healthcare and the freedom of arts and sciences as rights or principles, one can argue that they are on a lower rank compared to rights *stricto sensu*, such as the right to protection of personal data. The empirical assumptions should also be assessed as reliable, plausible or false,[110] but this assessment is not discussed in this work, as it largely differs on a case-by-case basis.

The practical outcomes of the balancing exercise will differ for each option presented in section V above. If processing continues on the basis of a new ground for lawfulness, the fairness of the separation between legal ground, the assessment of the legitimate interest to continue the processing and the admissible degree of limiting individual control over personal data will depend on the result of the balancing exercise. Concerning the layered system proposed as a means of exercising the right to withdraw consent, the lawfulness of the interference with the decision-making of the individual data subjects will depend on the result of the balancing exercise and on content and working of the standard options of withdrawal offered to the data subject.

IX. Safeguards

If the benefits do not outweigh the limitations, the controller should explore what safeguards are available.[111] A first example of a safeguard is to involve institutional research boards in making or reviewing decisions regarding the limits of withdrawal of consent. The board would make an ethical assessment of the measure and this would offer further protection to the rights of individuals.[112] This would bring a certain level of objectivity and will ensure that the research entities will not prioritise their own interests in deciding whether continuing the processing reconciles the interests at stake.

[110] Alexy (n 92) 447.
[111] European Data Protection Supervisor (n 89) 31.
[112] J Goebela and Ju Schellera, 'Do we need a biobank law?' 43 *Journal of Laboratory Medicine* 311, 313.

Another safeguard is a strict access policy. The controller can limit the access to the data to a restricted group of persons, on a need-to-know basis. If the reason for continuing the processing in the form of storage is to comply with standards of scientific integrity, then only in the case of an audit should the data be accessed. This way, the risk of unlawful disclosure will be limited. Yet another safeguard is to employ privacy-preserving technologies that can reduce the risks to the rights of the data subjects.

The harms related to autonomy and self-governance can be mitigated by improving the transparency of the processing. This can be done by employing information technology, such as a dynamic consent tool.[113] This consists of a personalised communication interface that enables the exchange of information between participants and entities processing their data. Dynamic consent offers increased flexibility, allowing the entities processing the data to present the information in various ways, for example through video content or through questionnaires.[114] The participants in the research can visualise how their data is processed, review the initially expressed consent and restrict certain processing activities. This can also contain several options of withdrawal, so that individuals are in a position to understand the repercussions of their actions. Finally, an important safeguard is an efficient system that ensures deletion of the data when it is no longer needed.[115]

X. Conclusion

If withdrawal is constructed as a bright-line rule, the costs of using consent for processing personal data in biomedical research are very high, jeopardising the interests of research entities, as well as the public interest. However, limiting withdrawal affects the control of the data subjects over the processing of their personal data. One solution would be to rely on an alternative ground for lawfulness from the beginning and disregard consent completely. However, in certain cases, such as international research programmes, this is not lawful, because there are no uniform Union or Member State laws supporting the research exemption in Article 9(2)(j) GDPR. Furthermore, eliminating consent would affect the autonomy of individuals and affect their privacy, especially considering the sensitive character of their data concerning health.

This chapter has argued in favour of determining the effects of withdrawal by means of a balancing exercise. This will involve both an analysis of the factual

[113] European Data Protection Supervisor, 'A Preliminary Opinion on data protection and scientific research' (2020) 14.

[114] H Teare, M Prictor and J Kaye, 'Reflections on dynamic consent in biomedical research: the story so far' (2021) 29 *European Journal of Human Genetics* 649.

[115] Gostin and Hodge (n 33) 1473.

elements, as well as legal arguments, and its result will differ on a case-by-case basis. This approach has the advantage of flexibility and promises a fair outcome, adapted for different contexts. Its downside is that is involves the high cost of compliance and brings a lack of legal certainty and foreseeability. As mentioned in *Evans*, promoting legal clarity and certainty is in the public interest. In the context of biomedical research, this might influence the trust of individuals in the entire research ecosystem, with consequences for their willingness to participate in research.

However, these disadvantages can be mitigated. Further clarifications from data protection authorities, the European Data Protection Supervisor or the European Data Protection Board on the interplay between consent and other legal grounds would be welcomed. In addition, the development of codes of conduct at industry level can increase the level of foreseeability of the outcome of the balancing exercise. Finally, encouraging the design and use of technology systems, such as dynamic consent, can help increase transparency, so that individuals are aware of the limits to their right to withdraw consent and have means of exercising their right in a meaningful way.

11

Proportionality and Civil Law Policy in Copyright: Criticism of Necessity Standard as Applied in CJEU Case *Poland v Parliament and Council* (C-401/19)

KONRAD GLIŚCIŃSKI

I. Introduction

The principle of proportionality is increasingly used in the context of copyright regulation and case law.[1] It has been noticed that the creation of exclusive rights, such as copyright or other intellectual property rights (IPR), restricts other fundamental rights and freedoms. An example of the application of this principle is the recent judgment of the CJEU of April 2022 (C-401/19).[2] This case concerns the new liability regime for the largest online content-sharing service providers (OCSSP). It was introduced in Article 17 of the Directive on copyright and related rights in the digital single market (DSM). This regime imposes an obligation to use automatic upload filters by service providers which enable preventive evaluation of uploaded content. Essentially, the case concerned the issue of permissibility of such a solution in the light of the freedom of expression and information, ie the fundamental rights of the European Union.[3] According to the judgment, this regime does limit the freedom of expression and information, but its introduction was permissible in light of the principle of proportionality. However, the reasoning

[1] *cf* OF Afori, 'Proportionality – A New Mega Standard in European Copyright Law' (2014) 45 *International Review of Intellectual Property and Competition Law* 889; T Mylly, 'Regulating with rights proportionality? Copyright, fundamental rights and internet in the case law of the Court of Justice of the European Union' in O Pollicino, GM Riccio and M Bassini (eds), *Copyright and Fundamental Rights in the Digital Age* (Edward Elgar Publishing, 2020).

[2] Case C-401/19 *Poland v Parliament and Council* [2022] ECLI:EU:C:2022:297.

[3] Art 11 Charter of Fundamental Rights of the European Union (CFR).

presented in this ruling raises a number of questions regarding the practical application of this principle.

The key question is how the principle of proportionality can help regulate intangible goods, particularly in a digital environment. For this purpose, I will try to juxtapose the concept of necessity appearing in the CJEU jurisprudence and Civil Law Policy. In section II, I will present the hopes placed in the principle of proportionality as a guide for regulation, briefly discuss the new liability regime introduced by the DSM Directive, and present the concept of Civil Law Policy. Section III is devoted to the analysis of differences in the understanding of the concept of necessity. In particular, I will focus on the significance of the purpose of the regulation for its recognition as necessary and the sources of knowledge on the necessity of regulation. Section IV discusses the differences in recognising a given regulation as necessary within the meaning of CJEU case law and Civil Law Policy. Against this background, conclusions regarding the new liability regime will be presented in section V.

A certain terminology must be formulated at this point. The concept of necessity may take on at least three different meanings. First, the concept can be understood as equivalent to the concept of proportionality. In this understanding, it appears in Article 52(1) CFR. For the sake of clarity, I will not use the concept of necessity in this meaning. In the second interpretation, the concept of necessity appears as one of the elements (tests) shaping the principle of proportionality. In this sense, I use the term *relative necessity* (appearing in case law regarding the principle of proportionality). In the last meaning, the term refers to *causal necessity* as a necessary condition for the occurrence of a given effect (characteristic of analyses based on Civil Law Policy).

II. A Hope: The Principle of Proportionality as a Regulatory Guide

The principle of proportionality is seen as a key mechanism for balancing equal rights. As Aleinikoff stated: 'It took blinders off judges' eyes and let them openly take into account the connections between constitutional law and the real world.'[4] The relationship between the principle of proportionality and empirical reality is also noticed in more recent literature. For example, Smolak points out that 'the analysis of proportionality indicates the empirical determinants of choices and weighting the law in terms of effectiveness, which to some extent frees the courts from making decisions based on some normative premises, including moral ones'.[5]

[4] TA Aleinikoff, 'Constitutional Law in the Age of Balancing' (1987) 96 *Yale Law Journal* 943, 1005.

[5] M Smolak, 'Analiza proporcjonalności, rządy prawa a kultura uzasadnienia' in M Smolak, W Sadurski and T Chirkowska-Smolak (eds), *Rozum publiczny – uzasadnienie sądowe – umysł sędziego* (Wydawnictwo Naukowe UAM, 2020) 105.

The importance of this principle is also apparent in relation to copyright law. In particular, it is emphasised that in the digital environment, due to the presence of various interests (rightsholders, users and intermediaries), it is not possible to regulate them precisely. Consequently, 'at EU level, proportionality is a general principle of EU law and therefore must guide the institutions, and the Member States in implementing EU law'.[6] Such a connection of the principle of proportionality with empirical facts is to prevent discretion.[7] In the following section, we will see whether such high hopes for applying this principle are justified.

III. New Liability Rules in Copyright and Freedom of Expression

The rules that have been in place so far (including Article 14(1) of the E-Commerce Directive[8]) assume that the responsibility for the content made available rests with the person who uploaded it, and the platforms themselves – if any – bear secondary liability. Article 17 of the new Directive on Copyright in the Digital Single Market changes these rules, once again extending the copyright monopoly.[9] In this way, a new right was created that falls within the scope of copyright.[10] It relates to the activities of specific OCSSPs. These are providers whose main purpose is to store and provide public access to a large number of copyright-protected works uploaded by users of these services that are organised and promoted by the platforms for commercial purpose.[11] Examples of such platforms include YouTube, Dailymotion, and Vimeo.

As the Advocate-General noted in his opinion, the EU legislator made a political decision in favour of copyright owners.[12] In consequence, works are made available to the public not only by those who publish a given work on the internet,

[6] Geiger and B Jütte, 'Platform liability under Article 17 of the Copyright in the Digital Single Market Directive, Automated Filtering and Fundamental Rights: An Impossible Match' (2021) 70 *GRUR International* 17.

[7] D Duarte, 'From Constitutional Discretion to the Positivist Weight Formula' in JR Sieckmann (ed), *Proportionality, Balancing, and Rights. Robert Alexy's Theory of Constitutional Rights* (Springer, 2021) 17.

[8] Directive 2000/31/EC of the European Parliament and of the Council of 8 June 2000 on certain legal aspects of information society services, in particular electronic commerce, in the Internal Market ('Directive on electronic commerce').

[9] M Husovec and JP Quintais, 'How to License Article 17? Exploring the Implementation Options for the New EU Rules on Content-Sharing Platforms' (2021) 4 *GRUR International* 325. *cf* on extending the copyright monopoly over the years: K Gliściński, *Wszystkie prawa zastrzeżone. Historia sporów o autorskie prawa majątkowe, 1469–1928* (Fundacja Nowoczesna Polska, 2016).

[10] M Husovec and JP Quintais, 'How to License Article 17? Exploring the Implementation Options for the New EU Rules on Content-Sharing Platforms' (2021) 4 *GRUR International* 325.

[11] Art 2(6) DSM Directive.

[12] Case C-401/19, *Republic of Poland v European Parliament and Council of the European Union* [2022] ECLI:EU:C:2022:297, Opinion of AG Saugmandsgaard ØE [136].

but also by the platform itself. As a result, OCSSPs become directly responsible for the content uploaded by their users (primary liability).

The main problem resolved in this ruling was whether this new liability regime violates the freedom of expression and information of platform users. The Court confirmed that the new liability regime provided for in Article 17 of the Directive interferes with the freedom of expression and information by users, guaranteed in Article 11 CFR and Article 10 ECHR.[13] In particular, the Court acknowledged that OCSSPs are required – by Article 17(4)(c) of the Directive – to use automatic recognition and upload filtering tools and that the use of these filters may lead to a problem of overblocking of the legitimate content.[14]

At the same time, the Court recognised that the freedom of expression and information is not absolute and may be subject to limitations.[15] According to the provisions of the Charter of Fundamental Rights, Article 52(1), such limitations are permissible as long as they are provided for by statute and respect the essence of the rights and freedoms with which they interfere. Moreover, any such restriction must comply with the principle of proportionality, ie, be necessary and genuinely meet the objectives of general interest recognised by the Union or the need to protect the rights and freedoms of other people.

IV. Civil Law Policy – A Brief Overview

In order for the proportionality principle to provide insight into reality in practice, it should be indicated how it can take into account elements of empirical knowledge. From a methodological point of view, such a possibility is provided by Civil Law Policy. The principle of proportionality and Civil Law Policy are linked by the search for legislative solutions that are necessary and adequate to achieve the intended goal. Civil Law Policy, however, is aimed at developing systemic solutions that allow one to evaluate the law through the prism of empirical knowledge. It is based on Petrażycki's Civil Law Policy[16] and supplemented by the theory of the rational legislator[17] and economic analysis of law (in terms of neoclassical and heterodox schools of economy).[18] The empirical knowledge gathered in this way about the purposefulness and adequacy of individual regulations may constitute the basis for normative considerations under the principle of proportionality. For this reason, I believe that (even) a brief presentation of the basic assumptions

[13] ibid [55], [58], [82].
[14] ibid [24].
[15] ibid [68].
[16] L Petrażycki, *Wstęp do nauki polityki prawa* (PWN, 1968).
[17] S Wronkowska, *Problemy racjonalnego tworzenia prawa* (UAM, 1982); J Wróblewski, *Teoria racjonalnego tworzenia prawa* (Ossolineum, 1985).
[18] M Lavoie, *Post-Keynesian Economics: New Foundations* (Edward Elgar, 2014); M Mitchel, R Wray and M Watts, *Macroeconomics* (Macmillan International Higher Education, 2019); S Birks, *Rethinking Economics: From Analogies to the Real World* (Springer, 2015).

of the Civil Law Policy may be helpful for better understanding the principle of proportionality.

The presented approach to Civil Law Policy is based on the assumptions regarding law-making policy in general and on specific assumptions regarding civil law. The general assumptions include: 1) the assumption about social sources of law and about the separation of law and morality – the separability thesis (positivist conception of law); and 2) the assumption about the duty of the legislator to act rationally (purposefulness of the established legal norms). In line with Petrażycki's approach, the following three detailed assumptions of Civil Law Policy can be distinguished.[19]

First, the assumption about the organisational function of civil law. The function of civil law is not reduced to the compensatory function (reacting to violations of rights) but consists of determining the forms of collective life. Second, the assumption of a socioeconomic point of view as the basis for shaping the content of civil rights. Civil law confers rights on certain individuals that are obligations of other individuals. Recognising that a given subjective right (or other right) is favourable to the individual that obtains it is not, however, sufficient to consider that such a right should be created. The justification of its existence must prove that the creation of such a right and the related obligations bring benefits not only to the entitled person but makes sense from a socioeconomic point of view. Therefore, it is important to justify it on a macro scale (not only a micro one). Third, the assumption about civil law as a mechanism of a decentralised economic system means treating the norms of civil law as norms relating to the decentralised system of distribution of goods. At the same time, it should be noted that although the norms of civil law deal with the regulation of such a decentralised system, Civil Law Policy itself must also analyse situations in which the decentralised system is not an appropriate means to achieve certain goals.

The basic task of Civil Law Policy is to determine the methods of adequate selection of means to achieve the assumed social goals. The basic instrument for achieving these goals in relation to private law are subjective rights. From this perspective, it can be assumed that: 1) private subjective rights are the basic (though not the only) mechanism used to achieve certain social goals; 2) the creation of these rights is intended to achieve these goals; 3) private rights are not an end in themselves, but instruments for the implementation of specific social goals. From the point of view of Civil Law Policy, it is important that the scope of the rights granted corresponds to the assumed goal of their creation. When assessing whether specific legal provisions constitute appropriate instrumental means to achieve the intended goals, one should be guided, inter alia, by the following criteria: adequacy – whether individual measures can achieve the assumed goal; and effectiveness – whether there is a motivational relationship between a given norm and human behaviour.[20] Such an instrumental assessment should include an

[19] Petrażycki (n 16) 133–39, 387–93.
[20] Wróblewski (n 17) 144–48.

analysis of given measures from the perspective of their causal necessity: whether the creation (existence) of a given measure is necessary to achieve the assumed goal (condition *sine qua non*).

V. The Concept of Necessity – Different Views

There are some similarities between the analysis of whether given regulations meet the proportionality principle and whether they are an adequate means to achieve the intended goals under Civil Law Policy. However, there are in fact significant differences between these two approaches. In the next section, I will focus on the concept of necessity understood as a relative necessity on the basis of the principle of proportionality and the concept of causal necessity, applied on the basis of Civil Law Policy.

A. Necessity and the Purpose of Regulation

The first difference that appears in the assessment of *relative necessity* and *causal necessity* is that related to the assessment of the purpose of the proposed regulations. Barak, in the context of the application of the proportionality principle, indicates that:

> The necessity test is based upon the assumption that the law's purpose is a proper one. Thus, while examining the requirements of necessity, there is no room for an examination of the constitutionality of the law's purpose. Similarly, there is no room to question the wisdom behind establishing that purpose, or the very need to establish it. The necessity test relates to the means chosen by the legislator to achieve the purposes and not to the need to achieve those purposes.[21]

At the same time, Article 52(1) CFR requires an analysis of the purpose of the regulation. However, this analysis takes place outside of the analysis on the basis of *relative necessity*. From the point of view of this provision of the Charter, a given regulation will be considered acceptable if it meets the following:

(1) the objectives of general interest recognised by the Union; or
(2) the need to protect the rights and freedoms of others.

The new liability regime was found in the analysed judgment to be compliant with the provisions of the Charter on the basis of the latter premise.[22] Referring to the case in question, the Court stated: 'Whether the restriction of freedom of speech by the new liability regime is (relatively) necessary to meet the need to protect intellectual property rights.'

[21] A Barak, *Proportionality* (Cambridge University Press, 2012) 320.
[22] Case C-401/19 (n 12) [83].

So, what justifies the restriction of the freedom of expression, in the opinion of the Court? On the one hand, the Court found that the restriction of freedom of speech by the new liability regime is necessary to meet the need to protect intellectual property rights.[23] From this perspective, it can be concluded that the purpose of this necessary limitation is precisely *the need to protect IPR.* This means that the Court treats the protection of IPR as an end in itself. On the other hand, it was argued that the purpose is 'to ensure that intellectual property rights are protected in such a way as to contribute to the achievement of a well-functioning and fair marketplace for copyright'.[24] In this case, one could attempt to argue that IPR protection is no longer an end in itself but is intended to serve a *well-functioning and fair marketplace for copyright.* This approach can also be found in the impact assessments prepared by the European Commission.[25] However, it can be concluded that such a formulation is a tautology: the creation of a new copyright regime fosters the creation of a well-functioning copyright market. Effectively, the creation of a new liability regime does not serve, for example, the development of creativity, but copyright. However, from this perspective, it can be inferred that, according to the court, IPR protection is an end in itself.

Of course, such a justification for a given regulation in light of the proportionality principle is normatively justified. However, it differs from the questions and the resulting answers which are important under Civil Law Policy. In line with this approach, the existing rights do not in themselves constitute the goal of introduction of a new regulation.

The proper goal of regulation is to achieve certain social states, to which various legal instruments are used (such as rights, privileges, orders, prohibitions, etc). Moreover, as has already been mentioned, in this approach, the goal is necessarily related to the measures taken to achieve it. In other words, it is impossible to judge the usefulness or necessity of a given measure (in isolation from a clearly defined goal. Consequently, from the point of view of Civil Law Policy, in the context of the analysed case, one could try to determine, for example: 'Whether the restriction of freedom of speech by the new liability regime is (causally) necessary to ensure the emergence of creativity'.

B. How Legislators and Courts Know that Something is Necessary

Usually, courts that examine the necessity test are forced to independently determine whether a given measure is necessary to achieve the assumed goal. However,

[23] ibid.

[24] ibid [82].

[25] Commission, 'On the modernisation of EU copyright rules' (Impact assessment)' COM(2016) 593 PART 1/3, 132 ff.

due to their limited research capabilities and the nature of the trial itself, the courts are forced to rely on the arguments presented by the parties to the dispute. 'However, these arguments may not necessarily be based on empirical facts. In most cases, the parties will not even provide any scientifically based elaboration underpinning their arguments that the measure in question is not the least restrictive alternative.'[26] Apparently, in the case under study, we dealt with such an approach. The decision lacks in-depth information in this regard. In short, the court concluded that 'the liability mechanism … appears necessary'.[27] Therefore, in the very content of the judgment, we do not find information upon which facts or analyses the court reached such a belief. We will not find a more extensive argument justifying such a statement in the opinion of the Advocate-General. It only shows that he is in favour of the statement made by the Parliament and the Council, that the compared alternative 'is clearly not *as effective*'.[28]

Even if we consider *relative necessity* to be the appropriate method of assessment of a given measure, the conclusions presented in the case investigated by the court raise doubts. This is because the assessment of the new liability regime against the *notice and take-down*[29] system leads to quite different conclusions on the basis of currently available empirical studies. The Court compared the new liability mechanism (de facto requiring prior automatic filtering of content)[30] with other obligations imposed on OCSSPs.[31] One of them[32] can be considered a a more complex version of the *notice and take down*. According to the court, the new liability regime is more effective than the *notice and take down*. The problem is that this assessment – as mentioned before – is based only on the court's assessment and is not supported by any evidence. It is obvious that the new liability regime imposes greater obligations on platforms, and thus further restricts the rights of users. However, just because it imposes more responsibilities does not mean that it is more effective (in any sense of the word). At most, you can say that it is more restrictive, which may implicitly translate into its greater effectiveness. In terms of efficiency, 'The current state of evidence suggests that, despite its flaws, the notice and take down regime is working'.[33] The Court did not refer to these studies, as neither the parties nor the Advocate-General indicated it.

Against this backdrop, it should therefore be noted that the key element[34] of the proportionality test was found to be met only on the basis of the subjective

[26] T-I Harbo, *The Function of Proportionality Analysis in European Law* (Brill Nijhoff, 2015) 14.

[27] Case C-401/19 (n 12) [83].

[28] ibid [124].

[29] According to the assessment, online hosts are not liable for the illegal content placed on their systems by a user, so long as the online host does not have 'actual knowledge' about it. Once such knowledge is acquired, in order to avoid liability, the online host must act expeditiously to remove or to disable access to the information (see Art 14 Electronic Commerce Directive).

[30] Art 17(4)(b) DSM.

[31] Set out in Art 17(4)(a) and (c) DSM.

[32] Art 17(4)(c) DSM.

[33] K Erickson and M Kretschmer, 'Empirical Approaches to Intermediary Liability' (2019) 17, available at doi.org/10.5281/zenodo.3473215.

[34] Barak (n 21) 337.

judgments of the Court and the Advocate-General and is not based on any objective premises. At least no such objective premises were disclosed in the text of the judgment and the opinion. What emerges in this context is a certain rhetorical feature of the principle of proportionality. On the verbal level, it is thought that a given measure is admissible because it is necessary, but this necessity is not a *causal necessity* in the strict sense, nor is it an objectively stated necessity.

Contrary to the approach presented in the Court, the analyses performed within the framework of Civil Law Policy must always be supported by empirical research.

> But how to gather appropriate empirical material, how to find out whether a given positive norm or a given civil code works good or bad at all? This is not an easy matter and not trivial. The science of Civil Law Policy will pay due attention to it as a serious matter and will develop an appropriate methodological theory showing how to collect and evaluate the usefulness of the collected empirical material.[35]

In this sense, economic sciences can be an inspiration and a source of knowledge for the development of Civil Law Policy. It should be emphasised, however, that Civil Law Policy is not equivalent to the so-called economic analysis of law. The latter concept should be understood as the application of the methods of orthodox (neoclassical) economic analysis to legal issues. Although such an analysis may constitute a point of reference, it is not suitable as a tool for a comprehensive understanding of the issues that are necessary for Civil Law Policy. Therefore, we should refer to the entire output of many economic schools, known as the heterodox approach.[36] Understandably, at the present stage of development of the approach presented here, neither precise methods nor a full body of empirical studies have been developed. Regardless of this, an existing set of such studies allows us to draw conclusions about the IPR system in general (see below).

C. The Concept of Relative Necessity in the Jurisprudence of the CJEU

In its case law, the CJEU, following other courts that referred to the principle of proportionality, adopted the specific meaning of the necessity test. It is also called the requirement of 'the less restrictive means'.[37] Generally speaking, the court treats the condition of *necessity in relative terms*. Consequently, it assumes that an 'interference can only be considered necessary in the strict sense where

[35] Petrażycki (n 16) 127.
[36] Compare more broadly the differences in assumptions between the orthodox and heterodox approaches in Lavoie (n 18) 5–27.
[37] T Lock, 'Article 52 CFR' in M Kellerbauer, M Klamert and J Tomkin (eds), *The EU Treaties and the Charter of Fundamental Rights. A commentary* (Oxford, 2019) para 14.

there is no less intrusive measure available that could achieve the legitimate goal pursued equally effectively'.[38] This means looking determining: 1) whether there are alternative measures; and 2) whether such alternative measures are as effective as the measure being assessed. This understanding of necessity is characteristic of the application of the proportionality principle in general.[39] At the same time, the literature suggests that such a relatively understood necessity may feature different meanings. It may mean that a given measure: 1) brings more benefits than others, with equal losses (gain necessity); 2) brings fewer losses than others with equal gains; or 3) has a better ratio of gains and losses (ratio necessity).[40] It is argued that when the necessity test is met, one position can be improved at no cost to the other. Such an understanding of that test, which will be important for further considerations, is treated as ensuring the implementation of Pareto efficiency.[41]

The *relative necessity* test was also adopted in the present case. The Court found that the new liability regime meets the necessity test because

> although the alternative mechanism proposed by the Republic of Poland, …, would indeed constitute a less restrictive measure with regard to exercising the right to freedom of expression and information, that alternative mechanism would, however, not be as effective in terms of protecting intellectual property rights as the mechanism adopted by the EU legislature.[42]

The concept of relative necessity is better captured by the statement that it is simply a requirement for a less restrictive measure. Jurisprudence notes that: 'The necessity test amounts to verifying whether alternative measures exist which would be *as effective as* the measure chosen to attain the objective pursued whilst being *less restrictive*.'[43] Consequently, it can be inferred that a given measure (M1) is necessary in the sense of the proportionality principle if:

- measure M1 achieves the assumed goal G at a given level of effectiveness of X at a given level of violation of other rights or freedoms at the level of Z; and
- there is no M2 measure that achieves the assumed goal G at the efficiency level of X with a lower level of violation of other rights and freedoms than Z.

Consequently, a given measure M1 is relatively necessary when the alternative measure M2:

(1) pursues goal G to the same extent as M1, but violates other rights and freedoms more than M1; or

[38] ibid.

[39] M Michalska and M Latacz, 'Zasada proporcjonalności' in M Florczak-Wątor and A Grabowski (eds), *Argumenty i rozumowania prawnicze w konstytucyjnym państwie prawa. Komentarz* (Wydawnictwo Księgarnia Akademicka, 2020) 987.

[40] Duarte (n 7) 30; *cf* Barak (n 21) 317.

[41] Lock (n 37) para 14.

[42] Case C-401/19 (n 12) [83].

[43] Case C-401/19, Opinion of AG (n 12) [124].

(2) pursues goal G to a lesser extent than M1 and at the same time violates other rights and freedoms more than M1; or
(3) pursues goal G to a lesser extent than M1, but at the same time violates other rights and freedoms less than M1; or
(4) pursues goal G to the same extent as M1, and violates other rights and freedoms to the same extent as M1; or
(5) pursues goal G to a greater extent than M1, and at the same time violates other rights and freedoms more than M1.

On the other hand, a given measure M1 will not be considered relatively necessary if the alternative measure M2:

(6) pursues goal G to the same extent as M1, but violates other rights and freedoms less than M1; or
(7) pursues goal G to a greater extent than M1 and at the same time violates other rights and freedoms to a lesser extent than M1.

Table 11.1 The concept of relative necessity in the jurisprudence of the CJEU – summary

No	Achieving the goal	Restrictiveness	Analysis results
(1)	M2 = M1	M2 > M1	M1 is relatively necessary
(2)	M2 < M1	M2 > M1	M1 is relatively necessary
(3)	M2 < M1	M2 < M1	M1 is relatively necessary
(4)	R = M1	M2 = M1	M1 is relatively necessary
(5)	M2 > M1	M2 > M1	M1 is relatively necessary
(6)	M2 = M1	M2 < M1	M1 is not relatively necessary
(7)	M2 > M1	M2 < M1	M1 is not relatively necessary

The above relative understanding of necessity means shifting the burden of analysis to the study of the alternative measure M2 and its effectiveness and impact on other rights and freedoms. However, such an analysis does not show that a given measure M1 is *causally necessary* to achieve the assumed goal G. Here, we only examine the relative effectiveness of measure M1 with measure M2 in achieving the goal G, and not whether measure M1 is a necessary condition for achieving that goal. From the first component of the proportionality principle, we only know that such a measure M1 is '*appropriate for contributing* to the achievement of that'[44] goal G.

[44] Case C-401/19, Opinion of AG (n 12) [120].

D. Relative Necessity and the Pareto Principle

Lock indicates that 'the necessity requirement thus aims to ensure Pareto efficiency'.[45] However, such a statement raises two serious concerns. The first is whether the application of the *relative necessity* criterion actually leads to the optimal Pareto situation. Secondly, whether using the Pareto principle is the right way to analyse political decisions behind the adoption of a given regulation.

On the first point, it is not fully understood why applying the criterion of *relative necessity* would lead to an optimal Pareto situation. Generally speaking, there are many ways of expressing the Pareto principle that affect the way it is applied. The literature suggests, among others, that the Pareto principle includes: 'changes which benefit some people without injuring other; a change which benefits or is approved by at least one person and to which no one else object; equilibrium; no further gains from trade; unanimity; consent; exchange; and voluntary exchange'.[46] For the purposes of further considerations, let us adopt the following definition of the Pareto principle: 'An allocation is considered Pareto optimal if no alternative allocation could make someone better off without making someone else worse off.'[47] Similar definitions are quoted in the literature that analyse the test of *relative necessity*.[48]

It should therefore be pointed out that the Pareto principle analysis is based on three concepts: Pareto improvement; Pareto superior; and Pareto optimum. A change from the initial state is a *Pareto improvement* if at least one person's situation improves and no other person's situation worsens at the same time. The situation resulting from this change is *Pareto superior*. As a consequence, the *Pareto optimum* is a situation where Pareto improvement is not possible, ie, the position of at least one person cannot be improved without deteriorating the situation of some other person. Consequently, the use of the measure M1 is a *Pareto improvement* over the M2 measure if the use of M1 does not worsen the situation of any person, and at the same time, one or more persons are strictly better off under M1.

From the above analysis, it appears that measure M1 is considered necessary relative to M2 if both M1 and M2 make the situation worse, but M1 worsens it to a lesser extent. However, the essence of the Pareto principle arguably consists of the fact that the application of a given measure M is permissible if it constitutes an *Pareto improvement*, ie the situation of at least one person is improved without deteriorating the situation of any other person. Just because measure M1 is

[45] Lock (n 37) [14].

[46] WJ Samuels, *Essays on the Methodology and Discourse of Economics* (Palgrave Macmillan, 1992) 132.

[47] WBT Mock, 'Pareto Optimality' in DK Chatterjee (eds), *Encyclopedia of Global Justice* (Springer, 2011), available at doi.org/10.1007/978-1-4020-9160-5_341.

[48] J Rivers, 'Proportionality and Variable Intensity of Review' (2006) 65 *The Cambridge Law Journal* 174, 198.

relatively better than measure M2 (because M1 is less harmful than M2), it does not follow that M1 is a *Pareto improvement*.

Characteristically, the source of the misunderstanding lies in the way in which the Pareto principle is formulated (applied). The formulations of this principle on economic grounds generally refer to a state of harm to a person. If the use of a given measure M1 benefits someone and at the same time it does not harm anyone, then M1 is a Pareto improvement. However, when this principle is applied on the basis of the test of *relative necessity*, the point of reference is not the harm to another person, but the manner of infringement ('harm') on a different (constitutional) principle.

Alexy gave the following example:

> The principle of consumer protection (*P2*) is broadly equally well satisfied by a duty to label (*M1*) as by a trade prohibition (*M2*). So for *P2* is it irrelevant whether *M1* or *M2* is adopted. This is not the case for freedom of profession (*P1*). *M1* interferes much more intensively with *P1* than does *M2*. In the light of what is factually possible (*M1* or *M2*), *P1* can be satisfied to a greater extent by choosing *M1* over *M2* without costing P2 anything. So the optimization of *P1* and *P2* prohibits the adoption of *M2*.[49]

According to this example: 'Thus the principle of necessity is an expression of the idea of Pareto-optimality as well. Because of the existence of a less intensively interfering and equally suitable means, one position can be improved at no cost to the other.'[50] However, such an approach is not entirely precise. Let us take a closer look at this claim. By 'one position can be improved', the author seems to be referring to the P1 principle. From the perspective of P1, the use of the measure M2 (less restrictive), relative to the measure M1, is an improvement. In turn, the term 'at no cost' refers to the P2 principle. From the perspective of P2, both measures M1 and M2 are identical. To put it another way, the principle of P2 principle would not oppose the use of M1 or M2 as both serve it. In my opinion, however, such an application of the Pareto principle differs from its standard interpretation. From the above example, it can be inferred that we introduce the measure M1 or M2 for the implementation of P2. M2 is less harmful to another P1 principle, so it is preferred (*relatively necessary*). However, the Pareto principle is conservative in nature (see below) as it protects the initial state. Thus, while for P2 the choice of M1 or M2 is 'no cost', for P1 the introduction of any measure M1 or M2 is associated with 'costs'. In other words, P1 has a legitimate veto right against the introduction of both measures M1 and M2. Consequently, from the point of view of P1, both M1 and M2 are not Pareto improvements. This is because the introduction of the measure M1 or M2 improves the situation of the P2 principle, but at the same time they harm the P1 principle (although M1 is less than M2).

[49] R Alexy, *A Theory of Constitutional Rights* (Oxford University Press, 2010) 399.
[50] ibid.

This conclusion leads to the second objection. The Pareto principle was created for the purpose of exploring the allocation of resources within welfare economics.[51] It is a very conservative principle that justifies the *status quo*. Situations in which it is possible to improve the situation of at least one person without adversely affecting others are very rare or simply do not exist in social reality.[52] (Theoretically, however, such situations may occur, to which we will come back later.) Its application is to limit the possibility of legislative interference in favour of changes based on free exchange.

Against this background, a question arises as to why the Pareto principle is invoked in the context of analysing the test of *relative necessity*. As Samuels points out: 'Paretians, like economists generally, desire to provide policy advice and recommendations with the aura of "science", vis-a-vis the more purely positive (but less glorious) explanation of the allocation of resources and other performance consequences of political economy.'[53] The supporters of the Pareto principle try to create a system of analysis that is detached from the concept of value. However, as it turns out: 'Efficiency questions appear to be inseparable from equity questions.'[54] In other words, one cannot hide behind the Pareto principle as a neutral test showing that a given solution is neutral from the point of view of various values.

Apparently, a similar function is played by the reference to the Pareto principle in the context of applying the principle of proportionality by the courts. Recognising that a given measure M1 leads to an optimal Pareto state also features important rhetorical implications. It follows from this statement that the use of M1 benefits at least one person without harming anyone. If so, a court of good conscience may decide that a given solution is constitutionally acceptable. The implication is that this solution is Pareto optimal, ie it does not harm anyone. However, the problem is that, as demonstrated above, the application of the *relative necessity* test does not give rise to the claim that the change to initial state given by M1 is Pareto optimal. A given initial state may not be an 'ideal' state for various reasons or values, but at the same time it may be a Pareto optimal state. In principle, it can be said that each initial state in this sense is Pareto optimal, because almost its every change, despite bringing benefits to someone, will always translate into losses for someone else.

E. The Concept of Causal Necessity under Civil Law Policy

First of all, it should be stressed that 'the rational legislator does not … set goals that, without his intervention, would have been achieved anyway'.[55] From this

[51] M Blaug, *Economic theory in retrospect* (Cambridge University Press, 1997) 573–74.
[52] J Stelmach, B Brożek and W Załuski, *Dziesięć wykładów o ekonomii prawa* (Wolters Kluwer, 2007) 31.
[53] Samuels (n 46) 132.
[54] M Blaug, *Economic theory in retrospect* (Cambridge University Press, 1997) 575.
[55] Wróblewski (n 17) 157.

perspective, necessity is understood strictly as a *condicio sine qua non*. In very simplified terms,[56] we can posit that the analysis of causal relations is related to the concept of a necessary condition, a sufficient condition, and combinations of these concepts. The *necessary condition* is a condition without the occurrence of which it would not be possible for a specific event, thing or feature to appear. We can consider a cause (A) as a necessary condition for the appearance of (B) only if (B) never occurs without the appearance of (A) first. If (A) is a necessary condition for the occurrence of (B), then the occurrence of (B) necessarily implies the existence of (A). However, at the same time, the occurrence of (A) does not in itself imply the existence of (B). A necessary condition understood in this way should be distinguished from a sufficient condition. A *sufficient condition* is a condition or set of conditions that will produce the event. We can regard cause (A) as a sufficient condition for the appearance of phenomenon (B) if (B) always appears when (A) appears earlier. If (A) is a sufficient condition for the occurrence of (B), then the occurrence of (A) implies the existence of (B). However, at the same time the occurrence of (B) does not imply the occurrence of (A). Thus, a sufficient condition will lead to the given effect, but the same effect may also appear due to other factors. Put differently, the condition is sufficient for the effect to occur, but not necessary for it to occur. Theoretically, we can distinguish conditions that are both *necessary and sufficient conditions* for the appearance of a given phenomenon. (A) is a sufficient and necessary condition for (B) to appear if (B) always appears and only when (A) appears.[57]

Translating the concept of a necessary condition into the language of Civil Law Policy, it should be acknowledged that without the application of a given measure (eg without creating a specific subjective right with the analysed content), it would not be possible to achieve the given (social) goal. Such a strict understanding of necessity makes it possible to distinguish between measures that are actually necessary and those that are, for example, only helpful for achieving the intended goals. This, in turn, translates, inter alia, into a cost–benefit analysis of a measure. Regulations that, for example, restrict certain rights, but are necessary for the achievement of a desired goal, should be assessed differently than those that are only helpful in its implementation.

Of course, in the analysis of Civil Law Policy, and more broadly the instrumental application of legal norms to achieve specific goals, it is very difficult to establish that a given condition actually meets the requirement of *causal necessity*. This is due, inter alia, to the fact that in the social reality we deal with situations in which only a combination of factors leads to a given effect and a given effect may result from different combinations of factors. That is why the simple division into sufficient and necessary conditions is not enough. In this context, it is necessary

[56] *cf* J Mahoney, E Kimball and K Koivu, 'The Logic of Historical Explanation in the Social Sciences' (2009) 42 *Comparative Political Studies* 114.

[57] *cf* A Sagan, *Metodologia badań ekonomicznych* (Wydawnictwo uniwersytetu Ekonomicznego, 2016) 35; S Stachak, *Podstawy metodologii nauk ekonomicznych* (Difin, 2013) 173.

to refer to the so-called INUS conditions: 'an *insufficient* but *necessary* part of a condition that is itself *unnecessary* but *sufficient* for the result'.[58] We must therefore consider the INUS condition on two levels. First, the INUS condition is part of a certain *set of conditions* that together are sufficient to produce a given effect but are not necessary for it, since there may be other *sets of conditions* leading to the same effect. In other words, condition (C) is an INUS condition under condition set No 1 that gives effect (E), but effect (E) can also be achieved by condition set No 2. Second, the INUS condition, within a given *set of conditions*, is necessary (not redundant) but at the same time insufficient. Put differently, for a given *set of conditions* to lead to the creation of a given effect, the INUS condition must exist, but other conditions must also appear (with properties different from the INUS condition). Effectively, condition (C) is an INUS condition within condition set No. 1, which also includes X, Y and Z conditions.

i. Incentive Theory as a Justification for IPR

One of the basic theories justifying the creation of exclusive rights in relation to intangible goods is the so-called incentives theory.[59] It is an attempt to apply the neoclassical theory of public goods for the purposes of regulating the processes of production and distribution of works and inventions. The logic of the incentive theory is based on the following reasoning. Works and inventions are intangible goods, and this means that they can be treated as pure public goods. Public goods, from the point of view of neoclassical economics, cause the so-called market failure. This is a situation where a market, in the absence of intervention, fails to allocate resources Pareto efficiently. This is because a given good 'is available to all people at no extra cost and consumption of the good by one person does not affect the good's availability to others. This makes it impossible to recoup the costs of provision by extracting payment from users'.[60] With respect to works and inventions from the perspective of incentive theory, the creation of exclusive rights in the form of copyright or patent law is a legitimate intervention. This is because such goods as works, the 'production' of which is expensive, can be 'cheap' and 'easily' copied by illegal entities (the so-called pirates) and then sold by them at lower prices than those of the rightholders. As a consequence, rightholders will

[58] J Mackie, 'Causes and Conditions' (1965) 2 *American Philosophical Quarterly* 245, 245.

[59] *cf* N Elkin-Koren and EM Salzberger, *The Law and Economics of Intellectual Property in the Digital Age: The limits of analysis* (Routledge, 2013) 57–114; K Gliściński, 'Digitalization vs. assumptions of the theory of incentives. Towards a change of the paradigm from exclusive rights to non-exclusive rights as part of the regulation of intangible goods' in 6th International Conference of PhD Students and Young Researchers Digitalization in Law, Conference papers (Vilnius University, 2018), available at ssrn.com/abstract=3250642.

[60] NSW Government, 'A guide to categorising market failures for government policy development and evaluation' (New South Wales Department of Industry, 2017) ii, available at media.opengov.nsw.gov.au/pairtree_root/41/eb/7e/1a/65/1b/4e/a2/b8/d8/68/9a/1d/8d/75/1a/obj/PUB17_509_Market__failure_guide.pdf.

not be interested in producing such goods, which will mean that new works will not be created. Authors, acting as rational individuals, do not create for their own or someone else's pleasure. They create only in order to earn money from their works. Thus, they ensure the supply of goods. Consequently, this theory assumes that incentives in the form of IPR are causally necessary either:

- for the production of creative goods in general (strong assumption); or
- to ensure a socially optimal level of production of creative goods (weaker assumption).

In other words, it is assumed that IPR are *causally necessary* because, without guarding the creators of such incentives, they will not devote their time, resources or effort to creative activities. At the same time, this theory assumes that they provide a sufficient (adequate) incentive for creators to create under all circumstances and that they are the most cost-effective means of achieving this goal.

The consequence of adopting the theory of incentives is the statement that increasing incentives (eg by expanding a monopoly) translates in a simple way into a greater amount of available creativity. This approach has been adopted, among others, in the documents of the European Commission concerning the DSM Directive. It indicated that the new liability regime would contribute to the fact that 'consumers may in the long term have an increased choice of content due to more incentives for rightholders to create new content'.[61] From this perspective, the incentive theory boils down to the fact that a larger number of incentives is desirable. This is where the key difference between the theory of public goods and the theory of incentives based on it becomes apparent.

First, the theory of public goods does not justify the claim that privatisation of these goods (eg, by creating exclusive rights) is desirable under all circumstances. In many cases, public goods should not be provided by private entities, and the financing of their creation should be a public task. Second, and important in considering the critique of the theory of incentives, the creation of exclusive rights to intangible goods solves one problem, but at the same time creates another. The neoclassical theory of public goods is based on the logic of efficiency. Generally, it is acknowledged that the creation of exclusive rights to intangible goods is economically ineffective. 'It is more efficient to distribute knowledge freely to everybody than to restrict its use by charging for it'.[62] From a technical point of view, this is due to the fact that the creation of an exclusive right in the case of intangible goods allows a fee to be charged in excess of the marginal costs (*price-setter*). This means that in the given case we are dealing with a monopoly. 'The excess of price over marginal cost is a measure of monopoly power. …

[61] Commission, 'On the modernisation of EU copyright rules' (Impact assessment)' COM(2016) 593 PART 1/3, 153.

[62] JE Stiglitz, 'Economic Foundations of Intellectual Property Law' (2008) 57 *Duke Law Journal* 1693, 1700.

A competitive firm (*price-taker*) cannot raise price above marginal cost and has no monopoly power.'[63] This is because in perfect competition, any profit-maximising producer faces a market price equal to its marginal cost. From this perspective, it is clear that the strict application of the theory of public goods does not produce the same effects as the incentive theory for the unlimited extension of exclusive rights. Put differently, in the theory of public goods, more of these incentives mean more monopoly power that is unfavourable to society.[64]

ii. Incentive Theory and Reality

As can be seen from the above, the incentive theory distorts the neoclassical theory of public goods. At the same time, it should be emphasised that the neoclassical theory, due to the assumptions it adopts, has little in common with reality[65] and can serve as a basis for shaping Civil Law Policy only to a limited extent (if at all).

From the perspective of the issue discussed here, one assumption of neoclassical economics is particularly important. More specifically, the *homo-oeconomicus* assumption, which is adopted (although often indirectly) also on the basis of the incentives theory. The statement that incentives in the form of exclusive rights are *causally necessary* to induce creators to work creatively under all circumstances is only sustainable with this assumption about the nature and cognitive abilities of man. It is obvious, however, that this assumption is wrong. As observed in the literature on heterodox economics:

> [T]here is no such thing as 'natural' human behaviour; rather, it is shaped and changed by institutions, culture and society. There is nothing inherently 'natural' about self-interested (or better, 'selfish') behaviour, nor would such behaviour be 'rational' in the neoclassical sense. Humans are social animals and in many cultures, selfish behaviour is punished and selfish individuals are ostracised.[66]

As far as creative goods are concerned, people have created and continue to create them for a variety of reasons. First, the history of the development of human creativity is longer than the history of the development of exclusive rights. Naturally, people created at a time when there was simply no copyright.[67] Second, even after copyright was invented, people have been creating and distributing creative works in various organisational models. Such observations are confirmed by examples of the organisation of production and distribution of goods, including creative

[63] D Begg et al, *Economics* (McGraw-Hill Education, 2014) 328.

[64] *cf* M Perelman, *Steal This Idea: Intellectual Property Rights and the Corporate Confiscation of Creativity* (Palgrave Macmillan, 2002) 181–82.

[65] *cf* S Keen, *Debunking Economics – Revised and Expanded Edition: The Naked Emperor Dethroned?* (Zed Books, 2011).

[66] Mitchel, Wray and Watts (n 18) 7.

[67] K Gliściński, *Wszystkie prawa zastrzeżone. Historia sporów o autorskie prawa majątkowe*, 1469–1928 (Fundacja Nowoczesna Polska 2016).

goods, described, among others, by: Ostrom; Bowles and Gintis, von Hippel; Benkler; Frosio; Lessig; and Ricolfi.[68] In addition, there are also models based on public financing.[69] These distinct modes of production can be called in INUS condition language as set conditions sufficient to achieve a given effect. However, they are not necessary in this sense, because, as can be seen from the above, there are different such sets and each of them can achieve a given effect in the form of creative goods. These individual sets require certain causally necessary conditions for their functioning. Within a given set, these particular conditions are INUS conditions. However, what will be an INUS condition for one production model, for another may be an irrelevant or even harmful condition. From this perspective, it can be stated that the existence of exclusive rights constitutes an INUS condition for certain models of creative goods production, but at the same time it does not constitute such a condition for others, and in the case of models, eg based on internal motivations, the existence of these rights may block their development. Consequently, there is no basis for the claim that the existence of exclusive rights is a causal precondition for the emergence of creativity in all circumstances (strong assumption). The issue of assessing the impact of IPR on the validity of a weak assumption requires further research.

VI. Conclusions

The conducted analysis of the concepts of *relative necessity* and *causal necessity* allows us to point out the following differences between them. First, *relative necessity* in practice is based on normative reasoning, while *causal relativity* is based on empirical data. Recognising a given regulation as *relatively necessary* is a derivative of argumentation (evidence) presented by the parties to the dispute. To recognise such a regulation as *causally necessary*, it requires scientific research, the subject of which is neither limited by the framework of court proceedings nor reduced to a single methodology.

Second, for a regulation to be *relatively necessary*, it is sufficient to refer to the need to protect some rights, while for regulation to be *causally necessary*, it is important to refer to some desired social statuses. In other words, rights are not an end in themselves, but a means (instrument) to achieve some goal.

[68] E Ostrom, *Governing the Commons: The Evolution of Institutions for Collective Action* (Cambridge University Press, 1990); S Bowles and H Gintis, *A Cooperative Species: Human Reciprocity and Its Evolution* (Princeton University Press 2013); E von Hippel, *Free Innovation* (MIT Press, 2016); Y Benkler, *The Penguin and the Leviathan: How Cooperation Triumphs Over Self-Interest* (Crown Business, 2011); G Frosio, *Reconciling Copyright with Cumulative Creativity: The Third Paradigm* (Edward Elgar, 2018); L Lessig, *Free Culture* (Penguin Press, 2004); M Ricolfi, 'The new paradigm of creativity and innovation and its corollaries for the law of obligations' in P Drahos (ed), *Kritika: Essays on Intellectual Property* Vol 1 (Edward Elgar, 2015).

[69] K Gliściński, 'Reclaim the state: public interest in copyright and Modern Monetary Theory' (2022) 3 *internet&sociedade*, available at revista.internetlab.org.br/reclaim-the-state-public-interest-in-copyright-and-modern-monetary-theory.

Third, the *relative necessity* is based on the comparison of one legislative solution with another, in this respect being gradational. In contrast, *causal necessity* explores the impact of a given solution on the occurrence of a specific effect. This makes it possible to distinguish between such measures which are *causally necessary* for the occurrence of a given effect, and those which merely serve as aids for its occurrence. This is important at the stage of justifying the restriction of other rights and freedoms by the measure in question.

Fourth and finally, *relative necessity* offers only a limited significance as a guideline for legislation, while *causal relativity* may be an existing source of knowledge in this regard.

Translating the above reasoning into the ground of the new liability regime, the application of *relative necessity* leads the CJEU to conclusions different from those to which it leads the application of *causal necessity* under Civil Law Policy. The Court came to the conclusion that this new regime is *relatively necessary* (compared to another normative solution) for the protection of IPR and, as such, justifies the restriction of freedom of expression and information. From the perspective of Civil Law Policy, it is clear that this new regime is not *causally necessary* for the production of creativity, and consequently its creation does not justify restricting the freedom of expression and information. The current state of the art in this field confirms that IPR is not *causally necessary* for the emergence of creation in all modes of production. In this respect, it can best be said that IPR is the INUS condition for the production of creative goods. Moreover, the current state of knowledge justifies the claim that the level of protection of copyright is too high and may negatively affect the possibility of producing creativity in other production models.

All things considered, it is worth quoting Aleinikoff once again; as he pointed out in the late 1980s, 'balancing, whatever its merits as a way out of formalism, has itself become rigid and formulaic. It gives answers, but it fails to persuade.'[70] In my opinion, the way the CJEU analyses the condition of necessity, relatively understood, will fit such a formal approach. For this reason, a causal necessity under Civil Law Policy may provide a better guide for law-making.

[70] Aleinikoff (n 4) 1005.

12

EU Digital COVID Certificate Regulation: A Retrospective Analysis on Proportionality and Data Protection*

FATMA SÜMEYRA DOĞAN[1] AND PAUL DE HERT[2]

I. Introduction

In December 2019 the novel coronavirus disease (COVID-19) was first identified, and it quickly turned into a global pandemic.[3] Restrictions of movement and curfews began sooner rather than later, aiming to prevent the transmission of the virus and reduce the burden on health systems.[4] However, these restrictions constrained individuals in exercising their fundamental rights, such as freedom of movement. COVID-19 vaccines were delivered at a record pace and countries competed to obtain them. Contract tracking apps were largely considered the most suitable way of monitoring and controlling the infection rate, and they also tracked the vaccination status of individuals once these started being rolled out. Although the Commission recommended a coordinated and interoperable approach from Member States,[5] several different application systems were adopted.[6] Denmark

* This work has been funded by the European Union's Horizon 2020 Innovative Training Networks, Legality Attentive Data Scientists (LeADS) under Grant Agreement ID 956562.

[1] PhD Researcher, Jagiellonian University (Krakow), Poland, fatma.sumeyra.dogan@uj.edu.pl, ORCID: 0000–0002–6774–0228.

[2] Professor, Vrije Universiteit Brussel, Tilburg, The Netherlands.

[3] WHO, 'Coronavirus Disease (COVID-19) Pandemic', available at www.who.int/europe/emergencies/situations/covid-19.

[4] WHO, 'Digital Documentation of COVID-19 Certificates: Vaccination Status – Technical Specifications and Implementation Guidance' 16, available at www.who.int/publications/i/item/WHO-2019-nCoV-Digital_certificates-vaccination-2021.1.

[5] European Commission, 'COMMISSION RECOMMENDATION of 8.4.2020 on a Common Union Toolbox for the Use of Technology and Data to Combat and Exit from the COVID-19 Crisis, in Particular Concerning Mobile Applications and the Use of Anonymised Mobility Data', available at health.ec.europa.eu/publications/commission-recommendation-eu-2020518_en.

[6] E Kursat Kaya, 'Safety and Privacy in the Time of Covid-19: Contact Tracing Applications' (Centre for Economics and Foreign Policy Studies, 2020), available at www.jstor.org/stable/resrep26089.

and France were first in developing national COVID-19 passes and other Member States expressed an interest in developing their own systems.[7]

During the pandemic, the European Commission established that maintaining harmonisation among the Member States was crucial to battling the virus. This led to the introduction of a European COVID-19 pass (more precisely a standard for all the national initiatives to comply with, also in terms of interoperability with the EU system of Digital COVID Certificates). The whole system was launched with the goal 'to facilitate safe free movement inside the EU during the COVID-19 pandemic'.[8] The EU Digital COVID Certificate Regulation ('EU Digital COVID Certificate' or 'DCC Regulation') was enacted on 14 June 2021 for one year, and stipulated three types of valid certification: (a) a certificate confirming that the holder had received a COVID-19 vaccine in the Member State issuing the certificate (vaccination certificate); (b) a certificate indicating the holder's result and date of a NAAT test or of a rapid antigen test carried out by authorised personnel (test certificate); and (c) a certificate validating that the holder had recovered from a SARS-CoV-2 infection following a positive NAAT test or a positive rapid antigen test (certificate of recovery).[9] The provisions of the Regulation were much-debated and raised several legal and ethical concerns.[10] Debates were multidimensional and the proportionality principle was central in the debates about individuals' rights and liberties being restricted by the DCC Regulation.[11] Fundamental rights such as the right to liberty and the right to move and reside freely within the territory of the Member States are protected under the Fundamental Rights of the European Union ('Charter') and the Treaty on the Functioning of the European Union (TFEU). These rights were significantly limited by the implementation of the DCC Regulation.[12]

Another right that was affected by the Regulation was the fundamental right to protection of personal data, since multiple types of data were to be processed in the name of fighting the spread of the virus. Concerns regarding the right to

[7] I Goldner Lang, 'EU COVID-19 Certificates: A Critical Analysis' (2021) 12 *European Journal of Risk Regulation* 9, available at www.cambridge.org/core/journals/european-journal-of-risk-regulation/article/abs/eu-covid19-certificates-a-critical-analysis/EE43E0AF68F827A72547FF1C05987DA4.

[8] 'Coronavirus: Commission Proposes a Digital Green Certificate' (European Commission), available at ec.europa.eu/commission/presscorner/detail/en/ip_21_1181.

[9] Regulation (EU) 2021/953 of the European Parliament and of the Council of 14 June 2021 on a framework for the issuance, verification and acceptance of interoperable COVID-19 vaccination, test and recovery certificates (EU Digital COVID Certificate) to facilitate free movement during the COVID-19 pandemic 2021. Art 3(1).

[10] HT Greely, 'COVID-19 Immunity Certificates: Science, Ethics, Policy, and Law' (2020) 7 *Journal of Law and the Biosciences*, available at doi.org/10.1093/jlb/lsaa035.

[11] E Paris, 'Applying the Proportionality Principle to COVID-19 Certificates' (2021) 12 *European Journal of Risk Regulation* 287, available at www.cambridge.org/core/journals/european-journal-of-risk-regulation/article/abs/applying-the-proportionality-principle-to-covid19-certificates/0EC45C68A4A9CB2828D481594D27F5E3; HD Gunnarsdóttir et al, 'Applying the Proportionality Principle to COVID-19 Antibody Testing' (2020) 7 *Journal of Law and the Biosciences*, available at academic.oup.com/jlb/article/doi/10.1093/jlb/lsaa058/5878809.

[12] Paris (n 11) 3.

protection of personal data had been explored by many scholars.[13] In particular, the EU's General Data Protection Regulation (GDPR) requires a more stringent protection regime for 'data concerning health'[14] and thus caused a lively discussion.[15] Yet, little work has been done to examine this issue in the context of the principle of proportionality.

This chapter wants to fill that gap. It is structured as follows: section II, after giving an explanation of the proportionality principle, examines the implementation of the COVID Regulation by Italy, France and Spain in light of the proportionality principle. Section III outlines the interplay between the right to protection of personal data and its limitation with the DCC Regulation under the proportionality principle. This discussion seeks to address whether the proportionality principle was taken into consideration during the adaptation of the DCC Regulation within selected Member States, and how the fundamental 'right to have a private life' was affected by this Regulation in terms of proportionality principle. Section IV concludes.

II. Proportionality and the Union's Response to the Pandemic: EU Digital COVID Certificate Regulation

A. The Principle of Proportionality

The principle of proportionality is one of the main pillars of EU law. It was initially adopted as an unwritten principle, but soon it found its place in the Charter (Article 52(1)) and the Treaty on European Union (Article 5(4)). Harbo explains that: 'the principle of proportionality is applied in judicial procedures to manage disputes involving an alleged conflict between two rights claims, or between a rights provision or private interest and a state/public interest'.[16] In contrast, Tridimas states: 'the principle of proportionality requires that a measure must be appropriate and necessary to achieve its objectives'. He also mentions two types of tests to examine whether the principle is followed: suitability and necessity tests. The suitability test assesses the relationship between the intended result and the

[13] H van Kolfschooten and A de Ruijter, 'COVID-19 and Privacy in the European Union: A Legal Perspective on Contact Tracing' (2020) 41 *Contemporary Security Policy* 478, available at doi.org/10.1080/13523260.2020.1771509; L Bradford, M Aboy and K Liddell, 'COVID-19 Contact Tracing Apps: A Stress Test for Privacy, the GDPR, and Data Protection Regimes' (2020) 7 *Journal of Law and the Biosciences*, available at www.ncbi.nlm.nih.gov/pmc/articles/PMC7313893.

[14] Regulation (EU) 2016/679 of the European Parliament and of the Council of 27 April 2016 on the protection of natural persons with regard to the processing of personal data and on the free movement of such data, and repealing Directive 95/46/EC (General Data Protection Regulation) 2016, Art 9.

[15] E Ventrella, 'Privacy in Emergency Circumstances: Data Protection and the COVID-19 Pandemic' (2020) 21 *ERA Forum* 379, available at www.ncbi.nlm.nih.gov/pmc/articles/PMC7521575.

[16] T-I Harbo, 'The Function of the Proportionality Principle in EU Law' (2010) 16 *European Law Journal* 158, available at onlinelibrary.wiley.com/doi/abs/10.1111/j.1468-0386.2009.00502.x.

instrument that is projected to be used to achieve that result. The necessity test measures competing norms or interests.[17] The application of the principle in EU law is debated among many scholars, as Sauter points out, but the principle plays a key role in filling a gap 'by allowing EU acts to be reviewed against fundamental rights'.[18]

B. Implementation of the Regulation by Member States

The DCC Regulation saw the light as a response to national initiatives to launch vaccine passports.[19] The DCC Regulation was enacted on 14 June 2021. The Regulation did not offer a transition period and became effective on the day of publication. Article 17 stated that the regulation had a one year of applicability,[20] although this was amended on 29 June 2022 to extend the applicability period until 30 June 2023.[21] At the time of writing (September 2023), the DCC Regulation had expired.[22]

The EU Digital COVID Certificate Regulation is binding in its entirety and directly applicable in all Member States. Member States therefore had to take the necessary steps to implement the Regulation in their domestic law.

Numerous Member States enacted further usage of certificates. Italy, despite its swift response during the early stages of the pandemic, was one of the most badly affected countries in Europe. From February and March 2020, decisions were made about locking down depending on the risk in each territory, while shutting down educational institutions, cinemas and museums, and forbidding public gatherings throughout the country.[23] It is also worth mentioning that Italy was the first country in Europe to introduce the compulsory vaccine for all health professionals in April 2021.[24] On 23 July 2021, a decree on the usage of the EU Digital

[17] R Schütze and T Tridimas (eds), *Oxford Principles of European Union Law. Vol. 1, The European Union Legal Order* (Oxford University Press, 2018).

[18] W Sauter, 'Proportionality in EU Law: A Balancing Act?' (2013) 15 *Cambridge Yearbook of European Legal Studies* 439, available at www.cambridge.org/core/product/identifier/S1528887000003128/type/journal_article.

[19] S van Erp, 'Who "Owns" the Data in a Coronavirus Tracing (and/or Tracking) App?' in A Nicolussi et al (eds), *Coronavirus and the Law in Europe* (Intersentia, 2021).

[20] Regulation (EU) 2021/953 (n 9) 953.

[21] Regulation (EU) 2022/1034 of the European Parliament and of the Council of 29 June 2022 amending Regulation (EU) 2021/953 on a framework for the issuance, verification and acceptance of interoperable COVID-19 vaccination, test and recovery certificates (EU Digital COVID Certificate) to facilitate free movement during the COVID-19 pandemic 2022.

[22] 'EU Digital COVID Certificate' (31 January 2022), available at commission.europa.eu/strategy-and-policy/coronavirus-response/safe-covid-19-vaccines-europeans/eu-digital-covid-certificate_en.

[23] F Robustelli, 'Locked down: In Their Quest to Fight the Covid-19 Pandemic, Have Italy, France and Spain Undermined the Principles of the Rule of Law as Enshrined in Their Constitutions?' (Master's Degree Thesis, Luiss Guido Carli 2021) 18–24, available at tesi.luiss.it/30399.

[24] M Antonini et al, 'An Analysis of the COVID-19 Vaccination Campaigns in France, Israel, Italy and Spain and Their Impact on Health and Economic Outcomes' [2021] *Health Policy and Technology* 100594, 6, available at www.ncbi.nlm.nih.gov/pmc/articles/PMC8702636.

COVID Certificate was passed.[25] Government officials stated that an incentive-based model and non-mandatory approach was being adopted while practicing the new regulations. However, this Decree also established the usage of the digital COVID-19 certificate for entering restaurants and museums, and attending public events; these rules applied to all those over 11 years old. Later, two other decrees made it mandatory for those who are attending schools and universities and for those with access to a workplace to have a green pass.[26] Under these regulations, workers without a valid certificate were considered inexcusably absent and did not receive payment for the days of their absence. Those who wanted to prove their negative COVID status in order to work were left to bear the financial cost of the tests. In November 2021, the Italian Government introduced an enhanced regulation on certificates, generally referred to as the 'Super Green Pass'. With this new regulation, the Super Green Pass certificates became obtainable only by individuals who had been vaccinated or had recovered from COVID-19 in the previous six months. In addition, the regular Green Pass was decreed sufficient for accessing the workplaces, while the Super Green Pass was required to access social activities. As such, usage of the certificates surged.[27]

Similarly to Italy, France introduced mandatory regulations throughout this period. Despite public outcry, the requirement of a certificate for long-distance public transportation and entertainment facilities was enacted.[28] Spain on the other hand, adopted a different approach and did not pass mandatory provisions. According to Antonini et al, 'no mandates to get the COVID certificate are in place in the country'. However, there were two exceptions: the autonomous communities of Galicia and the Balearic Islands enforced the requirement of a COVID pass for entry to night clubs from October 2021.[29]

Throughout this process, criticisms against the DCC Regulation were labelled as vaccine-hesitancy and were not taken seriously; subsequently, no proportionality assessment was conducted in relation to the DCC Regulation. However, the Superior Court of Justice of Galicia reached found the DCC Regulation unlawful based on its inability to satisfy the proportionality and suitability assessment principle. The fact that this decision was annulled by the Supreme Court of Madrid does not affect its importance, as it has become a reminder of the proportionality principle and how the principle is still a necessary tool for a democratic society.[30]

[25] C Reno et al, 'The Impact of Health Policies and Vaccine Rollout on the COVID-19 Pandemic Waves in Italy' [2022] *Health Policy and Technology* 100604, 3, available at www.sciencedirect.com/science/article/pii/S2211883722000107.

[26] P Stefanizzi et al, 'Vaccination Strategies between Compulsion and Incentives. The Italian Green Pass Experience' (2022) 21 *Expert Review of Vaccines* 423, available at doi.org/10.1080/14760584.2022.2023012.

[27] Antonini et al (n 24) 6.

[28] A Gagneux-Brunon et al, 'Public Opinion on a Mandatory COVID-19 Vaccination Policy in France: A Cross-Sectional Survey' (2022) 28 *Clinical Microbiology and Infection* 433, available at www.ncbi.nlm.nih.gov/pmc/articles/PMC8912915.

[29] Antonini et al (n 24) 7.

[30] L Roncati and M Roncati, 'COVID-19 "Green Pass": A Lesson on the Proportionality Principle from Galicia' (2021) 28 *European Journal of Health Law* 525, 531.

Initially, the intention of the European Commission was not to hinder people's ability to travel, which was stated in a communication paper:

> It is important to stress that people without such a certificate must still be able to travel and that being in possession of a certificate is not a prerequisite of exercising the right to free movement or other fundamental rights.[31]

However, as we have shown with selected Member States, the actualisation of the Regulation played out differently. It is exactly at this point where the proportionality principle is crucial in making an assessment between the restriction and its consequences. In Möller's expression, the aim of the proportionality principle is to 'instruct us to assess whether the cure might be worse than the disease'.[32] Moreover, there are studies which show that certificates used for immunity purposes have different effects on society when they have been used for different purposes.[33] Häkli argues that the obligation of certification has unforeseen effects on vulnerable groups of society.[34] These various effects indicate that not every possible outcome of the application of the certificates was foreseen.

The foregoing underlines the need of proper human rights testing of state interventions and to look at all the details in the light of the proportionality principle. However, to our knowledge, only one court decision – by the Supreme Court of Galicia – has discussed the proportionality assessment of the DCC Regulation. Given the large number of fundamental rights at stake,[35] this outcome is bizarre, to say the least.

The proportionality principle is not an easy principle to apply; however, it is one of the main principles which protect our democratic society. Harbo remarks in his thorough study that when the regulation under examination is about the health of the Europeans, courts may tend to rule in favour of the regulation. However, he explains that there should not be automatic decision-making in this regard. In his words, 'For, there is always a possibility that the same goal could be achieved by introducing less infringing regulations, i.e. that the object of securing health for European citizens could be achieved just as effectively by other means'.[36]

[31] European Commission, 'Communication from the Commission – a Common Path to Safe and Sustained Re-Opening', available at eur-lex.europa.eu/legal-content/EN/TXT/PDF/?uri=CELEX:52021DC0129&from=EN.

[32] K Möller, 'The Proportionality of Lockdowns' (Social Science Research Network 2021) SSRN Scholarly Paper 3973261, 10, available at papers.ssrn.com/abstract=3973261.

[33] K Bardosh et al, 'The Unintended Consequences of COVID-19 Vaccine Policy: Why Mandates, Passports and Restrictions May Cause More Harm than Good' (2022) 7 *BMJ Global Health* e008684, available at gh.bmj.com/content/7/5/e008684; CE Niculaescu et al, 'Why "One Size Fits All" Is Not Enough When Designing COVID-19 Immunity Certificates for Domestic Use: A UK-Wide Cross-Sectional Online Survey' (2022) 12 *BMJ Open* e058317, available at bmjopen.bmj.com/content/12/4/e058317.

[34] J Häkli, 'COVID-19 Certificates as a New Form of Mobility Control' (2021) 12 *European Journal of Risk Regulation* 362, available at www.cambridge.org/core/journals/european-journal-of-risk-regulation/article/abs/covid19-certificates-as-a-new-form-of-mobility-control/ED1937464CEEBC40B486FA7132705EF3.

[35] Paris (n 11) 4.

[36] Harbo (n 16).

This statement shows us the importance of considering the less intrusive methods while applying the proportionality principle.

III. The Proportionality Principle and Restricting the Right to Protection of Personal Data

In this section, we will examine the interplay between the right to protection of personal data and its limitation with the DCC Regulation under the light of the proportionality principle. The right to protection of personal data is guaranteed under Article 8 of the Charter.[37] Restrictions brought upon this fundamental right must also follow the principles of Article 52(1) of the Charter.[38] In an explanatory document the EDPS examined the proportionality principle from the perspective of limitation of the right to protection of personal data and expressed that:

> For a measure to respect the principle of proportionality enshrined in Article 52(1) of the Charter, the advantages resulting from the measure should not be outweighed by the disadvantages the measure causes with respect to the exercise of fundamental rights.[39]

Processing personal data, especially health data, was crucial during the pandemic. This was particularly evident in the early stages of the pandemic, especially with the proliferation of tracking apps. Several institutes noted the excessive gathering of personal data and drew attention to the matter.[40] The OECD noted that governments should not omit privacy and data protection principles when introducing new measures in their policy response. Furthermore, it stated that if contract tracking technologies were left unchecked, they were prone to cause challenging situations in terms of data protection and privacy.[41] The Data Protection Commissioner and the Chair of the Committee of Convention 108 of the Council of Europe published a joint statement pointing out that data protection principles must be respected even in difficult times.[42] The EDPB and EDPS also

[37] European Data Protection Supervisor, 'EDPS Guidelines on Assessing the Proportionality of Measures That Limit the Fundamental Rights to Privacy and to the Protection of Personal Data' 6, available at edps.europa.eu/sites/edp/files/publication/19-12-19_edps_proportionality_guidelines_en.pdf.

[38] European Data Protection Supervisor, 'Necessity Toolkit on Assessing the Necessity of Measures That Limit the Fundamental Right to the Protection of Personal Data' 4, available at edps.europa.eu/data-protection/our-work/publications/papers/necessity-toolkit_en.

[39] European Data Protection Supervisor (n 38) 9.

[40] European Union Agency for Fundamental Rights, 'Coronavirus Pandemic in the EU – Fundamental Rights Implications – Bulletin 2', available at fra.europa.eu/en/publication/2020/covid19-rights-impact-may-1.

[41] 'Ensuring Data Privacy as We Battle COVID-19' (OECD, 14 April 2020), available at www.oecd.org/coronavirus/policy-responses/ensuring-data-privacy-as-we-battle-covid-19-36c2f31e.

[42] Council of Europe, 'Joint Statement on the Right to Data Protection in the Context of the COVID-19 Pandemic by Alessandra Pierucci, Chair of the Committee of Convention 108 and Jean-Philippe Walter, Data Protection Commissioner of the Council of Europe', available at www.coe.int/en/web/data-protection/statement-by-alessandra-pierucci-and-jean-philippe-walter.

issued multiple opinion statements, starting from the proposal stage of the DCC Regulation; they stated at the beginning of their joint opinion that 'data protection does not constitute an obstacle for fighting the current pandemic'.[43] However, they also draw attention to potential problems which the Regulation presents to the data protection principles and to the lack of a data protection impact assessment as an essential part of the law-making process.[44] This fact that the Regulation was enacted without having an impact assessment was also criticised by Gstreint: as 'the Commission does not "practice what it preaches", this undermines the credibility of those European standards that it has fought for over the last decade all over the world'.[45]

A major problem was the presence of health data as an integral component of the DCC Regulation in the light of the GDPR's stringent protection measures for such data. Although there are GDPR provisions explicitly dealing with health data processing under emergencies,[46] the regime remains rather complex and strict. GDPR's lawful data processing principles must also be followed.

Article 10 of the DCC Regulation ('Protection of personal data') is dedicated to regulating its data protection aspects. Although its structure gives the impression of being extensive (it has eight subparagraphs), it neglects a couple of key factors, and it has thus received attention from the scholarship. Criticism revolves mainly around the way the DCC Regulation implements or respects important lawful data processing principles of GDPR, namely purpose limitation, data minimisation, transparency, storage limitation and scrutinisation of implications of these principles by tracking apps in the EU.[47]

Furthermore, during the implementation of the Regulation by Member States it was seen as crucial that the data acquired within the DCC system not be used for

[43] 'EDPB–EDPS Joint Opinion 04/2021 on the Proposal for a Regulation of the European Parliament and of the Council on a Framework for the Issuance, Verification and Acceptance of Interoperable Certificates on Vaccination, Testing and Recovery to Facilitate Free Movement during the COVID-19 Pandemic (Digital Green Certificate)' 4, available at edps.europa.eu/system/files/2021-04/21-03-31_edpb_edps_joint_opinion_digital_green_certificate_en_0.pdf.

[44] 'EDPB & EDPS Adopt Joint Opinion on the Extension of the EU Digital COVID Certificate Regulation | European Data Protection Board', available at edpb.europa.eu/news/news/2022/edpb-edps-adopt-joint-opinion-extension-eu-digital-covid-certificate-regulation_en.

[45] OJ Gstrein, 'The EU Digital COVID Certificate: A Preliminary Data Protection Impact Assessment' (2021) 12 *European Journal of Risk Regulation* 370, available at www.cambridge.org/core/journals/european-journal-of-risk-regulation/article/eu-digital-covid-certificate-a-preliminary-data-protection-impact-assessment/F51BABA3959C62E1EE9EFDB26D21EBB9.

[46] Art (9)(2)(c) and (i) GDPR: M Kędzior, 'The Right to Data Protection and the COVID-19 Pandemic: The European Approach' (2021) 21 *ERA Forum* 533, available at doi.org/10.1007/s12027-020-00644-4.

[47] M Bardus et al, 'Data Management and Privacy Policy of COVID-19 Contact-Tracing Apps: Systematic Review and Content Analysis' (2022) 10 *JMIR mHealth and uHealth* e35195, available at www.ncbi.nlm.nih.gov/pmc/articles/PMC9278406; D Dzurakova (nee Galatova) and O Gkotsopoulou, 'Data Protection Law and the EU Digital COVID Certificate Framework' in D Hallinan, R Leenes and P De Hert (eds,) *Data Protection and Privacy: Enforcing Rights in a Changing World*, vol 14 (Bloomsbury, 2021); S Wairimu and N Momen, 'Privacy Analysis of COVID-19 Contact Tracing Apps in the EU' in M Asplund and S Nadjm-Tehrani (eds), *Secure IT Systems* (Springer International Publishing, 2021).

other purposes. However, despite the Regulation's clear instructions,[48] the certificates were used for purposes other than maintaining public health, for example by the German police.[49] Maintaining the security of the data is another significant matter in terms of data protection principles and incidents happened in this regard, too.[50]

Nowhere in the course of the pandemic was time found at EU level for a proportionality assessment of the shortcomings in terms of rights of the DCC Regulation and its implementation. The EDPB and EDPS were clear on this requirement: 'A regular assessment on any measures to fight the COVID-19 pandemic should take place, having regard to the relevant scientific evidence and additional measures in place, in order to continuously evaluate which actions remain effective, necessary and proportionate'. Both the EDPB and EDPS emphasised that any restriction to the right to protection of personal data should be under constant scientific evaluation regarding measures. However, as a result of this research, we did not find such actions from Member States, but rather counter-actions, such as the use of data from the DCC system for other purposes and failure to ensure the security of the data collected.

IV. Conclusions

The COVID-19 global pandemic generated various direct outcomes on economic, social and environmental levels. In this chapter, we assert that while trying to keep up with the new developments, fundamental rights had to be prioritised as they are the main pillars of our democratic society. In this sense, we have offered an evaluation of the COVID-19 certificates in the context of the proportionally principle while specifically analysing its effects on the right to protection of personal data.

[48] Art 10(3) EU Digital COVID Certificate Regulation states: 'The personal data included in the certificates referred to in Article 3(1) shall be processed by the competent authorities of the Member State of destination or transit, or by the cross-border passenger transport services operators required by national law to implement certain public health measures during the COVID-19 pandemic, only to verify and confirm the holder's vaccination, test result or recovery. To that end, the personal data shall be limited to what is strictly necessary. The personal data accessed pursuant to this paragraph shall not be retained'.

[49] 'German Police Used a Tracing App to Scout Crime Witnesses. Some Fear That's Fuel for Covid Conspiracists.' *Washington Post* (13 January 2022), available at www.washingtonpost.com/world/2022/01/13/german-covid-contact-tracing-app-luca; 'German Restaurants Object after Police Use COVID Data for Crime-Fighting' Reuters (31 July 2020), available at www.reuters.com/article/us-health-coronavirus-germany-privacy-idUSKCN24W2K6.

[50] 'Data of Thousands of Dutch Citizens Leaked from Government Covid-19 Systems' (ComputerWeekly.com, 8 February 2021), available at www.computerweekly.com/news/252495983/Data-of-thousands-of-Dutch-citizens-leaked-from-government-Covid-19-systems; 'Dutch Authorities Defend COVID-19 Test System despite Security Flaw' (euronews, 19 July 2021), available at www.euronews.com/my-europe/2021/07/19/dutch-authorities-defend-digital-covid-19-testing-system-despite-security-breach.

Zwitter and Gstrein state that 'Constitutions and human rights … are designed with such crises in mind'.[51] The DCC Regulation and its implementation by Member States showcase the importance of the proportionality principle and the examples of excessive usage where the principle was not taken into serious consideration. Section II demonstrated that Member States did not hold back when introducing additional usage of the certificates, and section III demonstrated that owners of the apps did not hold back when exploiting the data of the certificates. Both trends clearly demonstrate the outcomes of the improper execution of the proportionality principle. Several scientific studies documented the controversial effects of the usage of immunity certificates. In these studies there was no additional assessment regarding the proportionality principle. More generally, we missed a proportionality discussion in many discussions about COVID measures. In the course of this study, we have been able to find only one proportionality assessment conducted by a court relating to the EU Digital COVID Certificate Regulation. This is a peculiarity considering the numerous fundamental rights which were affected by the implementation of the Regulation. Moreover, Member States brought additional restrictions to the standards of the Regulation and used the data from certificates for other purposes. The extensive implications which were carried by the Member States showed that the effects of the Regulation reached further than expected. Unforeseen consequences, as mentioned throughout this chapter, amplify the requirement for systematic proportionality testing by regulators, also in times of crisis.

[51] A Zwitter and OJ Gstrein, 'Big Data, Privacy and COVID-19 – Learning from Humanitarian Expertise in Data Protection' (2020) 5 *Journal of International Humanitarian Action* 4, 6, available at doi.org/10.1186/s41018-020-00072-6.

13

Is Prohibiting Targeted Ads for Minors under the Digital Services Act Proportionate? The Need for a Child-rights-based Approach to Protecting Children's Personal Data Online

MATEUSZ KUPIEC

I. Introduction

It is estimated that 80 per cent of children living in developed Western countries have left a digital footprint before they reach age two,[1] and one out of three internet users globally is a child.[2] Such general statistics demonstrate that children's activities and identity formation processes have already shifted to the digital environment through widely available information and communication technologies. The result is that children's data are shared on a large scale with third parties' online platforms and their business partners.[3] Some scholars even go as far as to declare that contemporary childhood is digital-by-default, as minors are likely to have a digital profile established even before their birth.[4]

The ongoing datafication of children's daily lives contributes to the loss of control by the youngest to create their own narratives about themselves in the

[1] UNGA, 'Artificial Intelligence and Privacy, and Children's Privacy. Report of the Special Rapporteur on the Right to Privacy, Joseph A. Cannataci' (2021) UN Doc A/HRC/46/37 13.

[2] UNICEF, 'Growing Up in a Connected World', available at www.unicef-irc.org/growing-up-connected. That tendency results from the fact that a child's digital identity is created even before they are born. For instance, many young parents eager to track pregnancy and early infancy use certain apps whose providers share information about the unborn child with other entities or data brokers.

[3] It is worth noting that data on children may also be transferred to such entities by individuals other than the children concerned, such as their relatives. See G Mascheroni and A Siibak, *Datafied Childhoods. Data Practices and Imaginaries in Children's Lives* (Peter Lang Verlag, 2021) 155.

[4] M Stoilova, S Livingstone and R Nandagiri, 'Digital by Default: Children's Capacity to Understand and Manage Online Data and Privacy' (2020) 8 *Media and Communication* 197, 197–98.

online environment (digital personas).[5] What happens instead is the growing socio-economic importance of their data doubles[6] developed by commercial entities. The digital environment in which children participate daily has been permeated with personalised advertisements that are displayed to children based on the automated analysis of their behaviour and preferences.[7] After all, how children perceive a particular company can indirectly influence their parents' purchasing behaviour or their own consumer decisions as (future) adults.[8] Assigning children to a predetermined profile created with automated analysis of their behaviour during a specific period may result in displaying only such information that the algorithm arbitrarily deems attractive to them (ie, corresponding to the profile). This may inhibit children's development,[9] for example, by limiting their opportunity to encounter different worldviews via online activities or reinforcing bad habits.

Since children are largely at the early stages of cognitive development, they may lack knowledge of the purposes of various business models based on processing personal data.[10] Therefore, they are perceived as data subjects who require additional safeguards to protect their privacy. The protection of children becomes an important policy objective. Lawmakers are expected to introduce mechanisms that would effectively regulate the extent of third-party interference in the information autonomy of the young. In an attempt to mitigate children's vulnerability to online risks, the EU legislator in the Digital Services Act (DSA)[11] has generally prohibited online platform providers, which will, with reasonable certainty, be aware that a minor receives their services from presenting the ads to children based on profiling.[12] Under Article 5(4) Treaty on European Union (TEU), the principle of proportionality mandates that the content and form of Union action must not surpass what is necessary to achieve the objectives outlined in the Treaties. This principle, fundamental to EU law, is essential in assessing the legality of EU institutions' actions. It aids in aligning various union law objectives with fundamental rights and acts as a standard for subsequent evaluation

[5] V Barassi, *Child Data Citizen. How Tech Companies Are Profiling Us from before Birth,* (MIT Press, 2020) 136–37.

[6] A digital duplicate of natural personal behaviour in a specific time period, recorded in data and distributed in information systems; see K Jones, 'What is Data Double', available at datadoubles.org/2018/05/01/what-is-a-data-double.

[7] V Verdoot, 'The Role of Children's Rights in Regulating Digital Advertising' (2019) 27 *International Journal of Children's Rights* 455, 455–56.

[8] ibid 455.

[9] S van der Hof et al, 'The Child's Right to Protection Against Economic Exploitation in the Digital World' (2020) 28 *The International Journal of Children's Rights* 839.

[10] A Roßnagel, 'Privatheit und Selbstbestimmung von Kindern in der digitalisierten Welt: Ein juristischer Blick auf die Datenschutz-Grundverordnung' in I Stapf et al (eds), *Aufwachsen in überwachten Umgebungen. Interdisziplinäre Positionen zu Privatheit und Datenschutz in Kindheit und Jugend* (Nomos, 2021) 168.

[11] Regulation (EU) 2022/2065 of the European Parliament and of the Council of 19 October 2022 on a Single Market for Digital Services and Amending Directive 2000/31/EC (Digital Services Act), OJ L 277/1.

[12] See Art 28(2) DSA.

of union measures.[13] Therefore, when implementing any legal action aimed at a legitimate objective, such as prohibiting online platforms from displaying targeted ads to minors, it is imperative to assess whether the action is proportionate to the objective's importance and necessary for its achievement.

I argue that the proportionality of Article 28(2) DSA is at least open to question as there are compelling reasons that it neither passes the least restrictive alternative test nor meets the criterion of proportionality *sensu stricto*. There may be less restrictive measures available to protect children from the negative impacts of behavioural advertising, especially since profiling children for advertisement purposes is not explicitly inadmissible under the General Data Protection Regulation (GDPR)[14] nor the UN Convention on Rights of the Child (CRC).[15] Furthermore, the prohibition could excessively affect the interests of both online platform providers and minors. Specifically, prohibiting online platforms from presenting minors advertisements based on profiling may adversely affect children-friendly platforms offering age-appropriate content and, paradoxically, limit minors' development into privacy-literate adults. Given these concerns, this chapter assesses the proportionality of prohibiting online platforms from displaying profile-based advertisements targeted at children. To put Article 28(2) DSA into the broader context of the safeguards established to protect children against negative aspects of online behavioural marketing, the chapter outlines the approach adopted under the CRC and GDPR to protect minors from the potential harms of targeted advertising. The analysis then focuses on the prohibition established under Article 28(2) DSA, examining it against the standard for proportionality review under EU law.

II. Prohibition of Displaying Advertising based on Profiling to Minors by Online Platform Providers under the DSA

A. The Aim and Scope of Article 28(2) DSA

Article 28(2) DSA stipulates that the providers of the online platforms[16] shall not present advertisements on their interfaces based on profiling, as defined in

[13] M Klamert, 'Article 5 TEU' in M Kellerbauer, M Klamert and J Tomkin (eds), *The EU Treaties and the Charter of Fundamental Rights: A Commentary* (Oxford University Press, 2019) 62.

[14] Regulation (EU) 2016/679 of the European Parliament and of the Council of 27 April 2016 on the protection of natural persons with regard to the processing of personal data and on the free movement of such data, and repealing Directive 95/46/EC (General Data Protection Regulation), OJ 2016 L 119/1.

[15] United Nations Convention on the Rights of the Child (adopted 20 November 1989, entered into force 2 September 1990) 1577 UNTS 3.

[16] Under Art 3(i) DSA, 'online platform' means a hosting service that, at the request of a recipient of the service, stores and disseminates information to the public, unless that activity is a minor and purely

Article 4(4) of the GDPR using the personal data of the recipient of the service when they are aware with reasonable certainty that the recipient of the service is a minor. Simultaneously, Article 28(3) DSA clarifies that providers are not obliged under the regulation to process additional personal data to assess whether their platform is accessible to children. Thus, online platform providers should take steps to identify if their services are likely to be accessed by children while complying with the data minimisation principle established in Article 5(1)(c) GDPR.[17]

While analysing Article 28(2) DSA it is important to note that its material scope is restricted only to profiling under Article 4(4) GDPR, meaning

> any form of automated processing of personal data that involves using it to evaluate certain personal factors of a natural person to analyze or forecast aspects of that person's work performance, economic situation, health, personal preferences, interests, reliability, behaviour, location, or movement.

A fundamental aspect of profiling under the GDPR involves assessing individuals to categorise them based on correlations identified from their actual or inferred characteristics, derived from personal data.[18] Consequently, the prohibition does not encompass the displaying of advertisements that are based on processing non-personal data or without predicting individuals' personal dimensions. Although a significant number of personalised advertising instances involve profiling, it is not a universal rule; for instance, when a media platform allows companies to target advertisements to its users based only on the data supplied by the users without inferring their characteristics or preferences, this approach does not meet the criteria for profiling.[19]

Even though the DSA explicitly introduces the prohibition on displaying children-targeted ads, it does not include objective and clear criteria to assess when an online platform's provider should be considered 'reasonably certain' as to the accessibility of their services by minors. Recital 71 DSA provides some guidance in this respect by introducing a non-exhaustive list of factors that may indicate the platform's openness to children: terms and conditions permitting minors to use the service the predominant use of the platform used by minors; or where the provider is otherwise aware that some of the recipients of its service are minors, for example, because it already processes personal data of the recipients of its for other purposes, which reveals their ages. However, the DSA does not clarify how such factors affect the assessment of online platform providers' level of 'certainty'.

ancillary feature of another service or a minor functionality of the principal service and, for objective and technical reasons, cannot be used without that other service, and the integration of the feature or functionality into the other service is not a means to circumvent the applicability of DSA.

[17] According to that principle, the 'personal data shall be adequate, relevant and limited to what is necessary in relation to the purposes for which they are processed'.

[18] M Hildebrandt, 'Defining Profiling: A New Type of Knowledge? Profiling the European Citizen: Cross-Disciplinary Perspectives' in M Hildebrandt and S Gutwirth (eds), *Profiling the European Citizen: Cross-Disciplinary Perspectives* (Springer, 2008) 19–21.

[19] B Duivenvoorde and C Goanta, 'The Regulation of Digital Advertising Under the DSA: A Critical Assessment' (2023) 51 *Computer Law & Security Review* 9–10.

If online platform providers possess information that directly or indirectly indicates that minors may access their services, they will have to comply with the prohibition established in Article 28(2) DSA. In turn, the authorities responsible for DSA enforcement will have to assess ex post each online platform's advertising practices and how likely it is that the targeted recipients seeing personalised advertisements are minors.

B. Contrasting Article 28(2) DSA with the Children's-rights-based Framework

In 1989, the United Nations General Assembly adopted the CRC, which established, for the first time in history, fundamental and universal protection of children, defined as persons up to 18 years, regardless of their background. Protecting the child's rights is one of the main objectives of the EU's external and internal policies, as is clear from Article 3(3) and (5) TEU. Although the EU as an organisation is not itself a party to the Convention, due to its ratification by all EU Member States, the Union is obliged to comply with its principles, at least about matters within its competence.[20] As Article 16(2) Treaty on the Functioning of the European Union (TFEU) explicitly entrusts the European Parliament and the Council with the determination of the principles of protection of natural persons about the processing of personal data and of the free movement of such data, it is reasonable to conclude that the CRC should be considered while adopting and then interpreting EU data protection legislation.

Although the CRC stipulates the minimum rights and freedoms that governments should enforce for all children on a non-discriminatory basis, this international treaty does not explicitly refer to children's rights in the informational society, including their right to data protection in an online environment. The UN Committee on the Rights of the Child reinterpreted the CRC's provisions by adopting General Comment no 25 on children's rights in relation to the digital environment.[21] The interpretation aims to ensure that rights enshrined in the Convention reflect challenges posed by the digital world. Assessing the legality of displaying the targeted ads to minors, the Committee points out that due to the vulnerability of children to manipulation and unclear data flow between the targeters and their partners, to pursue their best interests, parties to the CRC should 'prohibit profiling or targeting children for commercial purposes based on a digital record of their actual or inferred characteristics, including group or collective data, targeting by association or affinity profiling'.[22]

[20] European Agency for Fundamental Rights, *Handbook on European law relating to the rights of the child* (Publications Office of the European Union, 2022) 42.
[21] UNCRC, 'General Comment no 25 on children's rights in relation to the digital environment' (2021) UN Doc CRC/C/GC/25.
[22] ibid 7.

It is clear from the wording of General Comment no 25 that the UN Committee on the Rights of the Child endorses a restrictive approach to such online profiling of children that aims to bring the profiling entity economic benefits by displaying advertisements tailored to children's digital activity. However, the Committee strictly addresses commercially driven marketing practices aimed at 'promoting products, applications, and services'.[23] Consequently, its stance does not include non-commercial advertising, such as campaigns aimed at raising awareness about significant causes or social issues. This differs from the scope of Article 28(2) DSA, which, due to the broad definition of 'advertisement' under Article 3(r) DSA, encompasses all information intended to promote a message, regardless of whether it serves commercial or non-commercial purposes.

C. Contrasting Article 28(2) DSA with the GDPR Framework

The GDPR imposes additional requirements on controllers processing minors' personal data. For instance, among these are the conditions for the consent of the children in the case of information society services (Article 8 GDPR), and the obligation to communicate transparently with children as data subjects (Article 12 GDPR). Although Recital 38 GDPR explicitly stresses that the special protection of the youngest 'should apply primarily to the use of [their] personal data … for marketing purposes or for the creation of personal or user profiles', the GDPR does not contain separate rules that would explicitly govern using children's data for profiling them for marketing purposes. Under the Regulation, only subjecting data subjects (both adults and children) to automated decision-making processes, including profiling, that lead to legal or other substantial impacts on individuals are principally forbidden (Article 22(1) GDPR). Other forms of profiling are permissible under the general principles of the GDPR, eg after the controller performing such operations on the data fulfils the prerequisites for the lawfulness of processing set forth in Article 6(1) or Article 9(2) GDPR, respectively, depending on the categories of data that are used in the process.

The Article 29 Working Party has repeatedly stressed that controllers should refrain from profiling children for marketing purposes as the rules behind displaying behavioural advertising exceed children's cognitive abilities,[24] and they can be influenced by behavioural advertising.[25] This perspective was reiterated by the European Data Protection Board (EDPB), which underscored the necessity of applying 'specific protection to the use of personal data of children' for profiling as it significantly influences children's development, ultimately impacting

[23] ibid 7.

[24] Article 29 Working Party, 'Opinion 02/2013 on apps on smart devices' (WP202, 27 February 2013) 26.

[25] Article 29 Working Party, 'Guidelines on Automated Individual Decision-Making and Profiling for the Purposes of Regulation 2016/679' (WP 251 revised and adopted on 6 February 2018) 29.

their autonomy.[26] The national data protection authorities, including the Swedish Authority for Privacy Protection and the Data Protection Commission (Ireland), generally adopt a more child-rights-based approach. They emphasise that the use of children's data for marketing purposes, including profiling, should primarily serve the child's best interests and not impinge on their autonomy or rights.[27] Thus, Article 28(2) DSA goes further than the GDPR and the prevalent interpretation of the regulation by data protection authorities in protecting minors from the negative consequences of online behavioural marketing.

III. The Proportionality of Article 28(2) DSA

A. Article 28(2) DSA in the light of the Overall Standard for Proportionality Review under EU Law

The principle of proportionality is used as a tool to assess the legality of secondary EU law where a legitimate aim is pursued but there is another interest deserving of legal protection. In such cases, the Court of Justice of the European Union refers to the proportionality principle to determine whether an EU legal act pursues a legitimate aim (suitability or appropriateness), there are no other less restrictive but equally effective means available (necessity), and does not impose a disproportionate or excessive burden upon the individual to achieve its legitimate aim ('proportionality *stricto sensu*').[28] While protecting minors from the possible harms associated with behavioural advertising (such as manipulative deception and losing control of developing one's digital persona) should be considered a legitimate aim, it is at least uncertain whether introducing an absolute prohibition for online platform providers from presenting the minors targeted ads is necessary and proportional *sensu stricto* for achieving that purpose.

B. Alternative Means for Protecting Children from the Negative Impacts of Profiling

The necessity principle within the proportionality test is unambiguous, with its core meaning widely agreed upon – a measure that is necessary if its objective

[26] European Data Protection Board, 'Guidelines 8/2020 on the Targeting of Social Media Users' (adopted 13 April 2021) 8.

[27] Data Protection Commission (DPC), 'Children Front and Centre: Fundamentals for a Child-Oriented Approach to Data Processing' 57–58. The Swedish Authority for Privacy Protection (Integritetsskyddsmyndigheten), 'The Rights of Children and Young People on Digital Platforms. Stakeholder Guide' 38.

[28] T Harbo, 'The Function of the Proportionality Principle in EU Law' (2010) 16 *European Law Journal* 158, 158–59.

cannot be achieved as effectively by a less restrictive alternative to the affected rights.[29] Thus, it is crucial to analyse whether there are less restrictive but equally effective means for protecting children from the negative impacts of exploiting their data for marketing purposes.

At this point, it must be emphasised that the DSA contains another provision that constrains online platform providers from presenting their users with targeted advertising. Article 26(3) DSA explicitly prohibits them from displaying the recipients of their services advertisements based on profiling as defined in Article 4 GDPR using special categories of personal data referred to in Article 9(1) GDPR. The prohibition applies regardless of recipients' ages, and aims to prevent providers from exposing recipients of their services to marketing content optimised to match their interests and potentially exploiting their vulnerabilities (recital 69 DSA). The scope of data that fall under Article 9(1) GDPR (eg health data, data revealing sexual orientation, religion) in the context of online behavioural marketing is subject to a broader interpretation, potentially encompassing not only direct sensitive data but also source data from which sensitive inferences could be drawn.[30] The prohibition set forth in Article 26(3) DSA is less restrictive compared to a ban on displaying targeted advertisements to minors that applies regardless of the data intrusiveness used for profiling. Article 26(3) ensures, namely, that intimate information about individuals is not exploited for surveillance advertising, while simultaneously not excluding the use of neutral content data for such advertising purposes, thus maintaining the attractiveness of online platforms to advertisers.

While discussing the necessity of the prohibition stipulated under Article 28(2) DSA and its possible alternatives, one should also consider what makes children vulnerable recipients of ads based on profiling. Depending on the context and type of social interaction, an individual adopts different attitudes towards the sphere of their own informational autonomy.[31] Thus, children's vulnerability to the risks posed by being subjected to profiling techniques for marketing purposes should be balanced against their agency and evolving capacities. At the same time, one of the fundamental concerns associated with using children's data for digital marketing purposes is (the alleged) children's ignorance of the consequences of (over)sharing their personal data in the digital environment. When using information society services, such as online platforms, children often prioritise the immediately

[29] VA da Silva, 'Standing in the Shadows of Balancing: Proportionality and the Necessity Test' (2022) 20 *International Journal of Constitutional Law* 1738, 1739–40.

[30] L Zard and AM Sears, 'Targeted Advertising and Consumer Protection Law in the European Union' (2023) 56 *Vanderbilt Journal of Transnational Law* 799, 839. The CJEU's judgment in the *Meta Platforms* case supports a broader understanding of 'special categories of data' in online enviroment, as the Court acknowledged that data related to website or app visits can reveal special categories of data, even without user input during registration or online ordering (Case C-252/21, *Meta Platforms* [2023] ECLI:EU:C:2023:537 [70]–[73]).

[31] H Nissenbaum, *Privacy in Context: Technology, Policy, and the Integrity of Social Life*, (Stanford, Stanford University Press, 2010) 130.

apparent benefits of sharing their data over the distant and uncertain risks of violating their rights or freedoms in the future,[32] leaving many digital footprints that allow commercial entities to profile them for marketing purposes. However, as research indicates, children whose internet usage is confined to a few primarily ad-free websites demonstrate a reduced ability to recognise advertisements on unfamiliar sites compared to children with more varied online experiences.[33] Furthermore, while minors' perspectives on profiling for marketing purposes in the digital environment are underexplored, there are initial findings that some adolescents are not disturbed by being subjected to targeting and even find personalised ads helpful.[34] On the other hand, less mature children are not always able to discern profile-based advertisements and do not understand their consequences.[35]

Consequently, Article 28(2) DSA, which prohibits such advertising, seems more appropriate as a safeguard designed for younger children with limited digital and social competencies. A less intrusive alternative to the current prohibition could involve imposing graduated profiling restrictions on online platform providers, varying according to the user's age. For instance, providers could be obliged to completely exclude targeted advertising only for pre-teens, limiting users aged 11–15 to non-commercial targeted ads, and not restricting advertising profiling for users aged 16–17.

Another conceivable and less restrictive alternative to Article 28(2) DSA could be a requirement to provide children with additional information in the form of graphical or textual notifications tailored to their cognitive abilities.[36] Emerging research provides nuanced insights into children's age-specific needs to actively shape their privacy by leveraging personal resources and capabilities. Studies indicate children's desire for self-autonomy and age-appropriate support from service providers in managing their experience online as they seem to understand the consequences of datafication practices.[37] However, prevailing approaches to minors' protection, predominantly guided by adult perceptions of risk and protection, tend to overlook children's perspectives, potentially exacerbating their vulnerability by not adequately preparing them for informed decision-making.[38]

[32] M Stoilova, R Nandagiri and S Livingstone, 'Children's Understanding of Personal Data and Privacy Online – a Systematic Evidence Mapping' (2019) 24 *Information, Communication & Society* 557, 571.

[33] C Lampert, A Schulze and S Dreyer, '"This might be advertising": Perception, Understanding and Handling of Online Advertising by Children' (2021) 43 *MedienPädagogik* 1, 12.

[34] S Srivastava, TA Wilska and J Nyrhinen, 'Awareness of Digital Commercial Profiling Among Adolescents in Finland and their Perspectives on Online Targeted Advertisements' (2023) 17 *Journal of Children and Media* 559, 571–73.

[35] EA van Reijmersdal et al, 'Processes and Effects of Targeted Online Advertising Among Children' (2017) 36 *International Journal of Advertising* 396, 408–410.

[36] M Veretilnykova and L Dogruel, 'Nudging Children and Adolescents toward Online Privacy: An Ethical Perspective' (2021) 36 *Journal of Media Ethics* 128, 134.

[37] G Wang et al, '"Treat me as your friend, not a number in your database": Co-designing with Children to Cope with Datafication Online' (2023) 19–21, available at doi.org/10.1145/3544548.3580933.

[38] G Lansdown, *The Evolving Capacities of the Child*, Innocenti Insights, no 11 (2005) 39–40.

Following the children's best interest as required by Article 3 CRC,[39] it seems that such a solution could consist in requiring the online platforms to present children with additional information in the form of graphical or textual notifications tailored to their cognitive abilities about the possibility and foreseeable consequences of third parties using their data for personalised marketing. Such notifications could, for example, be displayed to minors when they decide to disseminate information about themselves in a digital environment (eg by sharing music on a social media platform). Motivating children to reevaluate their decisions about sharing personal information online and providing real-time assistance in adjusting their privacy settings could enhance their understanding of the impact their actions have on the digital content they receive.

The proposed alternatives to the total ban on displaying targeted advertisements to children by online platform providers would be less restrictive and more effective. Not only would they allow providers to maintain essential advertising revenue, but they would also better protect children. By offering age-appropriate advertising limitations or actively nudging them toward online privacy, these measures ensure children have the opportunity to take informed risks regarding their privacy, which is crucial for gaining a first-hand understanding of the rules and impacts of online advertising. This approach balances the commercial interests of platform providers with the need to protect minors online.

C. Consequences of Compliance with Article 28(2) DSA for Minors and the Online Platform Providers Accessible to them

In evaluating the strict sense of proportionality of a legislative measure, it is essential to conduct a balanced analysis of the public benefits derived against the infringement of rights incurred through the employment of the means chosen by the legislation to achieve its legitimate objective.[40] While banning online platform providers from profiling minors or displaying targeted advertisements may protect children from manipulative content, this restriction could also inadvertently impact their overall online experience and access to information. Furthermore, it could potentially disadvantage providers of child-oriented online platforms, resulting in unequal treatment compared to platforms that cater to a mixed-age audience.

Article 28(2) DSA material scope seems very broad, given that, under the Act, 'advertisement' means any information designed to promote the message of

[39] The best interest of the child is an overriding principle for interpreting children's rights. According to Art 3 CRC, 'all actions concerning children … the child's best interests shall be a primary consideration'. Within the realm of personalised online marketing, this directive can be interpreted as an obligation for entities analysing children's behaviour for targeted advertising to prioritize the best interests of the child and their evolving capacities.

[40] A Barak, *Proportionality: Constitutional Rights and their Limitations* (Cambridge University Press, 2012) 340.

a legal or natural person, irrespective of whether to achieve commercial or non-commercial purposes and presented by an online platform on its online interface against remuneration specifically for promoting that information.[41] Under the DSA, providers of online platforms are prohibited from presenting children with all kinds of marketing communication regardless of its content and purposes. Thus, the EU legislator discretionally presupposes that all advertisements based on profiling presented to children on the interfaces of online platforms may equally harm them on a societal or individual level, ignoring the fact that receiving some types of marketing communication tailored to their actual or inferred preferences may benefit children.

However, promoting services or products that may contribute to children's well-being and cognitive development is generally considered as pursuing the child's best interest.[42] For instance, providing minors with personalised communications informing them about counselling services or representative organisations tailored to their interests and localisation may reduce their need to undertake more extensive searching for such services or direct them to educational content that they might not have discovered otherwise. Considering that the national data protection authorities (DPC, The Swedish Authority for Privacy Protection) established to enforce the GDPR tend to accept applying profiling techniques when children are involved (including for marketing purposes) if the controllers can demonstrate that their actions serve the best interests of children or there is an overriding public interest for subjecting children to profiling,[43] the absolute ban on profiling children for displaying to them personalised ads on online platform interfaces seems too restrictive. It is also debatable whether banning online platform providers from profiling children for the purpose of displaying personalised advertisements, irrespective of their content or objective, aligns with the CRC, considering the position of the UN Committee on the Rights of the Child, which advocates for the prohibition of profiling or targeting children of any age only for commercial purposes. Such a recommendation from the Committee suggests a more nuanced approach to safeguarding children's well-being online may be consistent with the CRC, rather than a blanket ban on presenting minors all advertising based on profiling.

As Verdoot and Leviens observe, while discussing the legal framework for protecting children against possible harms associated with online behavioural advertising, it is crucial to recognise the significant role the advertising-based revenue business model plays in funding information society services content primarily directed at children.[44] The providers of such services (eg online platforms,

[41] Art 3(r) DSA.

[42] Data Protection Commission (DPC), 'Children Front and Centre: Fundamentals for a Child-Oriented Approach to Data Processing' 33.

[43] ibid 57–58. The Swedish Authority for Privacy Protection (n 27) 38.

[44] V Verdoot and E Lievens, 'Targeting Children with Personalised Advertising: How to Reconcile the (best) Interests of Children and Advertisers' in G Vermeulen and E Lievens (ed), *Data Protection and Privacy under Pressure: Transatlantic Tensions, EU Surveillance, and Big Data* (Maklu, 2017) 321.

mobile games) must engage in constant innovation to maintain users' interest and, therefore, need a considerable number of slack resources only for development. Currently, the primary business model for many providers consists of charging advertisers' fees for delivering online advertising that their users find relevant and that advertisers find cost-effective, enabling the individuals subjected to profiling to benefit from these platforms without incurring direct monetary costs. Some empirical studies suggest that the prohibition of targeted advertising within children's games on Android, introduced by Google in 2019, resulted in a decline in the release of feature updates, especially for games from undiversified and advertisement-reliant developers.[45] It was noted that the mobile games impacted by the ban were often removed from the Google Play Store and that developers tended to redirect their focus and resources on feature updates to their unaffected apps.[46]

Given the online platform providers' reliance on ad revenues, it is very likely that the prohibition stipulated under Article 28(2) DSA will similarly adversely impact these online platforms whose active recipients are mainly or predominantly minors. By depriving them of the income that would have been usually generated by displaying their underage audience the targeted ads, the providers of children-oriented online platforms will potentially have fewer financial resources for service development and competing with large or very large online platforms. Online platforms catering to age-diverse users can easily find or create alternative monetisation opportunities (eg by showing their adult users more personalised ads), whereas providers of online platforms oriented only for children (eg online video sharing platforms with age-appropriate content; niche social networks designed only for minors) may abandon their projects or adopt various paid subscription business models (resigning from providing free services) due to the limited number of active recipients. Such a transition could place them at a competitive disadvantage compared to larger providers that offer free access to their platforms.[47]

The issue becomes more pressing when considering the limitations of Article 28(2) DSA. Notably, Article 3(r) DSA does not categorise self-promotion by online platform providers as 'advertising'.[48] Accordingly, large or very large providers are free to profile minors to display messages on their platforms' interfaces promoting their own services (eg apps, communicators, virtual assistants) or additional features specifically designed for children, without violating Article 28(2) DSA, thus rendering their dominant position by attracting more underage users. Therefore, the prohibition of displaying targeted ads to minors under the DSA

[45] T Kircher and J Foerderer, 'Ban Targeted Advertising? An Empirical Investigation of the Consequences for App Development' (2023) 70 *Management Science* 1072, 1089.

[46] ibid 1083, 1088.

[47] ME Stucke, *Breaking Away: How to Regain Control Over Our Data, Privacy, and Autonomy* (Oxford University Press, 2022) 85.

[48] F Hofman, 'Artikel 3 Begriffsbestimungen' in Franz Hofmann and Benjamin Raue (eds), *Digital Services Act. Gesetz über digitale Dienste* (Nomos, 2023) 107.

may reduce the number of available children-oriented independent online spaces designed to provide minors with experiences adjusted to their age and interest. Consequently, there is a risk that compliance with Article 28(2) will result in limiting children's access to online platforms focused on delivering age-appropriate educational or counselling content.

The potential detrimental effects to the development of children-oriented online platforms that may result from compliance with Article 28(2) DSA are inadequately addressed by the exemption for micro and small enterprises defined in Recommendation 2003/361/EC,[49] as outlined in Article 19 DSA. This exemption applies to platform providers who have not been designated as very large online platforms, with fewer than 50 employees and an annual turnover under 10 million euros, focusing solely on economic criteria[50] that are subject to change based on the entity's development and evolving staffing requirements. Crucially, it overlooks child-centric factors such as the platform's risk to children, the number of active recipients who are minors,[51] its relevance to underage users and potential contribution to the child's best interests. As a result, micro and small enterprise children-oriented online platform providers, initially not covered by Article 28(2) DSA, may also need to consider alternatives to revenues from displaying ads based on profiling, such as freemium or paid subscriptions, even early in their development, especially if their growth leads to restrictions on targeted advertising to minors. Notwithstanding the aforementioned, some of these platforms might also strategically exploit this exemption to attract advertisers interested in targeting minors. Such a tactic could lead to a substantial increase in the prevalence of targeted advertising directed at minors within such platforms, not only impinging upon children's best interests but also potentially disadvantaging providers who qualify as medium enterprises and fall under the scope of Article 28(2)DSA.

IV. Conclusion

We mistake children as being constantly at risk and in need of protection from the consequences of their own behaviour and the actions of others.[52] Therefore, while discussing children's privacy, it is not uncommon to forget that gaining experience in deciding who uses information about them and for what purpose is necessary for the youngest to develop the capacity for self-determination. Laws aimed at protecting children's informational autonomy have generally undermined their other rights and limited their access to potentially beneficial information and

[49] Commission Recommendation of 6 May 2003 concerning the definition of micro, small and medium-sized enterprises (notified under document number C(2003) 1422) [2003] OJ L124/36.

[50] See Art 2(2)–(3) Recommendation 2003/361/EC.

[51] I Stapf et al, 'Strengthening Children's Rights through the Digital Services Act (DSA): Towards Best Practice Approaches' Zenodo (2023) 8, available at doi.org/10.5281/zenodo.10156939.

[52] G Dimopoulos, 'A Theory of Children's Decisional Privacy' (2021) 41 *Legal Studies* 430, 436.

interactions that would positively contribute to their development.[53] Unfortunately, it appears that the DSA's prohibition on displaying to minors targeted ads on the platform's interfaces should be viewed in the same way. The GDPR provisions for safeguarding children have been criticised for protecting minors only as the users of information society services without supporting their development into future adults, who will have to make various decisions regarding the shape of their information autonomy.[54] However, a similar statement can be made about the prohibition introduced in the DSA since it only reaffirms a paternalistic approach to children's protection online without considering the complexity of putting children's rights into practice. The EU legislator once again failed to recognise that childhood is not a homogenous phenomenon and therefore children at different developmental stages demand various levels of protection.[55]

There are compelling reasons for considering Article 28(2) DSA as a disproportionate means of protecting children online. Firstly, there are less restrictive alternatives to it, such as prohibiting online platform providers from displaying targeted ads based on special categories of data (already included in DSA) or imposing gradual restrictions on profiling varying by the user's age. Secondly, the ban seems not proportionate *sensu stricto* and may have unreasonable consequences to minors' online experience. Article 28(2) DSA is based on a misconception that displaying all kinds of targeted ads by providers of online platforms has the same negative impact on children regardless of the ads' content or aims. Furthermore, compliance with this prohibition may deprive platforms offering children-oriented content, especially those belonging to medium-sized providers, of necessary financial resources, potentially impeding their ability to further develop their services and maintain user attraction. The EU legislator should have adopted a more nuanced, children-rights-based approach to protecting them from the negative impact of advertising by introducing such means that would not only protect them as the users of online platforms but also contribute to their development as the individuals who consciously shape the scope about their informational autonomy. Even if the proportionality of Article 28(2) DSA is not formally questioned in the foreseeable future, it is reasonable to argue that the regulation constitutes another missed opportunity to reposition minors from passive consumers online to active participants in the online environment.

[53] SM Grimes, 'The Politics of Children's Privacy' (2022) 8 *European Data Protection Law Review* 14, 15.

[54] JC. Buitelaar, 'Child's Best Interest and Informational Self-Determination: What the GDPR Can Learn from Children's Rights' (2018) 8 *International Data Privacy Law* 293, 298.

[55] A Blecher-Prigat, 'Children's Right to Privacy' in JG Dwyer (ed), *The Oxford Handbook of Children and the Law* (Oxford University Press, 2020) 377.

INDEX

NB - Page numbers in *italics* refer to information in figures

www.ingramcontent.com/pod-product-compliance
Ingram Content Group UK Ltd.
Pitfield, Milton Keynes, MK11 3LW, UK
UKHW020242290926
15470UKWH00002B/698

9 781509 974511